PLANNED SHORT-TERM
PSYCHOTHERAPY

PLANNED SHORT-TERM PSYCHOTHERAPY
A Clinical Handbook

Second Edition

BERNARD L. BLOOM
University of Colorado

Allyn and Bacon
Boston   London   Toronto   Sydney   Tokyo   Singapore

Copyright © 1997, 1992 by Allyn and Bacon
A Viacom Company
Needham Heights, MA 02194

Internet: www.abacon.com
America Online: keyword: College Online

Library of Congress Cataloging-in-Publication Data

Bloom, Bernard L.
     Planned short-term psychotherapy : a clinical handbook / Bernard
L. Bloom.—2nd ed.
       p. cm.
     Includes bibliographical references and index.
     ISBN 0-205-19344-7
     1. Brief psychotherapy.   I. Title.
     [DNLM: 1. Psychotherapy, Brief—methods.   WM 420.5.P5 B655p 1997]
RC480.55.B56 1997
616.89'14—dc21
DNLM/DLC
for Library of Congress   96-48082
                                                      CIP

Whatever strengths can be found in this volume are due in large measure to my students at the University of Colorado and to workshop participants around the country who, over the years, have helped me enhance my understanding of planned short-term psychotherapy. Their compliments, their criticisms, but mostly their efforts to go beyond the material I have presented by extracting greater meaning from it, have clarified and enriched my grasp of the field. I am grateful to each and every one of them.

CONTENTS

PREFACE

Since the publication of the first edition of this book, new literature on planned short-term psychotherapy has continued to appear in unabated volume and is finding an ever increasing audience of mental health practitioners. The principal purpose of this new edition is to provide an up-to-date description, analysis, and perspective on the field of planned short-term psychotherapy by incorporating this new literature and by revising the first edition where appropriate. Three orientations to planned short-term psychotherapy now have their own chapters—the Palo Alto Brief Psychotherapy Program, solution-focused approaches to planned short-term psychotherapy, and crisis intervention.

This edition, like the first, is written primarily for the practicing clinician. As such, it concentrates on providing a comprehensive yet succinct analysis of different approaches to brief psychotherapy that take place in a wide variety of settings. Again, as in the first edition, the presentations are limited to those that appear to provide a unique orientation to theory or to technique. As will be seen, there are an increasing number of planned short-term psychotherapy practitioners whose theories are not only well articulated but whose approaches to time-limited psychotherapy also offer substantial food for thought.

At the same time that the growing literature base is having an impact on mental health professionals, the revolution in managed care and the accumulating evidence of the effectiveness of brief episodes of psychotherapy are serving as further impetus for mental health professionals to examine their therapeutic practices. They are being forced to think about time as never before in their professional lives, and most practitioners are developing an increasing respect for what they can accomplish in short episodes of care. Whether this new edition accomplishes its objectives can probably best be judged by its impact on this process, that is, on the clinical practices of mental health practitioners and by their attitudes toward these practices.

I have tried to follow the classic admonition to authors by being brief, clear, and bold. At the same time, however, I have tried to avoid being strident, superficial, or overly abstract. The descriptions of each of the approaches to planned short-term psychotherapy stand on their own, and mental health professionals should have no difficulty in grasping the essentials of each perspective. The references are sufficiently detailed, however, so that additional information regarding any particular approach can easily be located.

I want to express my admiration for the clinicians whose work I have cited. I have the greatest respect for the thinking of these mental health professionals who have so influenced the field of planned short-term psychotherapy. My enthusiasm for using psychotherapeutic time wisely is, if anything, stronger than it was 5 years ago, due in large measure to the writings of these clinicians whose discipline, wisdom, caring, passion, and willingness to take intellectual risks should serve as a model to us all.

I want especially to thank the following reviewers for their helpful suggestions and comments: Lynne Kellner, Private Practice, South Royalston, Mass., and Terrence J. Koller, Private Practice, Evanston, Ill.

ACKNOWLEDGMENTS

Material in Chapter 9 is reprinted from *The Complex Secret of Brief Psychotherapy* by James Paul Gustafson, with the permission of W. W. Norton & Company, Inc. Copyright © 1986 by James Paul Gustafson.

Material in Chapter 13 is reprinted from *Handbook of Cognitive Therapy Techniques* by Rian E. McMullin, Ph.D., with the permission of W. W. Norton & Company, Inc. © 1986 by Rian E. McMullin.

Material in Chapter 16 is reprinted from *Uncommon Therapy: The Psychiatric Techniques of Milton Erikson, M.D.* by Jay Haley, with the permission of W. W. Norton & Company, Inc. Copyright © 1986, 1973 by Jay Haley.

Material in Chapter 18 is reprinted from *Working with the Problem Drinker: A Solution-Focused Approach* by Insoo Kim Berg and Scott D. Miller, with the permission of W. W. Norton & Company, Inc. Copyright © 1992 by Insoo Kim Berg and Scott D. Miller. Other material is reprinted from *In Search of Solutions: A New Direction in Psychotherapy* by William Hudson O'Hanlon and Michele Weiner-Davis, with the permission of W. W. Norton & Company, Inc. Copyright © 1989 by William Hudson O'Hanlon and Michele Weiner-Davis. Material is also reprinted from *Solution Talk: Hosting Therapeutic Conversations* by Ben Furman and Tapani Ahola, with the permission of W. W. Norton & Company, Inc. Copyright © 1992.

Material in Chapter 22 is reprinted from *Rewriting Love Stories: Brief Marital Therapy* by Patricia O'Hanlon Hudson and William Hudson O'Hanlon, with the permission of W. W. Norton & Company, Inc. Copyright © 1991 by Patricia O'Hanlon Hudson and William Hudson O'Hanlon. Additionally, material is reprinted from *Fishing for Barracuda: Pragmatics of Brief System Therapy* by Joel S. Bergman, with the permission of W. W. Norton & Company, Inc. Copyright © 1985 by Joel S. Bergman.

THE HISTORY AND EVALUATION OF PLANNED SHORT-TERM PSYCHOTHERAPY

Planned short-term psychotherapy as a systematic field of inquiry and clinical practice began as part of the community mental health movement that emerged in the early and mid-1960s. Initially planned short-term psychotherapy was an uneasy compromise, promulgated as a strategy for coping with the mental health needs of the community without undermining the principles or reputation of time-unlimited psychotherapy.

But what began as a fairly single-minded interest in making psychotherapy available to larger numbers of people slowly expanded as it became increasingly clear that brief psychotherapy (sometimes as brief as a single interview) could be remarkably effective. Indeed, were it not for the consistent evidence of the effectiveness of planned short-term psychotherapy, the writings in this field might have ended up simply as a footnote in the history of psychotherapy.

Developing an appreciation of the usefulness of planned short-term psychotherapy is not easy for therapists who have devoted years to the study, practice, and mastery of time-unlimited therapy. But initial critical attitudes toward planned short-term

psychotherapy are undergoing a profound transformation as more and more clinicians are coming to the conclusion that short-term therapists are on to something—that somehow, perhaps as a consequence of our training, or the ways in which we earn our livings, we clinicians systematically underestimate how helpful we can be to our clients in brief periods of time. As the literature clearly shows, if we need confirmation of this state of affairs, we have only to ask our patients.

The single chapter in this section provides the context for the subsequent examination of clinical approaches to time-limited therapy by briefly reviewing the history and ideology of planned short-term psychotherapy and then examining efforts to evaluate its effectiveness within the specific framework of dose-response methodology. More generally, what testifies most persuasively to the importance of planned short-term psychotherapy is the extraordinary number of dedicated clinical practitioners who have devoted themselves to furthering their and our understanding of this increasingly accepted mode of psychotherapy.

CHAPTER 1

PLANNED SHORT-TERM PSYCHOTHERAPY: AN INTRODUCTION

Overview

The Essential Characteristics of Planned Short-term Psychotherapy

Therapist Attitudes Toward Time-Limited Psychotherapy

What Makes Planned Short-Term Psychotherapy Compelling

The Evaluation of Planned Short-Term Psychotherapy

Dose-Response Studies

Concluding Comments

Starting in the early 1960s, coincident with the formal beginning of the community mental health movement, a series of major volumes appeared (e.g., Bellak & Small, 1965; Malan, 1963; Phillips & Wiener, 1966; Wolberg, 1965b) that described and evaluated some particular form of what was first called "brief psychotherapy" but is now somewhat more commonly termed, "planned short-term psychotherapy." In spite of this relatively short history, a number of writers (Binder, Strupp, & Henry, 1995; Levenson & Butler, 1994; Magnavita, 1993a) have recently suggested that short-term psychotherapy theories and practitioners can be subdivided into a number of "generations"—first, the original early Freudians, whose work was often remarkably short-term; then, the second generation psychodynamically oriented short-term psychotherapists; followed by the third generation interpersonal, cognitive, and solution-focused psychotherapists; and, most recently, the short-term psychotherapists whose work is influenced by the development of managed health care.

The word *planned* in the phrase *"planned short-term psychotherapy"* is important. These early writers, and all who followed them, describe short-term treatment that is intentionally designed to accomplish a set of therapeutic objectives within a sharply limited time frame.

While the current rapidly increasing interest in planned short-term psychotherapy appears to be driven by changes in the organization, delivery, and payment mechanisms for health care services (see Chapter 25), it is important to remember that the beginnings of this interest far predated the beginning development of managed mental health care. Indeed, recent developments in the field of planned short-term psychotherapy should command the attention of mental health practitioners even if there were no changes underway in the mental health service delivery system.

It is no coincidence, of course, that interest in planned short-term psychotherapy grew rapidly at the time of the development of the community mental health movement. That movement, with its emphasis on making psychotherapeutic help available to everyone in need, puts a premium on delivering such services efficiently, effectively, and promptly. Planned short-term psychotherapy is thus short-term by design, not by default (Gurman, 1981; Weiss & Jacobson, 1981; Wells & Phelps, 1990), and should be distinguished from what might be called *"unplanned short-term therapy,"* that is, services that are brief typically because treatment is terminated unilaterally by the client.

The growing interest in short-term therapy can be seen as part of the constantly developing history of psychotherapy. Early clinicians who wrote about brief psychotherapy came out of a psychoanalytic or psychodynamic orientation, an orientation that started out as relatively short-term but that now represents the longest of the psychotherapies. Marmor (1979) has noted that Freud's initial therapy cases were often very short in duration. Bruno Walter, the conductor, was successfully treated for a chronic cramp in his right arm in six sessions (Sterba, 1951). The composer Gustav Mahler was treated for an obsessional neurosis and severe marital difficulties in a single four-hour session that took place while strolling through the town of Leyden in Holland (Jones, 1955; Vol. 2, p. 80; see also Strupp, 1980a, p. 379).

The current interest in short-term therapy can thus be seen in part as a response to growing dissatisfaction with the lengthening of traditional psychotherapy. Many writers in the field of time-limited psychotherapy are fully aware that psychotherapists do not ordinarily have the luxury of unlimited time with their patients. As a consequence, they have begun to search within their own experiences for wisdom they can share with those mental health professionals who have no alternative other than to try to be helpful to their patients in limited periods of time (Butcher & Koss, 1978, pp. 726-727).

THE ESSENTIAL CHARACTERISTICS OF PLANNED SHORT-TERM PSYCHOTHERAPY

Short-term psychotherapy, as this term is currently defined, ranges in length from a minimum of one interview to a maximum of around 20 interviews, with an average duration of about six sessions. Few people now talk about therapies longer than 20 interviews as short-term, although the upper limit is not really agreed upon. Talley (1992) has suggested the term "very brief psychotherapy" for treatment episodes of less than eight sessions, reserving the term "brief psychotherapy" for episodes of between 8 and 20 sessions.

At its simplest level, short-term psychotherapy can be defined as those therapies in which "the practitioner deliberately limits both the goals and the duration of treatment" (Wells, 1994, p. 2). To complicate this succinct definition somewhat, five fundamental components other than duration usually characterize planned short-term psychotherapy (Bauer & Kobos, 1984; Budman & Gurman, 1983; Budman & Springer, 1987; Koss, Butcher, & Strupp, 1986; Magnavita, 1993a; Manaster, 1989; Marmor, 1979; Svartberg, 1993). These components are: (1) prompt intervention, (2) a relatively high level of therapist activity, (3) establishment of specific but limited goals, (4) the identification and maintenance of a clear focus, and (5) the setting of a time limit. There are, however, considerable differences in how writers use the term focus, what they mean by therapist activity, and how they go about setting a time limit.

Eckert (1993) has suggested that the components of planned short-term psychotherapy can be grouped into four categories: planning (rapid assessment, identification of focal issues, goal clarification, and treatment selection), collaboration (building a therapeutic alliance), timing (promptness of intervention; number, frequency, and duration of therapy sessions; intersession tasks), and empowerment of the client (sharing control with the client, reducing the creation of dependency). Regarding empowerment, Trad (1991) has described the evolution from time-unlimited to planned short-term psychotherapy in terms of a fundamental change in the role of the therapist— from a passive one in which the gradual deconstruction of conflict is observed to a more active one in which the therapist takes a more directive stance. Thus, the move toward brief psychotherapy appears to have empowered both therapist and client.

Koss and Shiang (1994) have provided a summary of the common characteristics of most brief interventions (see Box 1-1).

THERAPIST ATTITUDES TOWARD TIME-LIMITED PSYCHOTHERAPY

Advocacy for planned short-term therapy stands in contrast to a deeply ingrained mental health professional value system (Aldrich, 1968; Gelso & Johnson, 1983; Haley, 1990; Karasu, 1987; O'Hanlon & Weiner-Davis, 1989; Ursano & Dressler, 1977; Weakland, 1990). In that value system, brief treatment is thought of as superficial, longer is equated with better, and the most influential and prestigious practitioners tend to be those who undertake intensive long-term therapy with a very limited number of clients.

Box 1-1: Common Elements in the Brief Psychotherapies

1. Prompt and early intervention to aid in resolving immediate problems, in part to avoid more serious and chronic problems in the future
2. Identification of limited but attainable goals designed to ameliorate the most disabling symptoms and improve coping ability
3. Contract for time-limited intervention designed to attain specified goals
4. Principal focus on the here and now rather than on early life events
5. Active and directive therapists who maintain the focus and organization of therapeutic contacts
6. Experienced therapists who keep goals in sight, provide rapid initial assessment of the nature of the problem and the client's resources, gather relevant information, develop a working formulation, and maintain a flexible approach to intervention

Adapted from Koss and Shiang, 1994, p. 674.

Social workers expressed some early interest in planned short-term therapy but adopted the Freudian long-term model as they sought a rationale for their own professionalization (H. J. Parad & L. G. Parad, 1968; L. G. Parad, 1971; L. G. Parad & H. J. Parad, 1968).

Psychotherapists differ in the extent to which they are drawn to the basic ideas of planned short-term psychotherapy, in part because they have differences of opinion regarding the modification of human behavior, as well as the psychotherapeutic enterprise itself. According to Budman and Gurman (1983), while long-term therapists generally seek to change basic character, short-term therapists seek more parsimonious, limited, and conservative interventions. While long-term therapists believe that significant psychological change rarely occurs simply on the basis of experiences in day-to-day living, short-term therapists believe that significant psychological change in everyday life is not only common, but is, in fact, inevitable.

In addition, long-term therapists tend to view presenting complaints as symptoms of deeper psychopathology, while short-term therapists tend to take presenting complaints seriously and see their removal as a legitimate goal of therapy. Long-term therapists tend to view therapy as always benign and useful, and therefore they believe that there can hardly be too much therapy. In contrast, short-term therapists believe that therapy can under some circumstances be counterproductive, particularly if it goes on too long. Finally, long-term therapists tend to view

being in therapy as the single most important aspect of a patient's life. In contrast, short-term therapists tend to view being in therapy as only one of many important activities in which patients are involved.

Hoyt (1985) has identified a number of related beliefs and tensions that may account for some of the continuing hesitancy of psychotherapists regarding short-term dynamic psychotherapy. The first of these beliefs is the conviction that more is better, that time-limited psychotherapy is necessarily inferior to time-unlimited therapy, simply because there can be less of it. A second belief is that some therapeutic techniques are simply impossible to carry out under time constraints and that these specific techniques, such as uncovering or the provocation of affect, are essential to effective therapy.

Among the sources of tension generated by the prospect of planned short-term psychotherapy, Hoyt has noted a mismatch between some therapists' convictions of the clinical superiority of long-term therapy and many patients' interests in having their therapy be as brief as possible. A second source of tension is the fact that time-limited psychotherapy is increasingly recognized as more demanding and often more difficult for the therapist than time-unlimited therapy. A third difficulty identified by Hoyt is the fiscal complexity inherent in trying to derive an adequate income from one's professional activities while encouraging a high turnover in patients. Finally, Hoyt suggests that a short-term therapy practice inevitably results in repeated psychological losses to therapists, a phenomenon that can often result in considerable personal stress and discomfort (see also Carmona, 1988; Hoyt, 1987).

WHAT MAKES PLANNED SHORT-TERM PSYCHOTHERAPY COMPELLING

In spite of these concerns, interest in planned short-term therapy is accelerating. This expanding attention has come about as a consequence of three interrelated factors: first, concern with efficiency and economy; second, changing concepts and theories of psychotherapy; and third, an accumulation of evidence that the effectiveness of planned short-term therapy appears to be indistinguishable from that of long-term treatment.

Efficiency and Economy

The efficiency and economy rationale for planned short-term therapy is stressed most notably by persons in the public sector. With limitations in both financial and staff resources, a community mental health facility, they argue, must derive the greatest possible effect from every available therapeutic hour. Treatment would then be more feasible for larger numbers of clients.

With the increasing demand for service, a planned short-term therapy orientation could result in the virtual elimination of waiting lists, a source of chronic tension for staff, clients, and the public (Kirkby & Smyrnios, 1992). Finally, for many clients, whether because of economic, cultural, or ideological considerations, planned short-term therapy is the only real alternative to no treatment at all (Avnet, 1965).

One setting that has attracted substantial interest in planned short-term psychotherapy is the university counseling center. Increased demand for psychotherapeutic services combined with reductions in budget allocations has drawn the attention of counseling center staff to research literature documenting the potential benefits of a time-limited approach to student counseling and psychotherapy. As a consequence, there is growing interest in establishing short-term counseling programs. A number of reports seem to suggest that such programs provide both effective as well as efficient care (Halligan, 1995; Pinkerton & Rockwell, 1994; Robbins & Zinni, 1988; Steenbarger, 1992a, 1993).

The private sector has also become interested in the efficiency and economy of planned short-term therapy, but for a somewhat different set of reasons. First, third-party insurance reimbursement for outpatient psychotherapy is being reduced as part of the efforts to cope with the soaring cost of medical care and of medical insurance. Second, new organizational forms of health care are being developed. These various models offer the promise of reducing the cost of medical care by reducing overtreatment. Third, primary care physicians, who until recently provided about two-thirds of all mental health services in the United States (Regier, Goldberg, & Taube, 1978), are continuing, if not expanding, their interest in providing mental health services. While surprisingly little is known about the nature of mental health services provided by primary care physicians, one thing is clear—those services are nearly always short-term in nature (see Chapters 20 and 21).

Changing Concepts in Psychotherapy

Among the relatively recent changes in psychotherapeutic theory pertinent to the growing interest in planned short-term therapy the following should be mentioned: (1) acceptance of limited therapeutic goals, (2) emphasis in ego psychology on strengths as well as weaknesses of the client, (3) impact of behavior modification techniques, (4) increasing centrality of crisis theory and crisis intervention in service delivery system planning (see Chapter 19), and (5) greater attention being paid to current precipitating circumstances in contrast to past predisposing circumstances.

These changes have resulted in making treatment more promptly available (Rosenbaum & Beebe, 1975, pp. 299–300); in the realization that when therapeutic time is limited, both client and therapist appear to work harder (Applebaum, 1975; pp. 427 ff.; Piper, Debbane, Bienvenu, & Garant; 1984), and in exploring the possibility that planned short-term therapy would in many circumstances be the treatment of choice even if it were not less expensive (Ewing, 1978; p. 19; Hoch, 1965; pp. 53-54; Sifneos, 1967; p. 1069; Wolberg, 1965c).

The treatment-of-choice argument comes in part from the growing realization that most treatment (planned or unplanned) is short-term (Garfield & Affleck, 1959; Hoffman & Remmel, 1975; Hoppe, 1977; H. J. Parad & L. G. Parad; 1968, L. G. Parad, 1971) and that there is some potential utility in making it intentionally short-term. While it is true that most outpatient psychotherapy is short-term (less than 20 sessions), it is important not to make too much of this fact. The 16 percent of clients who are in long-term psychotherapy account for nearly 63 percent of outpatient psychotherapy expenditures (Olfson & Pincus, 1994).

Mann (1973) states eloquently what a number of writers have noted

> There comes a point in the treatment of patients, whether in psychoanalysis or in psychotherapy, where time is no longer on the therapist's side insofar as the possibility of helping the patient to make further changes is involved, and where time serves far more the search by the patient for infantile gratification. (p. xi; see also Chapter 6)

THE EVALUATION OF PLANNED SHORT-TERM PSYCHOTHERAPY

A large number of evaluation studies of planned short-term psychotherapy have appeared in the literature. Indeed, there are so many evaluation studies that even the number of reviews and critical analyses of these evaluations has become quite large (e.g., Bloom, 1984; Casey & Berman, 1985; Crits-Christoph, 1992; Cummings & VandenBos, 1979; Johnson & Gelso, 1980; Koss & Butcher, 1986; Koss, Butcher, & Strupp, 1986; Koss & Shiang, 1994; McKay, Murphy, & Longabaugh, 1991; Parad, 1971; Ryder, 1988; Smith, Glass, & Miller, 1980; Strupp, 1980a; Svartberg, 1993; Svartberg & Stiles, 1991; Task Force on Promotion and Dissemination of Psychological Procedures, 1995; Wells, 1994; Woody, McLellan, Luborsky, & O'Brien, 1987).

These evaluation reports need to be understood in the context of the overall evaluation of psychotherapy. While research study results certainly make it appropriate to conclude that psychotherapy is better than no psychotherapy, its lack of more firmly established effectiveness, however, should make practitioners and educators somewhat uneasy (Gallagher, 1987). The most optimistic figures that have

appeared in the literature regarding the general effectiveness of psychotherapy are that about 75 percent of treated patients are doing better after therapy than the average untreated patient. While this sounds on the surface as a rousing endorsement of psychotherapy, in fact these findings mean that while three treated patients out of four demonstrate substantial improvement when contrasted with untreated patients, one treated patient out of every four ends up worse off than the average untreated patient. Furthermore, examination of the existing evaluation literature makes it clear that we cannot confidently identify in advance who that one patient out of four might be.

To return to planned short-term psychotherapy, the empirical evaluation studies of short-term outpatient psychotherapy have found that planned short-term psychotherapies are, in general, as effective and long-lasting as time-unlimited psychotherapy, virtually regardless of client characteristics or treatment duration (Koss & Butcher, 1986; Smyrnios & Kirkby, 1993) and are essentially equally effective (see, for example, Laikin, Winston, & McCullough, 1991). Almost identical findings have been reported for short-term inpatient psychiatric care (see, for example, Bloom, 1984, pp. 98–101; Gelso & Johnson, 1983; Miller & Hester, 1986; and Chapter 23).

Indeed, perhaps no other finding has been reported with greater regularity in the mental health literature than the equivalence of effect of time-limited and time-unlimited psychotherapy. Schlesinger (1994) has noted the implications of this finding by commenting that "government and insurers fear that if left to their own devices, psychotherapists would tend to go on indefinitely. They are convinced that the prescription of 'long-term psychotherapy' guarantees only higher cost, not better results" (p. 2).

Some of this evaluation literature is nonquantitative or based on very small samples (e.g., Barkham, 1989a; Gottschalk, Mayerson, & Gottlieb, 1967; Grand, Rechetnick, Podrug, & Schwager, 1985; Kaffman, 1963; Lewin, 1970; H. J. Parad & L. G. Parad, 1968; L. G. Parad & H. J. Parad, 1968; Sifneos, 1972; Strupp, 1980b, 1980c, 1980d, 1980e; see also Schlesinger, 1984). But many reasonably large well-designed evaluations of planned short-term psychotherapy have been published (see, for example, Bierenbaum, Nichols, & Schwartz, 1976;

Blowers, Cobb, & Mathews, 1987; Brockman, Poynton, Ryle, & Watson, 1987; Brodaty & Andrews, 1983; Winer-Elkin, Weissberg, & Cowen, 1988; Fisher, 1980; Gallagher & Thompson, 1983; Hawton et al., 1987; Husby et al., 1985; Lorr, McNair, Michaux, & Raskin, 1962; Meyer et al., 1981; Piper et al., 1984; Rosenthal & Levine, 1970, 1971; Shapiro, Barkham, Hardy, & Morrison, 1990; Stuhr, Meyer, & Bolz, 1981; Thompson, Gallagher, & Breckenridge, 1987; Waring et al., 1988).

In their review of the short-term psychotherapy evaluation literature, Berg and Miller (1992) have concluded:

> Research on treatment outcome has consistently demonstrated that such short-term treatment is as effective as traditional, long-term therapy—in spite of all of the predictions to the contrary. ...In fact, the results of a 12-year study recently published by the Menninger Clinic, a psychoanalytically oriented treatment and training facility, showed that clients who received brief, supportive treatment profited as much from that experience as those who had undergone extensive, long-term, psychoanalytically oriented treatment. (p. xiii)

Representative of the recent conclusions of the many reviews of the relationship of treatment duration to outcome is that of Koss and Shiang (1994), who commented:

> Brief therapy methods, once thought to be appropriate only for less severe problems, have actually been shown to be effective in treating a wide range of psychological and health-related problems, including severe and chronic problems....Contemporary comparative studies of brief psychotherapy offer little empirical evidence of differences in overall effectiveness between time-limited and time-unlimited therapy or between alternate approaches to brief therapy....Consequently, brief therapy results in a great saving of available clinical time and can reach more people in need of treatment. (pp. 664, 692)

Their conclusions are similar to those reported by Koss and Butcher in 1986 and by Butcher and Koss in 1978. In addition, Koss, Butcher, and Strupp (1986) have suggested that these findings may actually underestimate the effectiveness of planned short-term therapy since so few of the therapists participating in the evaluation studies had received formal training in brief therapy techniques.

We shall turn to the issue of training in the final chapter of this volume. But it is important to underline the importance of Koss, Butcher, and Strupp's suggestion by noting that in a recent study reported by Pekarik (1994) the role of training in improving clinicians' brief therapy skills can clearly be seen. Evaluating a 10-hour training program with a sample of 12 therapists who received the training program and a control sample of 10 therapists who did not, Pekarik found that in the case of 176 clients of these 22 therapists, in comparison with clients of the control group psychotherapists, clients of trained short-term psychotherapists received more brief therapy, reported greater treatment satisfaction, had lower dropout rates, and obtained better therapist ratings of outcome.

This general assessment of the evaluation literature is not meant to suggest that no further evaluations are needed or that no questions persist about the efficacy of brief episodes of psychotherapy. To the contrary, it may be as imprudent for mental health professionals to accept without question the implications of the research studies already conducted as to reject them out of hand. Gelso (1992), for example, who has written quite favorably about the effectiveness of brief episodes of care, still notes that more research is necessary before one should be entirely confident that planned short-term psychotherapy is as effective as longer episodes of care; that the changes noted in planned short-term psychotherapy are as long-lasting as those following longer episodes of care; or that, since improvement is noted so quickly after psychotherapy has begun, only a few sessions of therapy are ever needed.

Another review of the planned short-term psychotherapy evaluation studies will not make a significant contribution to the literature or to this volume, but it is important to accomplish two more clinically relevant tasks in this chapter—to review what has been found about the length of therapy and client satisfaction and to put the existing evaluation literature in the larger context of dose-response studies.

LENGTH OF THERAPY AND CLIENT SATISFACTION

Client satisfaction is perhaps the single most commonly accepted measure, although not necessarily the most valid measure, by which the effectiveness of psychotherapy has been judged. Haley (1987), for example, has suggested that neither clients nor therapists may be the best judges of therapeutic outcome: "Clients who have invested a great deal of money in therapy—or who like or dislike their therapists—will report 'facts' biased by that context. Similarly, therapists are hardly objective observers of a task in which they have a large personal investment" (p. 104).

The research literature linking length of psychotherapy and client satisfaction can be divided into two components: first, studies with clients who were judged to have completed a treatment episode at the time of termination and, second, the examination of client satisfaction in the case of clients who terminated treatment unilaterally, that is, who ceased keeping previously agreed-to appointments.

In their comprehensive review of the client satisfaction literature, Talley, Butcher, and Moorman (1992) concluded that the vast majority of clients were satisfied with their psychotherapy and that no client, therapist, or therapy variables were consistently related to the level of satisfaction. While there were some exceptions, their review suggested that neither client age, gender, socioeconomic status, income, occupation, nor prior psychotherapeutic experience were significantly related to satisfaction level. In addition, duration of psychotherapy and a variety of therapist variables, including profession, seniority, and judged level of warmth, empathy, and nurturance failed to be significantly linked to the level of client satisfaction.

As for studies examining level of satisfaction in the case of clients who unilaterally terminate psychotherapy, mental health professionals tend to view termination by these clients as a sign of therapeutic failure and client dissatisfaction. Professional attitudes toward unilateral termination of treatment by patients can be quickly discerned when it is noted that such clients are virtually always referred to as "dropouts." The importance of the dropout problem

can be seen in the fact that nearly half of all clients unilaterally terminate psychotherapy. While much is known demographically about how clients who drop out of treatment differ from those who remain in treatment until a mutual decision between therapist and client is made to end the treatment episode, relatively few studies have followed so-called dropouts to determine their current status or level of satisfaction with the treatment (Sledge, Moras, Hartley, & Levine, 1990; Wierzbicki & Pekarik, 1993).

The two most common clinician responses to a patient's unilateral termination of therapy are either to conclude that the patient was unsuitable for psychotherapy or that they themselves made some fatal error in their therapeutic interactions with the patient. Thus, it may be reassuring to know that empirical studies of client satisfaction and length of treatment consistently fail to support either of these hypotheses.

Starting with Kogan's early work, a number of investigations have examined patients who dropped out of therapy from the point of view of their level of satisfaction with the care they received. Kogan (1957a, 1957b, 1957c) examined the records of all new clients in the Division of Family Services of the New York Community Service Society for one month in late 1953. During that month, 250 new cases had a first in-person interview. Of these 250 cases, 141 (56%) were closed after one interview. Most of those closings were planned, that is, agreed upon in advance by client and therapist. But 30 percent were unplanned, in that the client failed to keep subsequent appointments.

Kogan was able to interview, either in person or by telephone, 80 percent of these 141 cases between three months and one year after the cases were closed. He had similar success in contacting cases with planned and unplanned closings. In addition, therapist evaluations prepared at the time of case closings were analyzed. Kogan's results are illuminating. In the majority of cases, therapists had attributed unplanned closings to client resistance or lack of interest. Follow-up interviews with these single-session clients revealed, however, that reality-based factors prevented continuance and also that improvements in the problem situations may have accounted for a substantial proportion of these unplanned closings.

About two-thirds of all clients felt they had been helped. There was no difference in this proportion when clients with planned closings were compared to clients with unplanned closings. In contrast, therapists considered that clients were, in general, helped, but they believed that those with planned closings were helped significantly more than those with unplanned closings. Therapists consistently underestimated the help that clients with unplanned closings judged they had received, and they consistently overestimated how helpful they had been to clients with planned closings (see also Fiester & Rudestam, 1975; Frings, 1951; Hoppe, 1977; Lazare, Cohen, Jacobson, Williams, Mignone, & Zisook, 1972; Littlepage, Kosloski, Schnelle, McNees, and Gendrich, 1976; Phillips, 1985b; Shyne, 1957; Silverman & Beech, 1979).

Finally, regarding the issue of length of treatment and patient improvement with particular reference to patients who terminate psychotherapy unilaterally, Pekarik (1983) contrasted pretreatment and post-treatment scores on a brief symptom inventory in a group of 41 dropouts and another group of 23 patients who were judged to have terminated treatment appropriately. Pekarik also examined these scores as a function of number of treatment sessions. Dropouts were defined as patients who were thought by their therapists to be in need of additional treatment beyond their last session. Initial scores on the symptom checklist did not differ substantially between dropouts and appropriate terminators, nor did the initial scores differ as a function of number of subsequent treatment sessions. The analysis, based on a follow-up assessment conducted about three months after the start of treatment, indicated that for those patients who had had only a single therapy session, those who were judged to be dropouts were functioning significantly more poorly than those patients judged to have terminated treatment appropriately. For all other patients, that is, for patients who had had two or more therapy sessions, no significant differences in symptom scores at the time of the follow-up assessment were found.

There thus appears to be virtually no support for the clinical assumption that patients who unilaterally terminate treatment are dissatisfied with their care, and there is little support for the belief that they are functioning more poorly than patients whose ter-

minations from therapy were mutually agreed upon ahead of time by therapist and patient.

DOSE-RESPONSE STUDIES

A number of studies of psychotherapy effectiveness have drawn on *dose-response methodology* from the field of pharmacology. That methodology examines the relationship between the amount of exposure to a treatment and the degree of improvement (see, for example, Howard, Kopta, Krause, and Orlinsky, 1986; Rush & Giles, 1982; Schlesinger, Mumford, Glass, Patrick, & Sharfstein, 1983). While invoking dose-response methodology in the evaluation of psychotherapy effectiveness raises a number of complex issues (Stiles & Shapiro, 1989), the growing interest in dose–response relationships is understandable since if it can be shown that there is a significant relationship between the amount of exposure to a treatment and the degree of improvement, the likelihood that the relationship is a causal one is increased (MacMahon & Pugh, 1970).

Dose-response studies seek to determine the relationship between the dose of a drug and characteristics of the resulting response. Response to psychotherapy has been studied as if psychotherapy were a drug, using number of sessions as a measure of dose. The linking of a well-established methodology from another field to the study of psychotherapy effectiveness is an important potential contribution of this line of inquiry. Dose-response concepts from the field of pharmacology clearly provide a promising framework for enriching the continuing evaluation of psychotherapeutic effectiveness, and suggestions for a planned short-term therapy research agenda that can be related to these concepts have already appeared (Koss & Butcher, 1986; Koss, Butcher, & Strupp, 1986).

Dose-Response Methodology

A number of standard pharmacology texts describe the fundamental importance of dose-response studies (Bochner, Carruthers, Kampmann, Steiner, & Azarnoff, 1978; Gerald, 1981; Gilman, Goodman, Gilman, Mayer, & Melmon, 1980; Shepherd, Lader, & Rodnight, 1968). Such studies plot the size of the dose against some measure of effect. Dose-response curves need not be linear, however, and are often found to be concave, convex, or even more complex.

Dose-response studies assume that drugs have some measurable effects on the body if they are administered in sufficient dose and seek to determine the characteristics of those effects. Efficacy is only one of those characteristics, however. In addition to efficacy, per se, dose-response studies examine treatment threshold, latency, potency, response variability and duration, treatment side effects, and margin of safety. Regarding factors that may be associated with variability in drug effects, dose-response studies have most commonly examined such variables as route and time of administration, rate of inactivation and excretion, interaction with other drugs taken at the same time, and such demographic factors as age, body weight, gender, drug tolerance, pathological state, genetic factors, and set, milieu, or other psychosocial factors (Gilman, Goodman, Gilman, Mayer, & Melmon, 1980).

Most of these parameters have their parallels, at least theoretically, in the study of the effectiveness of psychotherapy. It thus seems clearly appropriate to examine psychotherapy effectiveness studies as if one were conducting dose-response investigations, assuming, of course, that the studies being examined meet minimal dose-response methodology requirements.

As for these requirements, the following quotations from a standard text on drug evaluation principles (Tedeschi & Tedeschi, 1968) provide an adequate description:

> Perhaps the most important single principle in experimental design is randomization. Randomization is assumed in most data analyses, and can be omitted from a design only at the risk of biases in the conclusions....The simplest experimental design is a one-way classification in which the subjects or test animals, supposedly equivalent, are assigned at random to as many different groups as there are treatments to be tested. (p. 4)
>
> Especially in clinical experiments, a subject may react as much to the taking of a drug as to its pharmacological action. A standard correction for this effect is to include a placebo among the test preparations. For an unbiased response, the identity of each treatment must be unknown to both the subject and to those administering the drug or evaluating its effect, in a so-called double-blind test. (p. 11)

> An all-or-none reaction provides less information than a response that varies quantitatively. Several designs have been proposed for increasing the precision of such experiments. One is to score the degree of response, such as nausea in a study of seasick remedies, as none, mild, [or] severe...in subjects known to be susceptible to motion sickness. The response is then multinomial rather than binomial. (p. 14)

Examination of these excerpts reveals that from the point of view of experimental methodology, dose-response studies have the same set of minimum requirements as are generally proposed for well-designed studies of psychotherapy effectiveness (Ciarlo, Brown, Edwards, Kiresuk, & Newman, 1986; Cook & Ware, 1983; Frank, 1968; Hazelrigg, Cooper, & Borduin, 1987; Wortman, 1983). These requirements include: (1) random assignment of clients into at least two treatments of differing levels of intensity, one of which could be an attention placebo group; (2) development of evaluation measures that have adequate psychometric robustness and employ appropriate levels of discrimination and numbers of data collection points; and (3) evaluation of therapeutic outcome by judges who are not aware of the experimental study group to which any given client is assigned.

Special considerations in the evaluation of psychotherapy outcome should be noted regarding outcome judgments made by the treating therapist. Reports in the literature suggest, first, that the likelihood of finding long-term therapeutic interventions superior to short-term interventions declines dramatically as one moves from outcome judgments made by therapists to judgments based on objectively measured psychological symptoms or characteristics (Bloch, Bond, Qualls, Yalom, and Zimmerman, 1977; Gelso & Johnson, 1983; Johnson & Gelso, 1980). Second, even though a substantial minority of patients are reported by their therapists as showing improvement after a relatively small number of sessions, it has frequently been suggested that therapists tend to be biased toward long-term therapy (Budman & Gurman, 1983; Burlingame & Behrman, 1987). Without adequate controls, that bias can fully account for the positive relationship often found in early studies of therapy duration and judged effectiveness (Avnet, 1965; Fago, 1980; Howard, et al., 1986; Kogan, 1957a, 1957b, 1957c;

Robinson, Redlich, & Myers, 1954; Rosenthal & Frank, 1958; Shapiro & Shapiro, 1983).

Koss and Butcher (1986), in their critique of short-term therapy evaluation studies, specifically note that "many studies that purport to correlate therapy duration to outcome have methodological problems (e.g., confounding of time with time in treatment, biased raters or criteria, failure to utilize planned brief-therapy techniques) that render them irrelevant to the efficacy of brief methods" (p. 658).

Most early psychotherapy evaluation studies failed to meet dose-response methodological criteria. Untreated control or attention placebo groups were rarely created. Patients were rarely randomly assigned to treatment conditions of varying durations. Assessments of outcome were nearly always made either by the treating therapists, by judges (based on data provided by the treating therapists), or by the treated patients themselves, and only at the time of discharge. Finally, judgments of therapeutic outcome were generally made using procedures and measures of undemonstrated reliability and validity.

Early psychotherapy evaluation studies served primarily as psychotherapy process descriptions rather than as evaluations, and where data were available on therapy outcome and therapy duration, most authors were aware of the dangers of asserting any causal relationship between the two phenomena. For example, Rosenthal and Frank (1958) explicitly recognized the long-term therapy bias of most psychotherapists. Cappon (1964), Garfield and Affleck (1959), and Strassberg, Anchor, Cunningham, and Elkins (1977) have commented on the limited validity of outcome judgments made by the treating psychotherapists. In this connection, Phillips (1985b) has reported that therapist and client evaluations of psychotherapy are essentially uncorrelated. Cappon (1964), Cole, Branch, and Allison (1962), and Jones (1980) have expressed cautions about their dependent measures of therapy outcome. Brown and Kosterlitz (1964), as well as Cappon (1964), have recognized the limitations of their conclusions because of the absence of control groups in their studies.

Not all psychotherapy evaluation studies have these methodological limitations, of course, and more recent studies are usually more sophisticated than studies conducted decades ago. Indeed, with the growing number of individuals seeking mental health services there is no longer any reason why all dose-response methodological principles should not be fully implemented in psychotherapy outcome evaluation studies.

The Scope of Dose-Response Concepts

As has been suggested, the study of the relationship of therapeutic dose and therapeutic outcome does not exhaust the potential contribution of the dose-response model to the understanding of psychotherapeutic effectiveness. The conclusions regarding the relationship of individual therapy outcome to treatment characteristics, based on scores of reasonably well-conducted evaluation studies (see Butcher & Koss, 1978; Koss & Butcher, 1986 for an extensive review of these studies), can now be reframed by returning to the variables that have been given special consideration in dose-response investigations.

Efficacy

Efficacy is the maximum effect of a treatment employing its optimal dosage. Psychotherapy is unquestionably efficacious, but every psychotherapist would surely wish for its level of efficacy to be improved. While about two-thirds of treated patients are judged to have improved at the time of follow-up, one-third of untreated patients are also judged to have improved (Lambert, Shapiro, & Bergin, 1986). The treatment–no treatment dimension accounts for only 10 percent of the variability in outcome. Research findings have not yet made it possible to predict with any certainty which patients will benefit from psychotherapy and which will not. The efficacy of all forms of psychotherapy certainly needs to be increased, and it is encouraging to note that the search for ways to increase its effectiveness, is underway (see, for example, Lambert, Shapiro, & Bergin, 1986, pp. 178 ff.).

Threshold

Threshold is the lowest dose capable of producing a discernible effect. Psychotherapy appears to have an extremely low threshold. As few as two or three sessions of psychotherapy have repeatedly been shown to have a significant effect in a large minority of cases, and there are numerous empirical as well as anecdotal reports of a single interview having a remarkable positive impact on some clients (Bloom, 1981; Cummings & Follette, 1976; Follette & Cummings, 1967; Talmon, 1990; see also Chapter 8).

Latency

Latency is the speed with which discernible effects are produced. Psychotherapy appears to have a remarkably low latency, and its initial positive effects are commonly reported during or immediately after the first interview. Indeed, positive effects have been reported between the time the initial appointment is made and when it actually takes place.

Potency

Potency is the absolute amount of the treatment that is required to produce a specified effect. Psychotherapy has relatively high potency. Its maximum effects appear to be reached with small doses, and beyond that point, additional treatment appears to produce very little additional benefit (Bowers & Clum, 1988).

Duration of Effect

Duration of effect is the amount of time that a given treatment outcome is sustained. Regardless of the duration of the treatment, psychotherapy has a relatively long-lasting effect, and there is evidence that improvement continues for at least one year after the conclusion of an episode of brief psychotherapy (Cross, Sheehan, & Khan, 1982; Gelso & Johnson, 1983; Husby, 1985).

Variability of Effect

The effectiveness of psychotherapy in general, and of short-term psychotherapy in particular, appears to vary relatively little as a function of either therapist or therapy characteristics (Berman & Norton, 1985; Cross, Sheehan, & Khan, 1982; Durlak, 1979; Hattie, Sharpley, & Rogers, 1984; Parloff, 1982; Shiffman, 1987; Wolberg, 1965c; see also Chapters 24 and 25). This is not to suggest that therapists will

have the same results regardless of whom they treat or what therapeutic approach they use. But determining the most appropriate treatment for a given patient in the hands of a given therapist is a task of considerable complexity, one that cannot be expected to yield significant results unless it is approached with care and dedication.

Side Effects and Margin of Safety

While there is a literature describing the harmful side effects of psychotherapy (see, for example, Gross, 1978; Hadley & Strupp, 1976; Rush & Giles, 1982; Sachs, 1983; Strupp, 1989; Tennov, 1975; Zilbergeld, 1983), these reports consist mainly of the description of negative consequences associated with scandalously unethical therapeutic practices. Psychotherapy in the hands of an ethical psychotherapist, appears to produce few, if any, untoward side effects.

CONCLUDING COMMENTS

Planned short-term psychotherapy started out life 35 years ago as second best, offered to patients apologetically. Today, while there is continuing objection to across-the-board limitations on therapy duration, planned short-term psychotherapy is one of the most upbeat and professionally affirming developments in the field of clinical practice.

With the current concern about the high cost of medical care and with the growth of health maintenance organizations and other alternatives to fee-for-service health care (see Chapter 25), there is increasing interest in avoiding overtreatment, that is, in providing only those health-related services that are needed. The planned short-term therapy literature strongly suggests that the effectiveness of short-term psychotherapy is indistinguishable from that of long-term psychotherapy and that long-term encounters may very likely provide more psychotherapy than is needed (Budman & Stone, 1983; Cummings, 1986; Klerman, 1983; McGuire & Frisman, 1983).

Closer examination of the evaluation literature suggests that the basic reason for the equivalence in outcome of brief and long-term psychotherapy lies not in the fact that long-term psychotherapy is of such limited effectiveness but rather that brief psychotherapy seems to yield such remarkably positive results. In a way, this finding should not be surprising. By petitioning for help, therapy clients signal not only their acceptance of a psychological component to their difficulties but also their high motivation as well as a willingness to change.

One set of clues that can help explain the effectiveness of planned short-term psychotherapy can be found in the work of Piper, Debbane, Bienvenu, and Garant (1984), who found that relatively short-term individual psychotherapy (average of 22 sessions within 6-month maximum) was consistently superior to time-unlimited individual psychotherapy (average of 76 sessions within 2-year maximum) on a variety of outcome measures collected from patients, therapists, and independent assessors blind to treatment assignment. They reported that short-term therapy patients and therapists "felt the need to work hard and relatively quickly. Attention was concentrated and focused. Affective involvement was high....At completion most patients felt that they had received something valuable from the therapist" (p. 277). In contrast, long-term individual therapy patients and clinicians were less satisfied. "The length of time available coupled with the frequency of one session per week seemed to favor an increase in resistance and a decrease in working through. Thus, the patient tended to behave as if there was always plenty of time to work later" (p. 277).

It is important, however, not to promise more than can be delivered. Donovan (1987) has warned that when the proponents of time-limited psychotherapy suggest that their intervention is incontrovertibly the only reason for change in their patients' lives, they are engaging in clear speculation. People are in a constant state of change and they use a variety of situations and relationships to support that growth, including but certainly not limited to psychotherapy. In addition, Budman and Stone (1983) have reminded us that among the many development-promoting relationships are several courses of psychotherapy, not just one. Mental health professionals themselves seek an average of five therapies over their adult lives, even when one therapy has been a "full" psychoanalysis. These facts, according to Budman and Stone, throw into question the claim that one sequence of brief treatment should lead to definitive and permanent change (see also Budman, 1990). The question of how much psychotherapy is needed is not a trivial one, yet it has hardly been addressed in the theoretical or empirical literature.

In 1971, Parad concluded her review of the short-term treatment literature in the field of social welfare by noting that:

> For a variety of interlocking reasons—manpower shortages, demands for massive community mental health services, dissatisfaction with waiting lists, studies in goal-limited therapy, research on coping behavior and crisis phenomena—we are now witnessing a dramatic resurgence of interest in short-term approaches. Ours claims to be a pragmatic profession. If the level of outcome effectiveness evidenced in the recent studies is further substantiated in future large-scale experimental research, it would be logical to infer that short-term treatment should be the basic therapeutic approach for all but a relatively small selected group of applicants for family agency and child guidance services. (p. 145)

Research that has been reported since that paper was published has repeatedly affirmed the remarkable efficacy of planned short-term psychotherapy. Happily, mental health professionals are beginning to accept with grace the affirmation of their effectiveness in brief periods of time and are proceeding to develop strategies for institutionalizing that effectiveness.

PSYCHODYNAMIC APPROACHES TO PLANNED SHORT-TERM PSYCHOTHERAPY

In the next three sections we shall examine a number of remarkably different approaches to planned short-term therapy. This section will consider psychodynamic theories of planned short-term psychotherapy; the next will consider cognitive and behavioral approaches to planned short-term psychotherapy. Section IV will consider strategic and systemic approaches. As will be seen, there is fully as much variation in both the theory and practice of planned short-term therapy as in the theory and practice of long-term therapy.

It is useful to examine these various approaches for at least two reasons. First, a certain approach might prove to be superior for certain problems or certain types of clients, for certain clinicians, or under certain circumstances. In such cases, referrals or assignments to clinicians could be made on a more rational basis than is typical in most mental health agency settings, and one could anticipate general increases in therapeutic effectiveness. Second, exposure to different approaches to planned short-term therapy allows for the possibility that an individual clinician could develop a broader array of skills than might otherwise be the case; becoming effective with a more varied array of clients or problems.

At the same time, it is important not to exaggerate the importance of theory. Such an attitude can result in retaining a theory that is difficult to apply in a specific case or that, to use Gustafson and Cooper's (1990) words, "can be applied so elegantly that it explains everything and nothing" (p. 46). In order to be really useful, theories of time-limited psychotherapy must have both heuristic appeal and practical applicability.

CATEGORIZING APPROACHES TO PLANNED SHORT-TERM PSYCHOTHERAPY

There are a number of ways of categorizing approaches to planned short-term psychotherapy. In this book they are sorted into three major groupings—*psychodynamic, cognitive-behavioral,* and *strategic.*

Some effort has been made to integrate various approaches to psychotherapy into a single multidimensional unit. This is the case, for example, with Ryle's cognitive-analytic therapy (Ryle, Poynton, & Brockman, 1990), an approach that seeks to combine the best features of psychodynamic and cognitive and behavioral therapies. Regarding this integration effort, Malan (1979) has written:

> Any form of psychotherapy must be incomplete unless it incorporates the psychodynamic point of view. This applies particularly, of course, to learning theory and behaviour therapy. But the converse is also true: dynamic psychotherapy itself is incomplete unless it incorporates the theory and techniques of other forms of therapy, of which behaviour therapy is probably the most important. It seems to me incontrovertible, for instance, that the success of behaviour therapy in dealing with certain symptoms, without dealing with unconscious conflict, means that there is something missing in psychodynamic theory in this area; for instance, that some process such as self-reinforcement must be operating to maintain symptoms and give them autonomy. On the other hand, honest behaviour therapists will readily admit that their own explanation of the origin of symptoms—a question to which the psychodynamic approach has a fairly complete answer— is hopelessly insufficient. (p. 254; see also Phillips, 1985a)

But efforts to integrate various approaches are not very common. What is far more prevalent in the literature are texts that espouse the virtues of a single categorical approach. Burke, White, and Havens (1979; see also White, Burke, & Havens, 1981) have suggested that short-term therapies can be divided into those that are *interpretive,* in that they stress the role of insight; *existential,* in that they stress the salutary effects of a brief empathic encounter with a therapist; or *corrective,* in that they stress therapist-induced behavioral change.

Butcher and Koss (1978) divide brief therapies into those that are *psychodynamically oriented, crisis-oriented,* and *behavioral.* Bouchard, Lecomte, Carbonneau, and Lalonde (1987) have found significant differences in verbal activity among *psychodynamically oriented, gestalt,* and *behavior* therapists, suggesting that this differentiation represents a meaningful way of sorting therapy types. Peake, Borduin, and Archer (1988) group short-term therapies into three categories as this volume does—*psychodynamic, cognitive,* and *strategic-systemic* approaches (see also Burlingame & Fuhriman, 1987).

Further complicating this effort at grouping approaches to planned short-term psychotherapy is the fact that there are a number of eclectic time-limited psychotherapies as well (Duncan, Solovey, & Rusk, 1992; Fuhriman, Paul, & Burlingame, 1986; Norcross, 1986; Wells, 1994). The tripartite division employed in this volume, however, seems to account for most of the variance in the theories that are described (see also Bauer & Kobos, 1987; Budman & Gurman, 1988; Flegenheimer, 1982; Thorpe, 1987).

CHARACTERISTICS OF PSYCHODYNAMIC SHORT-TERM PSYCHOTHERAPY

Focusing specifically on psychodynamic theories of planned short-term psychotherapy, Marmor has described the psychodynamic perspective succinctly in terms of its five essential assumptions:

the recognition that human behavior is motivated; that the nature of this motivation is often largely concealed from awareness; that our personalities are shaped not only by our biological potentials, but also by experiential vicissitudes; that functional dis-

turbances in human cognition, affect, and behavior are the result of contradictory and conflictual inputs or feedbacks; and that early developmental experiences are of particular significance in shaping subsequent perceptions and reactions in adolescence and adulthood. (1968, p. 5)

These essential assumptions of psychodynamic psychotherapy—the fact that behavior is motivated, that people are not fully aware of the complexities of their intrapsychic lives, that experience is as important as biology in determining what we are like as human beings, that we are in conflict about many issues in our lives, and that our childhoods shape what we become as adults—hold true for all the approaches analyzed in this section of the book.

DIFFERENCES AMONG PSYCHODYNAMIC APPROACHES

The approaches of ten practitioners of psychodynamic time-limited psychotherapy are presented and illustrated in this section, and it may be difficult to keep each of them in sharp focus. Accordingly, some introductory comments and observations about how these approaches differ from one another are in order to provide an orientation to what lies ahead and to draw the reader's attention to specific approaches to planned short-term psychotherapy that might seem particularly pertinent in a specific situation (see also Barber & Crits-Christoph, 1991; Demos & Prout, 1993).

Since these approaches are all fundamentally psychodynamic, it should not be surprising that there is relatively little variability in some dimensions, such as the importance of attending to transference phenomena and other aspects of the therapeutic relationship, special attention to termination issues, and the importance of the concept of the unconscious. But there is also a surprising amount of variability among the approaches. Some approaches are particularly important because of the ideas that lie behind the therapeutic techniques used. Other approaches seem as remarkable because of the therapeutic techniques used as for their underlying ideas.

In general, theorists vary in their aspirations, perhaps their passion, for short-term therapy, ranging from those who see it as equal to time-unlimited therapy in terms of its potential effectiveness to those who see it as useful but likely limited in its effect. Theorists vary in their relative emphasis on the patient's history versus the present predicament as described by the patient. Theorists differ in terms of the transparency of their therapy, in the sense of how aware the patient is likely to be of the hypotheses motivating the therapist's behavior. Theorists also differ in their activity level and in the nature of their interventions—confrontation versus support, challenge versus patient exploration.

To be more specific, the theorists whose work is described in this section appear to differ in their fundamental attitudes toward planned short-term psychotherapy. Some, such as Bellak (Chapter 3) and Bloom (Chapter 8), assume that short-term therapy should be thought of as the treatment of choice, if not for every patient, certainly for almost every patient, and certainly at first before any longer treatments are undertaken. Others, such as Davanloo (Chapter 4), Sifneos (Chapter 5), and Gustafson (Chapter 9), see it as suitable only for certain patients and spend considerable time thinking about the criteria for suitability for planned short-term psychotherapy.

In addition to attitudinal differences, the therapists whose approaches are presented in this section vary in the methods of their practice of planned short-term psychotherapy. Contrasts and comparisons in the following eight areas are of particular interest.

Duration of Treatment

While most short-term therapists have a flexible approach to treatment duration, some consistent differences in attitudes toward optimal length of treatment can be found. At the low end of the duration spectrum can be found the work of Bellak (Chapter 3) and Bloom (Chapter 8). Durations in the mid range (10–14 hours) are espoused by Mann (Chapter 6), Horowitz (Chapter 10), and Klerman (Chapter 11). A number of therapists do not have an explicit number or range of sessions in mind. In addition, Mann's views of planned short-term psychotherapy have uniquely led him to develop a course of treatment that is fixed at exactly 12 hours.

Therapeutic Contract

A number of theorists assign special importance to an initial diagnostic study and therapeutic contract regarding the theme of the work to be done. This importance is particularly seen in the work of Bellak (Chapter 3), Sifneos (Chapter 5) and Mann (Chapter 6). The identification of a focal issue for the therapy is thought to provide a necessary boundary on the work to be done.

Interpersonal Approaches

Psychodynamic theories of psychopathology and psychotherapy have in recent years turned to interpersonal aspects of human behavior. Most contemporary views of psychopathology and its treatment, regardless of their similarities or differences on other dimensions, accord interpersonal factors more or less equal importance with intrapsychic factors in identifying pathology and in developing remediation programs. That is, most psychodynamic approaches to psychotherapy view psychopathology in an interpersonal context. The author whose theories stress the interpersonal aspect of behavior most clearly is Klerman (Chapter 11), and we shall deal most directly with interpersonal theory in that chapter. To a somewhat lesser extent, the writings of Wolberg (Chapter 2), Bellak (Chapter 3), Sifneos (Chapter 5), and Horowitz (Chapter 10) also make reference to interpersonal aspects of psychopathology and psychotherapy.

Attention to Transference Phenomena

Examination of transference reactions, both positive and negative, is one of the hallmarks of psychodynamically oriented psychotherapy. Among psychodynamically oriented brief psychotherapists there is a growing tendency to talk about attending to characteristics of the relationship rather than attending only to the transference reactions. The most common attitude toward transference phenomena expressed by short-term therapists is to use positive transference in the service of therapy and to try to avoid the development of negative transference reactions. The single and quite remarkable exception to this practice can be found in the work of Lewin (Chapter 7), who has developed a planned short-term therapy that is based on allowing, if not encouraging, the development of a negative transference and then examining its significance as part of the therapeutic process.

Diagnosis-Specific Approaches

While some approaches to planned short-term therapy are broad, in that therapeutic objectives and techniques do not vary significantly as a function of patient characteristics, a number of writers have suggested that their orientation, in either unmodified or modified form, may be particularly helpful for patients in certain diagnostic categories or who are facing certain life problems. Bellak (Chapter 3) has developed a number of suggestions for enhancing his approach with certain specific diagnostic problems. Horowitz (Chapter 10) has developed a type of brief psychotherapy that is specifically designed for patients who are coping with stressful life events, and within this group he has certain suggestions for how to be particularly helpful with patients with hysterical, compulsive, narcissistic, or borderline personalities. Klerman (Chapter 11) has developed a form of brief psychotherapy particularly suitable for patients who are suffering from nonpsychotic depressions. Lewin (Chapter 7) suggests that his approach is useful for treating patients with character disorders. Sifneos (Chapter 5) believes that his approach to brief psychotherapy is especially suitable for patients with oedipal issues who do not show evidence of significant regression.

The Mid-Session Intermission

While most theorists conduct traditional uninterrupted individual sessions, a relatively new approach to the organization of the initial therapeutic hour is well illustrated in the work of Gustafson (Chapter 9). This practice, which will also appear elsewhere, includes a somewhat longer initial interview appointment and a team of observers who, with the patient's permission, observe the interview through a one-way mirror. At some point midway through the initial session a brief intermission is taken during which time the therapist meets with the observers to share observations of the patient and to develop a consensus about the nature of the patient's problems and how best to be of help. The therapeutic session is then resumed, and the therapist discusses this assessment with the patient as part of the treatment planning process.

Planned Follow-Up Interviews

A consensus is developing among short-term therapists that a follow-up interview (usually a single interview by phone) can be a valuable part of the therapeutic encounter. This point of view, and its justification, can be found in the writings of Wolberg (Chapter 2), Bellak (Chapter 3), Mann (Chapter 6), Bloom (Chapter 8), and Klerman (Chapter 11).

Importance of Evaluation of Outcome

Finally, among the writers in this section are several who have described their efforts to examine the effectiveness of their work. This group includes Sifneos (Chapter 5), Lewin (Chapter 7), Bloom (Chapter 8), Horowitz (Chapter 10), and Klerman (Chapter 11). These efforts range from rather informal clinical follow-up assessments to quite sophisticated controlled outcome studies.

CHAPTER 2

WOLBERG'S FLEXIBLE SHORT-TERM PSYCHOTHERAPY

Overview

Therapeutic Goals

Therapeutic Techniques

Concluding Comments

Lewis Wolberg, a psychiatrist and psychoanalyst, founded and remained affiliated with the Postgraduate Center for Mental Health, a treatment and training facility in New York City from 1945 until his death in 1988. Reminding the reader that Freud practiced short-term therapy, Wolberg (1965a, 1965c, 1968, 1980), one of the earliest writers in the field, suggested that its virtues have not been fully appreciated. He argued that short-term therapy requires its own methodology and the development of its own theoretical concepts—it is not simply less of traditional long-term psychotherapy.

In approaching these requirements, Wolberg discussed the essential compromises in short-term therapy in terms of therapeutic goals, techniques, attitudes, and selection of cases and then presented an impressive rationale and set of principles for what he called "a flexible system of short-term psychotherapy" (1965a, p. 142). In doing so, Wolberg acknowledged the contribution of Karl Menninger, who in 1963 wrote, "The special merit of psychoanalysis is that from the painstaking long-continued treatment of some individuals so much has been learned that is helpful in the shorter treatment of other individuals" (quoted in Wolberg, 1965a, pp. 152–153; Menninger, 1963).

While Wolberg came from a traditional psychoanalytic background and clearly had not made peace with the issue of whether planned short-term psychotherapy could be as effective as time-unlimited psychotherapy,

his views of planned short-term psychotherapy were remarkably catholic. His 1980 handbook of short-term psychotherapy, for example, includes chapters on crisis intervention, hypnosis, use of dreams, relaxation techniques, and homework assignments.

THERAPEUTIC GOALS

Wolberg believed that abbreviated therapeutic goals must be accepted in short-term therapy. He mentioned specifically: (1) symptom relief, (2) restoration of prior level of functioning, (3) some understanding in the client of the factors operative in producing the problem for which help is sought, (4) beginning recognition of character traits that prevent a more satisfying life adjustment, (5) increased awareness of how early childhood experiences play a role in establishing these character traits, (6) recognition of some of the relationships between character traits and the current conflict, and (7) identification of some workable steps toward remediation.

With regard to techniques that have special salience in short-term psychotherapy, Wolberg identified the placebo influence, that is, the role of faith in the agency providing help; the therapeutic value of the relationship itself; the virtue of unburdening and emotional catharsis; the helpfulness of suggestion and teaching; and, finally, the unpredictable spontaneous forces and changes that arise from time to time with or without psychotherapy.

THERAPEUTIC TECHNIQUES

The most important changes in therapeutic technique that are needed when traditional psychotherapists begin doing brief psychotherapy include a higher activity level; open expressions of interest, sympathy, and encouragement; a willingness to try a variety of therapeutic strategies in a responsible manner rather than insisting on a single therapeutic approach; and a need on the part of the therapist to overcome (where it exists) the "prejudice of depth." According to Wolberg, this prejudice is founded in the belief that discussing the past is necessarily more therapeutic than discussing the present, that discussing material about which the client is unaware is necessarily more therapeutic than discussing experiences that are conscious, and that discussing attitudes toward the therapist is necessarily more therapeutic than discussing attitudes toward other important figures in the client's life.

When one examines Wolberg's system of short-term psychotherapy, his indebtedness to psychoanalytic concepts of personality development and of remediation is always clear. Wolberg made important use of such concepts as dream interpretation, transference, the psychodynamic hypothesis, and resistance. But he also made use of concepts that arise from learning theory, environmental analysis, and interpersonal psychology. In addition, he proposed that attention be directed to the establishment of life values and a life philosophy. That is, Wolberg's approach was itself an illustration of the responsible eclecticism that he suggested is needed by all therapists doing short-term psychotherapy.

The initial step in Wolberg's flexible approach to short-term psychotherapy is the rapid establishment of a working relationship through sympathetic listening, communicating understanding and self-confidence, reassuring clients who seem without hope, and taking an active role in structuring the therapeutic situation. While a relationship was being established, Wolberg would attempt to develop a diagnostic and psychodynamic formulation. In this process Wolberg drew heavily on psychoanalytic theories of personality development and psychopathology.

Formulation of the client's problem is followed by the identification of a specific area on which to focus. Often the focus is on the precipitating stress situation. Sometimes it is on the most distressing symptom or symptoms. Less often the focus is on characteristics of the relationship between the client and the therapist. Therapeutic techniques that were of particular importance to Wolberg include actions that help clarify and interpret the client's behavior.

In addition, Wolberg helped his clients learn how to increase their own self-understanding. He identified five particular strategies in working with his clients. First, he suggested that they relate their outbursts of tension, anxiety, and symptom increase to provocative incidents in the environment and to insecurities within the self. Second, he urged clients to become sensitive to the kind of circumstances that boost or lower feelings about themselves. Third, he encouraged clients to observe the vicissitudes in their relationships with other people. Fourth, he believed that clients should become more expert in understanding their own dreams and daydreams. Finally, he believed that clients can become sensitive to those occasions when they fail to put their insights into action.

Wolberg believed that annual follow-up interviews are important, either in person, by telephone, or by a letter from the client outlining feelings and progress. Plans for the follow-up are generally made as part of the termination phase of the therapy.

A General Guide for Short-Term Psychotherapy

Wolberg believed that a number of general principles of psychodynamic short-term therapy apply regardless of the therapist's specific theoretical point of view, personality, or level of skill. These 20 principles, identified and illustrated in Box 2-1, can be adapted to individual situations, but failure to employ these principles, however they are adapted, invites therapeutic failure. These general principles are enormously useful and have hardly been improved upon since their original formulation.

Wolberg summarized the stages that seem to occur in the resolution of an emotional problem in the process of short-term psychotherapy (see Box 2-2).

Box 2-1: Wolberg's General Principles of Short-Term Psychotherapy

1. Establish a Positive Working Relationship

Basic to achieving any significant therapeutic results is the establishment of a therapeutic alliance through the display of warmth, understanding, acceptance, and empathy.

Patient: I feel helpless about getting well. Do you think I can get over this trouble of mine?

Therapist: Do you really have a desire to get over this trouble? If you really do, this is nine-tenths of the battle. You will want to apply yourself to the job of getting well. I will point out some things that you can do, and if you work at them yourself, I see no reason why you can't get better. (1980, p. 36)

2. Deal with Initial Resistances

Among the causes of resistance that are commonly encountered, particularly early in the short-term therapy, are a mismatch between the patient's fantasies about an ideal therapist and the actual therapist, being referred to a mental health professional for a problem that is physical in its manifestations, and lack of motivation. Wolberg provides a number of illustrative examples of exchanges that deal with these resistances, among them the following:

Patient: Dr. Jones sent me here. I have a problem with stomach aches and have been seeing doctors for it for a long time.

Therapist: As you know, I am a psychiatrist. What makes you feel your problem is psychological?

Patient: I don't think it is, but Dr. Jones says it might be, and he sent me here.

Therapist: Do you think it is?

Patient: No, I can't see how this pain comes from my head.

Therapist: Well, it might be organic, but with someone who has suffered as long as you have, the pain will cause a good deal of tension and upset. *[To insist on the idea that the problem is psychological would be a poor tactic. First, the therapist may be wrong, and the condition may be organic though undetectable by present-day tests and examinations. Second, the patient may need to retain his notion of the symptom's organicity and even to be able to experience attenuated pain from time to time as a defense against overwhelming anxiety or, in certain serious conditions, psychosis.]*

Patient: It sure does.

Therapist: And the tension and depression prevent the stomach from healing. Tension interferes with healing of even true physical problems. Now when you reduce tension, it helps the healing. It might help you even if your problem is organic.

Patient: I hope so.

Therapist: So what we can do is try to figure out what problems you have that are causing tension, and also lift the tension. This should help your pain.

Patient: I would like that. I get tense in my job with the people I work. Some of them are crumbs. *[Patient goes on talking, opening up pockets of anxiety.]* (1980, p. 37)

3. Gather Historical Material and Other Data

Let patients tell their stories with as little interruption as possible. From the individual story the therapist should be able to develop a tentative diagnosis and psychodynamic formulation. Questions that could be kept in mind while listening to the history

(continued)

Box 2-1 continued

include: What is the most important problem to the patient? Why does the patient come to treatment at this time? What has the patient done about the problem so far? What theory does the patient have about the causes of the problem? What does the patient expect or want from the therapy?

4. Select the Symptoms That Are Most Amenable to Treatment

A focal problem needs to be selected and agreed upon by the therapist and patient in order to help organize the therapy. The therapist can then summarize the focus to make sure that the patient agrees.

Therapist: What you are complaining most about is a sense of hopelessness and depression. If we focused on these and worked toward eliminating them, would you agree?
Patient: I should say so, but I would also like to see how I could improve my marriage. It's been going downhill fast. The last fight I had with my husband was the limit.
Therapist: Well, suppose we take up the problems you are having with your husband and see how these are connected with your symptoms.
Patient: I would like that, doctor. (1980, p. 39)

5. Define the Precipitating Events

Identifying the precipitating factors that seemed to cause the present symptoms helps identify fruitful directions for exploration. It is not always easy to identify these events, but the therapist should try to do so even if the patient seems to be unwilling or unenthusiastic.

Therapist: It seems as if you were managing to get along without trouble until your daughter told you about the affair she is having with this married man. Do you believe this started you off on the downslide?
Patient: Doctor, I can't tell you the shock this was to me. Janie was such an ideal child and never was a bit of a problem. And then this thing happened. She's completely changed, and I can't understand it. (1980, p. 40)

6. Present a Working Hypothesis to the Patient

After the first session the therapist should have enough information to formulate a working hypothesis to account for the patient's presenting problem. This hypothesis should be suggested to the patient in a nontechnical way so as to maintain the patient's sense of confidence in the therapist.

Therapist: Is it possible that you are afraid your husband will do to you what your father did to your mother?
Patient: (breaking out in tears) Oh, it's so terrible. I sometimes think I can't stand it.
Therapist: Stand his leaving you or the fact that he had an affair?
Patient: If it could end right now, I mean if he would stop it. *(pause)*
Therapist: You would forget what had happened?
Patient: (pause) Yes, yes.
Therapist: How you handle yourself will determine what happens. You can see that your present upset is probably linked with what happened in your home when you were a child. Would you tell me about your love life with your husband? (1980, pp. 40–41)

7. Make a Tentative Diagnosis

Wolberg acknowledges that diagnostic categories are of limited usefulness and that sometimes the diagnosis is determined by the policies of reimbursement agencies.

(continued)

Box 2-1 continued

Nevertheless, he urges that a tentative diagnosis be made because it may be helpful in developing a treatment plan.

8. Enlist the Patient as an Active Participant in the Therapy

Many patients are unaccustomed to taking an active role in their therapy. In the case of primary medical care, for example, patients often have to do little more than to comply with the physician's directives. The situation is quite different in the case of psychotherapy, a matter of particular salience when the patient does not have a significant prior history of psychotherapy.

Therapist: There is no magic about getting well. The way we can best accomplish our goals is to work together as a partnership team. I want you to tell me all the important things that are going on with you and I will try to help you understand them. What we want to do is to develop new, healthier patterns. *My* job is to see what is blocking you from achieving this objective by pointing out some things that have and are still blocking you. *Your* job is to act to put into practice new patterns we decide are necessary, you telling me about your experiences and feelings. Psychotherapy is like learning a new language. (1980, pp. 41–42)

9. Make a Verbal Contract with the Patient

There should be an agreement with the patient about whatever characteristics of the therapeutic encounter can be specified in advance—particularly the frequency of appointments, the number of sessions, the fee, and the termination date.

Therapist: We are going to have a total of 12 sessions. In that time we should have made an impact on your anxiety and depression. Now, let's consult the calendar. We will terminate therapy on October 9, and I'll mark it down here. Can you also make a note of it?
Patient: Will 12 sessions be enough?
Therapist: Yes. The least it could do is to get you on the road to really working out the problem.
Patient: What happens if I'm not better?
Therapist: You are an intelligent person and there is no reason why you shouldn't be better in that time. (1980, p. 42)

10. Use the Most Effective Techniques to Help the Patient

Keeping in mind the need for flexibility and an active stance, therapists should implement the most effective techniques or combination of techniques at their disposal.

Therapist: At the start, I believe it would be helpful to reduce your tension. This should be beneficial to you in many ways. One of the best ways of doing this is by teaching you some relaxing exercises. What I would like to do for you is to make a relaxing cassette tape. Do you have a cassette tape recorder?
Patient: No, I haven't.
Therapist: You can buy one quite inexpensively. How do you feel about this?
Patient: It sounds great.
Therapist: OK. Of course, there are other things we will do, but this should help us get off to a good start. (1980, p. 42)

11. Study the Patient's Reactions and Defensive Patterns

Once the therapeutic program has been instituted, the patient will react. Attention to these reactions, including the ways in which the patient defends against the efforts of

(continued)

Box 2-1 continued

the therapist provides very useful information for the therapist and patient to examine together. In part the usefulness of this information is due to the fact that the reactions are in operation right in the office for both patient and therapist to see.

Therapist: I noticed that when I asked you to lean back in the chair and try relaxing to my suggestions, you were quite uneasy and kept on opening your eyes. What were you thinking about?
Patient: (emotionally) My heart started beating. I was afraid I couldn't do it. What you'd think of me. That I'd fail. I guess I'm afraid of doctors. My husband is trying to get me to see a gynecologist.
Therapist: But you kept opening your eyes.
Patient: (pause) You know doctor, I'm afraid of losing control, of what might come out. I guess I don't trust anybody.
Therapist: Afraid of what would happen here, of what I might do if you shut your eyes? *(smiling)*
Patient: (laughing) I guess so. Silly. But the thought came to me about something sexual. (1980, p. 43)

12. Be Sensitive to How the Past Is Influencing the Present

Every psychodynamic approach to psychotherapy makes use of the relationships between the past and the present, and Wolberg's approach is no exception. He does note, however, that it is important to avoid being trapped in a endless exploration of the past. Attempts are made to learn how established patterns of behavior have operated throughout the patient's lifetime, and interpretations are made at propitious moments when the patient seems to have some beginning awareness of connections between past experiences and present behavior.

13. Watch for Transference Reactions

Wolberg suggests that the therapist need not deal with positive transference, but that negative transference reactions should be dealt with rapidly and sympathetically, since such reactions can interfere with the therapeutic alliance and inadvertently lengthen the duration of treatment.

Therapist: (noting the patient's hesitant speech) You seem to be upset about something.
Patient: Why, should I be upset?
Therapist: You might be if I did something you didn't like.
Patient: (pause) No—I'm afraid, just afraid I'm not doing what I should. I've been here six times and I still have that panicky feeling from time to time. Do other patients do better?
Therapist: You seem to be comparing yourself to my other patients.
Patient: I—I—I guess so. The young man that came before me. He seems so self-confident and cheerful. I guess I felt inferior, that you would find fault with me.
Therapist: Do you think I like him better than I do you?
Patient: Well, wouldn't you, if he was doing better than I was?
Therapist: That's interesting. Tell me more.
Patient: I've been that way. My parents, I felt, preferred my older brother. He always came in on top. They were proud of his accomplishments in school.
Therapist: So in a way you feel I should be acting like your parents.
Patient: I can't help feeling that way.
Therapist: Don't you think this is a pattern that is really self-defeating? We ought to explore this more.

(continued)

Box 2-1 continued

Patient: (emotionally) Well, I really thought today you were going to send me to another doctor because you were sick of me.
Therapist: Actually, the thought never occurred to me to do that. But I'm glad you brought this matter out because we will be able to explore some of your innermost fears about how people feel about you. (1980, p. 43-44)

14. Examine Possible Countertransference Feelings
Wolberg cautions therapists that either persistent irritability, boredom, and anger or extraordinary interest in or attraction to any patient, on the other hand, may signal the presence of significant countertransference feelings that call for therapist self-examination. Some patients may remind therapists of important figures in their lives, and without an appropriate examination of these feelings, the therapy may fail. If self-examination does not cure the countertransference feelings, Wolberg suggests that the patient be transferred to another therapist.

15. Constantly Look for Resistances That Threaten Progress
Continuing resistances must be brought out openly in an empathic and nonblaming way if they are not to jeopardize the success of the time-limited psychotherapy. The therapist may want to help the patient identify the value that the resistance must have. Sometimes simply bringing the evidence of resistance to the attention of the patient may help dissipate it.

Patient: I didn't want to come here. Last time I had a terribly severe headache. I felt dizzy in the head. *(pause)*
Therapist: I wonder why. Did anything happen here that upset you; did I do anything to upset you?
Patient: No, it's funny but it's something I can't understand. I want to come here, and I don't. It's like I'm afraid.
Therapist: Afraid?
Patient: (Pause; patient flushes) I can't understand it. People are always trying to change me. As far back as I can remember, at home, at school.
Therapist: And you resent their trying to change you.
Patient: Yes, I feel they can't leave me alone.
Therapist: Perhaps you feel I'm trying to change you.
Patient: (angrily) Aren't you?
Therapist: Only if *you* want to change. In what way do you want to change, if at all?
Patient: I want to get rid of my headaches, and stomach aches, and all the rest of my aches.
Therapist: But you don't want to change to do this.
Patient: Well, doctor, this isn't true. I want to change the way I want to.
Therapist: Are you sure the way *you* want to change will help you get rid of your symptoms?
Patient: But that's why I'm coming here so you will tell me.
Therapist: But you resent my making suggestions to you because somehow you put me in the class of everybody else who you believe wants to take your independence away. And then you show resistance to what I am trying to do.
Patient: (laughs) Isn't that silly. I really do trust you.
Therapist: Then supposing when you begin to feel you are being dominated you tell me, so we can talk it out. I really want to help you and not dominate you.
Patient: Thank you, doctor, I do feel better. (1980, p. 45)

(continued)

Box 2-1 continued

16. Give the Patient Homework

Time-limited psychotherapy assumes that much of the treatment takes place between sessions. The therapist plays a role in how some of this between-session time is used by suggesting activities for the patient—for example, keeping a log or diary, establishing schedules of one sort or another, having a conversation with a specific person or persons, rewarding oneself for some positive action, thinking about a certain problem, reading a particular book or article, self-hypnosis, or writing to someone.

Therapist: What may help you is understanding what triggers off your headaches and makes them worse. Supposing you keep a diary and jot down the frequency of your headaches. Every time you get a headache write down the day and time. Even more important, write down the events that immediately preceded the onset of the headache or the feelings or thought you had that brought it on. If a headache is stopped by anything that has happened, or by anything you think about or figure out, write that down, and bring your diary when you come here so we can talk about what has happened. (1980, p. 45)

17. Keep Accenting Prearranged Termination

Time-limited therapy ends—often sooner than the patient wishes. But if excessive dependency needs are not to be encouraged nor fears of autonomy reinforced, it is important to remind the patient of the agreed-upon date of termination. Manifestations of regression that may occur as a consequence of these reminders need to be dealt with just as any other issue in therapy—by interpretation or any other appropriate maneuver.

Therapist: We have five more sessions, as you know, and then we will terminate.
Patient: I realize it, but I always have trouble breaking away. My wife calls me a holder-oner.
Therapist: Yes, that's exactly what we want to avoid, the dependency. You are likely to resent ending treatment for that reason. What do you think?
Patient: (laughing) I'll try not to.
Therapist: Well, keep thinking about it, and if you have any bad reactions let's talk about it. It's important not to make treatment a way of life. By the end of the five sessions, you should be able to carry on.
Patient: But supposing I don't make it?
Therapist: There you go, see, anticipating failure. This is a gesture to hold on.
Patient: Well, doctor, I know you are right. I'll keep working on it. (1980, p. 46)

18. Terminate Therapy on the Agreed-Upon Date

Wolberg treats the termination date very seriously and, except in the rarest of circumstances, terminates the therapy as scheduled. He does suggest, however, that patients write to him at some time in the future to let him know how things are going. They also know that if a problem arises they can call and arrange for an appointment.

Therapist: This is, as you know, our last session. I want you now to try things out on your own. Keep practicing the things I taught you—the relaxation exercises, the figuring out what brings on your symptoms and takes them away, and so forth. You should continue to get better. But setbacks may occur from time to time. Don't let that upset you. That's normal and you'll get over the setback. In fact, it may help you figure out better what your symptoms are all about. Now, if in the future you find you need a little more help, don't hesitate to call me and I'll try to arrange an appointment. (1980, p. 46)

(continued)

Box 2-1 continued

19. *Stress the need for continuing work on oneself*

Therapy continues beyond its formal end, and the therapist must not allow the patient to underestimate how important continuing self-therapy is for maintaining and improving upon therapeutic gains already made. The therapist may want to encourage the patient to isolate the past from the present and future, to accept tension and anxiety as a normal part of life, to recognize what can and cannot be changed, and to stop regretting actions and thoughts of the past and anticipating disaster in the future.

20. *Arrange for Further Treatment If Necessary*

If a patient exhibits very little improvement at the time of discharge from time-limited psychotherapy, continuing treatment may be necessary. The continuing contact does not need to be intensive or prolonged; the patient's needs can often be met by infrequent and short visits, for example, a 15- or 20-minute appointment every two or three weeks. Often it is only necessary that the patient know that a supportive person is available if needed. A social support group can be suggested, and occasionally a referral can be made to another therapist who may have some special skills, such as biofeedback, for example, that may be appropriate.

From L. R. Wolberg, *Handbook of Short-Term Psychotherapy*, New York: Thieme-Stratton, 1980. Used with permission from Thieme Medical Publications, Inc.

Box 2-2: Wolberg's Summary of the Therapeutic Process

1. Patients become reassured that they are not hopeless and that there is nothing so drastically wrong with them to prevent a resolution of their suffering.
2. They develop some understanding of reasons for their emotional breakdown and become aware of the fact that they have had problems within themselves that have sensitized them to their current upset.
3. On the basis of their understanding, they recognize that there are things they can do about their current environmental situation, as well as about their attitudes toward people and toward themselves.
4. They accept the fact that there are and probably always will be limitations in their environment and in themselves that they may be unable to change.
5. They fulfill themselves as completely as possible in spite of handicaps in their environment and in themselves, at the same time that they promote themselves to as great degrees of maturity and responsibility as are within their potential.

From L. R. Wolberg, *Short-Term Psychotherapy*, New York: Grune & Stratton, 1965, pp. 192–193. Used with permission from W. B. Saunders Company.

The Therapist as Educator

Wolberg also believed that clients can profit from knowing a few general principles that can assist in increasing life satisfaction. While values can change slowly in the course of long-term therapy, Wolberg wondered whether in short-term therapy, therapists can "expedite matters by acting in an educational capacity, pointing out faulty values and indicating healthy ones that the patient may advantageously adopt" (1965a, p. 183). Among these life principles that can be shared, Wolberg mentioned a dozen that seem particularly salient to him. They are presented in Box 2-3 in summary form as a series of aphorisms.

Box 2-3: Wolberg's Educational Aphorisms

1. What's past is past. Stop worrying about what happened long ago.
2. Learn to recognize when you are tense or anxious and try to identify the sources of these feelings.
3. A certain amount of tension and anxiety is normal in life.
4. All people have to live with a certain amount of anger and hostile feelings and should learn to tolerate those feelings.
5. Expect to be frustrated from time to time in life, and learn to accept those experiences.
6. If you find something in your environment that needs changing, get started correcting it.
7. Some life circumstances are irremediable. When something can't be changed, learn to live with it.
8. When you see that you are being self-destructive, figure out what you're doing. Remember, you have the power to change your behavior.
9. Keep the demands you make on yourself within realistic and reasonable limits.
10. People are different. Just because there are some things other people can do that you can't doesn't make you inferior.
11. Life is to be enjoyed. Get all the pleasure you can out of it.
12. Value the opportunities you have to build better relationships with people with whom you interact. Try to see the world through their eyes.

From L. R. Wolberg, *Short-Term Psychotherapy*, New York: Grune & Stratton, 1965, pp. 183–189. Used with permission from W. B. Saunders Company.

CONCLUDING COMMENTS

Wolberg was one of the earliest writers in the field of time-limited psychotherapy, and his work bears the unmistakable stamp of traditional psychoanalysis, with a full measure of compassionate flexibility added.

His work as a therapist was very eclectic, and it is astonishing how nondoctrinaire he was about the kinds of therapeutic techniques he recommended.

His list of such techniques included teaching, relaxation tapes, hypnosis, homilies, direct suggestion, psychoactive drugs, catharsis, faith, counting on good luck, dream interpretation, and crisis intervention—all in the service of accomplishing significant therapeutic objectives in as short a time as feasible. Yet, he did not stray too far from his psychodynamic base, and, while his fingers seemed crossed, his approach to time-limited psychotherapy was firmly rooted and at the same time was practical and broad.

CHAPTER 3

BELLAK'S INTENSIVE BRIEF AND EMERGENCY PSYCHOTHERAPY

Overview

Goals of Therapy

Therapeutic Techniques

Continued Development of Brief and Emergency Psychotherapy

Fundamental Aspects of Intensive Brief and Emergency Psychotherapy

Diagnosis-Specific Brief Therapy Recommendations

Concluding Comments

From 1958 until 1964, Leopold Bellak and Leonard Small (1965, 1978; see also Bellak, 1984) established and were associated with the Trouble Shooting Clinic, a service of the Psychiatric Department of the City Hospital at Elmhurst, Queens, New York. During its six-year life the clinic served as a 24-hour emotional first aid station, offering "immediate, walk-in care of emotional problems of minor or major degree, from advice to the lovelorn to care of acute psychoses" (Bellak & Small, 1965, p. 141). Its rationale was both therapeutic and preventive, in the sense that minor problems could be prevented from becoming more severe and helping a client deal with a problem might make it easier for that client to deal with a future problem without professional assistance.

GOALS OF THERAPY

Bellak and Small came out of a conservative psychoanalytic tradition and have tried to show in their volumes how psychoanalytic theory and therapeutic concepts can be used in providing brief and emergency psychotherapy. Rather than developing a separate theory, they argue that properly understood psychodynamic formulations can be successfully applied in brief psychotherapy. Bellak and Small use the term *brief* to mean between one and five or six

(depending on whether there is a follow-up contact) 50-minute therapy sessions.

In their earliest publications Bellak and Small suggested that "the goal of brief psychotherapy is limited to the removal or amelioration of specific symptoms: it does not attempt the reconstitution of personality except that any dynamic intervention may secondarily and, to a certain extent, autonomously lead to some restructuration" (1965, p. 9).

Brief psychotherapy seeks to help a client continue to function, so that nature can continue its work of healing, and also, when indicated, increase the client's ability to earn enough money so that more extensive psychotherapy can be undertaken. Bellak and Small, while acknowledging that relatively brief psychotherapy may be sufficient to help some clients continue growing on their own, actually favored more traditional, long-term therapy. They saw brief psychotherapy as having the potential for decreasing the sense of personal difficulty and increasing strength and adequacy of functioning so that improved earning power and increased motivation could lead the way to more substantial treatment. When circumstances would permit more prolonged treatment, Bellak and Small initially saw few if any instances where brief psychotherapy would be preferable.

THERAPEUTIC TECHNIQUES

Bellak and Small's most important contributions to the practice of brief psychotherapy are technical. They see the steps in brief psychotherapy as including: (1) identification of the presenting problem, (2) taking a detailed history, (3) establishing an understanding of the relationship between that history and the presenting problem, (4) selecting and applying appropriate interventions, (5) working through the problem from differing perspectives, and (6) termination. They believe that this process can take place most successfully in an atmosphere in which the therapist is seen in a positive light as likable, reliable, understanding, accepting, hopeful, benign, interested, and helpful.

Understanding the history and the details of the presenting problem is basic to the development of formulations and intervention plans, and Bellak and Small allocate virtually all of the first interview to that task. They conceive of the history as comprising two distinguishable parts—first, the history of the chief complaint and the life setting within which it arose and second, a comprehensive developmental history of the client. If the history is skillfully obtained, it should be possible to understand the onset of the present problem in dynamic terms, that is, in relation to genetic, developmental, and cultural events.

The process of establishing hypotheses linking current difficulties with past circumstances and events is, for Bellak and Small, clearly within the psychoanalytic theoretical tradition, a task that "requires every bit of intellectual and emotional equipment the psychotherapist can muster.... No unconscious process, no defensive reaction, no primitive quality in the human being can be alien to him" (1965, p. 49).

Bellak and Small describe the various intervention possibilities open to the therapist undertaking brief psychotherapy. The central intervention is the imparting of insight through judicious interpretations. Other interventions, often just as important as the increase of understanding, include increasing self-esteem; providing the opportunity for catharsis, that is, for the discharge of built-up emotions and tensions; helping repress and restrain drives that are destructive to adjustment, assisting clients to distinguish between what is fantasy and what is real, helping clients become more sensitive to warning signals that originate both inside of and outside them; providing clients with increased intellectual appreciation and understanding of salient issues they are facing; and providing reassurance and support.

The goal of brief psychotherapy is to strengthen the likelihood that more mature behavior will take place and that older neurotic modes of adjustment will be extinguished. In brief psychotherapy there is relatively little time for the application of therapeutic gains in the therapeutic setting. On the other hand, however, the client can continue to learn by applying the lessons of psychotherapy in real life.

Bellak and Small's comments about termination illustrate their own initial uncertainties about the definitive benefits of brief psychotherapy, in that they seem to suggest that these comments would not apply to long-term psychotherapy. They write:

> In brief psychotherapy, the patient must be left with a carefully cultivated positive transference and a clear understanding that he is welcome to return. The maintenance of the positive transference avoids a sense of rejection in the terminating process and permits the patient to retain the therapist as a benign, introjected figure. (1965, p. 73)

Bellak and Small stress that while clients should be urged to apply what they have learned from the brief psychotherapy, the therapist is available for additional help. The client should feel free to contact the therapist before future problems get out of hand, and the client can be urged to provide periodic follow-up reports.

CONTINUED DEVELOPMENT OF BRIEF AND EMERGENCY PSYCHOTHERAPY

Five years after the publication of the second edition of Bellak and Small's description of their brief psychotherapy, Bellak and Siegel (1983) extended the presentation of their ideas. In their new volume they included the adjective *intensive* in discussing their approach; they described it as an approach that draws on learning theory and systems theory as well as on psychoanalytic theory, and they suggested that it could be effective in working with "any and all problems brought to a clinic, an office, or a sick room" (p. 2). Bellak and his colleagues seem to have become more committed to time-limited psychotherapy as a strategy that by itself might fully serve the needs of the patient without lengthening the duration of the therapy—still five or six weekly 50-minute sessions with one additional follow-up session a month later.

FUNDAMENTAL ASPECTS OF INTENSIVE BRIEF AND EMERGENCY PSYCHOTHERAPY

Bellak and Siegel identify ten fundamental aspects of intensive brief and emergency psychotherapy:

1. Focusing on the crucial features of the presenting disorder
2. Understanding precisely why the patient came at this time for treatment, when the immediate problem began, and how such problems existed in the past
3. Identifying causal factors in understanding the presenting problems, that is, bridging the discontinuity between childhood and adulthood, between what is conscious and what is unconscious, and between symptoms and underlying personality conflicts
4. Establishing the fact that symptoms are attempts at problem solving and coping
5. Focusing on learning, on what has been poorly learned and on what needs to be unlearned and relearned
6. Identifying defensive mechanisms used by the patient
7. Focusing on the most disturbing symptoms within the broadest possible framework in order to provide the most precise conceptualization of the problem
8. Undertaking a systematic focused approach to the therapy
9. Acknowledging that the benefits of therapy may extend beyond the immediate focus
10. Accepting the suitability of intensive time-limited psychotherapy for a very wide variety of problems and disorders.

Bellak and Siegel select the problem they will treat, rather than selecting the patient they will treat. As for its principal tenets, Bellak and Siegel suggest that intensive brief and emergency psychotherapy relates to traditional long-term therapy the way a short story relates to a novel. They write: "Those of you who appreciate short stories know what a tremendous impact they can have and those who have actually tried to write a short story know what a terribly demanding task it is" (1983, p. 8). The novel and the short story are not in competition; each has its own strengths, and the writing of each requires its own set of skills. Bellak asserts that the therapist should try to understand everything, should know a great deal, and then should "do the one thing that will make the crucial difference" (1983, p. 8). Careful conceptualization makes time-limited psychotherapy possible.

Bellak believes that all patients can be helped, at least theoretically, by time-limited psychotherapy. Thus, brief therapy should be the first method of choice in working with any patient, whether someone with acute anxiety, a severe character neurosis, or a chronic psychotic. In order for time-limited therapy to be helpful, it has to take place within an understanding of the patient's history, current life situation, and general predispositions. Brief intensive therapy requires a careful historical exploration and psychodynamic appraisal of the person. Yet persons with relatively limited knowledge of psychodynamic principles can be taught to provide brief psychotherapy. Indeed, Bellak and Siegel suggest that a person specifically trained in brief emergency psychotherapy may be more effective than someone more broadly trained but without specific knowledge of brief intensive therapy.

Bellak and Siegel believe that emergency psychotherapy, in which the goal is clearly defined by whatever presents itself as the emergency, need not necessarily be limited to the goal of symptom removal. They believe that, despite the limited time that is available for the therapeutic encounter, there is an opportunity for the patient to achieve a higher level of psychosocial adjustment and maturity than before the emergency (see also Chapter 19). Bellak and Siegel suggest that in addition to its role in early treatment and in rehabilitation, brief psychotherapy may play a useful role in primary prevention in helping people work through the impact of a trauma, for example, before the trauma has had its full effect.

In addition, Bellak and Siegel believe that brief intensive therapy should be the treatment of choice whether the patient is seen in a public facility or in private practice. Finally, they urge the reader to understand that the demands on the therapist are far greater in doing intensive brief psychotherapy than in doing time-unlimited therapy, and that it may be especially difficult for a therapist who has been trained and who has considerable experience in a long-term therapeutic model to move comfortably into a setting where brief therapy is the more common modality.

Intensive Brief Therapy Intervention Techniques

Bellak and Siegel identify a number of specific intervention techniques that are generally appropriate in all psychotherapy but that seem to them unusually useful in their intensive brief therapy. This list of therapeutic techniques is an elaborated and useful extension of similar guidelines developed by them in their earlier publications. These techniques include:

1. Classical interpretation—one of the fundamental methods in dynamic psychotherapy
2. Empathic encouragement of emotional expression,
3. Auxiliary reality testing in which the therapist can clarify patients' distortions of reality
4. Advice and action directives, when patients proposed courses of action (or inaction) seem likely to be harmful to them
5. Increasing self-awareness in patients by sensitizing them to their own signals of conflict
6. Educating patients if they appear to lack information,
7. Helping patients develop an intellectual understanding of their problems
8. Support and reassurance
9. Involvement of the family network when that seems likely to be useful as a strategy for helping identified patients
10. Prescription of psychoactive drugs as appropriate, particularly in order to control anxiety, disturbed thought processes, or depression

DIAGNOSIS-SPECIFIC BRIEF THERAPY RECOMMENDATIONS

A special strength of the Bellak and Small volumes is the discussion of the role of brief psychotherapy in the case of specific psychiatric syndromes and life situations, including depression, panic, depersonalization, phobias, anxiety hysterias, feelings of unreality, suicidal danger, acute psychotic states, acting out, and in catastrophic life events. For each instance a variety of brief case histories is presented to illustrate the general therapeutic guiding principles (Bellak, 1984, Bellak & Siegel, 1983,). The recommendations associated with a number of these specific diagnoses will be presented here to illustrate their approach.

Depression

Bellak believes that where there is a depression, regardless of type, there is a precipitating factor. He identifies a number of major considerations in the management of depression (Box 3-1). These considerations, as can be seen, are firmly embedded within a contemporary psychoanalytic framework.

Suicidal Threats or Attempts

While the danger of suicide is unusually common among patients who are depressed, suicidal attempts are also found in patients who are in a panic, who are delusional or hallucinating or otherwise psychotic, or who are suffering from central nervous system disorders. It is particularly important to assess family history of suicidal thoughts, threats, or attempts and to determine whether other instances of violent acting out have occurred in the past. When patients are unambivalent about suicide, there is often little one can do to prevent the suicide from taking place. But, fortunately, most suicidal patients are ambivalent about their impulses and there are opportunities to provide life-saving clinical help. As for undertaking time-limited psychotherapy with suicidal patients, Bellak makes a number of specific recommendations, in addition to suggesting that therapists keep in mind the recommendations (Box 3-2), for dealing with depressed patients previously enumerated.

Box 3-1: Bellak's Brief Therapy Recommendations—Depression

1. Enhance self-esteem.
2. Reduce the punitive quality of the superego.
3. Reduce the patient's tendency toward intropunitiveness and self-denigration.
4. Help patients cope with loss, disappointments, and the sense that they have been deceived.
5. Help patients resolve their unrequited oral and dependent needs.
6. Help patients cope with the interpersonal aspects of their depression, particularly those related to frustrated narcissistic needs.
7. Identify how denial is used in the service of defense, particularly in obscuring the precipitating events of the depression.
8. Help patients cope with their disturbed object relations.

Adapted from Bellak & Small, 1965, 1978.

Box 3-2: Bellak's Brief Therapy Recommendations—Suicidal Patients

1. Assess the precipitating factors and the current situation, particularly level of hostility, oral needs, level of ego strength, and the specific dynamics of the suicidal impulses.
2. Determine how specific, concrete, and realistic the suicidal plans appear to be, and assess the level of impulse control.
3. Evaluate previous suicidal behavior and family history of suicidality and depression.
4. Abandon therapeutic neutrality under conditions of high lethality.
5. Expand the array of options apparently open to the patient.
6. Identify and involve members of the entire social support system as well as community resources in monitoring the patient and in providing ongoing support and reassurance.
7. Establish a liaison with the patient's primary care physician, and turn to medication and brief hospitalization as needed to control the suicidal impulses.

Adapted from Bellak & Small, 1965, 1978.

Acute Psychotic States

When the conditions are right, it is possible to provide very effective brief psychotherapy to acutely ill psychotic patients on an ambulatory basis. Bellak and Siegel (1983) suggest that when the patient is reasonably cooperative and nonassaultive, and can identify at least one stable current relationship and some socially supportive family nearby; when the therapist can establish a good working relationship with auxiliary therapists, emergency centers, and an inpatient facility; and when the patient has at least a minimally satisfactory housing arrangement, brief ambulatory therapy can be undertaken.

Bellak proposes a number of principles to keep in mind when treating acutely ill psychotics in time-limited psychotherapy (Box 3-3).

Catastrophic Life Events

Psychodynamic approaches play an important role in helping people who are attempting to cope with contemporary life crises (see also Chapter 19). Reactions to stressful life events can be viewed in a historical context just as can any other form of psychological disability. Since the precipitating events are known, however, special therapeutic considerations come into play (Box 3-4).

Box 3-3: Bellak's Brief Therapy Recommendations—Acute Psychotic States

1. Try to establish therapeutic contact with the patient and the patient's psychotic thinking.
2. Provide a rational perspective on how the patient's past plays a role in understanding his or her present predicament.
3. Reassure the patient that you will do everything you can to make sure that the patient will not be overwhelmed by his or her psychosis.
4. Reintroduce careful structure into the patient's life, when such structure has been lost.
5. Be available to the patient, if only by telephone, whenever needed, and provide supplementary therapeutic resources, such as crisis and emergency service addresses and telephone numbers.
6. Involve family members in the therapeutic effort, teaching family members as needed how to be of help to the patient.
7. Arrange for concrete help for the patient in the form of homemaking assistance or social services.
8. Serve as an auxiliary ego, testing reality for the patient, helping the patient make decisions, and confirming and supporting, where appropriate, decisions that the patient has made.
9. When needed, provide access to skilled recommendations regarding pharmacological treatments and hospitalization.

Adapted from Bellak & Small, 1965, 1978.

Box 3-4: Bellak's Brief Therapy Recommendations—Catastrophic Life Events

1. Provide the opportunity for catharsis.
2. Help the patient develop an understanding of the specific psychological meaning of the event, that is, the place of the event in the patient's unique life situation.
3. Explore the sense of guilt or responsibility that often occurs when catastrophic life events take place.
4. Be alert for evidence of long-term negative consequences of the event.
5. Pay particular attention to specific traumatic life events are unusually stressful, such as job loss, retirement, marital disruption, and bereavement. These life events is often associated with characteristic reaction patterns.
6. Catastrophic life events that have a violent component, such as robberies, muggings, rape, and severe disasters or accidents, require special therapeutic sensitivity.

Adapted from Bellak & Small, 1965, 1978.

General Principles of Diagnosis-Specific Recommendations

Inductive examination of these diagnosis-specific recommendations reveals an important set of general principles that Bellak espouses in undertaking time-limited psychotherapy. First, the therapist must find allies in the work to be done and find them quickly. These allies can be in the patient's family, the broader social support system, and the primary medical care system. Furthermore, the work of the outpatient psychotherapist may need to be supplemented with medication and even with periods of brief hospitalization. Second, the therapist must be available to the patient virtually unconditionally, and not just one hour a week, if severe psychopathology is to be treated successfully in limited periods of time. Third, the therapist must be active rather than passive, providing confident reassurance and support and temporarily taking over responsibilities that formerly were and once again will be those of the patient. Finally, Bellak believes that symptoms can be understood as responses to traumatic precipitating events and as part of a unique psychodynamic history. The belief that symptoms are intelligible is part of the great psychodynamic tradition and may provide the greatest reassurance of all to the patient whose symptoms can no longer be mastered without outside help.

CONCLUDING COMMENTS

In some ways the most interesting aspect of Bellak's writing is the illustration of how one's attitudes toward planned short-term psychotherapy can be modified over time. Initially Bellak kept faith with psychoanalytic theory and psychoanalysis. For him, planned short-term psychotherapy was not equivalent to traditional psychoanalytic treatment; it was something to tide patients over until they could enter into a real psychoanalysis.

Yet, Bellak worked for years to push the limits of a very brief psychotherapy—never more than six interviews. That was at the time a tremendous departure from traditional practice, and it must surely have caused many a raised eyebrow among his psychoanalytic colleagues. He kept his credibility, though, by his scholarly approach to his work and by his remarkably conservative approach to brief psychotherapy—as, for example, by allocating the entire first session to a diagnostic and dynamic assessment. His great initial and continuing contribution to brief therapy was his attention to how time-limited psychotherapy could be used specifically with a wide variety of differing diagnostic categories. Here Bellak was at his clinical best.

Five years later, as part of the overall growing interest and confidence in what could be accomplished with planned short-term psychotherapy, Bellak reappeared as a true convert. He asserted that brief psychotherapy was often all that was needed to be of significant help to a patient and, perhaps even more courageously, that doing brief psychotherapy was more difficult and demanding than traditional psychotherapy and that special training was a necessity. In terms of time, all he added to the planned short-term psychotherapy that he had developed five years earlier was a single follow-up session a month after the therapy had been completed. Thus, Bellak is in some ways the paradigm case of the radicalized psychoanalytically oriented long-term therapist.

CHAPTER 4

DAVANLOO'S INTENSIVE SHORT-TERM DYNAMIC PSYCHOTHERAPY

Overview

Davanloo's Psychodynamic Theory

The Seminal Work of David Malan

Therapeutic Techniques

Accelerated Empathic Therapy

Concluding Comments

Habib Davanloo (1978a, 1978c, 1979, 1980a, 1980b, 1980c, 1980d, 1980e; Laikin, Winston, & McCullough, 1991; Nahmias, 1991), founding editor of the *International Journal of Short-Term Psychotherapy*, is on the faculty at McGill University in Montreal and has been practicing short-term psychotherapy for nearly 30 years. He describes his intensive short-term dynamic psychotherapy as follows:

> It is a specific kind of dynamic psychotherapy with the aim of replacing the patient's neurotic pattern of behavior. It is based on psychoanalytic principles, using a special kind of focus interview. One focuses on the exploration of genetic [past history] material with the technique of confrontation, clarification, and exploration into conscious, pre-conscious, and the derivative of unconscious material. Dream interpretation and the analysis of transference reaction are used in varying degrees with an active attempt to avoid the development of transference neurosis. (1978c, pp. 23, 25)

DAVANLOO'S PSYCHODYNAMIC THEORY

Davanloo's (1980a) conceptualization of the therapeutic process draws on two sets of interrelated variables, earlier elaborated by Malan (1963, 1976, 1978b, 1979; Malan & Osimo, 1992). Malan, in turn, was trained and influenced by Balint (1957;

Balint, Ornstein, & Balint, 1972; Hildebrand, 1986), who between 1956 and 1961 was developing the initial ideas of what later came to be called *focal therapy*. Malan and Davanloo have been in close touch with each other over the years and have been much influenced by each other's clinical work. There are now few if any significant differences between the way each of them practices planned short-term psychotherapy.

Malan's ideas have, in fact, had a marked impact on an entire generation of short-term psychotherapists—not only Davanloo, but also Wolberg (Chapter 2), Sifneos (Chapter 5), Mann (Chapter 6), and Gustafson (Chapter 9), among others (see also Gustafson, 1981, 1986). The distinctions that Malan made between the goals and techniques appropriate to time-limited psychotherapy and those appropriate to long-term psychotherapy now constitute part of the foundation of most thinking regarding psychodynamic time-limited psychotherapy.

THE SEMINAL WORK OF DAVID MALAN

The clinical practice implications of Malan's and Davanloo's work are so similar (Migone, 1985) that a separate chapter on Malan will not appear in this volume. But both Malan's and Balint's seminal thinking justifies special review. Malan's thinking is examined here, while Balint's work is reviewed in Chapter 21 in conjunction with the discussion of brief contact therapy.

Malan (1963, 1976; Keller, 1984) wanted to call his brief therapy *radical*, but, warned away from that term by its unfortunate connotations in America, he chose the word *intensive* to describe the kind of brief psychotherapy undertaken by his group at the Tavistock Clinic in London and the Cassel Hospital in Richmond. Malan's studies of brief psychotherapy have been based on clients generally seen for between ten to forty sessions—certainly longer than the average number of contacts implied in the term brief—another reason for not devoting more space to his work in this volume.

Challenging Effectiveness of Long-Term Psychotherapy

Malan finds himself in strong disagreement with at least one aspect of traditional Freudian psychoanalysis, as can be seen in the following pithy paragraph:

> It needs to be stated categorically that in the early part of this century Freud unwittingly took a wrong turning which led to disastrous consequences for the future of psychotherapy. This was to react to increasing resistance with increased passivity —eventually adopting the technique of free association on the part of the patient, and the role of "passive sounding board," free-floating attention, and infinite patience on the part of the therapist. The consequences have been strenuously ignored or denied by generations of analysts and dynamic psychotherapists, but are there for all to see. The most obvious effect has been an enormous increase in the duration of treatment—from a few weeks or months to many years. A less obvious development is that the method has become, to say the least, of doubtful therapeutic effectiveness, a matter which has received little attention or proper investigation. A further practical consequence is the inability of most psychotherapeutic agencies to provide sufficient service; with most vacancies filled by long-term patients, there is little available for new patients who come seeking relief from their suffering. There is, then, a hidden disillusion with this method of treatment, one consequence of which may be called the "flight into training," a maneuver in which experienced staff give up practicing therapy to concentrate on teaching others to practice it, entirely ignoring the fact that the meth-

ods taught have never been shown to be effective. (1980b, pp. 13–14).

The Two Dynamic Triangles

Malan's first set of theoretically interrelated variables that has proven so useful to Davanloo has been referred to by Davanloo as the *triangle of conflict*. This triangle includes the three variables impulse, defense, and anxiety. This triangle represents the classical psychoanalytic theory of symptom formation—an unacceptable impulse generates anxiety, which is, in turn, defended against. Defenses, generally erected to avoid fear or psychic pain, have an associated cost in terms of somatization, depression, phobias, or other symptoms and their resultant anxiety. Thus, the presence of anxiety signals that there is some unacceptable impulse that is being denied expression. To the extent that psychotherapy can help clients cope with their fears, the need for defenses can be reduced with a subsequent reduction in symptomatology and increase in psychic energy.

The second of Malan's sets of interrelated variables that has been adopted by Davanloo is called the *triangle of person* and includes significant people in the past (most often parental figures), in the current social environment (e.g., spouse, friends, or work colleagues), and the therapist. The triangle of person can be noted, for example, when the patient's emotions or modes of behavior toward the therapist are similar to those the patient has had toward significant people in the past or has toward significant people in his or her current life outside of the therapeutic setting.

In each of these three-component sets, meaningful interpretations can link any two components. In the case of the triangle of conflict, connections can be made, as appropriate, between impulse and defense, between impulse and anxiety, and between defense and anxiety. In the case of the triangle of person, psychologically meaningful connections can be drawn between the patient's real or imagined interactions with important people in the past (e.g., parents, siblings) and present, between the patient's past and observed transference phenomena, and, finally, between the patient's life in the present outside of the therapist's office and transference phenomena noted in the office. It is important to clarify the nature of the client's conflicts in all three settings, but this is somewhat simpler than it sounds because very often the same patterns of anxiety, defense, and impulse occur in more than one setting.

With regard to the clinical aspects of the two hypothesized psychodynamic triangles that have become an important component of Davanloo's formulations, Malan (1976) has suggested, first, that the triangle of conflict should be explored before the triangle of person, and its major components should be developed in one area of the patient's life before being linked to another area. Second, within the triangle of conflict the defense—that is, the most manifest aspect of the triangle—should be interpreted first. The impulse and anxiety components of the triangle can be interpreted together later, with the ultimate goal of identifying the underlying impulses that ordinarily serve as the source of the psychopathology. Third, within the triangle of person the most important aim is to develop useful connections between the patient's past and observed transference phenomena in the present (Malan & Osimo, 1992).

Malan's brief psychotherapy differs from traditional long-term therapy in three important respects. First, it has a limited aim—specifically, to work through a particular conflict or set of conflicts partially and then see what results follow. Second, the client understands from the very beginning that the number of sessions is limited. Third, the technique has a remarkably single-minded focus on the agreed-upon therapeutic plan that guides the therapy as a whole. Malan's aim is ambitious—to "resolve either the patient's central problem or at least an important aspect of his psychopathology" (1976, p. 248).

The techniques of brief psychotherapy employed by Malan derive quite directly from psychoanalytic principles. That is, Malan sees the strategic aim of psychotherapy as bringing into consciousness the emotional conflicts the client is struggling with and helping the client experience and clarify them. Such conflicts are thought of as the result of the anxiety brought about by the unsuccessful or uneconomical use of defenses to ward off unacceptable impulses or intolerable feelings. Central to Malan's therapy is the therapeutic plan and the correct selection of clients (see Chapter 24). Malan says, "Put briefly, the best way of keeping interpretations focal is to select focal patients in the first place and then to for-

mulate a correct therapeutic plan" (1976, p. 263; see also Courtenay, 1968).

From a tactical point of view, the therapist is constantly acting on the basis of a judgment about (1) which of the components of the impulse-defense-anxiety triad to interpret, (2) in which of the three person settings would it be most therapeutic to examine that component of the conflict triad, and (3) how the most useful linking interpretations can be made between settings. With regard to this view of psychotherapy, Malan writes:

> It is the ability to formulate the patient's problem in terms of this kind that gives the therapist the opportunity to exert very considerable control over the course of therapy....Provided the initial formulation is correct, a good patient will follow these moves actively; that is, having received a partial interpretation, he will go on to complete it; and having received one interpretation in the sequence, he will spontaneously lead the therapist toward the next. This is part of what is meant by the "therapeutic alliance." It is the combination of a simple initial formulation, a responsive and well-motivated patient, and a therapist who intuitively understands these principles, that results in focal therapy. (1976, p. 262)

THERAPEUTIC TECHNIQUES

To return now to the short-term psychotherapy of Davanloo, we find that his therapeutic techniques are remarkably persistent and confrontive. He himself uses the term *relentless* to describe his approach (1978a), but others have used the terms *remorseless,* and even *bullying* (Hildebrand, 1986). Malan and Osimo (1992) describe Davanloo's work as involving "systematic challenge to the patient's defenses and minute attention to manifestations of transference." The technique is

> capable of breaking through the defenses of even the most resistant patients in a single interview,... enabling them to experience and express transference feelings directly. This in turn results in an 'unlocking' of the unconscious, which is followed by direct access to the hitherto repressed feelings about the past that have led to the patient's neurosis (p. 16; see also p. 326; Worchel, 1993, pp. 204–205).

Alpert (1992) has provided a useful overview of Davanloo's therapy model (Box 4-1).

Box 4-1: An Overview of the Davanloo Therapy Model

1. Therapist inquires into patient's problems.
2. Patient responds to inquiry.
3. Therapist focuses on a problem and labels defenses.
4. Patient experiences discomfort which causes increased resistance.
5. Therapist increases pressure for material and further challenges defenses.
6. Anger is experienced by the patient when his angry impulses become so intense that they break through the defenses erected against them.
7. After the experience of anger, previously unconscious material becomes accessible and the patient feels freedom, relief, sadness, and grief.

From Alpert, 1992, pp. 134–135.

Davanloo interprets transference reactions, thus avoiding the development of a transference neurosis that would require additional time to resolve. He challenges defenses. One result of this approach is that most patients experience feelings of anger, along with the defenses that they characteristically invoke in dealing with anger, such as denial, depression, or reaction formation (Migone, 1985). Perhaps because of the confrontive style of therapy employed by Davanloo, patients who one would consider most appropriate are those who maintain a relatively strong ego and who have not regressed significantly.

Davanloo suggests that his intensive short-term dynamic therapy is ordinarily suitable for patients with a predominantly oedipal problem or in whom the focus is loss (see Worchel, 1993), patients suffering from long-standing obsessional and phobic neuroses, and, finally and perhaps most remarkably, patients with severe forms of psychopathology and more than one focal conflict. Indeed, Davanloo is strongly affirmative about the broad applicability of brief psychotherapy. He writes:

I have never been convinced that short-term dynamic psychotherapy has a limited application and is a psychotherapeutic technique useful only in the treatment of mild neurotic cases. Nor have I ever agreed with those who see short-term dynamic psychotherapy as a technique which offers help best to those patients who are unable to deal with their emotional crisis and develop circumscribed neurotic conditions. Such therapy is of great value for this group of patients, but it has always been my conviction that it can be the psychotherapy of choice for patients suffering more severe psy-

choneurotic disorders of many years' duration, which have paralyzed their lives. (1978a, unpaginated preface)

An indication of the broad applicability of Davanloo's approach to planned short-term psychotherapy can be seen in the papers published by people who have been significantly influenced by his thinking. Among these papers are those of Snyker (1992) on the treatment of exhibitionism and Reitav (1991) and Della Selva (1992) on the treatment of character pathology.

Flegenheimer (1982) has suggested that Davanloo's technique in particular requires that therapists need to be comfortable with their anger and generally in complete control of their feelings. The therapist needs to maintain an emotional neutrality, regardless of what is being discussed, lest the patient "interpret the technique as either sadistic or seductive" (p. 162).

Davanloo's brief psychotherapy tends to average between 10 to 20 sessions but has varied from 5 to 40 sessions. He recommends 5 to 15 sessions for patients with a circumscribed neurotic conflict, 15 to 25 sessions for patients with multiple foci, and 20 to 30 sessions for patients with severe character pathology. These upper limits, like Malan's, are somewhat above what is ordinarily thought of as time-limited psychotherapy. Davanloo has reported, however, that improvement (as assessed by measures of patient's self-concept) tends to increase with the number of sessions up to a maximum of about 20 sessions. After 20 sessions, therapists may find themselves having lost the focal conflict that serves as the integrating rationale of the therapy and may thus compromise the outcome (Ursano & Hales, 1986).

Davanloo is clearly convinced, however, that shorter brief therapy can be quite effective. In his experience, in successful cases significant progress occurs in about eight sessions, as seen in shifts in the patient's interpersonal relationships and in reduction of presenting symptoms. When such progress has been found, it is time to terminate the therapeutic episode—a process that seems to take place without difficulty.

Box 4-2 presents excerpts from an initial interview that illustrate the persistently confrontive character of Davanloo's approach. The patient is a 29-year-old teacher who complains of depression, chronic anxiety, work difficulties, and disturbed relationships with men that have recently culminated in a breakup with a man she had planned to marry. In this excerpt the apparent components of the triangles of conflict and person are identified as they appear in the therapeutic interchange.

Box 4-2: Davanloo at Work—An Initial Interview Excerpt

Symbols in brackets represent corners of the two triangles referred to earlier in the chapter. The following abbreviations are used:

Triangle of Conflict:
   A = Anxiety
   D = Defense
   I = Impulse/Feeling

Triangle of Person:
   T = Therapist
   C = Current Figures
   P = Past Figures

Therapist: How do you feel about talking to me about yourself? [I; T]
Patient: I feel uncomfortable. [A] I have never done this before, so I don't really, you know, I feel I don't really know how to answer some of your questions. [D]
Therapist: Um-hum. But have you noticed that in your relationship here with me you are passive, and I am the one who has to question you repeatedly? [D; T]
Patient: I know....
Therapist: Is this the way it is with other people, or is it only here with me, this passivity, lack of spontaneity? [C]
Patient: Yeah. To some extent. I mean. I'm, there are a lot of things hidden, you know. Somebody once described me "like a hidden flower" or something. There are a lot of things about me that I don't think I have ever really, uh, explored that much. [C; D]
Therapist: Then from what you say you are passive with others. But from what you have told me you indicated that your mother has been a passive person. [P]...Going back to yourself, do you see yourself as a passive person?
Patient: Yeah. [I; D]
Therapist: You do?
Patient: In certain situations where I don't feel, when I get involved with a man, I find I tend to take a passive role, and I don't like that. [C]
Therapist: What specifically do you mean by not liking it?
Patient: I feel upset inside. [I; A]
Therapist: What is it that you experience? You say, "upset?"
Patient: Perhaps irritated, something like that. [I; D]
Therapist: But you say "perhaps." Is it that you experience irritation and anger, or isn't it?

(continued)

Box 4-2 continued

Patient: Ummm. Yeah. Yeah. I do.

Therapist: You say you take a passive role in relation to men. Are you doing that here with me? [T]

Patient: I would say so.

Therapist: You "would" say so, but still you are not committing yourself.

Patient: (long, awkward pause) Well, I don't, you see, I don't know how to, uh, I don't know about the situation, you know. I don't understand this whole situation, you know, I don't understand this whole situation yet. So I, I am here, and I am a passive recipient or a passive participant. I am not passive, really. I am active. I am participating, but I am—[D]

Therapist: Are you participating?

Patient: Well, sure.

Therapist: Um-huh. To what extent?

Patient: (Pause) I am answering your questions.

Therapist: What comes to my mind is, if I don't question you, what do you think would happen here? [D; T]

Patient: Well, I might, I might start to tell, I might start something which would indicate, would tell you where I am going. It might be very intellectual, though, because I don't really know, I don't really understand the source of my depression. [D]

Therapist: Um-hum. In relationship with me, then you are passive; and it is the same with all men. [C]...

Patient: (silent...pause)

Therapist: How do you feel when I indicate to you that you are passive?

Patient: I don't like it. *(The patient is laughing, but it is quite evident that she is irritated.)*

Therapist: But you are smiling.

Patient: I know. Well, maybe that is my way of expressing my irritation.

Therapist: Then you are irritated?

Patient: A little bit, yeah.

Therapist: A little bit?

Patient: Actually, quite a bit. *(The patient is laughing.)* [D]

Therapist: But somehow you smile frequently, don't you?

Patient: It is inappropriate.

Therapist: Let's look at what happened here. I brought to your attention your passivity, your noninvolvement. You got irritated and angry with me, and the way you dealt with your irritation was by smiling. [T; D]

Patient: That is right.

From H. Davanloo, *Short-Term Dynamic Psychotherapy,* Northvale, NJ: Jason Aronson, pp. 48–50. Used with permission.

Even when psychotherapy is proceeding without significant resistance, Davanloo remains consistently goal-oriented as illustrated by the initial treatment session with a client coming to grips with an unresolved grief reaction. Unresolved grief reactions are not only problems in their own right but can prevent the successful resolution of other neurotic conflicts. The psychotherapist tries to detect and treat the unresolved grief reaction by convert-

ing the pathological mourning into normal mourning and then must facilitate the expression of that normal mourning.

The client is a 37-year old Jewish man whose father worked six days a week in his small grocery store. His father suffered from asthma and chronic coughing and died of a heart attack when the client was 16 years old. The client, angry because his father's heart attack had disrupted his vacation, was

**Box 4-3: Excerpt from an Initial Interview with
a Client Suffering from Pathological Mourning**

Therapist: So you were there for your cousin, and all the other ones that got picked on, weren't you? Hmm?

Patient: Yeah.

Therapist: So then you were the one who stood up for the Jew who was being humiliated, but who stood up for you?

Patient: Nobody that I know of. Although…now here's something. When I was in college this friend of mine, we were like this *(two fingers intertwined)* and, ah, there was another guy who started to pick on me…

Therapist: You're fighting your feeling.

Patient: I'm just trying to tell a story.

Therapist: I know, but the feeling comes, let's look at the feeling.

Patient: Well, Jim told the guy he'd kill him if he,…whatever, and I remember he may have grabbed the guy and threw him against a wall.

Therapist: May have or did?

Patient: He did, and he got outraged that this guy was going to pick on me. *(tears in patient's eyes)*

Therapist: This is very moving to you.

Patient: Yeah.

Therapist: Why do you fight your feelings? Because it obviously brings a lot of painful memories from the past and…

Patient: Well, I don't know if it's painful…

Therapist: But that doesn't help.

Patient: No.

Therapist: You said the two of you were very close. Is he still alive?

Patient: Yes, he is in California.

Therapist: The other side of the country, that would be painful too.

Patient: It is. *(takes a deep sigh)* Yeah, I really miss him. He was just here in September, and I hadn't seen him for a few years.

Therapist: He was strong and willing to be there for you.

Patient: Right.

Therapist: Uh hmm. It's obvious that you've missed such a person in your life.

Patient: Yeah *(breaks into deep sobbing)* Yeah, I suppose the person could have been a father but wasn't.

Therapist: So obviously, there's a feeling that you wish you could have had a father like David.

Patient: Uh hmm, right. Instead, I just got…

Therapist: You take a deep sigh.

Patient: Hmm. Instead I just got yelled at. Unless I got good grades, and did this and did that, I got nothing.

Therapist: You mean from him?

Patient: Yeah. Yeah, that was, once I was of age where I could be a bad kid, I was always good, good, good, you know.

Therapist: Uh hmm. We can get to that change because it's important that we understand it, but what is clear is that you missed a person like David in your life, and that it could have been your father but wasn't. And now you are obviously feeling that.

Patient: Well, I'll tell you what! There was one episode when we were kids and my father, we were all driving to the beach and, ah, a policeman, a plain-clothed, ah, unmarked car,

(continued)

Box 4-3 continued

we were little...a car was chasing us and my father didn't know who it was...the guy pulled up behind us, and he ran up the side of the car and started yelling and screaming.... We were all crying, we didn't know who this guy was, like a bandit, or something. Even after he showed his badge, my father still laced into him for upsetting us.

Therapist: Your father was protective of you?

Patient: Oh, yeah!

Therapist: Exactly what did he say to this policeman?

Patient: He said, "Look how you've upset these kids."

Therapist: So then your father stood there, hmmm, and protected you, even in the face of the police?

Patient: Yeah. (*tears rolling down his cheeks*)

Therapist: So there was a wish he could have stood like that in your life and, ah . . .

Patient: Right. *(still crying)* Instead, it seemed like it was turned around at me.

From Worchel, 1993, pp. 209–211.

present in the hospital when his father died. Since that time, the client had become increasingly depressed, unable to relate to his mother or to establish a useful relationship with other women. He now was working six or seven days a week and had also developed asthma. This clinical excerpt is taken from the initial interview, during which time the identification of the unresolved grief reaction becomes quite clear. Immediately prior to this excerpt the client mentioned that he had protected a cousin when he was a child but that later in life there was no one to protect him.

ACCELERATED EMPATHIC THERAPY

A number of therapists have felt that the usefulness of Davanloo's ideas could be improved by allowing for greater expression of empathy by the therapist. These therapists (Alpert, 1992; Fosha, 1992) speak about therapist empathy as creating a more compassionate environment for the client and a stronger bond between client and therapist that can help the client unlock buried memories and their associated feelings. They refer to this expanded version of Davanloo's work as *accelerated empathic therapy.* It should be mentioned, in this connection, that therapists with very different theoretical perspectives have been aware that empathic responses seem to enhance the effectiveness of the psychotherapeutic

encounter (e.g., Burns & Nolen-Hoeksema, 1992; Free, Green, Grace, Chernus, & Whitman, 1985).

The techniques proposed by these therapists encourage expressions of appreciation by the therapist of work already done by the client, a willingness to follow the lead of the client, a sharing of perceptions and feelings by client and therapist, and a more empathic interaction with the client. These techniques include, for example, (1) having the client and therapist monitor each other's body language in order to increase awareness both in the therapist and the client of each other's emotional state; (2) developing greater intimacy and closeness between client and therapist by evoking themes of caring, sharing, attachment, tenderness, and connection; (3) viewing defenses as allies rather than as enemies by appreciating and reframing them as opportunities to explore new avenues of inquiry; and (4) discouraging the client's dependence on the therapist by creating a more egalitarian relationship. In contrast to the Davanloo approach outlined in Box 4-1, Alpert has proposed the analysis of accelerated empathic therapy shown in Box 4-4.

These modifications in Davanloo's approach proposed by Alpert (1992) and Fosha (1992) are hardly trivial, and in some ways can be thought of as a significant departure from Davanloo's original formulations. Accordingly, it should not be surprising that these ideas have generated criticism as

---

Box 4-4: An Overview of Accelerated Empathic Therapy

1. Therapist inquires into patient's problems.
2. Patient reacts to inquiry.
3. Therapist appreciates patient's work.
4. Patient feels cared for and appreciated.
5. Therapist shares his pleasure with patient's reaction.
6. Patient resists receiving what has been longed for or lost because it reconnects him or her with painful wounds.
7. Patient discovers that taking from the therapist is also giving back to the therapist. There is increasing closeness with reciprocal giving and receiving.
8. The therapist—patient interaction is constantly analyzed by the therapist and patient together in order to correct misperceptions. Therapist and patient both describe their cognitive and affective responses as well as physiologic sensations.
9. Patient has corrective emotional experiences.
10. Therapist and patient become caring and cared for peer-partners.
11. Patient and therapist now can work together to bear the trauma, loss, fear, anxiety, etc. that the patient has attempted to avoid.
12. Mastering separation, the patient achieves an adult view of relationships.
13. The transition from childhood to adulthood is worked through repeatedly.

From Alpert, 1992, p. 154.

---

well as support (see B. Foote, 1992; J. Foote, 1992; Land, 1993).

CONCLUDING COMMENTS

Davanloo's special contribution to the work of the planned short-term psychotherapist is his resolute and uncompromising fidelity to some of the most fundamental aspects of psychoanalytic theory. Davanloo treats time-limited psychotherapy as an intellectual task of the first magnitude. His use of the two triangles of conflict and of person as templates for understanding and treating a patient is an impressive example of how to put theory to work, and his insistence on remaining within the great traditions of psychoanalytic theory and practice demonstrates the utility of time-limited psychotherapy that does not compromise those principles.

Davanloo makes virtually unremitting demands on his patients to search within themselves, however difficult the task, and, as he would be the first to admit, his approach to time-limited psychotherapy cannot be tolerated by everyone. The therapeutic encounter must be taken on his terms, which emphasize the cognitive aspects of psychotherapy fully as much as the affective. But for those patients who can meet his terms, his approach provides an unparalleled opportunity to learn about themselves and to inaugurate significant change based on that learning.

CHAPTER 5

SIFNEOS'S ANXIETY-PROVOKING SHORT-TERM PSYCHOTHERAPY

Overview

Defining Anxiety-Provoking Psychotherapy

The Phases of Anxiety-Provoking Psychotherapy

Therapeutic Techniques

Evaluation of Anxiety-Provoking Psychotherapy

Concluding Comments

Peter Sifneos (1972, 1979, 1981a, 1984, 1985, 1987, 1990, 1991, 1992) practices at the Psychiatric Clinic of the Beth Israel Hospital in Boston and distinguishes two general types of psychotherapy whose suitability is determined on the basis of an assessment of the current anxiety level of the client. According to Sifneos, there is an optimal level of anxiety — if it is too high, it should be reduced in the therapeutic setting; if it is too low, it should be increased. Thus, Sifneos distinguishes between what he calls *anxiety-suppressing* and *anxiety-provoking* therapeutic styles. While Sifneos has written about anxiety-suppressing psychotherapy, most of his technical writings have dealt with short-term anxiety-provoking psychotherapy, a form of therapy with which he has been identified since the mid-1950s.

DEFINING ANXIETY-PROVOKING PSYCHOTHERAPY

Short-term anxiety-provoking psychotherapy was developed as a way of meeting the increasing demand for psychotherapy while at the same time, in Sifneos's words, counteracting "the prevailing—and I feel absurd—idea that long-term psychotherapy was the only way to change human attitudes and behavior" (1992, p. x).

While therapy that is anxiety-suppressive seeks to "decrease or eliminate anxiety by use of supportive

therapeutic techniques, such as reassurance, environmental manipulation, hospitalization, or appropriate medication" (Sifneos, 1972, p. 45), therapy that is anxiety-provoking is designed to increase anxiety in order to accomplish its dynamic goals of emotional reeducation and the enhancement of improved problem-solving skills.

Sifneos's anxiety-provoking psychotherapy is thought to be particularly useful in working with individuals who have developed circumscribed psychiatric symptoms superimposed on a reasonably healthy personality structure. Thus, clients with symptoms of anxiety, phobias, grief reactions, mild depression, and interpersonal difficulties are especially suitable. Its principal features are its brevity and limited goals and its focus on facilitating emotional maturation and problem resolution (Nielsen & Barth, 1991).

Both anxiety-provoking and anxiety-suppressive therapy may be of varying duration. Sifneos distinguishes between crisis support (anxiety-suppressive therapy generally lasting less than two months), brief anxiety-suppressive psychotherapy lasting between two months and one year, and long-term anxiety-suppressive psychotherapy that might last indefinitely and would most commonly be used to help seriously disturbed clients. Parallel distinctions are made in the case of anxiety-provoking therapy. Crisis intervention is conceived as anxiety-provoking therapy lasting less than 2 months; short-term anxiety-provoking therapy is conducted in between 12 and 16 weekly 45-minute sessions, (Ursano & Hales, 1986). Psychoanalysis, according to Sifneos, is "anxiety-provoking psychotherapy of long-term duration" (1972, p. 71). Sifneos is primarily identified with short-term anxiety-provoking psychotherapy, and the remainder of this chapter will be devoted to an examination of his ideas about this type of therapy.

THE PHASES OF ANXIETY-PROVOKING PSYCHOTHERAPY

Sifneos divides his psychotherapy into five phases: (1) the patient-therapist encounter, (2) early treatment, (3) height of the treatment, (4) evidence of change, and (5) termination. The first phase involves the building of a therapeutic alliance and the establishment of rapport. Sifneos takes advantage of initial positive feelings in order to interpret, as vigorously as seems necessary, the patient's resis-

tance to getting down to work. During the first phase Sifneos formulates a tentative psychodynamic diagnosis based on a careful developmental history and attention to the nature of the transference relationship as it develops. Sifneos and the patient come to a mutually agreed-upon focus—a definition of the problem to be solved—often by some form of negotiation that results in an acceptable compromise. Sifneos summarizes the first phase by outlining the mutually agreed-upon goals and making an assessment of the work that has to be done to resolve the core neurotic problem.

Identifying a focal issue is crucial to Sifneos's work, and requires not only the development of a psychodynamic formulation of the problem but also the ability to translate that formulation into a vocabulary that the client will understand and accept as the work to be done. Failure to identify the focus of the therapy significantly reduces the likelihood of success.

An example is provided in Box 5-1 of a summary statement skillfully presented by the therapist at the conclusion of the initial phase of the psychotherapy.

Box 5-1: A Summary Statement at the End of the First Phase of Treatment

Therapist: If I understand you right,…you say that the pain in your muscles and joints of your hand and your tendonitis in your elbow have something to do with your tendency to force yourself beyond your own limits. You suggested that your pain might have something to do with your being too nice a person, too easy to get along with. It is very easy for you to say yes, and you take too big a share of what should have been joint liabilities. This happens more often between you and your female friends and between you and your mother. *(The patient is listening attentively and nods her head.)*

For the last couple of months you have managed to diminish this tendency somewhat in relation to your mother. But that makes you feel guilty and also mobilizes some anxiety. *(The patient sighs in confirmation.)*

You mentioned particularly that you used to have more difficulties with women than with men in this respect, which corresponds with your feeling that it is generally easier for you to get along with men than with women. Remember your own words: "There is something delicate here." *(The patient nods.)* You also said that you hope that therapy will help you to discover new connections in your life which may help you say yes and no more according to your limits and your wishes. And I do agree. Let us therefore concentrate on finding out together what it is you call delicate in your relation with men on the one hand, and between you and women on the other, and maybe especially between you and your mother and father. *Patient:* Yes, fine. When can I see you again?

During the early treatment phase Sifneos continues to confront the patient as appropriate, particularly in the service of differentiating the adult, realistic aspects of the patient's personality from the magical infantile aspects of his or her personality. Sifneos is careful to limit the degree of regression by confronting the patient and interpreting the positive transference reactions. During the third phase, the height of the treatment, Sifneos focuses on the historical development of the patient's current difficulties, returning to examine the transference when it interferes with acceptable therapeutic progress. Anxiety-provoking questions are used to confront the patient, a process that often produces anger, a reaction that is mitigated by the existence of a continued strong therapeutic alliance. Sifneos takes a role that is part therapist and part teacher, putting the patient into a role that is part patient and part student. While he discourages lecturing, he certainly sees teaching as integral with therapy.

Sifneos asserts that every emotional symptom has a psychodynamic meaning that may be hidden from awareness. It is anxiety that can lead the client to explore that meaning. When that exploration is successful the client can gain insights that can lead to constructive behavior change, greater inner freedom, and greater resistance to both internal as well as external stress (Nielsen & Barth, 1991).

During the fourth phase, evidence of change, the therapist tries to determine whether there has been sufficient diminution of the presenting emotional problem so that termination can be considered. Evidence of change comes from four sources: reduction of tension in the interview, reduction of symptoms, changes in interpersonal behavior related to the focal issue, and evidence that the patient can generalize that progress to new situations and new areas. Finally, when the patient and therapist are in agreement that the initial goals have been achieved, termination can take place. The date for termination is set, and the therapist deals with the anxieties associated with the impending ending of therapy. As long as the therapist accentuates the positive gains that have been made, encourages the patient to apply what has been learned to new situations, and resists the temptation to broaden the original focus, termination is generally uncomplicated.

THERAPEUTIC TECHNIQUES

The therapeutic concept that sets Sifneos apart from many other brief psychotherapists is that of anxiety provocation. Sifneos describes the concept in the following way:

> Out of a variety of presenting complaints the patient is asked to assign top priority to the one emotional problem which he wants to overcome. The therapist…can obtain…enough information from the patient to…help him arrive at a formulation of the emotional conflicts underlying the patient's difficulty. Throughout the treatment he concentrates his attention especially on those conflicts in an effort to help the patient learn a new way to solve his emotional problem. To achieve these ends the therapist…must use anxiety-provoking questions in order to obtain the evidence he needs to substantiate or to modify his formulation. Also, by utilizing confrontations and clarifications, he must stimulate the patient to examine the areas of emotional difficulty which he tends to avoid in order to help him become aware of his feelings, experience the conflicts, and learn new ways of solving his problem. If the therapist is successful in his efforts, he achieves the stated goals of this kind of psychotherapy and is confident that the patient will use this novel experience and these newly developed problem-solving techniques to deal with the new critical situations in the future. (1972, pp. x–xi)

Box 5-2 illustrates the anxiety-provoking character of Sifneos's psychotherapy. A 25-year old social worker expressed concern at the start of the second interview because she claimed to have forgotten what the area of concentration for her therapy was going to be.

In the example in Box 5-2 the therapist's style is clear—a high level of activity, gentle yet unrelenting exploration, active confrontation, clarification, and interpretation. With regard to overall technique, Sifneos characterizes therapist activity as concentrating on areas of unresolved emotional conflicts by the use of anxiety-provoking questions, while at the same time avoiding involvement with deep-seated character defects, such as excessive passivity, dependence, or narcissism. Sifneos focuses on oedipal conflicts, and, while he deals with issues of loss, he does not believe that his psychotherapy is as suitable for such preoedipal issues.

Oedipal conflicts have a special place in psychoanalytic theory because their resolution is thought to

---

Box 5-2: Sifneos at Work— Provoking Increased Anxiety

Patient: I know that it may be significant, but the funny thing about it is that I cannot remember what we agreed to talk about last week.

Therapist: Why is it funny?

Patient: I meant it in the sense that it was peculiar.

Therapist: But you used the word "funny." What's so amusing in forgetting what we decided to focus on during your therapy?

Patient: Well, it must have something to do with wanting some guidance of sorts. If I don't remember, then you will help me.

Therapist: Yet, how can I help you when I don't know as yet why you have the problems that bring you to the clinic.

Patient: That's true.

Therapist: So, there is a part of you which nevertheless wants me to do something which you know only too well I cannot do. Now, assuming that I tried to tell you what to talk about, how would you feel about it?

Patient: I'd like it.

Therapist: Part of you would like it, but how would the other part feel? The part that knows that I cannot do it?

Patient: A little silly.

Therapist: Meaning?

Patient: (hesitating) That you are a little silly, doing something like that when you really don't know.

Therapist: Precisely! So, wouldn't it be funny then to see your therapist do something silly?

Patient: In a way, yes.

Therapist: So the word "funny" was used appropriately.

Patient: I suppose so.

Therapist: Now that we have clarified this point, let's return to your lapse of memory.

Patient: The funny thing is that I have just remembered what we have agreed to concentrate on during my treatment.

Therapist: There are a lot of funny things going on today!

From P. E. Sifneos, *Short-Term Dynamic Psychotherapy: Evaluation and Technique* (2d ed.), New York: Plenum Publishing Corporation, 1979. Used with permission.

---

be related to the consequent strengthening of the ego and the development of the superego, to gender identity, and to the management of feelings of competitiveness (Horner, 1985). In more general terms, Sifneos (1981a) has summarized what is required for short-term anxiety-provoking psychotherapy to be effective. These requirements are summarized in Box 5-3.

Recent Modifications to Sifneos's Approach

Sifneos's criteria for selecting clients for short-term anxiety-provoking psychotherapy are sufficiently strict so that perhaps only one quarter of clients who apply for this treatment are accepted (see Chapter 24). In an effort to make the treatment available to a larger proportion of applicants, Nielsen and Barth (1991) have relaxed the criteria somewhat by allowing for the possibility of their partial fulfillment. In order to provide a successful therapeutic experience to clients who do not fully meet the original acceptance criteria, a wider array of therapeutic interventions, including the provision of supportive techniques as well as cognitive and behavioral coping procedures, has had to be provided. Nielsen and Barth report that such modifications have allowed them to "make short-term dynamic psychotherapy a treatment of choice for a large number of patients encountered in [their] everyday clinical practice" (1991, p. 74).

Box 5-3: Requirements for Success in Short-Term Anxiety-Provoking Psychotherapy

1. The delineation of a psychodynamic focus that both therapist and patient agree to investigate
2. Presence of unresolved oedipal difficulties, problems relating to separation issues, or grief reactions
3. The establishment of a functional working alliance between patient and therapist
4. Active use of anxiety-provoking confrontation and clarification
5. The transference is dealt with explicitly and early
6. Avoidance of entanglements in pregenital characterological issues
7. Interpretations based on adequate prior data collection from the patient, particularly linking preexisting relationships with parents and transferred attitudes toward the therapist
8. Termination of therapy only after tangible evidence of change in neurotic behavior is found

From Sifneos, 1981a, pp. 47-48.

EVALUATION OF ANXIETY-PROVOKING PSYCHOTHERAPY

Sifneos has taken the task of clinical evaluation of his work very seriously, primarily by means of follow-up studies of formerly treated patients. Initially Sifneos (1972) reported that 50 patients had been treated by short-term anxiety-provoking psychotherapy and that 21 of them had been successfully located between one and one and a half years after the end of their brief therapy. All seemed to have benefited considerably from their treatment. Numerous evaluation studies have been conducted since 1972, the most recent of which was published in 1995 (Svartberg, Seltzer, Stiles, & Khoo, 1995).

Sifneos (1981a) reports that in these follow-up interviews, former patients indicate that: (1) they have a clear understanding of the conflicts underlying their difficulties; (2) they have a moderate degree of symptomatic relief; (3) there is a general improvement in their relationships with others; (4) there is a marked increase in their adaptive skills, problem-solving capacity, and self-esteem; (5) their feelings toward the therapist, who is viewed as an educator and friend, are predominantly positive; and (6) there is a feeling of achievement that is attributed primarily to the efforts of the patients themselves.

Similar findings have been reported from a series of evaluation studies conducted in Norway (Barth, Nielsen, Havik et al., 1988; Barth, Nielsen, Haver et al., 1988; Nielsen et al., 1988). These studies included not only clinical evaluations based on long-term follow-up interviews but also evaluation of score changes on a number of different psychological test instruments. No studies have as yet been reported, however, contrasting short-term anxiety-provoking psychotherapy with other forms of brief psychotherapy or with no-treatment controls.

Sifneos (1992) has recently described an interesting procedure for videotaping follow-up interviews. In this procedure, former clients are asked if they would like to view a past psychotherapy session. The follow-up session is videotaped in such a way that the past psychotherapy session and the follow-up interview can both be seen at the same time. In that way the patient can be seen describing presenting problems while commenting on the changes that have taken place since the end of therapy.

CONCLUDING COMMENTS

Sifneos believes, perhaps somewhat optimistically, that short-term dynamic psychotherapy "has eliminated, once and for all, several of the clichés or myths about psychotherapy in general" (1981a, p. 79). Among these myths, Sifneos identifies the following: (1) Long-term dynamic psychotherapy is the treatment of choice for all neuroses; (2) research regarding psychotherapy, its processes and its evaluation, cannot be done; (3) The transference should not be examined unless it takes the form of resistance; and (4) the only way for the therapist to relate to the patient is by minimal activity.

Sifneos has concluded that by selecting patients who have a circumscribed chief complaint, reasonable ego strength, and high motivation to change; by employing active interventions; and by conscien-

tious clinical examination of the therapeutic process and its consequences, therapists who practice short-term anxiety-provoking psychotherapy can be effective not only with patients who have mild neurotic disorders but also with patients with much more severe problems. Sifneos furthermore believes that short-term psychotherapy should be employed with children, with couples and families, with groups, and in psychosomatic medicine. As will be seen later in this volume, many of these applications are now being actively pursued.

CHAPTER 6

MANN'S TIME-LIMITED PSYCHOTHERAPY

Overview

Disadvantages of Long-Term Therapy

Theoretical Background

A Case Example

Concluding Comments

The critical word in Mann's (1973, 1981, 1984, 1991; Mann & Goldman, 1982) time-limited psychotherapy is the word time (see also Hoyt, 1990; Horowitz, Marmar, Krupnick, Wilner, Kaltreider, & Wallerstein, 1984, pp. 17–22; Kalpin, 1993; Rasmussen & Messer, 1986; Ursano & Hales, 1986, pp. 1510-1511). It is time with its many meanings that is not sufficiently understood, and it is the complex feelings toward the passage of time that help make the therapeutic relationship difficult for client and therapist alike. Mann's work, primarily at the Division of Psychiatry at the Boston University School of Medicine, is based on an insistence that time be faced squarely and that it be used purposefully in the service of psychotherapeutic gain.

Mann and Goldman (1982) write eloquently about time:

> Time is a source of confusion to us, and we express our ambivalence about it in many contradictory ways. Time is everything in our affective lives. Time is a…great teacher, a kind friend, a great leveler, a taskmaster,…money. It is fleeting, out of joint, the only comforter. Father Time is portrayed as an old man with a beard and scythe, whereas immortality is portrayed as a woman. In the unconscious, one finds the origins of the fantasy of immortality in the return to the early mother — to child time. (p. 7)

DISADVANTAGES OF LONG-TERM THERAPY

With the duration of psychotherapy left open, Mann has found that a "well-intentioned sabotage" (1973, p. x) often takes place in clinical settings where ther-

apists are trying to see more clients by shortening the length of treatment. Mann argues that long-term psychotherapy with insufficiently or inaccurately defined treatment goals, leads to a steady widening of and diffusion of content. This creates a growing sense of ambiguity in the mind of the therapist as to what he is about, and…it surely increases the patient's dependence on the therapist. The result is that patient and therapist come to need each other, so that bringing the case to a conclusion seems impossible. (1973, p. x) As a consequence, Mann suggests there comes a point in the treatment of patients when time is no longer on the therapist's side.

In an effort to counteract this nontherapeutic effect of time, Mann has established a short-term psychotherapy limited to exactly 12 treatment hours, with a fixed ending date agreed to in advance by both therapist and client. Setting a fixed ending date to psychotherapy continues a tradition invoked in the earliest writings about psychotherapy — particularly in the work of Freud and Rank (see Hoyt, 1979).

It should be noted that not all planned short-term psychotherapists believe that establishing a fixed ending date is an appropriate strategy (e.g., Binder, Henry, & Strupp, 1987). On the other hand, Gustafson (1981) has commented on how the fixed duration of therapy and termination date have influenced the field of planned short-term therapy: "We can get a little feeling for this in our own terms when we consider how psychotherapy has come to mean seeing the accepting doctor and talking endlessly. What a contrast when James Mann…tells his

patient that 12 sessions will be all that he will need"
(1981, p. 85).

Mann and Goldman (1982) note that all forms of
brief psychotherapy implicitly propose a time limit.
They write:

> The uniqueness of time-limited psychotherapy,
> beyond the specific limitation of treatment to
> twelve sessions, lies in the fact that the time limit
> directly influences the progress and process of treat-
> ment, because of the unconscious meaning and
> experience of time in the course of personality
> development and because of its enduring role in
> giving meaning to the past, present, and future
> affective life of each person. (p. 2)

THEORETICAL BACKGROUND

Mann views attitudes toward time developmentally.
In childhood, time seems infinite — the future seems
forever beyond reach. In adolescence we discover the
limits of time — decisions have to be made; they cannot be put off. The older we get, the more real and
inexorable becomes the passage of time. The special
paradise of timelessness is the paradise of the child.
With maturity comes a growing realization of the limits of time and of the ultimate separation of death that
time brings. Mann argues that there is a sense of
childlike timelessness within the unconscious of all
human beings and that all short forms of psychotherapy revive these complex feelings about time both in
the therapist and in the client.

Mann and Goldman distinguish between *categorical time,* the time of the clock and the calendar,
and *existential time,* the time that is experienced or
lived in. With development and the growth of the
sense of reality comes a growing appreciation of
categorical time and, later, a growing awareness
that time is limited. Life as lived daily includes a
fusion of eternal child time and categorical, finite
adult time.

Thus, there is a child time and an adult time, and
time-limited psychotherapy addresses them both.
Mann writes, "The greater the ambiguity as to the duration of treatment, the greater the influence of child time
on unconscious wishes and expectations. The greater
the specificity of duration of treatment, the more rapidly and appropriately is child time confronted with reality and the work to be done" (1973, p. 11).

The Goals of
Time-Limited Psychotherapy

According to Mann, the process of living includes
a series of separations from persons toward whom
one has feelings that are complex and often contradictory. Mann suggests that "it is as though each
individual feels that he needed something more of
the sustaining object when he was deprived of that
object. If only he were able to go back in time to
review negotiations with that object so that he
could gain what he had not previously" (1973, p.
27). Mann's time-limited psychotherapy is
designed to help reduce the negative self-image
that arose as a consequence of these separations
and losses.

Mann and Goldman (1982) summarize the clinical strengths of their time-limited psychotherapy
by suggesting that it is the only brief therapy that
aims at both a dynamic and a historical appreciation of (1) contemporary conflicts, (2) current attitudes toward the self, (3) residual childhood wishes
toward important figures from the past, and (4)
transference reactions toward contemporary figures
that derive from this past history.

Selection of the Central Issue

In addition to the setting of a time limit, the other
major objective during the start of therapy is identifying which of the patient's problems is to be at
the center of the task. At the initial session the
therapist attempts to identify the patient's chronic
pain associated with his or her self-image and
seeks agreement from the client that that theme
will be the focal point of the treatment. The issue
chosen for investigation is viewed in terms of its
historical as well as its current role in the client's
personality. The central issue concerns itself with
the patient's self-assessment; it has nothing to do
with conflictual interpersonal relationships. The
combination of the time limit and the identified
central issue brings to the forefront, according to
Mann and Goldman, the major private dilemma
associated with the human condition—"the wish to
merge with another but the absolute necessity of
learning to tolerate separation and loss without

undue damage to one's feelings about the self" (1982, p. 29).

Mann and Goldman describe the search for the central issue as a search for the patient's chronic pain. In this context they identify the goal of time-limited psychotherapy as to foster a resolution of this chronic pain and, in the process, to change the patient's negative self-image. In selecting the focal issue to work on, Mann draws heavily on psycho-analytic theory of personality and psychopatholo-gy. Mann believes that the number of such central unresolved issues is small, and he comments at some length on four such themes: (1) independence versus dependence, (2) activity versus passivity, (3) adequate self-esteem versus diminished or loss of self-esteem, and (4) unresolved or delayed grief.

Successful resolution of the central issue is thought to lead to a greater sense of independence and of self, a softening of the harsh superego, the introjection of the good object found in the therapist, reduced reliance on ineffective but automatic defense mechanisms, a broader vision of the rela-tionships of the client with others, and better ways of dealing with interpersonal stresses.

Examples of such theme statements (Box 6-1) presented to patients by Mann for their consideration all recognize the effort that the patient has made to effect change in the negative self-image, as well as the failure of that effort.

Phases in Time-Limited Psychotherapy

Mann has found that the 12 treatment sessions often divide themselves into roughly equal thirds. During the first three or four meetings, there is often rapid symptomatic improvement. Two factors seem to account for this improvement—the patient's optimism which helps create an unambivalent and positive relationship with the therapist, and a substantial relief of accumulated tension due to the abreaction that takes place when the patient begins to describe his or her troubling feelings and experiences. Mann suggests that this phenomenon can be understood as "consisting mostly in a surge of unconscious magical expectations that long ago dis-

---

Box 6-1: Examples of Central Themes as Conceptualized by Mann

I gather from all that you have told me that the greatest problem facing you at this time is your very deep disappointment with yourself to find yourself as you are at this time in your life. (1973, p. 18)

Your major difficulty is that you feel inadequate and chronically depressed as a result of your need to challenge and to pacify men who are important to you. (1973, p. 20)

Because there have been a number of sudden and very painful events in your life, things always seem uncertain, and you are excessively nervous because you do not expect anything to go along well. (1973, p. 20)

You have always feared that despite your best efforts you will lose everything. (Mann & Goldman, 1982, p. 35)

You seem to be a decent man and you have always tried to please others, and yet you feel and you have always had the feeling that you are not wanted. (Mann & Goldman, 1982, p. 33).

You have devoted yourself so completely to your husband and children, and yet you never lose the feeling that you are inferior and inadequate. (Mann & Goldman, 1982, p. 33)

You have always given of yourself to so many others and yet you feel and have always felt both undeserving and unrewarded. (Mann & Goldman, 1982, p. 84)

You have tried hard all your life to be and to do the acceptable things. What hurts you now and always has is the feeling that you are stupid and a phony. (Mann, 1991, p. 33)

appointments will now be undone and that all will be made forever well, as they should have been so long ago" (1973, p. 33).

During the middle phase of the therapy the client's initial enthusiasm begins to wane. Symptoms can return and a sense of pessimism about what will be achieved in treatment can be seen emerging. Old hurts are revived. Patients can begin feeling sorry for themselves. In addition, irrational feelings of antagonism, annoyance, and irritation begin to emerge as the specter of termination of therapy begins to loom. These feelings usually conceal strong dependency needs.

During the ending phase of the treatment the client's reaction to termination becomes the focus of discussion; it is during this last phase that the definitive work of resolution will take place. Separation from the therapist stands in direct symbolic relationship with all previous losses and separations, and resolution of this separation is the key to the therapeutic effect. Because of the importance of helping the patient develop an enhanced sense of adult time, Mann cautions that "it is absolutely incumbent upon the therapist to deal directly with the reaction to termination in all its painful aspects and affects if he expects to help the patient come to some vividly affective understanding of the now inappropriate nature of his early unconscious conflict" (1973, p. 36).

The termination phase, however, continues the exploration and resolution of the central issue identified at the start of therapy and helps patients psychologically differentiate themselves from the therapist and from figures from the past. This process results in a stronger ego, a greater sense of self, and a less punishing superego that at last permits patients to increase their self-esteem, to reduce their sense of guilt, and to feel better about themselves.

Follow-up Contacts with Patients

While Mann and Goldman deliberately make no mention of it during the treatment, they generally conduct a single follow-up interview by phone or letter six months to a year after the termination of therapy in order to learn how the patient is getting along. They report that patients experience the follow-up interview very favorably and have a remarkably accurate recollection of the therapy and of the

central issue as formulated by the therapist. Patients appear to be tolerating unpleasurable feelings, such as anxiety, anger, or shame, far better and seem to be more selective in how they deal with these feelings, in contrast with the virtually automatic way they invoked defenses at the start of therapy.

A CASE EXAMPLE

Excerpts from a case presented by Mann and Goldman (Box 6-2) give a sense of what transpires in Mann's time-limited psychotherapy. The case is that of a 32-year-old special education teacher who had taken leave from his job when his assignment to a classroom consisting of five disturbed children provoked extreme classical anxiety—physiological symptoms of perspiration, rapid heartbeat, and a sense of dread and a great "knot" in his stomach. The patient was now involved in a writing and research project that would come to an end in about two months. The patient was married and had two children and appeared to have a good marital and family relationship.

As a child the patient was big for his age and agreed to play football even though he was afraid of violent or uncontrolled behavior displayed by others. He loved a verbal fight, however, and did well in school. To make nine A's and one B in school meant that he was a "loser." His parents were business people and left for work early each morning. He remembered always being afraid of being left alone, and he dealt with his fear by engaging in some kind of activity, often losing himself in reading.

He appeared to be quite obsessional, and any kind of unstructured situation aroused pathological levels of anxiety. The disturbed children in the classroom were uncontrollable, unpredictable, and very aggressive; their behavior precipitated in him the sense that he had been abandoned; that he would be rendered helpless, subject to his own uncontrollable rage; and that he would soon be out of control. Mann formulated the central issue in the following words: "Although you are a big man physically and although you are successful in your work, you have long been plagued by the fear of helplessness if you are left alone" (Mann & Goldman, 1982, p. 65). Comments about the therapy (in italics) are those of Dr. Mann.

Box 6-2: Excerpts and Comments from a Case of Time-Limited Psychotherapy

Session 2

Patient: I've been thinking about our meeting last week and I really don't think that the fear of being alone was very prominent in my life. *[I had touched on his fear of being alone and now he was objecting. On the basis of the data, I recognized that his statement was defensive and that inquiry into his objection would be necessary. Perhaps he had had experiences of being alone that should be explored.]*

Therapist: Let's look into that. Were you ever away from home prior to going off to college?

Patient: Oh, yes. I went to camp from age eight to seventeen — first as a camper and then as a counselor.

Therapist: Tell me what you remember about camp.

Patient: That's funny — all I can remember is going to the railroad station and then getting off at the town nearest the camp. *[I regard this last statement as corroboration for him and for me that going to camp was indeed a struggle for him.]*

Session 3

[Structure and lack of structure, control and lack of control are central in the patient's personality structure, and whenever he refers to these topics, directly or indirectly, it is imperative that attention be directed to them.]

Therapist: Tell me what happens when one of the kids becomes uncontrollable.

Patient: Well, he must be removed physically into a quiet room.

Therapist: What is the quiet room like?

Patient: It's a padded room, no furniture. There is a small screen in the door, his belt is taken off, and he is left alone.

Therapist: And you know something about what it feels like to be left alone.

Patient: Do you think it's that that gets at me?

Therapist: What did you do when you were left alone?

Patient: I would try to get them not to leave me. I would ask them, sometimes I would tell them that my tummy hurt.

Therapist: Did you ever become angry at them?

Patient: No. I never raged at them or threw things or kicked or spit. *[This is the description, of course, of the uncontrollable children in the classroom.]*

Therapist: The most you could do was to complain that your belly hurt?

Patient: Yes, but it didn't work.

Therapist: It seems to me that the knot that you have described as coming on in your belly when you are in the classroom is the same knot that you felt when your mother left you in the morning.

Patient: You mean my body remembers?

Session 4

[And again the subject of control, the meaning of control or loss of control is to be scanned further. The central issue has now been enlarged and more clearly defined.]

Therapist: You become so badly frightened not only when a child loses control in reality but even when you think it might happen. Obviously, the element of control, of self-control, is a very touchy one for you. Tell me about that.

Patient: You know, I have always been afraid that I might lose control and that I might never come out of it.

Therapist: What do you mean, never come out of it?

Patient: Go crazy. Yet, something just hit me. There was a time when I deliberately chal-

(continued)

Box 6-2 continued

lenged control. In my third year at college, I drove two friends to the big city, stopping at every bar en route. Another time I sky-dived when I was drunk.

Therapist: Do you recall any such challenge even earlier?

Patient: When I was seventeen I raced a car at a track. I hit a tree and broke my neck.

Therapist: Have you felt any more of this kind of challenge since college?

Patient: No, not at all. The only way I sometimes imagine myself losing control these days, well, I come home and find a man raping my wife and I kill him. *[The patient has now given a more graphic picture of his attempts to break through the restraints of control, risking his life in the process. It is important to note that these attempts took place in his adolescence, a time when renewed efforts are made to master earlier conflicts. That he tried desperately bespeaks a degree of ego strength and a capacity for change, since an easier solution for him would have been not to struggle but rather to remain passive and restricted.]*

Session 6

[I felt that more aggressive attention must now be turned to the question of the classroom and his return to it. We had now passed the midpoint of the treatment and soon heightened resistance to termination, another abandonment, would increase his anxiety and harden his resistance to returning to the classroom.]

Therapist: Tell me more about your feelings for Mr. Z *(a scholar with whom the patient was currently studying and working).*

Patient: You remember that I said he was my guru. He is really a wonderful man.

Therapist: How else do you feel about him?

Patient: I have a lot of respect for him. I really feel as though he is like a father to me.

Therapist: Then, of course, he would be someone whose approval would be crucial to you?

Patient: Absolutely. You know I always felt that my father cared but he never showed it. We're closer now than we've ever been. I feel that closeness with Mr. Z and I can't afford to do anything to fail him.

Therapist: Then the appointment to the panel [by Mr. Z] means once more that you dare not allow nine A's and one B.

Patient: It has to be straight A's.

Therapist: So again, we see your need to be perfect as the only possible way for you to feel that you are approved, wanted, desirable — and since perfection of the kind you seek and need is impossible, there is a built-in guarantee of failure. In fact, your feeling about yourself is that you are a boy among the men. *[The phobic situation (return to the classroom) must be confronted regardless of the kind of treatment. In this interview a degree of pressure was exerted since I recognized that his need for my approval was important to him. Would he fail me and risk my disapproval?]*

Session 7

(The patient reported that he had gone back to the classroom the day before.)

Therapist: Tell me what happened.

Patient: I felt that I handled the kids pretty well. The only time that I really felt tense was when we had to place an out-of-control kid in the seclusion room.

Therapist: What was that like?

Patient: Another teacher and I took the kid and we literally had to stuff him into the room.

Therapist: You stuffed him into the room, like in a box, you were very very aggressive.

Patient: I was, but I felt good about it. I stayed in the class for about three hours and

(continued)

Box 6-2 continued

when I left I got rid of it all by busying myself with my other work. As a matter of fact, I had no further thought about it until I was on my way here....I think that I have made pretty good progress here. Do you think that I will need another five years of treatment back at my home base?

Therapist: How many sessions do we have left?

Patient: I don't know — four?

Therapist: No, five more and not five years. Do you recall the problem that I said you and I would work on?

Patient: Not at all, no recollection.

Therapist: It was how you feel helpless when you're left alone, and now you are concerned as to how you will manage when I leave you.

Patient: Oh, yes, I remember it now. *[It was not surprising that the patient indirectly raised the shadow of termination after the sixth meeting. The seventh meeting is one distinct step beyond the midpoint. It is not unlike the experience of being on a 2-week vacation: the first week is usually one of total anticipation of pleasure; the beginning of the second week forces the intrusion of the beginning of the end. In the case of the patient, his obsessional adherence to structure and to time would go along with a steady alertness to time....In the treatment situation, his anxiety about the end of our time and his subsequent aloneness forced him into a defensive position of denial. Nevertheless, the pressure of his anxiety was not to be thwarted, so he found himself speaking of the progress he had made (and progress must lead to a conclusion) and then wondering whether he would need five more years of treatment back home. This latter statement clearly indicated his feeling that twelve sessions would not be enough, that he needs more.]*

Session 8

Patient: Whenever I go to a conference without my wife I will stay up most of the night to avoid going to bed alone.

Therapist: You mean that you will keep busy with friends and colleagues until it is no longer possible to avoid going to bed?

Patient: That's right. Also, whenever I meet a new person and feel that I resonate with him, I feel that I must let the other person know all about me as quickly as possible. Then I can read the signals and learn immediately about the future of our relationship.

Therapist: You mean that you expose yourself in certain ways sufficient to be able to watch the reaction of the person and know right there whether he accepts you or not.

Patient: Yes. I didn't realize what I was really up to until now. It is so important to be accepted.

Therapist: And to feel wanted.

Patient: I should tell you of a dream that I had. In it Mr. Z offers me a job with him and I grab it. I sell my house back home and I come here. And then Mr. Z takes a job elsewhere and leaves. *[This is a transparent, almost childlike dream. He has found the people he wants to be wanted by and who appear to want him. Mr. Z and the therapist, but his joy will soon turn to despair. I related the feelings in the dream to his childhood experiences as they continue for him even today. I added that we would keep an eye on his reactions now that the time for him to leave Mr. Z and his institution was only two weeks away. All the data relate to the impending termination of treatment as well.]*

Session 9

Patient: I'm going to ask you again. Will everything fall apart again when I go back home?

(continued)

Box 6-2 continued

Therapist: I don't think you will lose any of your gains. More than that, you are addressing a plea to me not to let you go.

Patient: I guess that's it. I think I'm ready to look at my feelings about leaving.

Therapist: You and I have come to learn about the many different ways that you have been programmed to react to separation as a result of our work together, and we will have to deal with those feelings in the time that is left before we finish on Friday, July 12.

Session 10

(The patient asks the therapist for a prescription for sleeping pills, indicating that he has a painful back.)

Therapist: Let's talk about it.

Patient: I slipped handling my boat on Sunday and fell on my coccyx. It hurt and I immediately remembered the pain that I had had when I had multiple surgery for a pilonidal cyst. The pain keeps me from sleeping.

Therapist: A sleeping pill has no effect on pain.

Patient: From past experience I know that it works for me. I would like a ten-day supply. *[A ten-day supply would bring him precisely to the day of our final meeting.]*

Therapist: Suppose I say no.

Patient: I'll be angry. Gee, I'm surprised I said that. It came right out. If you don't give me the prescription it will mean you don't give a damn. I could go to the infirmary and get it, but why should I pay twelve bucks for a prescription when you can give it to me?

Therapist: You are asking me for succor. It is your indirect way of responding to my leaving you. If I say no, you become angry and it means I don't care. Yet you are asking me for a 10-day supply, exactly to the day that you leave me.

Patient: Last week, when I raised the question of transference and you said that I did have such feelings about you, when I was driving away from here I found myself saying that big shot is crazy. And then, maybe he knows what he is talking about.

Therapist: What are your feelings about me?

Patient: Mixed and strange. I know I'm angry. I say to myself, what has this guy done for me? What have I gotten for the bucks I pay? I'll be glad to save the money. Then I think that I've learned a lot about myself that I never knew before.

Therapist: Do you think that you will miss me?

Patient: Well, I know we have an agreement that said it would end on a certain date, but I did not at that time expect to feel this way.

Session 11

(The patient again wonders whether he might go back into therapy when he is home.)

Therapist: We've heard this before. You've been telling me that things are in control, so this is your way of saying that you do not wish to separate, to be left, that you want more.

Patient: I see that. But will things fall apart when I am back home?

Therapist: I know that you do not wish to leave, but I believe that you will do very well.

Patient: I do feel together. I don't feel so tied to Mr. Z and I feel that I will leave him with his respect but without pats on the head, like the little boy looking for approval.. . . I have thought again about winners and losers. I came to Boston with four goals to be met in seven months. I've done three of them. The other is uncertain and will have to wait for some months. It has never happened before that I could feel good about batting .750 and not 1.000.

Therapist: You remember that nine A's were wiped out by one B. You have sought for

(continued)

Box 6-2 continued

perfection in order to be approved, admired, wanted, and that desire could never be met or satisfied because you would simply have to make ten A's every day.

Patient: I've never been able to settle for less. I marvel at my contented reaction. I've really come to feel very differently about myself over the few months here. I didn't realize when I started what kind of intensity would be created by the time limit and how strongly I would feel about the end. Well, now I have only to deal with leaving you at our last session.

Session 12

[The patient is feeling "high." His work is all done and he was able to sit at his desk and read two books this morning. My suspicion is aroused. Is the "high" that he is feeling evidence of an inability to manage the separation? Is he moving into activity as a means of avoiding feelings that might merge into pathological overactivity?]

Therapist: You read two books this morning?

Patient: I read that way. It was not a driven feeling. I felt relaxed and I was able to reflect on how many aspects of my professional work have come together in a way that I've never been able to do before.

Therapist: How else have you been feeling?

Patient: Last night my wife and I had dinner with Mr. Z. Then we went home and I watched TV — something I rarely do. I slept "like a rock" all night and that's not too usual for me either.

Therapist: More?

Patient: I'm aware that maybe I'm warding off other feelings but I do feel that rather than this being only a termination — for me it is a beginning — a new world of options has been opened to me that I never knew before.

Therapist: I agree with you. Nevertheless, you might be avoiding other feelings. You may feel depressed or angry in the next days and if you do it will have to do with feelings about me.

Patient: I realize that your approval of me has become important. *[I used this remark to tell him that he has always sought approval, but since I am not in any position to promote him, give him references, or otherwise help his career, his feeling must be based on an old state of affairs. His wish for my approval is really the old wish for parental approval.]*

Therapist: Do you like me?

Patient: I really do.

Therapist: Then you may feel that since you worked so hard for me, why do I send you away, why do I leave you?

Patient: I know that I have made great gains and I know, too, about the gap between my head and my gut. Of course, you may have had better patients.

Therapist: Shall I give you an A or A plus?

Patient: I'm really satisfied with .750.

Therapist: But you see that there is the hint again of your wish for my approval.

Patient: You know, I've had the feeling of instant cure. I'm suspicious of that.

Therapist: You are not cured. You will run up against these problems again, but you will know what they are about and be able to handle them.

Patient: The compression of time is strange. What seemed so far in the future when we started is now about over.

Therapist: I warn you again that you may feel depressed, or angry, or both, and it will have to do with feelings about me.

Patient: I think I'm in control. I feel that way, and I'll handle it. *[And we say good-bye.]*

From J. Mann and R. Goldman, *A Casebook in Time-Limited Psychotherapy*, New York: McGraw-Hill, 1982, pp. 63–77. Used with permission from McGraw-Hill, Inc.

CONCLUDING COMMENTS

No theorist in the field of planned short-term psychotherapy has thought more about the word time than has Mann. In fact, except in a very specific and limited sense, no other theorist seems to have thought much about the term at all. Yet, time is central to the concept of time-limited psychotherapy, and its thoughtful consideration has had a significant impact on most short-term psychotherapists. The importance of the concept of time may, in fact, be felt most powerfully by older writers who sense their own time coming to an end. Indeed, the early writing in the field of planned short-term psychotherapy was undertaken by established therapists who were considerably older than the average therapist who would be reading what they wrote.

But the literature contains a good deal of controversy about the wisdom of establishing a specified number of sessions and termination date in advance (see Mann, 1991, pp. 36–37). Many therapists would like more flexibility regarding those two decisions than Mann's approach provides. Yet, if one is to take Mann's views about both conscious and unconscious aspects of time seriously, then the notion of setting that ending date unequivocally seems quite logical.

Mann's work is an excellent example of what is commonly called clinical research—the careful, often quite detailed, examination of clinical material with an eye toward inductively identifying common phenomena across patients. In this connection Mann's systematic use of follow-up interviews as a way of collecting information on the vicissitudes of the therapeutic process after its formal conclusion is exemplary. The follow-up contact, in Mann's case conducted without prior indication of his intent to do so, provides an excellent way of accomplishing two objectives at the same time—enhancing the effects of the therapy while at the same time enhancing one's understanding of the therapeutic process.

CHAPTER 7

LEWIN'S BRIEF CONFRONTIVE THERAPY

Overview

Theoretical Background

Therapeutic Techniques

A Case Example

Concluding Comments

Karl Lewin's (1970) brief psychotherapy is based on the application of a set of specific concepts in psychoanalytic theory to the process of brief psychotherapy. Because the theory and the therapeutic strategy that Lewin subscribes to are inseparable, a brief review of those aspects of psychoanalytic theory that are most important to Lewin in understanding what takes place in the therapeutic process is necessary.

THEORETICAL BACKGROUND

Lewin's therapeutic strategy deliberately concentrates on superego issues, that is, issues of guilt, shame, and conscience, or what has been called "psychic masochism" (Bergler, 1949). This emphasis is based on the importance to Lewin of the process of introjection, that is, the "process of incorporation of another person, usually a parent, into the child's self, the assimilation of another's personality" (1970, p. 13). Lewin believes that that process begins within the first year of life and that it can continue throughout adulthood. A previous introject can be extruded and replaced, although with increasing age the process becomes more difficult.

How the process of introjection takes place is not well understood. Why some children incorporate a loving, tender, accepting mother, while other children incorporate the cold disapproving, rejecting aspect of that same mother, remains a mystery. The choice of introject does not necessarily follow the real, objective attitude of that mother. Lewin notes that position in the family can dictate the choice; if

the role of the good child has already been filled by a sibling, another child might well become the bad child by introjecting less giving aspects of the mother. Most often children introject that view of their mother that they feel they deserve. Lewin suggests that if children are ashamed or feel guilty about aspects of themselves, they are more likely to introject a disapproving, punitive mother.

The importance of the nature of the introject to psychological well-being cannot be overemphasized. Lewin writes:

> The presence of a good introject sustains us in times of privation. A good introject constantly replenishes our capacity to give love, to think well of ourselves and of others, and to have an optimistic view of life. It allows us to be alone without the oppression of loneliness. Conversely, the child who does not incorporate, or who ejects that which he previously incorporated without replacement, very likely is schizophrenic, and his loneliness is a terrifying void, regardless of life circumstances. While the child with a good introject is happy within the limits of his actual life situation, experiencing the pleasures of living, the child with a bad introject is in constant psychic pain, suffering in the midst of plenty. (1970, p. 15)

Based on the nature of the introject, shame and guilt can play vastly differing roles in a person's psychological functioning. Shame and guilt can serve constructive purposes for the child with a good introject. Shame, by producing anxiety when children have not measured up to their ego ideal, spurs them to useful action. Guilt, by producing anxiety when children have hurt others, encourages them to do better by them in the future. For the child with a bad introject, shame and guilt serve no constructive purposes and become weapons for self-punishment. Shame nags them with the humiliation of their failure to achieve their ego ideal, and guilt serves as punishment for their wrongdoing. Shame and guilt do not improve their future actions; rather, they merely convince them that they are hopelessly bad.

As the reader might anticipate, Lewin sees the principal goal of psychotherapy as countering the client's psychic masochism, the internalized guilt and shame—as exposing and replacing the client's bad introject and disabling sense of right and wrong. The therapist sides with the client's ego, as it were, against the common enemy, a punishing and vindictive conscience. In this process the therapist is active, confrontive, and, if necessary, critical.

> Confrontations in brief therapy must be made in such a way that the patient sees them as helpful though painful. The doctor should emerge as a strong figure of assistance who is not afraid of, or repelled by, those traits of the patient about which he comments. The therapist represents both ego and healthy conscience. (Lewin, 1970, p. 37)

THERAPEUTIC TECHNIQUES

Perhaps most unusual from the point of view of therapeutic technique is Lewin's handling of negative feelings a client might have about the therapist, that is, what is commonly called negative transference. This one characteristic sets Lewin's thinking apart from that of all other brief therapists (e.g., Bauer & Kobos, 1987, pp. 176 ff.). Lewin (1970) writes:

> This method of brief therapy depends precisely on the development of initial negative transference. After all, people get sick from unpleasant feelings—envy, jealously, greed, and anger—and those will surface immediately, if given a chance. The exposure of the patient's negative feelings toward him enables the therapist to confront the patient with his masochistic response to anger....Almost invariably, patients react to any confrontation with anger, evident to the therapist only in the manner in which the patient defends against expressing it openly to the doctor. This is the characteristic masochistic maneuver of turning anger inward

upon the self. The patient may flush, fall silent, cry, fumble with fingers, clench his fist, or show suppressed rage in some other fashion. At that point, the therapist confronts the patient, not merely with his anger, but with the patient's reluctance to express the anger openly out of fear of antagonizing the therapist, the figure upon whom the patient depends for help in his illness. He is asked, if he has so much conflict about his expression of anger at his doctor, a relatively unimportant stranger in his life, how much worse are his conflicts about his family and loved ones? (pp. 35–36)

The purposes of Lewin's brief psychotherapy are to restore the clients' functioning, help them understand how their conflicts have led to their self-destructive actions, and to suggest other ways of handling their conflicts. As much as possible, the therapy seeks to replace clients' punitive introjects with less pathological ones. Temporarily the therapist's model of an introject is offered as a substitute. Success of the therapy depends in part on the ability of the client to accept the substitute. Lewin comments, in discussing the evaluation of his brief psychotherapy, that the results are good and are generally comparable with the results of long-term therapy.

Lewin's book is rich with powerful clinical illustrations. His examples are not verbatim interview transcripts, such as might be made from a tape recording, however, but reconstructed interactions based on shorthand note taking. Yet they dramatically illustrate how the work of the clinical interview follows from the theoretical formulations just described.

A CASE EXAMPLE

In Box 7-1 is an example of Lewin's presentation of his clinical work. The context of this case illustration was the legal requirement, in effect at the time of the interview, for a woman who had an unplanned pregnancy and wanted a therapeutic abortion to obtain a written statement from two physicians that her continued pregnancy would be injurious to her physical or emotional well-being. Lewin believes that the physician who provides the written statement would do the patient a disservice if the request is treated simply as a formality rather than as a therapeutic encounter. Lewin believes that women who do not use or do not insist that their partners use contraceptives and who manage to get themselves pregnant against their conscious will are displaying clear evidence of masochism. He writes:

No matter what other neurotic conflicts are being enacted through pregnancy, the need to hurt themselves is paramount....Very likely, their unwanted pregnancy will be only one of the first serious episodes in what will become a life-time of self-destructive acts. Since, characteristically, most of these patients are under thirty years of age, the psychiatrist could conceivably spare them that life-time of suffering were he to confront them with their need to punish themselves before they ruin their lives irreparably. (1970, pp. 88–89)

Box 7-1: Case Example of Lewin's Brief Confrontive Therapy

(Miss R.A., a 20-year-old high school graduate, was referred by a gynecologist for evaluation for therapeutic abortion. A very pale, distraught young girl, she barely acknowledged my greeting and slumped into the chair. Her eyelids were puffy, her eyes were bloodshot, and her nose was red and swollen as though she had been crying recently and copiously. Her breathing was rather shallow and jerky, and her thin chest heaved spasmodically from what soon appeared to be vain efforts to control her sobbing.)

Therapist: What brought you to see me?
Patient: I don't want to have this baby—I'm going on three months. I can't sleep, I can't eat, I just cry all the time.
Therapist: Tell me about the circumstances of your getting pregnant.
Patient: I don't care about the person from whom I'm pregnant. I had too much to drink at a party. Usually, we just dance at those parties. I never have more than one drink.
Therapist: What made you behave differently this time?
Patient: (weeping uncontrollably) I found out the person I was in love with was getting married to someone else. I used to see him a couple of times a week. Tom is twenty-five—he's nice and understanding, a fiberglass laminator. I hadn't wanted to marry right away. I'm too young. I have a sister who married young and she missed out on life. But that isn't the reason he broke off with me. We argued over stupid things that I started. I was too demanding and bossy. Like I expected him to call me at certain times.
Therapist: You recognize that you were driving him away. It sounds like a part of your personality is trying to see to it that you don't get what you want. *(At this point she stops crying.)*
Patient: I couldn't seem to stop doing it. I knew that I was doing it, I told myself what would happen, but I kept doing it. Then one day he told me that he was marrying the girl he used to go with—that was one week before I got pregnant.
Therapist: How did you feel when he told you?
Patient: I cried. At first I was angry and then I just didn't care any more.
Therapist: Did you express any anger to him?
Patient: No. In fact I even forgot that I was angry until right now. All I thought was—just not caring about anything any more.
Therapist: You were angry at him and took it out on yourself. He's not suffering from this pregnancy; you are—look at you! You have the kind of conscience that punishes you for angry feelings. And I suspect it was working on you even before, forcing you to drive him away from you in the first place.
Patient: Looking back on it, it does seem almost deliberate. I got myself drunk, which I never do, went out with a guy I don't even like after the dance, let him park and have intercourse with me, when I never did that before with anybody. And even drunk I knew

(continued)

Box 7-1 continued

he wasn't using any protection, but I didn't stop him. I thought of killing myself so as not to tell my parents. I always wanted to make my father proud of me. We're very close. He was disappointed in my sisters. My mother and father were divorced and both remarried. I'm living with my father and stepmother. I have two sisters, thirty and twenty-seven, two stepsisters, twenty-six and twenty-five, a stepbrother twenty and half-brother, sixteen. My mother lives by herself now. She's very sick with a nervous condition. She can't work—she has pains in the head. I was a baby when they were divorced. I don't know anything about that. I lived with my mother and two sisters until I was six. During that time I visited my father a lot. He had a big house and had lots of toys for me to play with. It was lots of fun. Whatever I wanted was given to me. I moved in with my father when I was six.

Therapist: What made you leave then?

Patient: I don't know. It was my idea. My father had remarried about two years after the divorce. My mother remarried when I was five. My sisters didn't get along with her husband, but I did.

Therapist: That sounds like more than a coincidence. You'd been mother's baby and then she remarried and a year later you move out for no reason. Is it possible you were jealous of her new husband and the attention he took from you for your mother?

Patient: I don't remember ever feeling jealous.

Therapist: Have you had any feelings about your having left her?

Patient: I do feel guilty about her being sick. Maybe I could have helped her if I stayed. My mother's all alone. She divorced again about ten years ago. They didn't get along and my sisters didn't get along with him.

Therapist: I don't know whether this is part of the guilt that makes your conscience punish you, but it could be. Your present predicament also followed someone's getting married, hurting you.

Patient: I think I'm an awfully nervous person. *["Nervous" is the adjective she used to describe her mother's illness.]* I get impatient, like when I'm stuck in traffic. I feel like screaming. Maybe it's my spoiledness, getting what I wanted all the time as a child. Sometimes I'm afraid of ending up like my mother.

Therapist: Your conscience would be pleased with that—it would feel that's your just reward for jilting your mother. You seem to feel disloyal, living a soft life with your father.

Patient: I was in no hurry to marry. If I found the right guy—I wouldn't settle for just anyone—I planned to marry for security reasons. *[From one foster mother to another.]*

Therapist: You mean some day your father will die and you'll need someone else to take care of you.

Patient: (flushing) You know, I never considered how babyish and selfish I'm being until I heard you say that. That's exactly what I've been feeling. He's taken care of everything for me. He had to find out anyhow for me to have this pregnancy ended because I'm under twenty-one. He accepted it very well—both my sisters had to get married—but I know I let him down. He expected better of me. But he's paying for everything. I feel guilty about the expense I'm putting him to. *[Notice the double meaning of "he's paying for everything."]*

Therapist: You were angry at what I said, but you're afraid of antagonizing me, because you need the letter. I intend to write it regardless of what you say, so go ahead.

Patient: I came here feeling sorry for myself. Maybe I needed a good spanking. All right, it did hurt, hearing you say it. I sound like a terrible person. But you didn't say anything

(continued)

Box 7-1 continued

that isn't true. I guess it's time I grew up. I'm twenty years old, I shouldn't be a baby any more. I have to do it on my own.

Therapist: I'll write the doctor today. I wonder if you'd mind letting me know how things are with you after you get out of the hospital. You could call or drop me a note.

Patient: Mind? It's kind of you to care. You've opened my eyes to something I didn't want to see.

From Lewin, 1970, pp. 89–92.

In concluding his presentation, Lewin returns to the issue of the negative transference. He suggests that the most common reason given by clinicians for avoiding the negative transference is that it makes the rapid resolution that should take place in time-limited psychotherapy far more difficult. Needless to say, Lewin disagrees with this assertion. Rather, Lewin suggests that the negative transference is more typically avoided because it is unpleasant to both therapist and patient.

Lewin believes that patients can tolerate far more than most therapists think and can understand most therapeutic propositions if they are presented clearly and accurately. Thus, the therapeutic interpretation "You must be very upset that you want to injure your brother in a fit of jealousy," a proposition that recognizes the feeling of guilt as well as of conflict, is far more acceptable than "You hate your brother." Similarly, while the interpretation "You think I'm stupid" will probably lead nowhere, the alternative "You must feel very badly that the person you've come to for help seems so inept" can lead to a continuing productive therapeutic relationship. In that relationship, patients can come to grips with their conflicts as well as their guilt and can learn that it is possible to change their feelings about another person and that in the meantime it is possible to dislike someone and still work with him or her.

CONCLUDING COMMENTS

Lewin's ideas about psychic masochism, the role of the superego in making people ill, the importance of the bad introject, and the way brief psychotherapy that can help the patient come to grips with these issues are of paramount importance in enriching the clinician's alternative views of psychopathology and its treatment in brief periods of time. It is hard to find another orientation to time-limited psychotherapy that draws so productively and so uncompromisingly on a specific, infrequently invoked aspect of personality theory.

The psychoanalytic concept of the introject helps us understand enduring personality traits of optimism or pessimism, as well as many aspects of character structure. Lewin uses these concepts to identify the most important purposes of his time-limited psychotherapy—to counter psychic masochism, to extrude the bad introject, and to temper a vindictive and overly punitive conscience.

These more stable aspects of the person are the ones most therapists think of as unusually difficult to modify; yet Lewin deals directly with these character issues. Reading about his theoretical orientation and examining his case examples lead one to be impressed with the considerable effect his approach has with people who might commonly be thought of as very demanding and difficult patients.

CHAPTER 8

BLOOM'S FOCUSED SINGLE-SESSION THERAPY

Overview

The Effectiveness of a Single Therapeutic Session

Focused Single-Session Therapy: A Personal Reminiscence

Therapeutic Techniques

A Case Example

Concluding Comments

The ultimate case of planned short-term psychotherapy is the therapeutic episode that is designed to be completed in a single session. Single-session episodes of care are very common, of course, but virtually all of these episodes are unplanned. Phillips (1985a) has noted that about half of the patients who come to a clinic do not come back again at that time. They may come again months or years later or may go to another clinic, but a very large minority of clinical contacts take place in a single session. Similar findings have been reported in many different clinical settings (Bloom, 1975; Fiester & Rudestam, 1975; Hoffman & Remmel, 1975; Littlepage, Kosloski, Schnelle, McNees, & Gendrich, 1976; Sue, Allen, & Conaway, 1978; Talmon, 1990). Single-session episodes of care seem almost as common in university mental health facilities as in community agencies (Dorosin, Gibbs, & Kaplan, 1976; Glasscote & Fishman, 1973).

THE EFFECTIVENESS OF A SINGLE THERAPEUTIC SESSION

Not only is the occurrence of single sessions of therapy underestimated, but, more importantly, their therapeutic impact appears to be underestimated as well. Such encounters frequently appear to have remarkably positive consequences, whether their primary objective is therapy or evaluation, and, as Rubin and Mitchell (1976) reported some time ago, interviews whose primary purpose is research may have substantial clinical impact on subjects as well.

Successful single-session therapy case histories (sometimes including verbatim transcripts of portions of the interview) have appeared in the literature. In chronological order these case histories include Freud in the 1890s (Breuer & Freud, 1895/1957), Tannenbaum (1919), Groddeck in 1927 (Groddeck, 1951), Reider (1955), Kaffman (1963), Rosenbaum (1964), Gillman (1965), Seagull (1966), Lewin (1970), Oremland (1976), Davanloo (1978c), Scrignar (1979), Sifneos (1979), Bloom (1981), Springmann (1982), Sifneos (1984), Shulman (1989), Powers and Griffith (1989), Talmon (1990), Mahrer and Roberge (1993), Rosenbaum (1993), Lankton (1994), Rosenbaum (1994), and O'Hanlon & Hudson (1994).

Such assertions and case histories do not, of course, substitute for more objectively conducted empirical research studies. A small number of such studies have been reported, however, and they uniformly support the conclusion that a single interview can have significant therapeutic impact.

In what is perhaps the most comprehensive study of single-session psychotherapy, Talmon (1990) reported that more than three-quarters of 200 patients whom he had seen only once reported that they were improved or much improved. Based on this observation, Talmon, and two colleagues attempted to conduct single session psychotherapy with 60 randomly assigned adults who appeared for noncrisis routine intake appointments. The three therapists differed substantially in their general approaches to psychotherapy, and the patients were a very heterogeneous group in terms of severity of presenting complaint, race, ethnic background, age, and education. Between 3 and 12 months later, 58 of the 60 patients were reached by telephone for a follow-up interview conducted by someone other than the patient's therapist.

Of the 58 patients who were contacted, 34 (58%) were, in fact, seen only once. That is, in these cases, patient and therapist mutually agreed that no additional appointments were necessary. Of the 34 patients seen only once, 88 percent reported that they were either improved or much improved—a figure slightly and insignificantly greater than among the 24 patients seen more than once (see also Chick, Ritson, Connaughton, Stewart, & Chick, 1988; Chapman & Huygens, 1988; Edwards, Orford, Egert, Guthrie, Hawker, Hensman, Mitcheson, Oppenheimer, & Taylor, 1977; Getz, Fujita, & Allen, 1975; Malan, Heath, Bacal, & Balfour, 1975; Zweben, Pearlman, & Li, 1988).

FOCUSED SINGLE-SESSION THERAPY: A PERSONAL REMINISCENCE

Focused single-session therapy (Bloom, 1981) builds on these earlier observations by creating, examining, and evaluating encounters designed to provide a significant therapeutic impact in a single interview. The theoretical orientation of focused single-session therapy is psychodynamic. While in a sense the objective of focused single-session therapy may seem outrageous, it is not greatly different from the ways that more traditional time-limited psychotherapists describe their objectives. For example, Strupp and Binder (1984) write: "We propose that each session be viewed as a minitherapy, with palpable progress as its aim" (p. 304). Butcher, Stelmachers, and Maudal (1983), in their overview

of crisis intervention and emergency psychotherapy, write: "Every crisis psychotherapy session should be conducted as though it may be the last contact with the patient" (p. 591).

During the fall semester of 1978 I was on sabbatical leave from the University of Colorado. The major task I had set for myself that semester was to write a chapter on planned short-term psychotherapy for the second edition of my community mental health textbook. I had become persuaded that one strategy by which community mental health practitioners could provide for the mental health needs of the community was to increase the efficiency of psychotherapy. I wanted to explore what people were saying about brief interventions, since I knew very little about this newly emerging field. Accordingly, I assembled a rather large number of carefully selected books and journal articles that I hoped to read and compress into that single chapter.

My first surprise was that there was already such a large literature on the topic of planned short-term psychotherapy. My second surprise was that an astonishing number of people, including people long associated with a traditional psychoanalytic orientation, were very enthusiastic about the usefulness of planned short-term psychotherapy. My third surprise was that the outcome evaluation studies that had been published seemed to be virtually unanimous in their findings that short-term psychotherapy appeared to be remarkably effective. It was clear that people who were practicing time-limited psychotherapy were enjoying what they were doing.

In addition, as I read through the books and articles, I kept coming across references to psychotherapy conducted in a single interview. Often these references were throw-away lines, literally parenthetical, as in, "Short-term psychotherapy (often as short as one interview) has been found to be indistinguishable in its effects from far longer...." Other comments were couched as if describing an anomaly, a fluke, a case as noteworthy because of its rarity as its results. This kind of comment was usually associated with a case history presentation in which the author described a positive outcome as some kind of miracle, hardly to be trusted, but still remarkable enough to justify describing to a professional audience (e.g., Scrignar, 1979).

Other references to psychotherapy undertaken in a single session were in the context of a set of reality constraints that made additional therapy impossible, and favorable results were presented somewhat apologetically, with the clear but unspoken subtext that had additional time been available results would surely have been even more favorable. That is, these references rarely described the deliberate use of a single session to accomplish some therapeutic goal.

My work during the sabbatical resulted not only in the completion of the chapter on planned short-term psychotherapy that appeared in due course in the second edition of the community mental health book (Bloom, 1984), but also in a resolution to review more completely whatever literature I could find on single-session psychotherapy, and even to try it out. For me the idea of deliberately undertaking a piece of psychotherapeutic work in a single interview represented a potentially exciting clinical adventure and, I hoped, a useful strategy for testing some of the beliefs associated with the growing short-term psychotherapy movement. I did not know how helpful a single session of psychotherapy could be, but I saw the clinical study of single-session psychotherapy as a way of testing the ideas of short-term psychotherapy by examining its limiting case—single-session psychotherapy was as brief as brief therapy could be.

My initial explorations in single-session psychotherapy took place at the local community mental health center where I volunteered my services one morning a week shortly after returning from my sabbatical year. I typically saw two clients each morning, ordinarily for an hour each, and I tried to get enough done so that they would not need to come back, at least not immediately. At the same time, I saw a number of clients from time to time in my office at the university. My working hypothesis was that a single session of psychotherapy could be effective if I were only smart enough to figure out how to be helpful. From the beginning I ruled out blaming the client if the therapeutic intervention was unsuccessful. I did my best to blame the therapist.

My strategy for evaluating my work was a primitive one. I invited my clients to contact me whenever they wished, and I arranged to contact the clients in two or three months, if I had not heard from them in the meanwhile, to find out how they were doing and how they felt retrospectively about the interview. I tape recorded most of the interviews and many follow-up telephone contacts.

After some months it was clear that one such session was often not enough, so I lengthened the available time to two hours. Since then I have found that a single therapy session has been judged by clients to have been sufficient most of the time, and I now find myself thinking about extended treatment as a series of single-session therapies.

In my work at the mental health center, after introducing myself to the patient, getting the patient's permission to tape record the interview, and explaining my volunteer status, the contractual agreement I made with each patient was that I would try to be as helpful as possible during the interview. If at the conclusion of the interview we both felt that another appointment was necessary, we would schedule it for the following week. If not, I would give the patient my card and invite him or her to call me if there was a need to get in touch with me for any reason—with a problem or a progress report, for example. Finally, I arranged for a follow-up telephone contact in the event that the client had not contacted me. I have learned that most found the intervention helpful, are doing well, and have not sought additional professional help.

I had been back in Boulder a year or so when I get a call from Si Budman at the Harvard Community Health Plan. He was organizing a major symposium on brief psychotherapy and he had heard from someone that I had become interested in single-session psychotherapy. Would I come to Boston and present my work? During the next few months I finished my review of the scattered literature on single-session psychotherapy, transcribed an example of my single-session psychotherapy cases, and prepared a manuscript describing my preliminary results. Not long thereafter I was in Boston—the city that had become for American psychoanalysis what Vienna had been for European psychoanalysis—talking to a couple of hundred traditionally trained mental health professionals about what it was like to try to do a significant piece of psychotherapy in a single interview (Bloom, 1981). I found the meeting exhilarating and the audience gracious and deeply interested.

There are two general principles that I have arrived at in conducting these extremely brief therapeutic interventions. First, I try to help clients become wiser about themselves; that is, I try to learn something about them that they might not know but that they would likely find useful and pertinent if I could successfully communicate it to them. Second, I work with clients to identify a course of action that they have the capacity and the willingness to carry out, that is, a direction for the continuing work that they can do on their own.

Neither principle needs to be very grand to be helpful. Indeed, my impression is that it may only take a "teaspoonful" for clients to get unstuck and get on with their lives.

THERAPEUTIC TECHNIQUES

The examination of focused single-session psychotherapy interviews has revealed a number of recurring technical objectives that seem particularly important in the therapeutic process. While most of these goals are not dramatically different from those that might be identified in time-unlimited dynamic psychotherapy, their importance in short-term psychotherapy seems unusually striking.

The objectives divide themselves into the two major categories mentioned above: (1) those that play a role in helping patients discover something significant about themselves and (2) those that play a role in starting a therapeutic process that can continue after the interview has ended. O'Hanlon refers to these same two overall therapeutic goals far more poetically—"changing the viewing, and changing the doing" (1990, p. 86).

Uncovering New Material

Perhaps the most fundamental aspect of psychodynamic theory concerning the process of psychotherapy is concerned is the importance of helping clients understand more about themselves—how their past experiences have influenced their motivations, their affect, and their conflicts, and how these experiences, if they are unassimilated, continue to influence their daily lives. Here are some of the clinical techniques that I have found to be useful in helping clients learn more about themselves.

Identify a Focal Problem

I try to identify a piece of psychological reality that is pertinent to the patient's presenting problem, below the patient's initial level of usable awareness and yet acceptable to the patient in the form of an interpretation or observation. In doing so, I am careful not to focus too early or foreclose too quickly. The success of the session seems to depend on my ability to identify and focus on one salient and relevant issue. As has been noted elsewhere in this volume, the briefer the psychotherapy, the greater the need to focus on a limited number of issues (Bauer & Kobos, 1987, pp. 157 ff.).

The focal problem is sometimes issue-oriented and sometimes process-oriented. Thus, a patient may present a problem that seems to be related to something more fundamental and less obvious. For example, a patient may come in complaining about his marriage and leave with some beginning realization that his own low self-esteem is making it hard for him to decide whether to try to save his marriage. Or a patient may come in complaining about her lack of progress in graduate school and end up being more aware of her anger toward her parents because of their lack of support for her professional aspirations. In these cases the goal of the therapeutic encounter is to help patients become more aware of some aspect of their cognitive or affective lives.

In contrast, other patients may not know how to share their feelings about themselves with other people. These patients can profit from the opportunity to do so in the therapeutic hour, not only because of the positive effects of that experience, but also because the process can serve as a model for how to talk about themselves with others (see Box 8-1 as an example).

The concept of a salient issue is similar to French's notion of a focal conflict (see Balint, Ornstein, & Balint, 1972, pp. 10–11). French distinguished between what he termed a *nuclear conflict,* that is, a dormant and repressed conflict originating during crucial developmental periods in early life, and a *focal conflict,* by which he meant a preconscious derivative of these deeper and earlier nuclear conflicts, which is able to explain much of the clinical material in a therapeutic interview.

A related concept can be found in the work of Balint (Balint, Ornstein, & Balint, 1972) who used the term *focal psychotherapy* to mean therapy with a focal aim (see Chapter 21). The aim, according to Balint, could be psychodynamic, that is, to interpret a specific conflict. But it could also be interpersonal, that is, to bring about a specific kind of interaction with the therapist that could lead to a new kind of mastery for the patient. Finally, the aim could be existential, that is, to help the patient confront and bear previously unbearable feelings (see Gustafson, 1981, p. 122).

I have no reason to believe that there is only one correct focal issue to be discovered in working with a particular patient. There are many ways of being helpful to a patient during a therapeutic interview. What is important is to develop a sense of how the patient is in the world and what processes can be started that can make a difference (see also Grand, Rechetnick, Podrug, & Schwager, 1985, pp. 131 ff.).

Do Not Be Overambitious

I try not to do too much. If I can find just one issue, just one idea, that is useful to the patient, the intervention can be a successful one. My experience, from listening to both my own interviews and those of others, is that it is hard for patients to make real use of more than two or three ideas in a single interview. Consequently, the choice of which ideas to explore and how to explore them is very important. In addition, it is important to keep the ideas simple. My personal rule of thumb is to try to formulate any comments I make in ten words or less.

What seems absolutely counterproductive in focused single-session psychotherapy is to leave the patient reeling from a great many different interpretations, however accurate the interpretations might be. In contrast, to leave the patient sobered by the power and salience of a single observation is quite a different matter. A patient can chew on that observation for weeks and continue to make use of it long after the interview is over.

Be Prudently Active

Most people who write about planned short-term therapy seem to agree that it requires a higher level of activity on the part of the therapist than is typically reported in time-unlimited psychodynamic therapy (e.g., Bauer & Kobos, 1987, pp. 149 ff.). I too have found it useful to be more active than I have been accustomed to being, but active in specific ways, and primarily during the latter half of the interview. I am not more active, certainly not early in the interview, if activity level is measured by how many words I utter. I generally ask questions rather than make statements. I do not make speeches or lecture. I do virtually no self-disclosure. When I do ask questions, I make them open-ended; that is, I avoid those that have yes or no answers. When appropriate I give information, but in the context of the patient's presenting problem, and I keep it simple. I try to use the patient's language, as soon as I think that I understand what is meant by the key words and phrases he or she uses.

During the first half or so of the interview the real risk is that the therapist can talk too much, can be too active. Even during the last part of the interview it is important to be economical with the words you use, in order to have the client retain primary responsibility for communicating.

To the extent that activity is an internal cognitive process, it is certainly important to be active. I begin the interview knowing nothing about the patient, and I have relatively little time to try to figure out a way to be helpful. That challenge requires a good deal of effort and is what can make time-limited psychotherapy very hard work. Thus, the higher level of activity is measured by internal intellectual and strategic thought rather than by who holds center stage for the longest period of time.

Explore, Then Present Interpretations Tentatively

In making interpretations, I try to do all the necessary exploration first and then tentatively present an idea in such a way that it is persuasive yet may be disagreed with without jeopardizing my potential effectiveness. I say something like "Do you think it is possible that…or "Have you ever wondered why…or "I wonder if…. It is easy to move too quickly in time-limited psychotherapy. I have become increasingly aware that it is not necessary to rush, even when there is very limited time available for the therapeutic encounter.

Never Underestimate the Power of an Empathic Remark

I encourage and explicitly recognize the expression of affect and use its expression as a way of pointing to important life events or figures. "It's ok to cry," "That really upsets you, doesn't it," and so forth. Similarly, when it seems timely, I point out incongruities in affect: "You're laughing, but there doesn't seem to be anything to laugh about." In my experience with focused single-session therapy I have not found any technique more effective than the explicit and accurate recognition of the feelings that the patient is carrying around.

These feeling states—whether of sadness, or anger, or frustration, or disappointment, or loneliness, or desperation—are usually easy to recognize and label, and, in my experience, identifying them often has very salutary consequences. In these instances the ability to be empathic has an enormous payoff. I have learned by listening to the tapes of my own interviews and those of colleagues to expect the appearance of new and important material immediately after the therapist makes an accurate, sincere, and timely empathic statement.

Keep Track of Time

There is a tempo, a pacing, to an interview. When two hours are available, there is enough time. Yet, I have to be aware of the passing time and keep planning how to use it. It is important to estimate how much time will be needed to discuss a particular topic and to make sure that there is a reasonably good match between the time that is needed and the time that is available.

In addition to the question of making sure of the availability of time, there is also the issue of the phases through which the interview passes. I have begun to think in terms of the introductory material, the middle identification and development of important themes, the planning period, and the gradual closing of the interview. It is something of an exaggeration, to be sure, but in a way I think about minutes the way I used to think about hours.

Similarly, I tend to judge how much or how little anxiety patients bring with them to the interview and how much seems to be generated by the interview. I act accordingly, now exploring in a way I know will raise anxiety, now modulating the anxiety, now introducing humor, now being very serious—all this in an effort to keep the interaction at its optimal level—enough anxiety to ensure progress but not so much as to be disabling.

Keep Factual Questions to a Minimum

I avoid collecting demographic information or doing a traditional mental status examination. It is my experience that the answers will nearly always be forthcoming without my having to ask the questions. Asking such questions can be intrusive, and the most important information will emerge in the normal course of the interview. Sometimes, however, it is useful to ask for identifying information as a way of reducing a momentarily excessive level of anxiety or in order to change the subject.

Except for these occasions, the quest for demographic information about the patient and significant people in the patient's life seems a poor use of time. I am nearly always sorry when I ask for such information, since it seems to produce so little useful data.

Do Not Be Overly Concerned about the Precipitating Event

Focused single-session therapy is not crisis intervention, so I feel no necessity to identify a crisis or event that has precipitated a patient's coming to the mental health agency. In many cases, patients seem not to know exactly why they came in. So I simply begin an interview by asking, "What can I do to be helpful?" The patient has come in because something is wrong for which help is needed, not because he or she has a regular appointment at that time every week. Since the patient has inaugurated the therapeutic encounter, the therapist has every right to expect the patient to get to work, to describe the problem, and to begin moving toward its resolution. No interview has more leverage in this regard than the first interview, and that leverage is further enhanced by the fact that both patient and therapist know that it is possible that it will be the only interview.

Avoid Detours

I have had to learn to avoid attractive detours and to remain single-minded about what I am trying to accomplish. There are numerous occasions in every intervention when I find myself wishing I could explore some little phrase for just a few minutes, but such diversions nearly always turn out to be errors. Initially, of course, I have no idea where I am heading, so I keep all my options open. I try to narrow the domain of inquiry in proportion to what I am learning about the patient, and I do not single out a particular issue or conflict to concentrate on until I have every reason to believe that it is an appropriate target for investigation and clarification. All this means that not only is there no time to explore side issues, but that such exploration detracts from the potential effectiveness of the therapy.

Do Not Overestimate a Patient's Self-Awareness

Finally, I am continuing to learn not to overestimate how much patients know about themselves. Patients may be totally oblivious of something about themselves that seems perfectly obvious to me and would, I believe, be perfectly obvious to almost everyone who knows them. I have had patients scream at me that they are not angry and tearfully tell me that they are not sad. While patients in one sense are experts on what is going on inside them, they are often unable to label, acknowledge, or use that knowledge effectively. Increasing a patient's useful self-awareness, even in only one critical area, can have an important impact on the adequacy of his or her functioning. In working toward that objective an accurate appraisal of what patients do or do not know about themselves is critically important.

Starting a Therapeutic Process

The effectiveness of brief psychotherapy is enhanced to the extent that the therapeutic episode inaugurates a process that the client can continue after the

episode has been concluded. Virtually from the beginning of the interview the therapist needs to consider not only what the client doesn't know that he or she needs to know, but also how to enhance the likelihood that the client will keep working on the issues that have been identified during the psychotherapy.

Affirm Therapeutic Work Done So Far

Schlesinger (1994) has described a not uncommon situation in which the relatively inexperienced therapist seems to have quickly run out of topics to discuss with the client. Detailed examination of this situation frequently reveals that such clients have come to their first session with the therapist not to begin therapy but to end it. That is, the client has completed the self-treatment phase of psychotherapy and is interested in a professional evaluation of the progress already made. Schlesinger observes that "to invite someone into a continuing attachment who has already accomplished his therapeutic goals, but who has strong relationship needs, is to invite an interminable relationship, but probably not a therapy" (1994, p. 11).

Thus, one of the first objectives in inaugurating a therapeutic episode is for the therapist to evaluate and comment, as appropriate, on the work already done by the client. The therapist must be alert to the situation in which the client seems to have accomplished a great deal thus far without the help of a formal therapeutic episode of care and the therapist's task is to acknowledge that accomplishment, make a suggestion or two as appropriate, and reassure the client that should anything go wrong in the future, the therapist would welcome the client to return.

Use the Interview to Start a Problem-Solving Process

I try to identify important unresolved issues and the figures in the patient's life pertinent to those issues and start or encourage a process of getting some of that unfinished business taken care of. "Have you ever told your mother that when you were a little girl you used to be so frightened of her?" "Have you ever talked with your sister about that?" "Do you think your father could shed some light on why you used to do that?" "Does your mother know how upset you are about her divorce?" In a way this effort gives the single session some increased longevity by attempting to internalize a process that can continue for a period of time.

It is important to identify the types of unfinished business that can be finished. Two judgments have to be made. First, what myths or false beliefs do patients carry around about themselves and important figures in their lives? Second, can additional experiences with these important figures convert those myths or beliefs into a less distorted appreciation of reality? In a way this strategy is a kind of behavior modification. The repertoire—talking, sharing, questioning—exists. It need only be explored with appropriate targets.

Do Not Underestimate Patients' Strengths

I think of the therapy session as having the potential for breaking through an impasse in patients' psychological lives, so that they can resume the normal process of growth and development. I count on patients' abilities to work on an identified issue on their own, particularly if I can be helpful in identifying what that issue might be. I count on patients' ego strength and on their abilities to mobilize those strengths.

Trying to identify an impasse in patients' lives is an intellectually and technically challenging task, one that makes focused single-session psychotherapy exciting. It is as if I am trying to answer the question "What have these patients failed to understand about their lives that could make a difference in how they are conducting themselves now and in how they might manage their lives in the future?"

Patients find their way to the mental health center all by themselves, most of them are holding down jobs, and they are generally able to manage major parts of their lives without help from others. The purpose of the psychotherapeutic encounter is to provide significant help in a useful way at a crucial time, and to do it as quickly as seems appropriate, acknowledging all of the strengths that a client brings into the therapeutic episode.

Help Mobilize Social Supports

Some of the important people in a patient's life may play supportive roles. Others may not currently but could do so if asked. The research literature on the positive effects of a strong social support system in minimizing the negative consequences of stressful life events or chronic stressful life circumstances is so persuasive that it seems critically important to encourage the patient to mobilize available social supports wherever that is possible.

Some family members or friends may potentially play a sounding board role. Others may have information that the patient may not have, and they may willingly provide that information if asked. Still others may be helpful by encouraging the client to continue doing what the client alone may have to do.

Educate When Patient Appears to Lack Information

Therapists can easily assume that patients know more than they really do about psychopathology or psychotherapy in general or factors related to their own particular disorder. If therapists remain alert for evidence that a patient lacks pertinent factual information, they can be helpful by providing that missing information in a sentence or two. Lectures or extended comments are rarely helpful, but a pithy, pertinent statement can often be just what is needed. Some patients, for example, may not understand that some disorders are genetic, or how stress can affect the body, or how different varieties of child rearing have consequences for children's development. A strategically placed factual comment or suggestion about something patients might profitably read can often serve as a useful supplement to the therapeutic process.

Negotiate Additional Therapeutic Contacts as Needed

On those occasions when additional sessions seem indicated, the therapist should be able to describe in simple terms why such additional contacts seem appropriate and what the client needs to do between the conclusion of today's session and the start of the next session to ensure that the next contact will be as productive as possible. Additional sessions can thus be specifically contracted in terms of their objectives, rather than simply scheduled.

Such negotiated appointments provide therapists with an opportunity to describe their understanding of their clients' predicaments, however tentative that understanding might be, and to educate clients regarding the envisioned psychotherapeutic process. Ordinarily, subsequent sessions are best negotiated one at a time.

Make Audiotape of Interview Available to Client

The tape recorder I use to record interviews is in plain sight, and on occasion clients have asked me for a copy of the recording. My practice has been to make a copy readily available to all clients who ask for it. This decision is based on the fact that clients invariably talk about a great many important matters during the session, many of which they may not have talked about or even thought much about before. Thus, it is possible that clients can make good use of the recording as they review their therapeutic encounter.

I tell clients that I will make a copy of the tape and send it to them within a day or two. Inexpensive tape reproduction equipment is readily available that allows a copy to be made of a tape in a matter of minutes. I have not gathered enough follow-up data to make any assertions about the use that clients actually make of the recording, but I feel quite comfortable about the decision to make the tape recording available on request.

Build in a Follow-up Plan

The development of a plan for problem solving ties in with the follow-up procedure I have developed (see Malan, 1980c). If the patient does not call me following the interview, I call the patient. The plans we made or talked about for dealing with unfinished business can be one of the matters discussed in the brief follow-up conversation. The conversation is not a request for a recital of accomplishments, nor does it attempt to instill a sense of obligation in undertaking a process that the patient may not be ready for. But it can be couched in terms of "Did it make sense to you to try to do what we talked about?" If the patient indicates that it did, we can talk about what that experience was like and what the patient learned. If not, the patient can be reminded that finishing that unfinished business can be something the patient can keep in mind for the future, whenever the time seems right.

A CASE EXAMPLE

In order to provide an example of the clinical process that takes place in focused single-session psychotherapy, the annotated transcript of the beginning 11 minutes and the final 12 minutes of an 80-minute interview is presented in Box 8-1, along with a transcript of portions of the telephone follow-up conversation conducted four months after this interview occurred. The patient, a 27-year-old male, was seen in the adult outpatient clinic of the Boulder County Community Mental Health Center. He came into the office carrying a cup of hot coffee that he had just obtained in the admitting office. Italicized comments in brackets represent an effort to reconstruct my thoughts during the interview.

Box 8-1: Excerpts from a Single-Session Psychotherapy

Therapist: Tell me what I can do to be helpful.
Patient: Well, I don't know. I didn't want to come here, but my girlfriend told me I should come here and do something. But I'm not sure what to say now. I had it all planned out. *(pause)* I don't know what to say now. *[The patient has rehearsed what he wants to say— that seems a positive sign to me because it indicates that the patient thought that the*

(continued)

Box 8-1 continued

appointment was important enough to prepare for it. But he is hesitant about getting into what he rehearsed. So he is likely quite ambivalent about being in the mental health center. I will have to be careful.]

Therapist: Take a sip of coffee.

Patient: (after taking a sip) Um, let's see. I guess I have a lot of stuff built up inside of me and I don't have anybody to talk to. I get tired of talking to some people, unless they're strangers. I don't know if that's normal or not. And, I've been under a lot of pressure lately, both at work and with, with her and another girl. I'm real indecisive. I don't know what the hell to do with myself here, and, I don't know what else to say. *[We are off to a very shaky start. This patient is clearly reluctant and uneasy about coming to the mental health center and talking about his difficulties even though he knows he needs to. I have to get him engaged in the process of talking about himself and my potential virtue is that I am that "stranger" he needs to talk to—his word that I file away to be used later when and if it is needed.]*

Therapist: Why don't you tell me a little bit about yourself.

Patient: You mean what do I do? *(therapist nods)* I work in a gun shop as a gunsmith downtown. I live by myself in a house. A three-bedroom house for a hundred bucks a month in Boulder is pretty good.

Therapist: It certainly is.

Patient: (pause) I've been going out with this girl for quite a while, less than a year, but it's been quite a while. And, let's see. We've had a good relationship and stuff. *["Stuff" is a generic term that the patient uses as a shorthand for inner tension. I file that word away too.]* And, oh, about a month ago, this old high school girlfriend of mine stopped by for a week, or for five days. And I told my other girlfriend, "Oh, there's nothing to worry about, you know. We're just old friends. We've always been friends." She's somebody I can talk to. And a much different kind of relationship developed than what I ever thought, whatever either one of us had ever thought. I got in big trouble with my girlfriend here in Boulder. And she's going to break up with me and stuff. *[There's that word again.]* And I didn't want that, because this other girl lives in _____ and I didn't want that, yet I'd like to be able to see this other girl any time I want it. And, I don't know. I just don't know what to do as far as that, and then at work I feel like, well, this is our busy time of year, because it's hunting season. And I get lots of pressure to get stuff done. And, I don't know, for a while here, somehow I feel like the two guys I work for are going to get rid of me after hunting season for some reason, just by the way they act. One of the guys I've known for about ten years, and he just doesn't even hardly talk to me anymore. I don't like that, because I like where I work a lot, because it's a real small shop, and it's friendly. Everybody's got time to shoot the shit, but, it doesn't seem like we have it anymore. Like I say, maybe I shouldn't be here, because maybe I've just got to thrash things out in my head. But the only way my girlfriend would stay with me is if I came to see someone. *[This is a fine opening statement from this man who is not sure he should be talking with me at all. In spite of the fact that he isn't sure he should have come to the interview, he does lay out his problems. But, for the moment, he is there only because his girlfriend has insisted. I can't help noticing the parallels between his descriptions of his work situation and his home situation, even though there are two entirely different casts of characters. Thus, it could be that it won't make any difference whether we talk about his home or work situation. Since the patient returns to the situation with his girlfriend, I choose to return to that theme. Again, the patient seems to be saying that he thinks he can be helped if he can do during the interview what he ordinarily doesn't do—"thrash things out" in his head.]*

(continued)

Box 8-1 continued

Therapist: What do you think she was thinking when she said to go to the mental health center? *[This can be a very difficult question for someone who is not psychologically minded, since it requires that this patient put himself inside the head of another person and try to figure out that other person's thought processes. The question, then, is somewhat risky, but it provides a good test of this patient's psychological mindedness and willingness to take the position of another person.]*

Patient: Oh, she said, "At least talk to somebody." *(pause)* Well, she told me she, let's see, she told me that I didn't know what I really wanted, and I got to thinking about that and I guess I don't. And I think the thing that kicked it off was when this girlfriend of mine from _____ was over, I knew my girlfriend in Boulder was going to come over one night, and she caught us in bed, and I knew she was going to come over. It was like I wanted to get caught, but I didn't want to get caught, because it was a big thing. And then last week she found a letter I wrote to this girl in _____. And I had it in my daypack for over a week and a half. I never sent it, and I know she always goes in there. So maybe I want to, I don't know, maybe I do want to break up with my girlfriend in Boulder. I don't know. I got a bunch of other pressures, too. I found out yesterday she's pregnant. I had known that, I guess, for a couple of weeks. (pause) So you see, maybe I shouldn't be here. Maybe I should just sit back and think stuff out, but...*[The patient does fine with my question, and continues to present new material. We learn two important additional pieces of information. First, the patient clearly wanted to precipitate the crisis he is in by virtually arranging to get caught; and, second, his girlfriend is pregnant. He certainly does have a lot to talk about and think about, and I see my task as helping him do that. I'm not sure yet how to go about that, however, or what to focus on in terms of content or process. So I continue trying to make it easier for him to talk about himself.]*

Therapist: I think sometimes it helps to think things out out loud.

Patient: Yes.

Therapist: And you said you think you don't have anybody to talk with.

Patient: That's right. I, like I say, we've been going together for a long time, but we just, we don't talk a lot about what goes on inside of my head. I think a lot. She's always asking me what's going on. And I just say, "It's nothing." And...

T: But there is stuff going on in your head. *[I deliberately use his word, "stuff."]*

Patient: Oh, yes.

Therapist: But you just don't talk with her about it.

Patient: Yes. I don't talk with too many people unless I, like I said, they're strangers. *[That's the second time he has used this word. I would make a mistake not to use it myself in the proper context.]* Because, I don't know why. Because probably you don't know them, and they aren't involved or something.

Therapist: Yeah.

Patient: (pause) Work's been bothering me a lot, though. *[The patient simply won't acknowledge that his problems with his girlfriend are more (or less) important than his problems at work. So I had better make sure to cover both areas during this interview.]*

Therapist: Well, you've got some time right now—with a stranger. *[I think it is appropriate to label this use of the word "stranger" by describing myself that way quite overtly. While it might seem obvious that I am a stranger, the connection between that obvious fact and what the patient has said about it being easier to talk with a stranger may not be obvious to the patient. Thus, explicitly labeling myself as that stranger can help the patient see that there is psychological significance and coherence to what he says, and that he can learn more about his psychological self by using this opportunity to talk about himself as freely as he can.]*

(continued)

Box 8-1 continued

Patient: Yes, I don't know what else to say though.

Therapist: Sure. What's, when you say there's a lot of stuff going on in your head, what are you talking about mainly? *[Here I decide to continue my risk taking with this patient by testing out the degree of access he has to his own thought processes. So I start exploring how he is able to talk about his inner life.]*

Patient: Oh, I'm always thinking about something, but not a whole lot—if we're watching television or sitting around the house or something. I'm usually pretty quiet around her. (pause) I just think of stuff. Since that other girl came to visit, I've been thinking of her a lot. And, I think I fantasize a hell of a lot.

Therapist: What's that mean?

Patient: Fantasize? Picture yourself doing something else, or being somebody else, or whatever.

Therapist: What do you fantasize? When you say you fantasize a lot, what do you mean?

Patient: That's hard to explain. *(pause)* Characters in books, or whatever book I'm reading, or—

Therapist: Can you give me an example?

Patient: Characters from Ray Bradbury books, something like that, or...

Therapist: Do you remember the last time you fantasized being a character in a book? *[I'm not at all sure here that it was such a good idea to push him about his fantasies. Nothing much is happening.]*

Patient: Yes. I don't really get, you know, I don't get carried away where I just don't hear what anybody says. You know, you're just thinking about that stuff all the time.

Therapist: Tell me what you think about when you think about that stuff. *(pause)* Just as an example. *[I am about ready to quit this line of inquiry. The patient is getting a trifle defensive and I think I have gone about as far as I can go.]*

Patient: I don't know, they just come and go all the time. Probably a good one is when there's a John Wayne movie on. Everybody likes John Wayne. That's a common one, I guess. I've always liked John Wayne. *[Bingo! John Wayne—the strong, silent hero figure for this patient who is a gunsmith by profession. This movie figure is a fine symbolic representation of this patient, whose feelings run deep but who doesn't talk about them.]*

Therapist: So you fantasize being him, or being that character.

Patient: Yes, I guess...

Therapist: Is that what you mean?

Patient: Yes. Not John Wayne, but just being a character like that.

Therapist: Right.

Patient: Or, jeez, I don't know.

Therapist: *[I decide to review here, to make sure I've understood the situation thus far, to give the patient a chance to catch his breath, to let the patient know that if he talks, I'll listen, and to get a clue as to what direction to move toward.]* Ok. Well, you've got a ____ girlfriend who's pregnant, and a ____ girlfriend who's...

Patient: (interrupting) who's not pregnant.

Therapist: (continuing) who's new and who is far more appealing to you than you ever thought would be the case.

Patient: Right. And, I think the grass looks greener on the other side, but maybe it's not. *[The patient is with me now in this reviewing process, and I think we are going to do just fine.]*

Therapist: Yes. And you feel some pressure at work, and you're not sure just what your status really is on the job. *[I am deliberately even-handed about giving work-related problems the same importance as girlfriend-related problems.]*

(continued)

Box 8-1 continued

Patient: Yes. And I know I could go take off and work for somebody else. But I guess I lack the confidence to do it. I've always had a big confidence problem in myself. I have to be pushed into some things.

Therapist: [*Now I make a major decision, to help the patient tell me the story of his life, particularly as it revolves around work and around heterosexual experiences. I have come to the tentative conclusion that he has probably never had an opportunity to be autobiographical in this way and that among the therapeutic gains that could come from such an inquiry would be that he would become less of a stranger to himself, he would see the continuity between the past and the present, and he would see that talking and thinking about himself out loud might be more productive than living the life of the strong, silent man who doesn't look inward—in a word, that if the decision is a good one, he might be able to talk with his girlfriend the way he will, I hope, talk with me.*] How long have you lived in Boulder?

[*About 50 minutes elapse. He has told me the story of his life, and then we have returned to talking about the events leading up to his decision to come to the mental health center*]

Therapist: How is it that ____ got pregnant? [*Now it is time to look at the pregnancy in light of what we have learned about this patient's history and his characteristic ways of dealing with his thoughts and feelings—that is, his habitual pretending that if he doesn't think about something or talk about something, it isn't there.*]

Patient: It just happened. I don't know. She didn't use her diaphragm for a while there.

Therapist: Why was that, do you know?

Patient: No.

Therapist: Did she, did you know she wasn't using a diaphragm when you were making love?

Patient: Uh-hum. She would just love to have a baby, and to be with it too.—She just loves little kids. So do I, but I'm not ready for it, I tell you that. I suppose nobody ever is, but I just don't…

Therapist: I don't think that's true. [*I gently disagree with the patient.*]

Patient: No? Some people are ready?

Therapist: Sure.

Patient: Well, I'm sure if you're married and plan it out. That's what I'd rather do. But I'm just not ready for this at all.

Therapist: Well, you guys are, you and ____ both are doing some things very deliberately…[*I begin a kind of recapitulation of the main issue in this interview—the patient's habitual way of communicating by action instead of by words.*]

Patient: (interrupting) Yeah, I know.

Therapist: (continuing)—that, uh, I guess you're not really acknowledging. I think you're trying to get caught. I think you wanted, the only way to interpret it is that you wanted to get caught in bed, and you wanted ____ to read the letter. How else can you interpret it?

Patient: Yeah.

Therapist: And it sounds like ____ wanted to get pregnant.

Patient: Yeah. That's what I think too, because she's said stuff like that to me before when we go over to her friend's house for supper. These friends of mine, they have a nice new baby and she just loves it. She gives you one of those looks that says, "Oh, let's have one of these." I really don't want to have a baby.

Therapist: ____ knows that?

Patient: Yeah.

Therapist: What's she thinking about doing in regards to the baby? [*I think we have to discuss the reality issues pertinent to this pregnancy.*]

(continued)

Box 8-1 continued

Patient: She says she wants to keep it. And, it's hard for me because I think both ways on the subject. I was kind of neutral about abortion. I said it just depends on the circumstance. I don't want to have a baby, that's for sure. I would like to someday, but not now.
Therapist: Well, I think you are doing a lot of communicating. Instead of by talking, which is the way people usually communicate with each other, you're doing an awful lot of it by…
Patient: *(interrupting)* By other ways.
Therapist: *(continuing)* by what you do in life. And you have to, the trouble with that is that somebody then has to try to figure out then what you're trying to say.
Patient: Yeah.
Therapist: It's like with _____ *[a previous girlfriend].* You don't really know what happened to her, or what's going on in her head, what went on with her. It's like the girl you lived with for two years in _____. You never knew what was going on in her head, and every time that happens it sets things up for people not to be very honest with each other.
Patient: Yeah. See, you know, I realize all these things. In the back of my head I know, I didn't want to get caught, but I did. You know, that's so dumb. I don't know why I just can't say stuff out.
Therapist: It's not like you're not aware of what is going on inside your head. I think you, you know pretty well what you really do believe. It may be hard to admit it, but I think you know. It's not like you're a stranger to yourself.
Patient: Yeah.
Therapist: I mean, you could really tell _____ about the girl who went to _____ , about _____, and about _____ *[previous girlfriends].* You, you're aware, pretty aware of your feelings. Sounds like you've grown up in a way where you don't talk about things very much. *[We have not talked at all about the patient's early childhood, and this comment is meant to give the patient an opportunity to say a word or two about his early years and his family.]*
Patient: So that's, my family are big talkers.
Therapist: They are?
Patient: Yeah. But I've never been that way. My dad's a real intellectual. He likes to have heavy discussions, and I don't. Doing a pretty good job today, though. *[This last comment is a nice confirmation that the interview is going well.]*
Therapist: You feel like you are?
Patient: Yeah, I think I'm talking pretty good today. I don't do that. Um, my sister in _____ is a big talker. I just never have been, I just, do a lot of thinking inside my head.
Therapist: Like John Wayne. Never said very much, carried a gun, the strong, silent man. *[The metaphor is repeated.]*
Patient: Yeah. *[This discussion continues for a couple of minutes.]*
Therapist: Do you think you could talk with, talk with _____ more like you are talking here today?
Patient: Yeah. I've been trying, this last week, to talk quite a bit. Talked last night, pretty good, and it's coming around.
Therapist: It's even ok to say, "I'm mixed up. I don't know what I think. I don't know what I want. And I want to be a father and I don't want to be a father. I want to get married and _____
Patient: *(interrupting)* and I don't want to get married.
Therapist: And "I don't want to hurt anybody."
Patient: Yeah.
Therapist: Those are all ok things to say. Whatever.

(continued)

Box 8-1 continued

Patient: Yeah. Just some sort of communication. *(pause)* Yeah. If a guy would just pay attention, he could tell a lot more about himself by what's going on around him.

Therapist: So what did, what did _____ have in mind when she said to come on in and talk to someone—"Go on in and talk to somebody." What did she have in mind? *[The recapitulation of the first moments of the interview serves as the beginning of the ending phase of this encounter.]*

Patient: Sitting down and talking to somebody, like this. I'm sure. And she said, I said if I go on in and talk to somebody, will you stay, will you not, will you see me some more? She said, "Yeah, only if you go see somebody." I said, "Ok, I'll do it." So, I called the next day.

Therapist: And why, why do you think she wanted you to talk to somebody?

Patient: Because she knows I got a lot going on in my head, and I haven't been able to talk to her about it. I think I'll see this pregnancy through OK, whatever way it goes. I just feel a lot of pressure, if she felt, if she wants to keep the baby. (pause) And I don't want to.

Therapist: So right now, if you had your wish, you'd kind of encourage her to have an abortion. *[The discussion continues for another minute or two.]* Well, have you done enough talking for today?

Patient: Yeah.

Therapist: Let me make a suggestion to you. Uh, call me up and let me know how you're doing. Call me up in about a month. I'll give you my phone number.

Patient: Okay.

Therapist: And I want to get your phone number. In case I don't hear from you, I'll call you up and see how you're doing.

Patient: Okay.

Therapist: And I'd be happy to have you give me a call in a month or so and let me know how you're doing. Call me, feel free to call earlier if there's some reason you want to.

Patient: Will you remember who I am?

Therapist: Yeah.

Patient: Ok. You must see a lot of people.

Therapist: I do, but I think I'll remember. And if you have to remind me, it won't take long to remember you.

Patient: All right.

Therapist: Just tell me you're John Wayne.

[Four months later, I contact the patient by telephone]

Therapist: I was just listening to the tape recording of the interview we made together. Jeez, it was a long time ago. And I realized I hadn't gotten back to you as quickly as I intended to. So I thought if you had a few minutes, I'd like to ask you how you're doing.

Patient: Oh, I'm pretty good. *(pause)* Um, me and _____ are getting married.

Therapist: Are you!

Patient: Yeah, in June.

Therapist: Are you pleased about that?

Patient: Yeah.

Therapist: Good, good. How's _____ feeling? *[I assume that _____ is considerably further along in her pregnancy.]*

Patient: She's fine.

Therapist: Good. How did it work out that you decided to do that?

Patient: Um, oh, I don't know. We talked about it a couple of times, and I didn't want to do it and I held off for a long time. And we broke up a few times, and then finally I just

(continued)

Box 8-1 continued

said, "The hell with it. Instead of messing around and changing my mind all the time, I should just go ahead and do it."

Therapist: Well, it sounds like it wasn't awfully hard to decide that, but it wasn't easy either.

Patient: No. It wasn't very easy for me. I was kind of reluctant. But I figure, what the hell, I might as well do it.

Therapist: Yeah. When's the baby due?

Patient: Um, ____ went ahead and had the abortion.

Therapist: She did? *[I am genuinely surprised.]*

Patient: Yeah, she sure did.

Therapist: Hmm. That's funny, when you said you were going to get married, I assumed that she was going to keep the baby.

Patient: No. We just decided to get married about four weeks ago.

Therapist: So, in other words, the decision to have the abortion came earlier.

Patient: Yes.

Therapist: How did that work out?

Patient: It was pretty rough.

Therapist: I bet it was.

Patient: I held out again till the last minute, and, I don't know, like the day before the abortion date, I decided to go ahead and keep it, and then, that morning we woke up, ____ said that she'd just wanted to go ahead and have it. She wanted to have the baby real bad, and then she decided she wanted to have the abortion.

Therapist: Yeah.

Patient: She thought that would be better.

Therapist: So, even toward the end you weren't sure whether to go ahead and have the abortion or not. So why do you think ____ decided to have the abortion?

Patient: I'm not sure. I think she, she just decided that she didn't want to have the baby. *[I don't have a good understanding about how they decided to go ahead with the abortion, but I don't think any more questions about it will play a useful role.]*

Therapist: And then you kept seeing each other, and you say you, you broke up a couple of times.

Patient: Well, yes. We just had a few hassles. She wanted to get married, and I didn't, and she said, "Well, ok, see you later." And then a week later we'd see each other. And we did it one more time, and finally I went back over to her house and I said, "I'm through holding out. I give in."

Therapist: That's how you think of it? *[I hoped there was more to his decision to get married than simply giving in.]*

Patient: Well, no.

Therapist: That's the words you used.

Patient: Yeah. I just figured the hell with it, I guess I really want to do this....I just figured I wanted to do it because I don't want to, I don't want to move. I don't want her to be out of my life.

Therapist: Yes. Well, that's a good reason to get married....Things still going okay on the job?

Patient: Yes. Going real good.

Therapist: Good. This time of year was the time that you said things slowed down a little bit.

Patient: Yes, but they haven't slowed down a bit.

Therapist: No kidding.

Patient: Yes. We're still five weeks behind.

Therapist: Is that right?

(continued)

> **Box 8-1 continued**
>
> *Patient:* Work is going better than ever.
> *Therapist:* Is that right?
> *Patient:* I'm making better money, getting along better with the people I work with.
> *Therapist:* You mentioned, when we saw each other, that you weren't sure how well you were getting along with the guys you were working with.
> *Patient:* Right. Well, after I saw you, about a week after I saw you, um, just before we closed down to go hunting, it must have been right at the end of October, I sat down and talked with the guy I worked with downstairs. And I asked him what was bugging him, and he told me, and I told him what was bugging me. And, then we, this was like a day before we closed down to go hunting, he said, "Well, think about it when you're hunting." And, we came back and talked about it some more. I decided to stay, and they decided to keep me, and things are going really good. I don't feel as much pressure, near as much pressure as I did before hunting season. And I'm keeping up with five weeks worth of work. We're just swamped.
> *Therapist:* Is that right?
> *Patient:* Yes. And I, I don't feel any pressure at all. Very little. And I've been trying to get myself physically fit, so that helps me too. Exercising. Running. Things are just going much better, much better.
> *Therapist:* Well, I'm really delighted to hear that. It sounds like the hour and a half we spent together was well worth it.
> *Patient:* Yeah, I think so. Jeez, it only cost me fourteen bucks. It was worth it.
> *Therapist:* *(laughs)* Well, good. I'm glad you found it useful.
> *Patient:* Yes. But things just seem to be falling in place, going much better. But after we had that talk at work, um, he told me that, see, back at that time I was getting some work back, and some complaints.
> *Therapist:* Oh, I see.
> *Patient:* And, I told him what was going on, what was bugging me, like ____ being pregnant. And, that was a lot of pressure. And I guess he took that as a, you know, he gave me some time to think about it, like when I was hunting, and then when we came back, he said, "Well, let's just start with a clean sheet." And, I talked to him about some things that I didn't like, too, at work. So I guess we both got it out in the open. *[I'm very glad that I asked about his work situation. I think that the problems at work were every bit as important to this patient as were the problems with his girlfriend.]*
> *Therapist:* Well, that's fine.
> *Patient:* I thought the interview was real good. It laid a lot of, it showed me things that I already knew that I wanted to do. I thought about that quite a bit.
> *Therapist:* Oh, good.
> *Patient:* Me and ____ are talking more. It's still hard to talk. We have to work on that.

CONCLUDING COMMENTS

Focused single-session therapy tests the fundamental principles of planned short-term therapy by deliberately creating and examining the extreme case. As such, it attempts to accomplish enough therapeutic work in a single interview to start a therapeutic process that can continue without additional direct intervention of the therapist. Happily, other clinicians are now exploring the usefulness of single-session psychotherapy (Block, 1985; Brown, 1984; Ellis, 1989; Erstling & Devlin, 1989; Feldman, 1994; Hoyt, 1994c; Hoyt, Rosenbaum, & Talmon, 1992; Lankton & Erickson, 1994; Littrell, Malia, &

Vanderwood, 1995; Mahrer & Roberge, 1993; Öst, 1989; Powers & Griffith, 1989; Rockwell & Pinkerton, 1982; Rosenbaum, 1993, 1994; Rosenbaum, Hoyt, & Talmon, 1990; Shulman, 1989; Talmon, 1990; Wells, 1994).

To be sure, many patients—perhaps most—will require more than a single therapy session in order to attain significant relief. But what can be exciting to the therapist is to keep open the possibility throughout the initial contact with a patient that it may be the only contact that is necessary. Indeed, working on the assumption that one session can and perhaps should be sufficient may be an increasingly useful mode of functioning for today's clinician, given the evidence that so large a proportion of patients are, by plan or otherwise, seen only once. The understanding of the therapist and the patient is that the patient can always return for another interview when whatever benefits have been derived from the previous session have been exhausted.

Focused single-session therapy matches the general ways in which primary medical care is delivered. The therapist provides some form of remediation that is judged to be pertinent to the presenting problem, with the understanding that the patient should feel free to return if the remedy does not appear to be sufficiently effective. Thus, focused single-session therapy can be thought of as primary mental health care. As such, it can appropriately be followed by additional contact between the patient and the therapist, if and when that additional contact is needed.

CHAPTER 9

GUSTAFSON'S BRIEFER PSYCHOTHERAPY

Overview

The Brief Therapy Clinic Treatment Program

A Case Example

Concluding Comments

James Gustafson's (1981, 1986, 1990, 1992, 1995) clinical ideas come from two important sources: (1) his careful analysis of psychoanalytic and psychodynamic writings pertinent to time-limited psychotherapy and (2) his clinical experiences at the Brief Therapy Clinic at the University of Wisconsin.

Gustafson's book (1986) draws primarily on his experiences with patients who are mildly disturbed college students. He writes as if his descriptions are not pertinent to patients who may be more seriously disturbed, but it may be useful to keep this possibility in mind when considering his ideas. In describing his orientation to time-limited psychotherapy, Gustafson writes:

> Many of the cases in this book are taken from the teaching practice of the Brief Therapy Clinic at the University of Wisconsin, which routinely offers about a semester of once-a-week sessions to its individual patients. But since I see few major differences in principle between brief and long-term therapy, individual and family therapy, the reader will also find illustrations from all these domains. This book could rightly be described as being about *briefer* therapy. (1986, p. 4)

Given the specificity with which Gustafson describes his approach to short-term psychotherapy, he is remarkably nondoctrinaire about his work. He clearly believes that there is no universal method of time-limited psychotherapy and that every way of

examining the process of therapy has its advantages. Indeed, in his major work on time-limited psychotherapy (1986) he allocates more than half of the pages to a description of a variety of what he calls "observing positions"—ranging from Freud, Breuer, Ferenczi, Rank, and Reich to Alexander and French, Sullivan, Winnicott, and Balint, and finally to Gedo, Havens, Malan, Sifneos, Davanloo, Bateson, Selvini Palazzoli, and Maturana, many of whose works are not discussed in this volume because they are not directly pertinent to our relatively narrow definition of planned short-term psychotherapy.

Gustafson likens his approach to brief psychotherapy to the approach employed by skilled chess players. In chess, he notes,

> there are many kinds of opening moves and many kinds of defenses against these opening moves.... No serious player of chess would enter a match merely prepared for a single line of play....Yet we do this with patients in our field, as if being well educated about psychotherapy were some kind of liberal education that a skilled tactician could forgo. (1990, p. 408).

Gustafson's concluding comments in his book underline this catholic view of psychotherapeutic thinking:

> The first principle is to take the entire tradition of psychotherapy as our province for learning. The

point is not to amass knowledge. No, it is rather to become familiar with what is powerful and deep in the many different guises, genres, and schools which are possible in such a diverse tradition. (1986, p. 344)

Gustafson's view of brief psychotherapy is what he calls "the entire field of small moves with large effects" (1990, p. 408), that is, knowing where, how, and when to have the most meaningful impact on a client. Thus, for example, when clients have issues in the work domain, it is well to remember that they (1) must work from their own conceptions of what they want to bring into the world, (2) have to face whatever weaknesses of preparation they might have, and (3) must find a work place where they can do well. When clients face pathologies in their own behavior, such as alcoholism or drug abuse, to cite another example, therapists must (1) help clients position themselves so that the pathological behavior is impossible;(2) persuade clients to continue in an abstinence mode when they can tolerate giving up their self-destructive behavior; and (3) have faith in their clients, giving them responsibility for their own behavior as soon as they are ready to accept it.

When clients' problems are multidimensional, when many problems exist side by side and are interconnected or, when the client may be suffering from a character disorder, meaningful effects must be obtained in a somewhat different way. First, Gustafson suggests that it is important to identify the greatest source of preoccupation at the start of every therapeutic session. Second, if the level of disability is so great that no special problem can be identified, the client must be helped to identify a specific area in which to work, perhaps by identifying the most recent problem that the client remembers being concerned about. Third, the therapist must meter the client's level of optimism or hope. Frequently lack of hope can be countered by a remark like, "You feel so bad about lacking self-confidence. This must mean you once felt a great deal of self-confidence, or you would not feel the lack of it so deeply," or "You would like to break up with her without giving her any pain whatsoever, as if surgery could be carried out with no suffering at all" (1990, p. 429). These therapeutic comments combine a deep understanding of human behavior with a remarkable sense of compassion.

THE BRIEF THERAPY CLINIC TREATMENT PROGRAM

Time-limited psychotherapy at the Brief Therapy Clinic takes place in three distinct phases. First there is a preliminary interview. If the prospective patient is deemed suitable to continue, there is a two-to-three hour trial therapy session, which is perhaps the most unusual aspect of this approach. If that session seems to be helpful, the patient is invited to complete a one-semester therapeutic program. Like many other psychotherapists, Gustafson spends a good deal of time thinking about who might and who might not be suitable for his time-limited psychotherapy (see Chapter 24).

The Preliminary Interview

Before the preliminary interview the clinician has an opportunity to examine the patient's medical chart and the responses to an open-ended questionnaire and a symptom checklist that were completed just before the interview. The open-ended questionnaire includes such questions as "What specific reasons made you come to the clinic now?" and "Describe your major problem or difficulty in your own words."

Preliminary Questions

The therapist looks for answers to three questions during the preliminary interview, which lasts about 30 minutes. First, is the patient looking for the kind of help that is available at the clinic? If it appears that there is a good match between the patient's interests and the clinic's program, then two additional questions are posed—what Gustafson refers to as the "best news" and the "bad news" questions. The best news comes from the determination of how the patient has been able to allow others to be of help in the past. The bad news comes from the answers to the question of how patients feel, think, and act when they are at their worst.

Gustafson thinks of the program at the Brief Therapy Clinic as most suitable for students with some recurrent distress that they want to talk over he writes, "If the patient is after something we might give, if the patient has gotten help in a serious way from other people, if the patient at worst has been in no serious danger, then we are likely to offer a trial therapy" (1986, p. 281). Gustafson reports that about half of the patients referred to the Brief Therapy Clinic are accepted for treatment, a rate that seems just about right to him.

Preliminary Interview Errors

Gustafson describes a number of errors that can occur during the preliminary interview. The first is to pass on to the trial therapy session a patient who either has an unrealistic idea of how brief time-limited therapy might be, given the nature and history of the problem, or who is offended at the idea that a charge will be made for all subsequent therapeutic sessions. The second is to pass on to the trial therapy session a patient who has had past experiences in psychotherapy that are inconsistent with the Brief Therapy Clinic program, such as someone who talks endlessly, as he or she did in previous psychotherapy, and is startled to discover that the clinician becomes somewhat impatient. The third is to ignore the parents' objections to the patient entering psychotherapy, since their ideas can frequently be at great variance with those of the prospective patient.

Another group of errors occurs because the clinician underestimates the severity of the problem as initially presented by the patient. Many initial presentations can be quite routine and can obscure profound psychopathology, such as described in the following excerpt.

> A 29-year old, single graduate student was referred to us for depression. He complained to us that his girlfriend had broken off with him, which was bothering him more than usual because the girlfriend would not allow him to see their one-year-old daughter....When I asked [him] what went through his mind when he thought of missing his daughter, he told me he thought of shaving his head so he

could place it in a noose. When I asked him what kept him from this proceeding, he cried and said his little daughter was the only person he loved in the world. When I asked when he would get to see her again, he cried again and told me that his girlfriend had just proposed to leave the state in a few months. (1986, p. 289)

At the other extreme are patients who give an unusually pathological or generally negative initial impression but who may, in fact, be far healthier than they admit. Often this occurs when the patient-therapist relationship is not positive, such as might occur when the patient doesn't like or is frightened by the therapist.

The Trial Therapy Session

The trial therapy session is divided into three components: an initial individual interview, a discussion between the interviewer and one or more members of the clinical team who have been observing the interview behind a one-way mirror, and a concluding individual interview. The entire trial therapy session may last as long as three hours. Its rationale is to determine whether some significant progress can be made in a brief period of time. If so, it is thought likely that additional significant progress can be made in additional brief periods of time; if not, it is thought unlikely that significant change will occur in brief psychotherapy.

The initial individual interview begins with the presenting problem and attempts to develop a history starting when the patient seemed to be functioning satisfactorily, then continuing to when things started to go wrong. In Gustafson's words the interview attempts to "reach what is worthwhile about the individual," attempts to "reach the illness," and at the same time tries to determine why the patient has had to be exactly as he or she has been (1986, p. 296).

The team discussion, which can produce much anxiety and confusion in the therapist if it is not skillfully managed by all participants, is designed to give the therapist an opportunity to describe his or her impressions of the patient and for the other observing team members to provide their impressions—optimally for the benefit of the therapist. Such team discussions usually last about 20 minutes.

The concluding individual interview, which usually lasts about an hour, is more future-oriented—for example, what if the patient entered psychotherapy, or didn't enter psychotherapy, or what if the presenting problem were to continue, or were to disappear. By the end of the trial therapy session the therapist is in a position to offer or not to offer a continuing therapeutic experience, and the patient is in a position to accept or decline the offer, if made.

The Continuing Psychotherapy

Gustafson (1986) describes the continuing therapeutic sessions as "first sessions which are given over as often as they are needed by the patient" (p. 315). It is worth quoting him on this point, since it is important in understanding his rationale for continuing beyond the trial therapy session.

> Only if you are ingenious about separations can you retain the thrill and scope of first meetings....This is exactly what happens in many relations between patients and doctors. The relations become routine when the connection is assured. No longer standing back from one another, doctor and patient locate smaller points of interest. But what if the doctor has a method for meeting his patient many times as if their meeting were the first meeting?...You give a "therapeutic consultation" and then you repeat it several more times if necessary....Single meetings could be repeated and still be singular if they could be far enough apart. (1986, pp. 316–317)

What seems to distinguish the continuing psychotherapy from the initial interview and trial therapy session is its complexity. The patient and therapist need to examine several life variables at the same time, keeping in mind their multiple interactions and multiple contradictions. Gustafson tries to locate a current problem in every session; find a useful perspective for examining the problem; clarify and revise hypotheses that serve to organize how the problem is best understood; appreciate the complexity of the patient's life, identifying all of the significant players and their roles; and at the same time assess the patient's psychological status more or less continuously.

Termination Issues

Like nearly all psychodynamically oriented psychotherapists, Gustafson is drawn to examine the termination phase of the psychotherapy. According to him the danger of an unskillful termination is that the gains will be lost, either through the patient's provocation of others to undo what has occurred in the therapy or through a kind of hopeless self-debasement. Hence, the final comments from the therapist have the goal of blocking that self-defeating behavior, by helping patients develop the capacity to enlarge the number of possibilities that might be open to them in the future.

A CASE EXAMPLE

An example of the work of Gustafson's group is given in Box 9-1. It is the beginning section of the initial individual interview that constitutes the first portion of the trial therapy session, along with a brief commentary about the mid-session discussion with the observer and the beginning of the resumed trial therapy session following the mid-session break. The patient is a 22-year-old woman who complained of feelings of insecurity and a low self-image and who was afraid that she might never be able to have a normal relationship with a man. She was chronically self-deprecating. During the preliminary interview she met all the criteria for eligibility for a trial therapy session. She was troubled but sound; she had a good support system; she had a problem she wanted to explore. It was also learned that a year earlier she had had two near disasters. She was struck by an automobile and had nearly died of complications while being treated in the hospital. An offer of continuing psychotherapy was made and accepted by this patient, who subsequently entered into a complex and helpful course of time-limited therapy.

This excerpt provides an excellent illustration of Gustafson's thought processes during the initial interview and his uncommonly high level of clinical skill. Note in particular how often Gustafson's comments have an educational objective, helping the client make sense out of her reactions to her life experiences and to this therapeutic encounter (see also Gustafson, 1995).

Box 9-1: Beginning of Gustafson's Initial Trial Therapy Session

Therapist: Where do you think we ought to start today?

Patient: I guess what I really want to know is—I was hoping you guys would give me some good ideas on how to improve my self-image.

Therapist: OK, then we need to have some idea of what you think is wrong with that. So that's what you'd like to get out of us today—how to improve your self-image?

Patient: I guess that's my biggest problem. It's that I have a low opinion of myself.

Therapist: You come across as a person with a certain amount of confidence, nevertheless, so I would imagine that at one time you felt pretty good about yourself.

Patient: Well, no. I mean I do like some things about myself. I think I'm intelligent; I guess that gives me some confidence. I feel OK about my looks. I guess it's my personality I think is wrong.

Therapist: All right, should we see about that? We can hardly make any suggestions unless we understand what is wrong.

Patient: I don't know. Like I said before, I feel like I'm boring. I feel like what I have to say isn't worthwhile.

Therapist: OK, so you feel you're boring and what you say isn't worthwhile. What do you mean?

Patient: You know, like it's stupid. Like it seems like a contradiction because on the one hand I say I feel intelligent but I say stupid things, so it's like I'm good at learning. I'm good at taking tests. I'm good in school.

Therapist: School intelligent?

Patient: Yeah.

Therapist: But you don't feel smart outside?

Patient: Right. Like I'm good at regurgitating—that's why I'm good in school.

Therapist: Well, that's no mean talent. So you're good at that but you don't feel…

Patient: But it's like I'm not really original.

Therapist: You don't feel original? Compared to whom?

Patient: I don't know.

Therapist: Who's original?

Patient: I don't know—some people just are.

Therapist: Well, whom do you admire?

Patient: I don't know. Nobody in particular.

Therapist: Well, one is always comparing oneself to other people, and you look like you're comparing yourself with someone who is original, compared to you.

Patient: Let's see. OK, like my friend Harry. It's like he is really funny. He just finds funny things to say. *[For me there are two crucial statements here which catch this woman by surprise. "You come across as a person with a certain amount of confidence." She may have jumped in her seat when I said that to her. I thought she did. Here she was saying she had a "low opinion of myself," and I was saying I didn't think she did. But I also say that I accept her "low opinion" and I am interested in how she arrives there: "You don't feel original. Compared to whom?" Here she may have jumped again. Again, I thought she did. The eye for her confidence and the eye for her comparing herself badly, together, give a double description which brings depth of field and then depth of feeling. We drop down fast into what is most painful to her, because we have a hold on what is right about her. We are "working the opposing currents."]*

Therapist: So Harry is funny?

Patient: Yeah.

Therapist: So you admire that in a man?

(continued)

Box 9-1 continued

Patient: Yeah. Like at work it kind of bugs me because there's this man, but I feel really weird that it bothers me so much. *[She begins to cry.]*

Therapist: Yeah, but it does. There's some Kleenex right here.

Patient: He's just so friendly, everyone likes him. I guess I compare myself to him because he's so comfortable with himself and it seems like he's just so friendly, he's just so like outgoing, just easygoing.

Therapist: So this is painful to you by comparison to yourself. How would you describe yourself?

Patient: Just really afraid.

Therapist: So you criticize yourself for being too fearful? What are you fearful about?

Patient: Like afraid of rejection.

Therapist: Why shouldn't you be afraid of rejection?

Patient: Because I'm so afraid that I don't take risks, so I don't gain anything either. I'm always protecting myself and by doing that I don't get what I really need.

Therapist: Like what?

Patient: Like I'm afraid of people not liking me so I don't really try so they don't—

Therapist: Sometimes a person learns to be a little cautious or protective and that's a good thing.

Patient: But why is it good?

Therapist: You can get hurt.

Patient: Yeah, but I think it's better not to be afraid than to get hurt.

Therapist: Really?

Patient: No pain, no gain. *[Now I'm leading into history. She proposes she "should not be fearful." I propose that she had to have had good reason. I propose we appreciate the necessity of her fearfulness. She tells me very clearly about her family.]*

Therapist: It depends on what the experience has been. Some people have had an easy time of it or a pleasant time of it or a protective time of it. So you know, you've had some rough hits already. But you criticize yourself for your caution. I was quite impressed that you've already been through two terrible things.

Patient: But they don't seem terrible to me.

Therapist: They're a lot harder than what most people go through. There must be some reason why you're cautious and you don't take risks. I mean this just didn't—this must have a history.

Patient: I don't think I ever have. Nobody in my family builds anybody else up; it's more like cutting down.

Therapist: So your family doesn't give each other much appreciation.

Patient: No. Its kind of weird. I don't know if that's the way I take it because I'm the youngest and so I was always called the baby of the family. I was always told that I was spoiled, and like my sister and two of my brothers always called me a little brat, and my older brother, Sam, I liked him because he was my favorite. My brother, Jim, and I, he's the second oldest, we always used to fight and I used to get him in trouble, like I'd do something to him and he'd do something back and I would start crying and my dad would yell at him. But my dad was like the head of the family so I always got the better end of it, and like my dad would be yelling at my brother and my mom would tell me what a brat I was. And like now, those are the things I remember. Sometimes she would say, "Oh, you're such a good kid," but the feeling that I got was that I wasn't and like now she says, "When people called you a brat nobody meant it," she's kidding but it's like—you just don't say things like that.

Therapist: Did she think you were a brat?

(continued)

Box 9-1 continued

Patient: If I was a bad person, or how I interpret it?

Therapist: What did she think was bad about you?

Patient: That I was getting my brother in trouble and acting that way.

Therapist: Your view is that she was siding with Jim and seeing you as being a troublemaker?

Patient: I was, it was true, but I think a lot of kids are like that.

Therapist: That's not unusual, the youngest fights back. But your mother was pretty harsh, you felt.

Patient: Yeah, she was. I don't think she realized. It was hard because I think she is very good at not remembering things that she doesn't want to. I'll tell her stuff she did and she'll say, "I said that to you and I did that? I don't remember that." On the one hand I feel like maybe I exaggerated it, but on the other hand I think that maybe she is just protecting herself because she really did do those things.

Therapist: You certainly feel it very keenly from your demeanor. It sounds like we got into that because we were talking about this self-image of yours and you were saying to me why you might be afraid and might even be a devil.

Patient: Yeah.

Therapist: I mean the fight with your brother and ordinary things like that. Maybe it dates back to taking a lot of criticism from your mom for fairly ordinary things.

Patient: I know she has a really low self-image too. I never thought she did, but she has told me.

Therapist: Maybe you got cautious somewhere back there. It sounds like you were actually taking some risks in the family there for a while, a fight with your brother and all that.

Patient: How is that taking a risk?

Therapist: You could have been sweet and nice. Instead you were having fights with your older brother. Isn't that taking a risk? You could have been a nice little girl. *[She describes being run down by her mother, which allowed her to be close to her father. But she also describes her mother's disconfirming that she ran her down. I could see how she could have been quite confused, being disconfirmed about being a worthwhile kid, but also disconfirmed about being run down.]*

[At the conclusion of the first hour of this trial therapy session the therapist suggests taking a break that will allow him to discuss the session with the observer. Two technical problems were discussed with the observer during the break. One was the missing history of what had gone wrong lately that had resulted in her seeking therapy. The other was the risk that her family would run true to form, that is, would not want her to undertake therapy, even if she felt she was making progress. A compromise was chosen by the therapist. He would ask for information about the events that precipitated her coming to therapy but would also discuss the family. The therapist knew that if he did not establish the right relationship with the family in the therapy with the patient, she would not continue in therapy. After that discussion the interviewer summarizes the thinking and suggests how to proceed for the remaining 45 minutes of time available to them.]

Therapist: The picture we have so far is that you came here to ask us what we thought about your self-esteem, your self-image, and how it could be improved, and so far we have this picture that there are two things that have put holes in your self-esteem. One is that there is this kind of reflex to think you have done something terribly wrong on minimum evidence. And then there have been times where people have really let you have it. Both of those things would tend to weaken your confidence—both letting people hit you

(continued)

Box 9-1 continued

and what you're regularly hitting yourself with. That's so far. We've got another 45 minutes right now, you and I, and hopefully we can understand some more about you. So then, the question is: There are so many things we could talk about, so we have to choose where to take a look in the next 45 minutes. I have several thoughts about that. One is to look at what's been going on this fall when you chose to come in. Maybe we should attend to that. I mean you were distressed about it enough this time, and I don't have clear enough sense of what was so painful this fall that made you come here. Can we start there?

From Gustafson, 1986, pp. 300–308.

CONCLUDING COMMENTS

Without question, Gustafson is the one of the most literary and literate of the contemporary writers in the field of planned short-term psychotherapy. His book is worth reading if only for its review of the thinking of earlier scholars. But Gustafson is clearly more than a chronicler. He has developed a unique, very sensitive, thought-provoking approach to planned short-term psychotherapy that makes a substantial demand of time and energy on a team of therapists but that seems organized to allow for a maximum effect on the patient. Indeed, one question that future clinical research might seek to answer is the issue of when to choose to offer continuing therapy to a patient who has demonstrated considerable gain during the trial therapy session. The trial therapy session is clearly more than simply an opportunity to identify a focal issue and to develop hypotheses to account for the client's current predicament. That is, under what conditions, if any, might a successful trial therapy session be therapy enough?

There is a strong commitment to training at the Brief Therapy Clinic that adds time to what would be required were Gustafson describing the same clinical activities in a context that did not involve an active training component. It is not clear how his specific form of clinical practice was developed and what aspects of the clinical work that is described would not be necessary were training not a significant part of the setting.

Gustafson works in an academic institution, and his patients are mainly college students—one would assume most of them to be bright, in reasonably good psychological shape, and motivated to do more with their lives. It is not clear how his approach would need to be modified, if at all, to make it possible for him to work productively with patients who were far less bright and accomplished. On the university campus he apparently chooses to reject patients who do not meet his admission criteria. But that rejection may not be as necessary as seems indicated to him. Gustafson (1986) notes that he routinely refuses to treat people who have made suicidal attempts in the past, who are borderline in terms of their adjustment, or who have had extremely difficult childhoods (1986, pp. 291–292)—potential patients whom other short-term therapists would certainly attempt to treat. It may well be that Gustafson's approach will be found to be useful for a far greater proportion of potential patients than it might seem at first.

CHAPTER 10

HOROWITZ'S STRESS RESPONSE PSYCHOTHERAPY

Overview

Goals of Stress Response Psychotherapy

The Stress Response

Therapeutic Techniques

Personality Styles and the Therapeutic Process

Therapeutic Outcome

Concluding Comments

Based on their review of the psychotherapy evaluation literature and on their own clinical experience, Mardi Horowitz and his colleagues (1976, 1991; Horowitz & Kaltreider, 1978; Horowitz, Marmar, Krupnick, Wilner, Kaltreider, & Wallerstein, 1984; Horowitz, Marmar, Weiss, DeWitt, & Rosenbaum, 1984; Horowitz, Marmar, Weiss, Kaltreider, & Wilner, 1986; Marmar, Horowitz, Weiss, Wilner, & Kaltreider, 1988; see also Kleber & Brom, 1987) at the Langley Porter Psychiatric Institute at the University of California Medical School believe that "brief therapy can be expected to ameliorate focal symptoms, to change delimited irrational beliefs, and, perhaps, to put the person back on the track of adaptive life development" (Horowitz, Marmar, Krupnick, et al., 1984, p. 31).

Because the most unequivocal focal symptoms arise in conjunction with stressful life events, Horowitz initially chose to study time-limited psychotherapy with patients who entered treatment because of stress response syndromes, or what are now called post-traumatic stress disorders. His specific interest was in following one particular stressful life event—the death of a parent (Horowitz, Wilner, & Alvarez, 1979). This event, according to Horowitz and his colleagues, heightens issues related to self-concept and to interpersonal relationships. Thus, learning about the process of time-limited psychotherapy with this group of patients

might likely be pertinent to more general psychodynamic issues as they relate to difficulties in current relationships.

Horowitz (1991) does believe, however, that many of the techniques developed in this approach are applicable to a variety of disorders other than those associated with specific stress response syndromes, since how one masters stress, whether of external or internal origin, is usually pertinent to understanding any disorder. But studying the stress response syndrome is particularly useful because one component of the etiology is known. The stress response syndrome is at least in part, a consequence of an identifiable injury, loss, or major threat. In addition, Horowitz notes that one of the advantages of studying brief psychotherapy and its consequences is that the time between the onset of the treatment and its evaluation is quite compressed, allowing for outcome data to play a role in modifying the therapeutic approach that is used.

GOALS OF STRESS RESPONSE PSYCHOTHERAPY

The goal of Horowitz's stress response psychotherapy is to help people work through their reactions to the stressful event, that is, to help them improve their current level of functioning while eliminating any symptoms associated with the event. The treatment can help clients return to their previous level of functioning and resolve whatever impediments exist that inhibit further psychological and interpersonal development. In the words of Horowitz and his colleagues: "Working through to master the personal consequences of loss eventually changes schemas and leads to a relative completion, a restoration of equilibrium from the extremes of denial and intrusion that exemplify stress response syndromes" (Horowitz, Stinson, Curtis, Ewert, Redington, Singer, Bucci, Mergenthaler, Milbrath, & Hartley, 1993).

There is some similarity between Horowitz's stress response psychotherapy and the work of people who are concerned with crisis intervention (see Chapter 19). In both cases the approach is based on a prompt case formulation designed to understand the personal meanings of the stressful life event and the inability of the patient to cope successfully with it. The premise governing the work of Horowitz and his colleagues is that a pathological reaction to a stressful life event indicates that the event stands in some meaningful relationship to current developmental issues facing the patient.

The case formulation employed by Horowitz is a fairly formal process (Horowitz, 1987) involving an analysis of the recurrent states of mind of the patient, of self-concepts and role relationships, and of cognitive and affective functioning and expression at three points in time—before therapy, during therapy, and at the conclusion of therapy. Regarding states of mind, Horowitz looks for evidence of experiences intruding into the psychological functioning of the client, or of evidence of denial or numbing. The therapist selects interventions that are pertinent to these states of mind—aiding self-regulation, reducing excessive self-imposed controls, and confronting contradictions and conflicts—as appropriate.

As for clients' views of themselves and others, traumatic stressful life events often require changes that clients may not be able to implement. New realities need to be recognized, and new ways of thinking and acting must be developed. Planned short-term psychotherapy can help patients begin these needed changes. Finally, cognitive and affective expression can be significantly impaired by traumatic life events, and new coping skills may need to be developed.

THE STRESS RESPONSE

A stressful life event usually brings with it a psychological, if not literal, outcry, often followed by intrusive thoughts and denial. Under normal circumstances these reactions yield to successful coping with the event and a return to the preevent equilibrium.

If the reaction to the event is excessively intense or prolonged, pathological stress reactions can occur. The initial event can result in a feeling of being overwhelmed. The outcry can manifest itself as panic, confusion, and exhaustion. Denial can result in maladaptive withdrawal, suicidal thoughts, counterphobic frenzy, selective inattention, amnesia, or numbness.

Normal intrusions can become unmanageable states of sadness, fear, rage, or guilt or can result in sleep disturbances, inability to concentrate, confusion, anxiety, or intropunitiveness. Instead of coping productively, the person can become constricted or frozen or can develop psychosomatic reactions. Instead of the return to the preevent equilibrium, permanent character disturbances can occur that can result in an inability to act or to love (Horowitz et al., 1993).

Horowitz proposes that "inner psychological structures of meaning," otherwise called the "inner model" (Horowitz, Marmar, Krupnick, et al., 1984, p. 39), must be modified in the process of coping with a serious stressful life event such as the death of a parent. Until this modification is completed, the stressful life event and all associations with it reside in active memory where they will remain and produce those strong emotional reactions that are collectively called the stress response syndrome. Until the event is incorporated within this inner model, unconscious decisions are made (in traditional psychoanalytic terminology, defenses are erected) to avoid pain. In Horowitz's brief therapy the therapist "aims to facilitate the patient's mastery of experience by bringing about a gradual, in-depth contemplation of the personal implications of the event" (Horowitz, Marmar, Krupnick, et al., 1984, p. 40). The therapist assists the patient in differentiating realistic appraisals of the event from fantasy-based appraisals. The therapist focuses both on the stressful life event and on the set of associations related to it. Horowitz and associates write:

> After the death of a parent, various preexisting fantasies about the relationship with that parent, as well as actual memories of interactions, will be activated for review. This provides an occasion to do a kind of differentiation between reality and fantasy, now with an adult mind, that the individual may not have accomplished since the original fantasies were established during childhood. (Horowitz, Marmar, Krupnick, et al., 1984, p. 41)

Horowitz notes that stressful life events often serve as a precipitant for people to enter into psychotherapy, even if the events are not catastrophic— events that might include separations, failed love affairs, being fired from a job, or inadequate role performance as a parent. If the therapeutic relationship is viewed by the patient as a safe one, a gradual modification of the defenses can take place that will allow the patient to reappraise the stressful life event and its associated meanings. With this reappraisal, patients will be able to revise their inner models of themselves and of their world and will be able to make new decisions and to engage in other adaptive actions. Among these adaptations, patients will have to cope with the loss of their therapists, a loss that can become a replay of the earlier loss.

Basing their therapeutic program on the prior work of Davanloo and Malan (see Chapter 4), Sifneos (see Chapter 5), and Mann (see Chapter 6), Horowitz and his colleagues have developed a brief psychotherapy program with a time limit of twelve sessions. The overview of the twelve-session stress response psychotherapy program can be found in Box 10-1.

THERAPEUTIC TECHNIQUES

Within the traditional context of the therapeutic relationship, Horowitz and his colleagues pay particular attention to what they call transference potentials (1984a, p. 42), by which they mean evidence that role relationship models with important figures from the past, including the lost parent, are being repeated with people in the present, including the therapist. If there are inappropriate or maladaptive aspects of

past role relationships that appear to characterize current relationships, those parallels become important subjects for therapeutic intervention.

In stress response psychotherapy it is important to identify and help modify defensive styles observed in the transference relationship. Patients with hysterical personality characteristics often look for remediation of their entire history of psychic injuries. Patients with narcissistic personality characteristics often construe the therapeutic relationship as one of entitlement, in which the therapists must do whatever is asked of them. Under any of these circumstances, therapists have to be supportive without promising unlimited gratification. Patients with obsessive-compulsive character traits represent therapeutic challenges because of their tendencies to keep relationships at an unemotional intellectual plane.

When one is working with patients who are coping with stressful life events, a number of themes appear frequently enough so that they can be considered virtually universal. These themes include: (1) sadness over the loss; (2) fear of repetition; (3) fear of merger with the deceased; (4) shame and rage as a consequence of the realization of one's vulnerability; (5) rage at the source of the event; (6) rage at those who have not suffered the stressful life event; (7) guilt, shame, or fear of loss of control of aggressive impulses; (8) guilt because of survival; and (9) guilt stemming from an exaggerated sense of responsibility for the event. These themes interfere with a patient's sense of competence and require therapeutic intervention in the form of reconstructive interpretation designed to help patients place their memories and affects in an orderly sequence, make appropriate linkages, and differentiate reality from fantasy.

Finally, it is important for the therapist to help patients become more aware of their defensive patterns that can inhibit or distort both affective and cognitive functioning. Therapeutic techniques that appear to be helpful include gentle but detailed questioning, labeling of emotions, helping patients put imagery into words, staying with a theme to encourage conceptual mastery of it, tactful pointing out of reality distortions, and clarification designed to help reappraisal, all within the context of empathic support.

Box 10-1: Overview of Stress Response Psychotherapy Program

Session	Relationship Issues	Patient Activity	Therapist Activity
1	Initial positive feelings for helper	Patient tells story of event	Preliminary focus discussed
2	Lull as sense of pressure is reduced	Event is related to previous life	Takes psychiatric history; gives patient realistic appraisal of syndrome
3	Patient testing therapist for various relationship possibilities	Patient adds associations to indicate expanded meaning of event	Focus is realigned; resistances to contemplating stress-related themes are interpreted
4	Therapist alliance deepened	Implications of event in the present are contemplated	Defenses and warded off contents are interpreted, linking latter to stress event and responses
5		Themes that have been avoided are worked on	Active confrontation with feared topics and reengagement in feared activities are encouraged
6		The future is contemplated	Time of termination is discussed
7–11	Transference reactions interpreted and linked to other configurations; acknowledgment of pending separation	The working through of central conflicts and issues of termination, as related to the life event and reactions to it, is continued	Central conflicts, termination, unfinished issues, and recommendations are all clarified and interpreted
12	Saying goodbye	Work to be continued on own and plans for the future are discussed	Real gains and summary of future work for patient to do on own are acknowledged

From Horowitz, 1991, p. 180.

As the period of therapy comes to an end, termination is discussed in the context of yet another loss. The therapist can encourage the continuation of the process of therapy by focusing on the future work that patients will be able to undertake on their own in order to continue with the task of problem resolution.

Horowitz provides a simplified and idealized model case (Box 10-2) that outlines what has to take place in stress response psychotherapy.

PERSONALITY STYLES AND THE THERAPEUTIC PROCESS

As noted in the previous section, Horowitz and his colleagues (1984a) have described their approach to planned short-term psychotherapy as it applies to patients who present differing personality and information-processing styles. They identify for particular emphasis the hysterical, compulsive, nar-

---

Box 10-2: Prototypical Case of Stress Response Therapy

Patient: I am angry with my father for dying before he apologized for declaring me a bad person, and before he declared me to be a good person.

Therapist: Why does that trouble you?

Patient: Because now I will go on feeling like a bad person forever.

Therapist: Are you a bad person?

Patient: No.

Therapist: Do you think your father died on purpose, in order to deprive you of his blessings?

Patient: Yes.

Therapist: Is that rational?

Patient: No. He just died, not on purpose. So I will change my mind about the idea that he died on purpose.

Therapist: Can you call yourself a good person on your father's behalf?

Patient: Yes. He actually would like me as I am. There are some bad things, but I'm pretty much ok.

Therapist: Can you forgive your father?

Patient: Yes. He had problems of his own.

Therapist: Can you accept yourself for being angry with him?

Patient: Yes. My anger was based on an irrational belief that he died on purpose, in order to deprive me of his blessing. But that is the way the mind works, and I know that it is not true. That cuts down the anger now. But my feeling angry did not hurt him. So I have changed my mind and do not feel that I am to blame for his death.

Therapist: Then I think we can terminate therapy.

Patient: Yes. Thank you.

From Horowitz, Marmar, Krupnick, et al., 1984, pp. 58–59.

---

cissistic, and borderline personality styles. Personality style is defined as "a repertoire of states of mind, self-concepts and patterns of relationships, and ways of coping with stress and defending against threat …[including] characteristic patterns of regulating perceptions, thought, feelings, decisions, plans, and actions" (Horowitz, Marmar, Krupnick, et al., 1984, p. 68). All the cases they discuss involved symptoms of stress response syndromes following the death of a parent. In addition, however, many of these patients had quite discernible personality styles, which have significant implications for how time-limited psychotherapy should be conducted.

The Hysterical Personality

The *hysterical personality* (the term preferred by Horowitz and colleagues) is officially referred to as the *histrionic personality disorder* in the *Diagnostic and Statistical Manual of the American Psychiatric Association (DSM-IV)*. Such persons have rapidly shifting emotional expression and a style of speech that is excessively impressionistic and lacking in detail, are characterized by self-dramatization, have a high degree of suggestibility, feel uncomfortable or unappreciated when they are not the center of attention, are often inappropriately sexually provocative, and use physical appearance to draw attention to themselves (American Psychiatric Association, 1994, pp. 655–658).

Such character traits present a variety of problems for time-limited psychotherapy, mainly in the form of special demands on the therapist to be active and to be a liberator or redeemer. Horowitz and colleagues suggest that such patients tend to inhibit their verbal expression of key ideas and feelings. They write:

As the therapist tries to focus on a specific problem, the patient will avoid clarity, limit associational connections, and abruptly change mood. If the therapist persists with a specific focus, the patient is prone to feel neglected or misunderstood, forget what just happened, or simply comply without real efforts at understanding or changing....If the therapist provides clarification and insight rather than solace, the patient will feel neglected and believe that the therapist is insensitive to his or her needs. If the therapist tries to give "more," the patient will feel that a special "beyond therapy" relationship has been established. When it turns out that this is not so, the patient may respond with shock, disbelief, sadness, or rage. (Horowitz, Marmar, Krupnick, et al., 1984, p. 73)

In dealing with patients with a hysterical personality style, the therapist needs to counter patients' tendencies to be diffuse, global, and inhibited by being focused, repetitive, concrete, and specific. The therapist needs to counter a patient's habitual tendency to say, "I don't know" by restating what the patient has just said, requesting details about events and feelings, keeping topics open for further discussion, clarifying vague statements, providing labels for unclear terms, interpreting warded-off feelings when data for such interpretations are sufficient, and being supportive and hopeful without accepting the role of caretaker.

Some hysterical personalities may be so disturbed that they become depressed, disorganized, erratic, jealous, possessive, confused, emotionally labile, and aggressive. In addition, they may suffer a significant drop in self-esteem and sense of self-efficacy. Under these circumstances the therapist can easily feel overwhelmed. But if the therapist slows down the pace, it can be possible to help the patient work through a limited set of problems. Techniques that can be particularly helpful under these circumstances include the request for details and careful reconstruction of sequences of events and behaviors, again while being supportive. Rather than working toward exploring aspects of patients' behavior that may be unconscious, with particularly disturbed hysterical personalities, the therapist can restore stability by helping the patient forge links between conscious memories, fantasies, wishes, and fears.

The Compulsive Personality

The essential features of the *compulsive personality* (currently referred to as the obsessive-compulsive personality disorder) are the restricted ability to express warm and tender emotions, excessive dominance, perfectionism, and pathological devotion to work. Such people are often stingy with their possessions as well as with their emotions; are preoccupied with rules, procedures, and trivial details; are indecisive and inordinately fearful of making mistakes; are inflexible and overconscientious, and are often unable to experience or tolerate pleasure. They are miserly, rigid, stubborn, and unable to delegate tasks to others and are often so devoted to work and productivity that they sacrifice friendships and leisure-time activities (American Psychiatric Association, 1994, pp. 669–673).

Patients with compulsive personalities often view psychotherapy as an intellectual exercise in which they present issues in excessive detail while at the same time displaying a pathological inability to be spontaneous. The relationship with the therapist can quickly become adversarial and the patient, fearing the loss of control that is associated with any feeling of dependence upon the therapist or fearing hostile impulses, can precipitously bolt from therapy. Under these circumstances it is usually very difficult to develop a workable therapeutic alliance.

Therapists need to be active and somewhat directive while at the same time maintaining a relatively neutral stance, avoiding their own countertransference feelings of frustration and hostility. Interpretations need to be presented carefully not as "elementary or obvious, but as interesting observations" (Horowitz, marmar, Krupnick, et al., 1984, p. 163) that the patient might want to think about.

The Narcissistic Personality

Patients with narcissistic personality styles (now referred to as the narcissistic personality disorder) have a grandiose sense of self-importance, are exhibitionistic and preoccupied with fantasies of their potential great successes, and have an insatiable need for constant attention and admiration. They exploit others, lack empathy, are extremely self-centered and self-absorbed, and may lie or fake feelings in order to impress the therapist (American Psychiatric Association, 1994, pp. 658–661). Horowitz, Marmar, Krupnick, and colleagues (1984) suggest, quite understandably, that there may be "less than the usual gratification for the therapist in treating this type of patient" (p. 208).

Narcissistic personalities have a kind of immature dependence, expecting the therapist to act as a parent and rescue them from whatever distress they may be experiencing. Faced with feelings of hostility toward their therapist and, at the same time, shame and sadness because of their attitudes toward the therapist, such patients often act as if the therapist can do them no good, while guarding against the expression of the very needs that brought them into therapy. In spite of expressions of derision, narcissistic patients are very vulnerable and need therapists who can be unusually tactful while also being firm.

Tact is needed to avoid forcing the patient into a position where lying might be necessary and to ensure that confrontations are presented palatably. Narcissistic patients are simultaneously frightened of the therapist because they expect criticism for what they have said and afraid that they will fool the therapist so easily that the therapist will not be capable of understanding them and thus will be unable to help them.

The Borderline Personality

The patient with a borderline personality, or borderline personality disorder, is characterized by intense and unstable interpersonal relationships, marked shifts of emotion and attitude over time, impulsive and unpredictable behavior that may be physically self-damaging, and unstable moods. Such personalities are uncertain about their gender identity, self-image, long-term goals, and values. They are often self-destructively impulsive and angry, and they have difficulty tolerating being alone. They may be suicidal, self-mutilating, and suspicious and suffer from chronic feelings of emptiness, abandonment, and boredom (American Psychiatric Association, 1994, pp. 650–654).

Patients with a borderline personality cannot usefully manage ambivalence. The world is either dangerous and chaotic or is all good. The threatened emergence of ambivalent feelings precipitates enormous anxiety. Accompanying that anxiety are massive confusion, temporal disorientation, and often a sense of depersonalization. Often supplementing this near psychotic behavior pattern are severe projection, isolation of affect, undoing, and other evidence of loss of cognitive control. As can be expected, the relationship of a borderline patient who has suffered parental loss with the therapist is intense and unstable. Such patients can neither engage in self-observation nor establish any sort of useful relationship with the therapist.

Undertaking time-limited psychotherapy with a borderline patient is problematical and hardly to be recommended, except under special circumstances, such as to deal with a stress-related regression following successful long-term psychotherapy. The therapist needs to help the patient distinguish between reality and fantasy and modulate the extreme feelings of undervaluation or overidealization that such patients often ascribe to the therapist. Therapeutic work has to be carefully focused and has to remain in that limited focal area, ordinarily the stressful life event that led to the entrance into therapy. Brief therapy rarely provides enough time for the repetitive working through of the complex good and bad images of others that borderline patients hold, but it may provide a restorative relationship within which a stressful life event may start to be mastered.

THERAPEUTIC OUTCOME

Horowitz and colleagues (1984a) have examined therapeutic outcome, both in terms of changes in presenting symptoms and in more general character structure in the same three topical areas that they use in case formulation—states of mind, self-concepts and role relationships, and cognitive functioning. Not surprisingly, changes in presenting symptoms are found more commonly than changes in character structure. In the case of states of mind, stress response psychotherapy has been noted to convert explosive rage into anger, panic into anxiety or dread, and self-tormenting despair into sadness and a sense of poignant loss. As for changes in character traits, Horowitz and his colleagues have found that some patients who formerly could not mourn are able to feel and express grief at the conclusion of therapy, and that other patients are able to enter into intimate relationships far more freely and successfully than before the therapy began.

In the area of self-concepts and role relationships, Horowitz and colleagues have found that maladaptive views of the self and of others are often transformed into views that are more differentiated and more under control. Views of the self become more complex and modulated, affects are more accessible, coping with ambivalent feelings is more successful, and formerly unacceptable aspects of the self are integrated with the entire view of the self into a more realistic whole. Finally, symptom reduction is a common consequence of therapy, and changes in defensive patterns have been noted through increased awareness of how those patterns are invoked and function.

Horowitz and colleagues summarize their findings by noting:

> The principal aim of these brief therapies—to work through stress-related and personality-related problems of a focal nature—often could be accomplished within the specified time limit. Major revision of character style seemed to be a goal seldom accomplished....Some types of personality change were noted in patients who gained from new experiences with the therapist and then continued developmental progress after completing the brief therapy....The more flexible the personality, the more the therapy process can focus on working through trains of thoughts to reduce strain. The more restrained, rigidly stereotyped, and limited the person's personality style, the more this style itself impedes the working-through process. (Horowitz, Marmar, Krupnick, et al., 1984, p. 329; see also Horowitz, 1991, pp. 188–189)

CONCLUDING COMMENTS

Horowitz and his colleagues have created a psychodynamic time-limited psychotherapy that has two remarkable attributes. First, it is presented as partic-
ularly suitable for persons who are coping with parent loss, a specific stressful life event; second, it proposes that personality style variations among patients have important implications for how time-limited psychotherapy should be conducted.

It is not yet clear how generalizable stress response psychotherapy may be, that is, whether it can be successfully employed with patients who have not had to come to grips with parent loss or, perhaps by extension, with any other major life stressor. The underlying theory that Horowitz proposes, namely, that pathological reactions to stressful life events occur because the events are psychologically related to chronic unresolved problems, would suggest, however, that stress response psychotherapy will be shown to be appropriate for a wide variety of issues that may not involve such events. Thompson, Gallagher, and Breckenridge (1987) have already found that Horowitz's approach to planned short-term psychotherapy can be successfully adapted to the treatment of depression. Furthermore, the large research literature on stressful life events (e.g., Bloom, 1984) indicates that stressful life events are remarkably common and that they often precipitate psychiatric disorders in persons who are healthy but vulnerable.

As for personality style variations, Horowitz and his colleagues have performed an important intellectual task in considering how different character types can best be treated by psychotherapists or, in other words, how the diagnostic and statistical manual of the American Psychiatric Association can be more useful to mental health professionals. Few other time-limited psychotherapy theorists have yet given significant consideration to how their ideas about therapeutic technique should be modified by diagnostic considerations, and Horowitz's work may be the harbinger of similar efforts in the future.

CHAPTER 11

KLERMAN'S INTERPERSONAL PSYCHOTHERAPY

Overview

Gerald Klerman, who died in 1992, served on the medical school faculties at Harvard, Yale, and Cornell and in the 1980s was the head of the Alcohol, Drug Abuse, and Mental Health Administration of the U.S. Department of Health and Human Services. He and his colleagues (Klerman & Weissman, 1982, 1993; Klerman, Weissman, Rounsaville, & Chevron, 1984a, 1984b; Neu, Prusoff, & Klerman, 1978; Rounsaville & Chevron, 1982) developed a psycho-dynamic time-limited psychotherapy designed specifically to meet the needs of depressed patients who are not psychotic and whose depressive disorder is not complicated by manic symptoms. The central assumption of his time-limited psychotherapy is that the precipitation and perpetuation of many psychiatric disorders are closely related to disturbances in current interpersonal functioning (see Horowitz & Vitkus, 1986).

Treatment duration averages about fourteen weekly one-hour sessions, and the therapy is designed to educate the client about depression—its causes, and its available treatments — and to improve the quality of the patient's current interpersonal functioning.

Since its central belief is not necessarily specific to the diagnosis of depression, interpersonal psychotherapy has been modified, as appropriate, for use in treating other psychiatric conditions (e.g., Rounsaville, Gawin, & Kleber, 1985). But the most common psychiatric diagnosis that has been of interest to planned short-term psychotherapists in general—and to interpersonal therapists in particular—has been depression (e.g., Cornes, 1990, 1993; Rush, 1982). The reasons for this high level of interest are not hard to discern. Depressions are unusually common: Perhaps as many as 15 percent of the total population will be significantly depressed at some time in their lives. In addition, depressions are the most lethal of all psychiatric disorders, putting patients at high risk for suicide (Yapko, 1988).

Klerman and colleagues describe interpersonal psychotherapy of depression as a "psychological treatment designed specifically for the needs of depressed patients. It is a focused, short-term, time-limited therapy that emphasizes the current interpersonal relations of the depressed patient while recognizing the role of genetic, biochemical, developmental, and personality factors in causation of and vulnerability to depression" (1984b, p. 5).

The crucial aspects of interpersonal psychotherapy that set it apart from other psychotherapies are its emphasis on brevity, its proactive rather than reactive therapeutic stance, and its single-minded focus on interpersonal relationships. Depression, like most other forms of psychopathology, is embedded in a social matrix; Klerman and his colleagues believe that if therapists avoid that social matrix, their effectiveness will suffer.

BASIC CHARACTERISTICS OF INTERPERSONAL PSYCHOTHERAPY

Klerman and his colleagues are convinced that clinical depression occurs in an interpersonal context and that therapeutic interventions directed at this interpersonal context will help the patient recover from the acute episode and possibly prevent relapse and recurrence. The psychotherapy can be divided into three phases: (1) the initial sessions, during which time the therapist helps the client understand the concept of depression and evaluates the need for medication; (2) the intermediate sessions, during which time the therapist deals with the major components of the depression—grief, interpersonal disputes, role transitions, and interpersonal deficits; and (3) the termination, during which time the therapist and the client discuss termination and work toward the recognition of the client's independent competence (Klerman & Weissman, 1993). As can be noted, Klerman's interpersonal psychotherapy has a rather strong pedagogical component.

In contrast with many other psychotherapies, interpersonal psychotherapy: (1) is time-limited, not long-term; (2) is focused, not open-ended—that is, it is directed toward one or two agreed-upon problem areas in the patient's current interpersonal functioning; (3) is interpersonal, not intrapsychic—that is, the patient's predicament is explored in terms of interpersonal relations rather than as a manifestation of internal conflict; (4) deals with current, not past, interpersonal relationships; and (5) tries to change the ways the patient reacts in interpersonal relationships rather than other behaviors, such as distorted thoughts, excessive guilt, or negative cognitions that may be troublesome to the patient in their own right and in settings that do not involve other people. Interpersonal psychotherapy does not aspire to have a significant impact on personality or character struc-

ture. Accordingly, while recognizing the personality of the patient, the therapy does not focus on personality. The personality of the patient may have an effect on the patient-therapist relationship and may be a determinant of the interpersonal difficulties that are the focus of the psychotherapy. But personality factors have not been found to be significantly related to short-term outcome of interpersonal psychotherapy and are treated as secondary in importance.

Klerman and his colleagues contrast interpersonal psychotherapy with other psychodynamic psychotherapies by means of the summary statements shown in Box 11-1.

While interpersonal psychotherapy differs from traditional psychodynamic therapies in certain important ways, it has many similarities as well, since the nature of social relationships has become increasingly important in the thinking of most psychotherapists. While traditional psychodynamic therapy concentrates on unconscious mental processes, interpersonal psychotherapy concentrates on social roles and interactions in the patient's past and current life experiences. Klerman and his colleagues write: "The psychodynamic therapist is concerned with object relations while the interpersonal therapist focuses on interpersonal relations. The psychodynamic therapist listens for the patient's intrapsychic wishes and conflicts; the interpersonal therapist listens for the patient's role expectations and disputes" (1984b, p. 18). Yet both interpersonal and psychodynamic therapies have a life-span orientation, attend to transference issues when they appear to be interfering with therapeutic progress, and respect the importance of early experience.

DIAGNOSTIC CONSIDERATIONS IN INTERPERSONAL THERAPY

Four specific interpersonal difficulties have been identified as being of particular importance in the treatment of depression—grief, interpersonal role disputes, role transitions, and interpersonal deficits (Rounsaville & Chevron, 1982). Each of these problem areas presents its own diagnostic and treatment challenges.

**Box 11-1: Comparison of Interpersonal Psychotherapy With
Other Psychodynamic Psychotherapies**

Interpersonal Therapy	*Other Psychotherapies*
What has contributed to this patient's depression right now?	Why did the patient become what he or is and/or where is the patient going?
What are the current stresses?	What was the patient's childhood like?
Who are the key persons involved in the current stress? What are the current disputes and disappointments?	What is the patient's character?
Is the patient learning how to cope with the problem?	Is the patient cured?
What are the patient's assets?	What are the patient's defenses?
How can I help the patient ventilate painful emotions, talk about situations that evoke guilt, shame, resentment?	How can I find out why this patient feels guilty, ashamed, or resentful?
How can I help the patient clarify his or wishes and have more satisfying relationships with others?	How can I understand the patient's fantasy life and help him or her get insight into the origins of present behavior?
How can I correct misinformation and and suggest alternatives?	How can I help the patient discover false or incorrect ideas?

From Klerman et al., 1984b, p. 17.

Grief

Klerman, like Horowitz (Chapter 10), believes that grief reactions, particularly in connection with the death of a loved one, have much in common with depression, but it is only abnormal grief reactions, either in the form of delayed or distorted reactions, that require psychological intervention. Normal grief reactions include sadness, disturbed sleep, agitation, decreased ability to carry out normal responsibilities for a two to four-month time period, and a gradual letting go of the loved one.

Abnormal grief reactions, in the form of pathological mourning, can be expected when there are overwhelming multiple losses or significant absence of social support during the bereavement period. Such reactions can be suspected when normal grief reactions are absent, when there is avoidance of

commonly expected behaviors such as visiting the gravesite, when physical symptoms that mimic those of the deceased are reported, when reactions to the loss are pathologically prolonged or are precipitated too easily or frequently, when phobic behavior is displayed toward the cause of the death, when the environment of the loved one is scrupulously preserved, or when there is a radical change in the survivor's lifestyle.

The two general goals in the treatment of persons who are depressed following the loss of a loved one are to facilitate the normal mourning process and to help the survivor reestablish interests and social relationships that can substitute for those that have been lost, using such procedures as nonjudgmental exploration of feelings, reassurance, exploration of the patient's relationship with the deceased and the development of increased awareness about that relationship, and the encouragement of appropriate subsequent behavior change.

Interpersonal Role Disputes

Role disputes, in the form of conflicts with important people in one's life, are an inevitable consequence of social interaction and are not often associated with depression. But when such disputes seem to be chronic or insoluble, they can lead to a sense of demoralization and a loss of the sense of self-efficacy that can result in significant depression. Thus, in working with depressed persons it is important to look for evidence of conflicts with the spouse, children, parents, colleagues or superiors in the work setting, neighbors, or other significant figures and to evaluate the extent to which these conflicts may be responsible for feelings of worthlessness, failure, or apathy.

Goals in the treatment of interpersonal conflict are to help the patient become more aware of the dispute and its characteristics; develop a plan for resolving the dispute; and, if maladaptive behaviors can be identified, make those changes in communication patterns that are necessary.

Role Transitions

Life changes often bring with them the need to develop new roles, for example, from that of wife to that of widow, or from husband to divorced person, or from employed person to job seeker. To some extent we all are our roles. Thus, role transitions are not easy for anyone to make, and in some cases, role transitions may be so difficult that they threaten the psychological equilibrium of the person. In treating depressed persons, the therapist needs to be alert to the possibility that the patient is not coping well with changes in roles that must be undertaken.

Two general goals in the treatment of depression associated with role transitions have been identified; enabling the patient to regard the challenge of establishing a new role or set of roles as an opportunity for growth, and restoring the sense of self-esteem by helping the patient master the demands of the process of role transition.

Interpersonal Deficits

Some patients have never developed the social skills necessary to maintain satisfying interpersonal relationships. This failure is often the result of longstanding interpersonal deprivations or difficulties and may be associated with chronic social isolation. When a patient does not appear to have any close or intimate interpersonal relationships, it is likely that this deficit may be causally related to the depressive symptoms. In this case, dealing with the interpersonal deficit is critical for the successful management of the depression.

The goals of treatment must include efforts to reduce social isolation through the therapeutic review of past social relationships, analysis of the relationship with the therapist, and encouragement of the formation of new relationships.

SPECIFIC THERAPEUTIC TECHNIQUES

While downplaying the uniqueness of the techniques that are particularly important in interpersonal psychotherapy, Klerman and colleagues (1984b) devote considerable attention to a discussion of those techniques that seem to be most helpful to patients. They organize their discussion of these techniques in the order in which they are most often used as the therapeutic relationship develops: (1) exploratory techniques, (2) encouragement of affect, (3) clarification, (4) communication analysis, and (5) facilitating behavior change.

Exploratory Techniques

Gathering information about presenting symptoms and problems is part of the beginning work of the therapy. Information is gathered through nondirective exploration, supportive acknowledgment, and continuing discussion of topics already brought up. Direct inquiry can include the use of formal questionnaires and, of course, stresses the elicitation of information about important relationships the patient has with others. Questions generally proceed from the general ("Tell me about your husband") to the specific ("How did you feel when your husband said that?").

Encouragement of Affect

Deliberate encouragement of the expression of affect is a special attribute of most dynamic psychotherapies, including interpersonal psychotherapy, and is pursued by: (1) helping patients acknowledge the existence of painful but appropriate feelings, (2) helping patients identify emotional experiences that are associated with difficult interpersonal relationships, and (3) encouraging the development of new emotions that may facilitate growth and change in interpersonal relationships.

Among the techniques that Klerman and his colleagues identify as particularly important in the encouragement of affect are: (1) acceptance of painful affects, (2) using affects in interpersonal relationships, and (3) helping the patient generate suppressed affects. Klerman and colleagues caution, however, that when a patient shows signs of being overwhelmed by diffuse and intense emotional experiences, it may be prudent to suppress the expression of such affects until the patient is strong enough to tolerate their expression constructively.

Clarification

Clarifying remarks by the therapist serve to reformulate and feed back material previously presented by the patient. Clarification increases the patient's awareness of what has been communicated, facilitating the continued exploration of previously suppressed material.

Among the clarifying techniques that Klerman and colleagues have identified are: (1) asking patients to repeat or rephrase what they have said, (2) rephrasing patients' statements, (3) calling attention to the logical implications of patients' statements, (4) identifying contrasts or contradictions in patients' statements, and (5) pointing out extremes in patients' beliefs when more modulated points of view seem more appropriate.

Communication Analysis

The interpersonal therapist can examine and identify communication failures in order to help patients communicate more effectively. Such an analysis is central to the objectives of a therapist who is interested in increasing the interpersonal skills of patients. By exploring the details of an interpersonal interaction, it should be possible to identify how faulty communication may be responsible for disputes or other interpersonal difficulties. Among the most common communication difficulties are: (1) using ambiguous indirect nonverbal messages instead of direct verbal messages; (2) assuming that one has communicated to another person when in fact no such communication has taken place; (3) assuming that a communication has been understood when no such understanding has occurred; (4) being unnecessarily ambiguous in verbal communications; and (5) remaining silent when communication is needed.

The fundamental purpose of communication analysis is to guide patients in developing increased awareness of the nature and consequences of their methods of interpersonal communication. Successful communication analysis will increase patients' awareness of how their communications are received by others, particularly when disputes arise as a consequence.

Facilitating Behavior Change

According to Klerman and colleagues, lasting improvement from depression depends on helping patients make changes in their interpersonal behavior. Major therapeutic techniques that are available to the interpersonal therapist to help patients change their interpersonal behavior include directive techniques, such as educating, advising, modeling, limit setting, and direct suggestion; decision analysis by expanding the array of available choices open to the patient and helping the patient decide on a course of action from among those choices; and role playing, in which the therapist takes the role of a person with whom the patient is in some interpersonal difficulty.

Klerman and colleagues believe that directive techniques should be used sparingly and only in the context of expanding options available to the patient, as in the phrase "One thing you might consider is…." Suggestions should not be too specific or direct and should not undermine the patient's sense of autonomy and self-esteem. When the therapist is engaged in decision analysis, premature closure should be avoided. The therapist should make sure that choices are not too narrow and that the consequences of choices are fully explored. The principle seems to be that, when in doubt, continue exploring decision alternatives. Role-playing techniques should also be used sparingly, but they can be helpful in providing an opportunity for patients to practice a course of action and to learn more about their feelings in specific interpersonal situations.

BECOMING AND BEING AN INTERPERSONAL PSYCHOTHERAPIST

Klerman and his colleagues see interpersonal psychotherapy as a set of skills built upon prior traditional training and experience in any one of the mental health clinical disciplines—clinical psychology, psychiatry, social work, or psychiatric nursing. Training in interpersonal psychotherapy requires the mastery of their training manual (Klerman, et al., 1984b), participation in a week-long didactic seminar, and conducting a small number of cases under careful supervision. The central focus of the training is to help clinicians determine what aspects of their previous clinical experience and orientation are functional for undertaking interpersonal psychotherapy and what aspects need to be modified. The principal emphasis in interpersonal psychotherapy is on symptoms and present behavior. Clinicians whose previous training has been in psychodynamic therapy tend to focus on historical, childhood phenomena without connecting these issues with the here and now and tend to spend too much time in overly long exploration of past history determinants of current behavior. Clinicians with previous training in behavior or cognitive therapy may find interpersonal psychotherapy difficult to master because of its commitment to understanding current behavior in a historical context.

The interpersonal psychotherapist takes a therapeutic stance that is both similar to and different from the general psychotherapist role. In interpersonal psychotherapy the therapist is not neutral; rather, he or she functions as an advocate of the patient. The therapist, according to Klerman and colleagues, is a "benign and helpful ally" (1984b, p. 214). By not taking a neutral, withdrawn stance, the therapist discourages regression and excessive dependence on the part of the patient. Rather, the therapist remains nonjudgmental, warm, supportive, gentle, accepting, and optimistic in the sense that the message is conveyed that a patient's problems are resolvable and not necessarily permanent.

In interpersonal psychotherapy the relationship between the therapist and patient is realistic rather than based on previous relationships with others. Transference issues are dealt with only when they appear to be impeding therapeutic progress.

In interpersonal psychotherapy the therapeutic relationship is not a friendship. If a patient wants the therapist to be more self-disclosing, this is permitted, provided that the therapist explores the patient's reasons for requesting such self-disclosure. While the therapist might appropriately become involved in helping a patient deal with life problems, or might testify on behalf of the patient in a court action, or might make arrangements for other medical or mental health professionals to play a role in the treatment of the patient, the therapist would not become involved with the patient in social or business relationships.

The interpersonal therapist is active. At the start of therapy that activity might reflect itself in helping the patient focus on the presenting interpersonal problem, in eliciting the salient aspects of the patient's history, and in setting therapeutic goals. In intermediate sessions the therapist actively guides the patient using appropriate therapeutic techniques as previously discussed. Yet, the therapist leaves in the patient's hands the decisions that must be made if interpersonal change is to take place.

EFFICACY OF INTERPERSONAL PSYCHOTHERAPY

Klerman and his colleagues have made a major commitment to evaluation of their therapy. In one of their early studies, 81 depressed patients were randomly assigned to one of four groups: (1) interpersonal psychotherapy, (2) antidepressant medication (amitriptyline), (3) a combination of interpersonal psychotherapy and amitriptyline, and (4) treatment on demand. All treatment programs lasted 16 weeks, and outcome was assessed by the patients and treating clinicians and by a clinician who was blind to the treatment the patients were being provided.

Interpersonal psychotherapy, with or without medication, was found to be superior to nonscheduled treatment. Improvement in the treated groups continued to increase after the treatment was concluded, and at the one-year follow-up, patients who had received interpersonal psychotherapy were functioning at a less impaired level in social activities and with their spouses, children, and other relatives. The rate of improvement was similar in the groups who had received interpersonal psychotherapy and medication alone, but the specific nature of improvement differed. Patients in the interpersonal psychotherapy group demonstrated greatest consistent improvement in mood, work performance and interest, and reductions in suicidal ideation and guilt. Amitriptyline had its most notable effect on reducing sleep and appetite disturbances and somatic complaints. Patients who were in the group that received interpersonal psychotherapy and medication showed the highest level of improvement, specifically including reduced symptoms and lower attrition rate (Weissman, 1979).

The use of interpersonal psychotherapy for maintenance treatment was also evaluated (see Klerman et al., 1984b). A sample of 150 women who were recovering from depressive episodes after having been treated for six to eight weeks with medication were then randomly assigned to either interpersonal psychotherapy or to low-contact control employing either amitriptyline, placebo, or no medication. Maintenance interpersonal psychotherapy significantly improved social and interpersonal functioning, but, at the same time, the medication was more efficacious than the interpersonal psychotherapy in preventing symptomatic relapse. The effects of the interpersonal psychotherapy and the medication were additive; that is, patients who received both interpersonal psychotherapy and medication showed the lowest rate of relapse and highest rate of social improvement.

The maintenance experiment was concluded after eight months, but patients were followed for up to four years. At the one-year follow-up, 30 percent were totally symptom-free, 60 percent had mild symptoms at some time during the year, and 10 percent remained chronically depressed. Additional studies of the efficacy of interpersonal psychotherapy are being conducted e.g., Elkin, Parloff, Hadley, & Autry, 1985; Elkin, Shea, Watkins, et al., 1989; Foley, O'Malley, Rounsaville, Prusoff, & Weissman, 1987; Rounsaville, Chevron, Prusoff, Elkin, Imber, Sotsky, & Watkins, 1987; Rounsaville, O'Malley, Foley, & Weissman, 1988).

The effectiveness of interpersonal psychotherapy in dealing with stress and distress in primary medical care settings has recently been examined, with encouraging results, employing nurse practitioners in six 30-minute sessions (Weissman & Klerman, 1993) and in dealing with patients who abuse drugs, with somewhat equivocal results (Rounsaville & Carroll, 1993). In addition, Fairburn (1993) has examined the effectiveness of interpersonal psychotherapy in the case of patients with bulimia nervosa. In studies contrasting interpersonal psychotherapy with cognitive-behavioral therapy, both treatments were found to be effective, with interpersonal psychotherapy having a slower onset but a longer duration of improvement. Improvement in the interpersonal psychotherapy group continued beyond the termination of treatment. Thus, short-term focal psychotherapies with an emphasis on current interpersonal problems appear to be a promising alternative to other psychotherapies.

CONCLUDING COMMENTS

The single greatest contribution of Klerman's interpersonal therapy to the field of planned short-term psychotherapy is its emphasis on interpersonal relationships and on how disturbances in those relationships can set the stage for significant psychopathology, particularly nonpsychotic depression. Based on this point of view, Klerman and his colleagues have set about working with patients for the purpose of analyzing and improving their interpersonal relationships.

In some ways, interpersonal psychotherapy holds a middle ground between psychodynamic therapy, with its focus on intrapsychic phenomena, and cognitive and behavior therapy, with their focus on external behavior that so often concerns itself with behavior in interpersonal settings.

Perhaps the most interesting development in Klerman's work is its growing applicability to disorders other than neurotic depression. The strategies employed by Klerman seem quite broad in nature, in no sense specific only to depression, and thus quite applicable to the treatment of patients with other conditions.

COGNITIVE AND BEHAVIORAL PLANNED SHORT-TERM PSYCHOTHERAPY

Cognitive and behavioral approaches to planned short-term psychotherapy have shown enough evidence of a productive union so that it seems appropriate to discuss them together. Cognitive theory has been significantly influenced by behavior therapy in the form of such techniques as social skills and relaxation training. At the same time, behavior therapy has become increasingly cognitive (Arkowitz & Hannah, 1989; Dobson, 1988). There is so much overlap between these two related forms of psychotherapy that many writers use the term "cognitive-behavioral" as a label for a single general approach to psychological treatment.

Indeed, Koss and Shiang (1994) have suggested that it is sometimes difficult to separate the techniques of a behavioral approach from those of a cognitive approach. Both approaches try to identify the client's present predicament and the variables that maintain inappropriate behaviors as well as inappropriate cognitions.

According to Dobson and Block (1988), cognitive and behavioral therapies share three fundamental beliefs: Cognitive activity affects behavior; cognitive activity may be assessed and altered; and desired behavior change may be effected through cognitive change. The main attributes of both cognitive and behavior therapy are "a clear focus on the patient's complaints, devising specific treatment for specific problems, relatively brief periods of treatment, and systematic appraisals of outcome" (Bergin & Garfield, 1986, p. 6).

The radical behaviorist approach (see Wilson, 1978, 1981), identified with the work of Skinner, essentially held that all behavior is under the control of environmental factors external to the person.

More contemporary views of behavior therapy include the social learning perspective, with its emphasis on cognitive mediational processes and self-regulatory capacities (e.g., Kendall, Vitousek, & Kane, 1991; Lewinsohn, Sullivan, & Grosscup, 1982; Liese, 1995; Marks, 1986; McLean, 1982; Mc Mullin, 1986; Rush, 1982, 1984). Thus, how external events determine behavior is mediated by internal cognitive processes and capacities that are, in turn, based on prior experience.

The use of cognitive and behavioral therapies has increased rapidly in the past two decades, in part because of their successes with such a wide variety of clients, many of whom have presented problems that have been difficult to treat from a psychodynamic orientation (Phillips, 1985a). If we begin with the assumption that thinking, feeling, and behaving are interdependent, then changes in one of these components have the potential of bringing about changes in the others. If we change how we think about something or someone, we shall likely change how we feel about and how we behave toward that something or someone. Cognitive and behavioral therapies focus on altering thought and behavior in the service of modifying emotional responses. To say it differently, emotional and behavioral responses are mediated by perceived meanings or cognitions (Bedrosian & Bozicas, 1994, pp. 26 ff.).

All the theories analyzed in this section share a central interest in the modification of contemporary behavior and thinking and share a set of values that dramatically distinguish cognitive and behavioral theories from psychodynamic viewpoints (Jones & Pulos, 1993).

While the psychodynamic approach views the origins of symptoms as unconscious and thus not easily accessible to clients, cognitive and behavioral theory suggests that clients are most often aware of these origins. According to cognitive and behavioral theory, dysfunctional feelings and behavior are largely due to ideas that produce biased judgments and cognitive errors, rather than to pathological motivation.

Cognitive and behavioral theories and therapy also differ from psychodynamic theory and therapy in their central interest in the present, on the one hand; and their relative disinterest in the patient's past, in helping the patient achieve insight, in determining causes, or in exploring transference relationships, on the other hand.

Cognitive and behavioral theories have a number of important common elements including a careful and active assessment of current problems, the establishment of attainable and contracted therapeutic goals, obtaining prompt relief from the most pressing problems, and use of a wide variety of empirically based interventions that increase the patient's sense of self-efficacy (Peake, Borduin, & Archer, 1988).

Cognitive and behavioral interventions can be thought of in three steps. First, clients are helped to find the thoughts and beliefs that are associated with their psychological problems and destructive behaviors. Second, clients are helped to analyze their thoughts and beliefs to determine their validity and functionality. Third, clients are helped to change their irrational thoughts, perceptions, and beliefs in the direction of greater rationality and usefulness so that the emotions associated with them will also change (Mc Mullin, 1986).

Schuyler (1991) has described these steps in terms of the principal goals of cognitive therapies, which are to seek to: "(1) identify cognitions relevant to the presenting problem; (2) recognize connections among cognitions, affects, and behaviors; (3) examine the evidence for and against key beliefs; (4) encourage the patient to try out alternative conceptualizations; and (5) teach the patient to carry out the cognitive process independently" (1991, p. 29). As will become evident in the following chapters, cognitive behavior therapy differs from psychodynamic therapy as much in terms of its specific intervention strategies as it does in terms of its underlying theories.

The four approaches to cognitively oriented short-term psychotherapy presented in this section are in no sense carbon copies of each other. Phillips and Wiener's approach exemplifies the resolute application of reinforcement theory in the clinical setting. Ellis insistently points out self-defeating beliefs and forcefully encourages changes in these beliefs and in their associated behaviors in a remarkably hortatory yet supportive manner. Farrelly is Machiavellian, using a kind of psychic jujitsu to disarm patients and to help them get well if only to spite their therapist. Beck combines rationality with empathy in his efforts to help patients change their cognitions.

CHAPTER 12

PHILLIPS AND WIENER'S STRUCTURED BEHAVIOR CHANGE THERAPY

Overview

Therapeutic Approach and Plan

Time-Lapse Protocols

Alternative Behavior Change Therapy Approaches

Concluding Comments

E. Lakin Phillips, who died in 1994, and Daniel Wiener's (1966) approach to short-term therapy, perhaps the earliest of the cognitive-behavioral approaches, proceeds from their basic premise that the goal of all therapists is the efficient production of significant behavior change. With this emphasis on prompt behavior change, they assert that

> long-term therapy is not, in fact, the most desirable, not even for those who can afford it or who prefer it. It is not a matter of efficiency alone that makes us favor short- over long-term therapy. Instead, our belief is that structured therapy (which tends to be short-term) is better than long-term, conventional therapy for this reason: structured therapy is purposely as short-term as possible. By "purposely", we mean structured to solve specific problems—regardless of whether they are chronic and serious or only mildly disabling. (1966, p. 2)[1]

Phillips and Wiener believe that short-term therapies are particularly appropriate for dealing with current problems in living. With an emphasis on current functioning, psychotherapy can become more effective and more efficient. Time-limited psychotherapy, they believe, should have little, if any, concern with the past or with the inner life of the patient, or with a "broad philosophical search for hidden meaning" (1966, p. 11).

---

[1] This quotation and boxed excerpts in this chapter are from E.L. Phillips and D.N. Weiner, *Short-Term Psychotherapy and Structured Behavior Change*, New York: McGraw-Hill, 1966. Used with permission from McGraw-Hill, Inc.

To Phillips and Wiener, it is not simply that short-term therapy can be supportive, provide guidance or the opportunity to discharge pent-up emotions, or fulfill dependency needs. They believe that short-term therapy can produce substantial and long-lasting behavior change, and they contend that the help most people need to develop more satisfying lives may be far more modest than therapists have been led to believe. In contrast to psychodynamic therapies that tend to emphasize person characteristics in understanding and modifying behavior, Phillips and Wiener's approach emphasizes characteristics of the external world and of the responses a person makes to it.

THERAPEUTIC APPROACH AND PLAN

Many consequences follow from this emphasis on externals and response patterns:

1. Since the focus of interest is on behavior change, there is relatively little concern with the origins of a person's difficulties—that is, with the original stimuli for the problem.
2. After the therapist and the patient have agreed upon the objectives of the therapy, patients can be taught to develop new responses to troublesome situations by changing their behavior, their environment, or both.
3. Other people can be involved in the therapeutic process whenever they might be able to function as change agents.

4. With the emphasis on behavior change procedures, there is relatively less need for traditional verbal, insight-oriented practices.

5. Any and all problem-solving procedures should be encouraged.

6. Rather than allowing undesired behavior to occur so that it might be studied and extinguished, it should be prevented from occurring whenever possible.

7. The general therapeutic task is to find, institute, and reinforce new desired behavior to substitute for the old problem behavior.

8. Behavior change, like all learning, can be expected to take place step by step rather than by sudden bursts of insight.

9. Corrective measures should be forward-looking and specific. The technical skills of the therapist should come into play in the process of identifying and promoting newly sought behavior patterns, with the use of such procedures as desensitization, operant conditioning, and aversive stimulation.

10. There is no need for a language that is not tied directly to behavior—that is, for such concepts as diagnosis, anxiety, complexes, defenses, or the unconscious.

Phillips and Wiener take the position that, since it is behavior change that the patient is seeking, the most direct approach to that goal is not only the most efficient, but it might very well also be the best. Their ideas and approaches would have less applicability in the case when behavior change is not the primary goal or not even a goal at all. Some therapists argue, for example, that the goal of psychotherapy is to increase a patient's self-understanding, and that changes a patient might make as a consequence of that increased understanding are of only secondary importance. But to the extent that behavior change is one of the major goals of psychotherapy, Phillips and Wiener's work provides an impressive justification for therapists to become skilled in the techniques of behavior analysis and behavior modification.

The principal purpose of the initial meeting with the patient is to develop a *therapeutic plan.* Such a plan ordinarily has three components: the change object, the change agent, and the change plan. The *change object* is the identified patient—it can be a specific individual or couple or family, for example, or a classroom of disturbed children. The *change agent* is the person or persons through whom changes can be attempted in the change object. In many cases the agent and the object are the same. But creating the concept of the change agent calls attention to the fact that there may be a potentially more effective but indirect way of bringing about change in the change object. Thus, a teacher or parent may be the change agent for an identified child who is the change object. In some situations several change agents may be identified and may work collaboratively to bring about change in a specific change object. Any person, condition, or situation can serve as a change agent, depending on the specific situation. The change plan identifies the behavior that has to change and develops the strategy and tactics for bringing the desired change about, including who, besides the therapist, should be involved in the process.

Behavior change is brought about through invoking the most appropriate learning theories. Certain behaviors can be modified through the use of classical conditioning theory, using such procedures as extinction, differential reinforcement, or desensitization. Other behaviors can be modified by employing operant learning theories—by concentrating on modifying the consequences of behavior as a way of modifying the behavior. It is the task of the therapist to develop a plan that makes the most intelligent use of learning theories and that has the best chance of success in changing behavior in the desired direction.

In Box 12-1 is a brief case history that exemplifies the process of developing a treatment plan.

TIME-LAPSE PROTOCOLS

Phillips and Wiener are, of course, interested in showing the special potential advantages of structured behavior change in affecting current behavior. They select key moments in the therapeutic experience (similar to time-lapse photography) and examine four different prototypical approaches to dealing with these moments—psychodynamic, nondirective, eclectic (more or less directive), and their own structured behavior change approach. The statements made by the patients are accurate, in that they were actually made in the course of therapy. Statements

---

Box 12-1: Developing a Treatment Plan

Mrs. T sought help for her 9-year old daughter who was a soiler (encopresis). The problem had existed for several years, but had worsened over the months just prior to referral. The child was scholastically able...was accepted socially by her peers except when the odor was strong, and she had good relations with adults....Laxatives and suppositories did not help....The parents alternately scolded, cajoled, and ignored the child, without success. The child responded by being alternately contrite, impervious, or angry....She soiled only at home, during play inside or out, and never at school....The mother revealed that she had tried, without success, to get the child to sit on the toilet a few minutes after breakfast; but since the mother was easily discouraged, she had soon abandoned this tactic when it was unsuccessful.

The hypothesis derived by the therapist...was that the child was too busy playing to heed the cues related to defecation....The child "let go" to a small extent, thus allowing herself to continue to play uninterruptedly and to reduce somewhat the internal pressure at the same time....The parents were told that they should not mention the habit, but that the mother should tell the child that she was to sit on the toilet a few minutes after each meal. If, after ten minutes, there was no bowel movement, the parent was advised by the therapist to say nothing, but to have the child come back after about one hour of play and sit on the toilet again. The child was to do this each hour until there was a movement. Then the child was to be free to play without another "sitting" that day unless continued observation showed that a second or third movement appeared to be necessary or likely.

In the second interview, three weeks later, the mother reported that the child had become symptom-free after two days of this regimen. In the next follow-up conversation, one year later, she reported that the child had had only one relapse, that otherwise the problem had disappeared, and that the child was continuing in a normal fashion with school and other activities. The mother said, "Well, I guess you trained me first and the child second, but it certainly worked!"

From Phillips and Wiener, 1966, pp. 72-73.

---

attributed to the therapists are not made in the form displayed. Rather, they are examples of statements that could be made by therapists from each of the four therapeutic orientations in response to the patient's statement. In Box 12-2, Box 12-3, and Box 12-4 are examples that illustrate their position about the potential usefulness of structured behavior change therapy.

ALTERNATIVE BEHAVIOR CHANGE THERAPY APPROACHES

Phillips and Wiener (1966) carry their concepts of structured behavior change therapy to the logical limit of envisioning therapy without the immediate presence of the therapist. Two examples that they examine are using principles from pedagogy to develop teaching approaches to therapy and conducting therapy by having the patient write rather than talk. Both approaches can result in the more efficient use of the therapist and in the development of useful adjuncts to the more traditional verbal interactional psychotherapies.

Programmed Therapy

The nature of structured behavior change therapy lends itself to thinking about therapy as teaching and to considering the use of teaching techniques for carrying out therapeutic objectives. One example of this possibility is the use of step-by-step programmed instruction as a therapeutic adjunct. These programmed instructional steps could be presented to the patient in pamphlet form, or even on a com-

---

Box 12-2: Four Approaches to Psychotherapy—Protocol I

Patient: I've got this problem, you see, being homosexual and all that. I'm afraid about it. I go to church and I feel guilty and I can't confess. And I'm nervous all the time. Can you help me get over this nervousness? I'm afraid I'll lose my job and all.

Therapist Responses:

Psychodynamic Orientation: Tell me about your home and family. What were they like? How did you feel toward your father? And mother? What dreams have you had lately? Do you see how this fear of getting too close to your mother, with her seductive ways, can make you fear women? And fear what your father would do if you loved your mother too much?

Nondirective Orientation: You feel very nervous about your homosexuality and don't know what to do about it. I wonder whether this feeling can be clarified. If I catch it correctly, you seem to be saying that you're worried more about being caught and about your guilt, than of the sex act itself.

Eclectic Orientation: Don't worry about homosexual thoughts. Everyone has them some time. And almost everyone has at least one homosexual experience. But try to control it or forget it. You should go out with girls. Keep busy. And try going to church, where you can get a grasp of good principles of living. If you feel too nervous to control the impulse, you can take a tranquilizer I'll give you a prescription for.

Structured Behavior Change Orientation: Can we decide, even tentatively, what your problem is and what you want to do about it? As a beginning, do you want to get over being a homosexual, or do you want only to get over your nervousness connected with it? You have this choice, and you must make it sooner or later if you want to get over your nervousness. You may not like the consequences of being homosexual, but you have to accept and suffer the consequences in terms of social dangers and penalties, if you practice it.

From Phillips and Wiener, 1966, pp. 143-144.

---

puter screen, and, if the patient can read and follow directions and is willing to cooperate in this type of learning process, significant behavior change can take place.

For example, if a patient's presenting problem is that he loses his temper too often and too easily, it should be possible to develop a programmed instructional experience that could result in desired behavior change. Initial steps in such a program might look like those shown in Box 12-5.

Occasional meetings with the therapist would be desirable to reinforce progress that has been made and to deal with issues that are not included in the programmed instruction.

Writing Therapy

Another example of an alternative approach to structured behavior change therapy is a procedure that Phillips and Wiener call writing therapy (see Phillips, Gershenson, & Lyons, 1977; Phillips & Wiener, 1966, ch. 9). Such a procedure could be particularly appropriate for patients who are articulate and who can write clearly; it has been used for some years in college settings. It should be noted that there is evidence that some patients prefer writing to being in a face-to-face situation and can be more open and more direct when they write than when they speak (see Phillips & Wiener, 1966, pp.

Box 12-3: Four Approaches to Psychotherapy—Protocol II

Patient: I can't stand it when my husband orders me around. He never really hits me or anything like that, but he's just terrible the way he raves and rants. And I can't ever please him. Nothing does, by me or the kids. I just can't do anything about it. It makes me feel terrible all the time.

Therapist Responses:

Psychodynamic Orientation: Apparently there's a great deal of hostility between you and your husband, and you can't stand it, so you develop symptoms and get sick. Now, why shouldn't you get angry when he treats you badly? Why shouldn't you even hate him at times? But tell me also, is this the way you felt toward your father?

Nondirective Orientation: You can't stand to be ordered around. And you feel pushed around and unappreciated no matter what you do. So you end up feeling bad, and getting sick, is that it?

Eclectic Orientation: Your husband probably doesn't mean anything by it. He's good to you otherwise, isn't he? Maybe he really loves you, but doesn't know how to show it. You'll have to try to pull yourself together. Have you tried this new drug yet?

Structured Behavior Change Orientation: Your husband orders you around and acts unreasonable, and you feel terrible because of the way he is. But if that's the way he is, and he's not about to act differently just because you want him to, then you have to look at yourself to change, to learn what you can do differently so that you don't end up feeling so terrible. Can you sometimes handle him in a way that brings him around?

From Phillips and Wiener, 1966, p. 151.

160–162). Recently White and Epston (1990) have discussed another aspect of the usefulness of writing by describing the many uses to which it can be put as part of the psychotherapeutic encounter.

Writing therapy is intended to help people with their personal, social, or academic problems. Patients have regular weekly appointments just as would be the case with traditional psychotherapy, but during the hour they are expected to write in a special notebook that is kept under lock and key and is available only to them and to their therapist. Patients are instructed to be as frank, complete, and cooperative as possible, and to write as clearly as they can about themselves, their observations, their problems, and how they have tried to cope with their difficulties in the past. The therapist reads and replies in writing to what the patient has written, and

thus an exchange between therapist and patient takes place.

Phillips and Wiener report that dealing with written communication is about twice as efficient as dealing with oral communication, that the technique is unusually helpful for beginning therapists, that there is remarkably little wasted time in the interaction, and that the written protocols are always available for reconsideration as well as for evaluation of change in the patient. Both therapist and patient have access at any time to everything they have previously written.

In an evaluation of time-limited writing therapy, Phillips, Gershenson, and Lyons (1977) employed the technique with 17 undergraduates who had not had previous therapy and who volunteered to try writing therapy instead of face-to-face therapy for

---

Box 12-4: Four Approaches to Psychotherapy: Protocol III

Patient: Well, I've been trying to think along the lines we talked about last time, and it just doesn't make sense to me. I admit that you've done me some good but my life still seems like such a mess and so hopeless that I can't see any use to going on with these interviews. So I've decided that this will be my last session.

Therapist Responses:

Psychodynamic Orientation: You seem to have reached a point where you're anxious about going on. I wonder why this is, what it is that's too threatening for you to face. And you have some positive feelings toward me, but also apparently some negative ones, and you have some resistance about going on with me. But wouldn't it be better to analyze these feelings? You don't have to be afraid of them. You can talk freely to me about them.

Nondirective Orientation: You have been trying to follow through on what we've been talking about, but you just can't figure it out. And you feel so hopeless that you've decided to give up at this point, and quit, is that right?

Eclectic Orientation: You're feeling pretty depressed, aren't you! Many patients have periods like this. But why quit now, when you've begun to get out of the woods? Of course, you could quit for awhile and see how it goes. Maybe your life isn't really such a mess as it seems right now. Perhaps you could go off on a vacation for awhile, and then come back and reconsider.

Structured Behavior Change Orientation: You're having trouble moving ahead along the lines we've been setting up, and you want to fall back on your old habits. But isn't that what got you into trouble in the first place and made you decide to see me? It is hard work to change long-time habits, of course. And you will always have periods of being discouraged. But if we go over your program again, and perhaps try to improve on it, you can get back to work on it. Then if you can continue to succeed with it as you began to do—instead of falling back on the old ways—you know that in a week or a month you'll be much more likely to feel good about yourself than if you follow your impulse of this moment.

From Phillips and Wiener, 1966, pp. 155–156.

---

10 sessions. Personality inventories were administered to the patients both immediately before and after the writing therapy process. In addition, experienced therapists rated the patients' writings in terms of the degree of successful problem resolution that was reported and the extent to which the patients' reactions to the therapy were favorable.

Patients wrote on average about 1200 words at the initial session. The number of words decreased fairly regularly, until at the final session an average of about 600 words were written. Therapist's written comments averaged about 300 words for each session. Significant improvements in a number of per-

sonality dimensions were found when the pretherapy and posttherapy personality test results were compared. The personality dimensions that exhibited the greatest improvement were in psychasthenia, hypomania, social introversion, and in becoming more assertive, more outgoing, independent, and self-directed. Most patients had favorable reactions to the writing therapy, and when asked if they would continue writing therapy if given the opportunity, nine said that they would, seven said they would not, and one had no opinion. Of the seven who said they would not, four said that that they had already solved their problems and needed no further help.

Box 12-5: Initial Steps in a Programmed Therapeutic Process

1. Loss of temper is better described as "loss of self-control." One may notice this tendency when tired, ill, or highly irritated by another person's behavior. Whatever the reason, one has to develop ways of showing better s_____ c_____. (Write in correct answer) Answer: self control.

2. People experience "loss of temper or self-control" in more than one type of situation. I tend to lose self-control of temper most commonly in the following ways: (write in replies) _____

3. Given knowledge of a situation in which loss of self-control is common, one can then attempt to foresee such situations and develop means to counteract this tendency. One does not need an "explanation" of the temper loss, only ways and means of c_____ the temper. Answer: controlling or counteracting.

4. To prepare in advance for a troublesome situation is the best way to offset a tendency to lose one's temper. One can use humor or delay his external action to someone when he is provoked. If one thinks ahead about his probable reaction, he can often _____ a tendency to react with anger or temper loss. Answer: change.

From Phillips and Wiener, 1966, p. 120.

CONCLUDING COMMENTS

Phillips and Wiener have proposed a highly rational behavioral cognitive therapy that is derived directly from data-based and theory-based learning approaches to the understanding and modification of behavior. Their uncompromising focus is on examining and changing behavior, and their belief is that most people who enter into psychotherapy do so because there is some aspect of their internal or external behavior that they wish to modify.

Structured behavior change therapy incorporates the essence of planned short-term psychotherapy—it is structured to solve specific problems as quickly as possible and to make use of every available therapeutic resource in order to accomplish that goal.

Structured behavior change therapy is upbeat in its orientation and democratic in its view of the legitimate actors in the therapeutic process. It carries with it the light baggage of learning theory, but none of what it considers the excess baggage of intrapsychic approaches. It professes no interest in the remote past, in developing insight, in making diagnoses, in establishing causes, or in such concepts as defenses, conflicts, or the unconscious.

Finally, Phillips and Wiener have courageously gone where their theories have led them—to the initial development of pedagogical approaches to psychotherapy that can be automated so as to give therapists the opportunity to use their skills and their limited time in those situations in which they can be most effective.

CHAPTER 13

ELLIS'S RATIONAL-EMOTIVE PSYCHOTHERAPY

Overview

Rational-Emotive Theory

Rational and Irrational Beliefs

The Belief System Between Stimulus and Response

Cognitive Restructuring Therapy

Concluding Comments

Rational-emotive therapy (RET) is a relatively brief form of psychotherapy that, according to its proponents, is appropriate to consider for treating the vast majority of emotional disorders. Developed originally by Albert Ellis in 1955 (1962; see also Dryden & DiGiuseppe, 1990; Ellis, 1989, 1990, 1992, 1993; Ellis & Abrahms, 1978; Ellis & Bernard, 1983; Ellis & Grieger, 1977; Ellis & Harper, 1961; Wiener, 1988), RET is advocated as a treatment of choice for anxiety, depression, inadequacy, hostility, and low frustration tolerance and has been used in the treatment of a far wider array of disorders (see Dryden & Hill, 1993).

RET assumes that certain disorders, for example, borderline and psychotic conditions, have both biological as well as environmental origins and usually require relatively longer periods of psychotherapy, but that "a large number of neurotic individuals can be significantly helped in 5–12 sessions and can...appreciably help themselves by continuing to practice the main RET principles they learned during these sessions" (Ellis, 1992, p. 36).

Ellis had been trained as a psychoanalyst and practiced psychoanalysis for several years until he concluded that much of what he had been trained to do was irrelevant in the lives of his clients. Specifically, he felt that the psychoanalytic approach ignored how clients constructed and maintained their own dysfunctional behavior. From this realization, Ellis designed his rational-emotive method as a brief and efficient approach for most neurotic clients.

RET is a comprehensive and multimodal cognitive behavioral approach that is based on the theory that people's disturbance-creating beliefs underlie their self-defeating actions. Emotionally dysfunctional people, in Ellis's picturesque language, "catastrophize, awfulize, overgeneralize, personalize, jump to invalid conclusions, use emotional reasoning, dichotomize, damn themselves and others, and make other major unrealistic, anti-empirical, often false inferences and attributions" (1993, p. 7). Or, to use a more pedestrian vocabulary, overt difficulties are due to underlying psychological mechanisms that are often expressed as irrational beliefs about the self (Persons, 1989).

RET is designed for efficiency by stressing a high degree of activity by the therapist and specific homework assignments for patients to perform in between sessions. Not only can RET help clients become free of their presenting symptoms, but it can potentially minimize other disturbances, reduce the discomfort clients feel about their symptoms, and reduce the risk of upsets in the future (Ellis, 1993).

RATIONAL-EMOTIVE THEORY

Six principles form the foundation of RET:

1. Cognition is the most important determinant of human emotion—we feel what we think.
2. Dysfunctional thinking is a major determinant of emotional distress.
3. Since personal distress is a product of irrational thinking, the best way to conquer distress is to change our thinking.
4. People seem to have a natural predisposition to think irrationally.
5. The primary focus in therapy is the continuing self-indoctrination that maintains irrational thinking.
6. Irrational beliefs are modified by active and persistent efforts to recognize, challenge, and revise one's thinking (Walen, DiGiuseppe, & Dryden, 1992, pp. 15–17).

The goal of RET is to help a patient achieve full self-acceptance—the acceptance of one's self, one's aliveness, one's existence—without requirements and unconditionally. Self-acceptance is achieved, according to RET theory, by pure choice; no special reasons are required. Full self-acceptance implies that one's characteristics or personal traits can be evaluated, but not one's self. In the case of a person with severe hypochondriasis, for example, full self-acceptance would mean that the person: (1) believes that having the disorder is undesirable, perhaps unfortunate, but that it is not horrible; (2) can tolerate the symptoms of the disorder without extreme anxiety, depression, or rumination; (3) can cope with a medical examination or medical treatment; and (4) can apply the behavioral methods learned in the psychotherapy sessions to prevent or overcome similar symptoms in the future.

From this point of view, every person ought to be able to say:

> First, I am alive. That is fairly evident and observable. Second, I choose to stay alive. Why? Simply because I choose to do so. Third, I desire, while alive, to live fairly happily, with relatively little pain and much pleasure. Because that seems conducive to my staying alive—and because I simply like being happy rather than miserable. Fourth, let me see how I can manage to decrease my pain and increase my short-range and long-range pleasure. (Ellis & Abrahms, 1978, p. 7)

Self-acceptance is achieved to the extent that people can give up their inordinate needs to do well and to win the approval of others. The vignette in Box 13-1 illustrates how RET assists in achieving unconditional self-acceptance.

RATIONAL AND IRRATIONAL BELIEFS

The distinction between rational and irrational beliefs is central to RET theory. The principal goal of RET is to help patients discover their irrational beliefs about themselves and others and abandon them if these beliefs are having negative consequences. According to RET theory psychological problems arise from irrational beliefs, that is, from misperceptions and misconceptions, from emotional underreactions or overreactions, and from dysfunctional behavior patterns. Rational thoughts, appropriate feelings, and effective behaviors are defined as those that aid human survival and happiness. RET actively and vigorously confronts cognitive, emotional, and behavioral pathology, principally by focusing on the rational and irrational intervening beliefs that lie between the activating experiences and the emotional consequences.

Ellis (1962) identified ten common irrational beliefs that, in his judgment, are ubiquitous in Western civilization and would seem inevitably to lead to widespread neurosis. These dysfunctional beliefs are listed in Box 13-2.

More recently, Ellis (1993) has suggested that these ten irrational beliefs can be grouped into three major headings: (1) I must perform well and win significant others' approval or else I am an inadequate, worthless person; (2) you must be nice and fair to me or else you are a rotten, horrible person; and (3) conditions under which I live must be comfortable, safe, and advantageous or else the world is a rotten place,

The A-B-C-D-E Model

Ellis has suggested an acronym to describe the five steps in the therapeutic process in summary form—the A-B-C-D-E model. According to this model, an

---

Box 13-1: Working Toward Unconditional Self-Acceptance

Patient: Why do I have to take those crummy pills? I can see that the doctors are right. I know that the drugs stop me from hearing voices. And I'm sure I'd be back in the hospital if I stopped taking my medicine. So I take the pills. But I think *it's terrible* to take them!

Therapist: Why is it terrible to take medication?

Patient: Because I have to remember to take it, and I have to take time to see you for appointments—and sometimes I get side effects from the medicine.

Therapist: And that's why it's *inconvenient* for you to take the pills. That's a rational Belief— "I don't like to take the pills because I find some of their effects unpleasant." If you stayed only with that rational Belief— that taking medication is *inconvenient* or *unfortunate*—how would you feel?

Patient: I'd feel less depressed.

Therapist: Yes. You'd probably, if you only stressed the inconvenience or unfortunateness of taking the pills, feel sorry, or sad, or regretful about taking them. And that would be ok, or what we call "appropriate" in RET. For if you find something inconvenient, you certainly don't want to feel good about it! So when you feel depressed, you really have two feelings: first the appropriate feeling of sorrow or regret, because you don't *like* to take the pills and yet you know that you'd better take them; and second, the inappropriate feeling of depression. And this second feeling, your inappropriate feeling, doesn't come from that rational Belief, "I don't like to take the pills because I find some of their effects unpleasant." It comes, instead, from a second belief, or what we call an irrational Belief in RET. What do you think your irrational Belief is?

Patient: (30-second pause) The irrational Belief that causes me to be depressed? I guess, "It's *terrible* to take the pills!

Therapist: That's exactly right. When you say to yourself irrationally, "It's *awful, horrible,* or *terrible*" to do anything, such as take pills, you're really creating your own depression.

Patient: Then what do I do to feel better about myself?

Therapist: First, understand exactly what you are telling yourself irrationally, in the manner that we're now going over it; and then give up these irrational ideas.

From Ellis and Abrahms, 1978, pp. 9–10.

---

activating event triggers a rational or irrational *belief* that leads to emotional or behavioral *consequences*. If the belief is irrational, a therapeutic episode can be designed to create *disputation* in the client in the form of internal challenge or debate about the irrational belief, which can lead to a positive *effect* compatible with appropriate problem solving. In this context the goal of RET is to help clients become their own therapists.

Two Case Examples

The best way to exemplify RET is to examine excerpts of representative interviews. An example of the use of RET in the treatment of chron-ic pain is presented in Box 13-3. In this case the therapist works toward replacing the identification of the problem as an external event (the pain) with the identification of the problem as an internal event (the beliefs). First, it is essential that patients understand that the pain cannot be eliminated, and that life is not a matter of simply trying to "hang in there." Rather, the therapist attempts to suggest that not only does chronic pain have psychological consequences but that these consequences can add to the experience of pain. While the pain itself cannot be taken away, the psychological consequences can be modified so that the pain can become less intrusive.

Box 13-2: Ellis's List of Common Irrational Beliefs

1. It is a dire necessity for an adult human being to be loved or approved by virtually every significant other person in his community.
2. One should be thoroughly competent, adequate, and achieving in all possible respects if one is to consider oneself worthwhile.
3. Certain people are bad, wicked, or villainous, and they should be severely blamed and punished for their villainy.
4. It is awful and catastrophic when things are not the way one would very much like them to be.
5. Human unhappiness is externally caused, and people have little or no ability to control their sorrows and disturbances.
6. If something is or may be dangerous or fearsome one should be terribly concerned about it and should keep dwelling on the possibility of its occurring.
7. It is easier to avoid than to face certain life difficulties and self-responsibilities.
8. One should be dependent on others and need someone stronger than oneself on whom to rely.
9. One's past history is an all-important determiner of one's present behavior, and because something once strongly affected one's life, it should indefinitely have a similar effect.
10. One should become quite upset over other people's problems and disturbances.

From Ellis, 1962, pp. 61–85.

Box 13-3: Using RET in the Case of Chronic Pain

Patient: I don't get it. My pain hurts. Of course, I feel lousy because of the pain. If there were no pain, I'd feel great.

Therapist: Can you see the difference between you now, with depression and anger and a you, still with pain but calmer and friendlier?

Patient: Yeah. My wife would sure like that.

Therapist: How about you? A calmer and more relaxed you, still in pain, but just feeling better.

Patient: That makes sense, but how can I do that? The pain will always be there.

Therapist: Probably, but what happens is that your upsetness makes the pain feel worse. Don't you feel even worse when you are depressed about what's happening to you?

Patient: Yes.

Therapist: If we can help you reduce your emotional reaction to the pain, you'd be better off, right?

Patient: Yes.

Therapist: OK then. Let's work on how you can reduce your emotions that get out of hand, because anything we do that can help you feel better will be all to the good.

Patient: Yeah.

[The patient, now accepting that it makes sense to work on the problem, may still believe that not much can be done about his emotional responses because they are "natural" consequences of the pain.]

Therapist: Suppose you were the sort of person who loved pain. Do you think that you would be depressed and angry? Not at all.

(continued)

Box 13-3 continued

Patient: That would be crazy.

Therapist: Perhaps, but the point is that different people could have different reactions to the pain. Reactions to it seem to be in the person, not the pain.

Patient: Well, I see your point, but I'm the kind of person who hates pain.

Therapist: Sure, but that might be the problem. Perhaps you get so busy hating whenever you notice it that you inadvertently produce the emotional discomfort.

From Rothschild, 1993, p. 111, in W. Dryden and L.K. Hill (Eds.), *Innovations in Rational-Emotive Therapy*, Newbury Park, CA: Sage, 1993. Reprinted by permission of Sage Publications, Inc.

Box 13-4: Rational-Emotive Therapy in Action

Therapist: You seem to be terribly afraid that you will fail to make good initial contacts with a woman and also succeed sexually.

Patient: Hell, yes! To say the least, I'm scared stiff on both counts.

Therapist: Because if you fail in either area…

Patient: If I fail, I'll be an utter slob!

Therapist: Prove it!

Patient: Isn't it obvious?

Therapist: Not for me! It's fairly obvious that if a woman rejects you, socially or sexually, it'll hardly be a great thing. But how will that prove *you,* a total person, will be no good?

Patient: I still think it's obvious. Would this same woman reject *anyone*?

Therapist: No, probably not. Let's suppose that she accepts many men, but not you. Let's also suppose that she rejects you because she finds that, first, you're not terribly good at conversation and, second, you come quickly in intercourse. So she finds you doubly deficient. Now, how does that still prove that you're no good?

Patient: It certainly proves that I'm no good for *her.*

Therapist: Yes, in a way. You're no good for her conversationally and sexually. You have two rotten *traits*.

Patient: And she doesn't want *me,* for having those traits.

Therapist: Right. In the case we're assuming, she rejects *you* for having those two traits. But all we've proved is that one woman despises two of your characteristics; and that this woman therefore rejects you as a lover or a husband. Even she, mind you, might well accept you as a nonsexual friend. For you have, don't forget, many other traits—such as intelligence, artistic talent, reliability, et cetera.

Patient: But not the traits she *most* wants!

Therapist: Maybe. But how does this prove that *all* women, like her, would find you equally wanting? Some, actually, might like you *because* you are shy and *because* you come quickly sexually—when they don't happen to like intercourse, and therefore want to get it over rapidly!

Patient: Fat chance!

Therapist: Yes, statistically. For *most* women, presumably, will tend to reject you if you're shy or sexually inadequate, in their eyes. But a few, at least, will accept you for the very reasons that most refuse you, and many more, normally, will accept you in spite of your deficiencies, because they nonetheless become attached to you.

(continued)

Box 13-4 continued

Patient: Who the devil wants *that*!

Therapist: Most of us do, actually, if we're sane. For, since we're all highly imperfect, we're happy that some people accept us *with* those imperfections. But let's even suppose the worst—just to show how crooked your thinking is. Let's suppose that, because of your shyness and fast ejaculation, all women reject you for *all* time. Would you still be a worthless slob?

Patient: I wouldn't exactly be a great guy!

Therapist: No, you wouldn't be Casanova! But many women, remember, wouldn't want you if you were. Most women, at least today, wouldn't want Casanova just *because* he was so sexy and promiscuous. Anyway, we're evading the question; *would* you be a total slob?

Patient: Well, uh, I—no, I guess not.

Therapist: Because?

Patient: Well, because I'd still have other, uh, good traits. Is that what you're getting at?

Therapist: Yes, partly. You'd still have other good traits. And you, if you were to rate yourself at all, would equal *all* of your traits, not merely two of them.

From A. Ellis and E. Abrahms, *Brief Psychotherapy in Medical and Health Practice,* pp. 41–42, New York: Springer Publishing Co., 1978. Used by permission.

The excerpt in Box 13-4 comes from the second interview with a 27-year-old man whose symptoms included shyness and social inhibition, particularly around women; rapid ejaculation in intercourse; and hostility to authority figures, including his parents and his supervisor at work.

THE BELIEF SYSTEM BETWEEN STIMULUS AND RESPONSE

Between the stimulus and the response is a complex belief system consisting of both rational and irrational components. The rational component in the previous case (Box 13-4) was the belief that the client might be rejected if he approached a woman and that the rejection would be unfortunate and annoying and would make him feel sorry, regretful, and frustrated. The irrational component was the belief that the rejection would be awful and that he could not bear it.

This irrational component earned that description because it treated the possible rejection as unbearable, because it signified that the patient was worthless, and because the patient viewed these self-descriptions as permanent. That is, the patient was evaluating himself as an entirety rather than evaluating his traits or his social performance. In a subsequent therapeutic session, after Ellis had pointed out the philosophic foundation of the patient's inhibitions and anxiety, the patient asked how he could get rid of his irrational beliefs. The excerpt in Box 13-5 demonstrates how this fundamental question was dealt with.

As can be seen from the case vignettes, RET stresses the cognitive, philosophic, value-oriented aspects of human personality. RET holds that people largely manufacture their own psychological symptoms and have the ability to eliminate or minimize these symptoms and make themselves much less easily disturbed. It does not strive for symptom removal so much as for a profound philosophic solution to people's fundamental emotional problems. As such, RET is a significant example of the rapidly developing field of cognitive behavior therapy.

This underlying theory of RET makes certain requirements of clients to increase the likelihood that it will be helpful to them. Clients have to believe that thoughts cause emotions and have to be able to distinguish their thoughts from their emotions and both from external situations. Clients must find that their core beliefs are linked to their emotional responses, both positive and negative, and must be able to achieve sufficient distance from their

Box 13-5: Rational-Emotive Therapy—Prescribing Homework

Therapist: For ten minutes every day, take *any* irrational or nutty belief that you have, such as the one that it's terrible for you to be rejected by a woman you find attractive, and practice giving it up, even when you are not being rejected.

Patient: How?

Therapist: By using the logical and empirical method of seeing whether your hypothesis is consistent with your other goals and hypotheses, and by asking for factual evidence to sustain or invalidate it.

Patient: Can you be more specific?

Therapist: Yes. In my group therapy sessions, recently, I have been giving most of the members of the group disputing assignments...to help them carry out these ten-minute-a-day disputations....The point is for you to decide exactly what hypothesis or nutty idea you want to work on for at least ten minutes a day. And, in your case, it would be the idea, again, that it's terrible for you to get rejected by a woman you find attractive. You would take this idea, and ask yourself several basic questions, in order to challenge and dispute it.

Patient: What kind of questions?

Therapist: Usually, four basic questions—though they have all kinds of variations. The first one is "What am I telling myself?" or "What silly idea do I want to challenge?" And the answer, in your case, is "It's terrible if a woman whom I find attractive rejects me." The second question is, "Is this, my hypothesis, true?" And the answer is...

Patient: Uh, well, no, it isn't.

Therapist: Fine. If you had said this was true, the third question would have been "Where is the evidence for its being true?" But since you said it isn't true, the third question is, "Where is the evidence that it's not true?" Well...?

Patient: Well, uh, it's not true because, as we said before, it may be *inconvenient* if an attractive woman rejects me, but it's not *more* than that...it's *only* damned inconvenient!

Therapist: Right. And there's other logical and empirical evidence that it isn't terrible. For one thing, because *this* woman rejects you hardly means that *all* will. For another, you obviously have survived even though you have been rejected. For still another, lots of other people in the world have been rejected by the woman they most love, and it has hardly been terrible for all of them, has it?

Patient: I see. There are several evidences that my being rejected isn't awful. And there is no reason, as we again noted before, why I *should* not get rejected. The world simply isn't a totally nonrejecting place!

Therapist: Yes, I think you're getting that well. Now, the fourth question is "What is the worst thing that could happen to me, if an attractive woman rejects me?"

Patient: Very little, I guess. I was at first going to say that the worst thing that could happen to me was that I would be very depressed for a long time. But I now see that such a thing would not happen from any rejection but from my *view* of the horror of being rejected.

Therapist: Really, then, not so much could happen to you, if you got rejected. Is that right?

Patient: Yes. As a matter of fact, I would learn something about approaching an attractive female. And I might learn something valuable about myself.

Therapist: Right. Now, this method of asking yourself these four questions, and persisting until you get sensible answers to them, is something you can do at least ten minutes every single day, even when there is not much going on in your life and you are in no danger of being rejected.

From A. Ellis and E. Abrahms, *Brief Psychotherapy in Medical and Health Practice,* pp. 43–45, New York: Springer Publishing Co., 1978. Used by permission.

own thinking so that they can appreciate their thoughts objectively. Clients need to be able to analyze the validity of their ideation, see the similarities and differences among their various thoughts, and be able to agree that if a thought is logically false, it may be useful to change it (Mc Mullin, 1986, pp. 303–305).

COGNITIVE RESTRUCTURING THERAPY

One of the most important developments in cognitive psychotherapy that has served to supplement Ellis's work has been Mc Mullin's cognitive restructuring therapy (1986). Mc Mullin's work systematically describes cognitive interventions in terms of their general principles and most appropriate uses. That is, Mc Mullin has concentrated on identifying the wide variety of interventions that can be employed in treat-

ing clients. Of these, the most important are countering, perceptual shifting, and classical conditioning.

The first general category of cognitive intervention, countering, is the term given to arguing against irrational beliefs. As a therapeutic intervention, countering, is based on the assumption that when clients argue with themselves repeatedly against an irrational belief, the irrational belief weakens in intensity. That is, countering emphasizes talking to the self, or self-language. The ideal counter is identified by the client rather than by the therapist; it is forceful, realistic, and logical and consistent with the client's fundamental philosophical belief system—"It is impossible to succeed in everything I do." Counters are effective in direct proportion to how many can be identified for each irrational belief, and they need to be applied consistently and repeatedly. An example of countering can be found in Box 13-6.

Box 13-6: Countering as a Cognitive Intervention

(The client is a 22-year old woman who was having trouble becoming independent from her parents. In addition, she reported chest pains and difficulty breathing. Repeated medical examinations were negative but she still feared she might have heard disease or lung cancer. This excerpt is from the tenth session.)

Therapist: Do you think there is any connection between your belief that you have a heart problem and the situation that happened at work?
Patient: Well, yes! That's when I first noticed the chest pains.
Therapist: How could this situation have given you a heart problem?
Patient: Well, I've been under a lot of strain recently and maybe the strain that day was the last straw for my heart.
Therapist: If you do have a heart problem, why have scores of doctors been unable to find anything wrong?
Patient: I don't know. Maybe the whole thing is just my imagination, but I really feel the pain in my chest. I know I'm not just imagining it.
Therapist: I don't doubt for one moment that you really have a pain in your chest. What we are trying to find out is why you have it. Can you think of any other explanation of your chest pains besides having a heart attack?
Patient: No.
Therapist: Have you noticed any connection between your chest pains and anxiety?
Patient: Well, yes. The more chest pains I have, the more anxious I am.
Therapist: How about the more anxious you are, the more chest pains you have?
Patient: Are you saying the whole thing is caused by my anxiety?
Therapist: I am asking you, not telling you. Granted, I have some ideas about what's going on with you, but I want you to find the fallacies in your own thinking. What strikes me

(continued)

Box 13-6 continued

most about your situation is you say your heart problem spontaneously developed three months ago. It was at work and a very stressful day. You are only 22, have no history of heart problems in your family, and scores of doctors haven't found a scintilla of evidence that there is anything wrong with your heart. So how can we determine whether your chest pains are due to a heart problem or something else?

Patient: Well, I know I don't have any real evidence for believing it's my heart. But every time I have the chest pain I get scared.

Therapist: Sure, but what are you saying to yourself every time you have chest pains?

Patient: (pauses for 30 seconds) That I am having a heart attack. *(another pause)* Yeah! I see what you mean. Maybe I'm scared because I am telling myself it's my heart.

Therapist: Maybe. For the sake of argument, let's assume that's true; you are scared because you have called one of the symptoms of your anxiety a serious heart problem. But can you remember what you think right before you feel chest pains that might cause them? How could the same thought—that you have a heart problem—cause the chest pains, which would in turn cause you to conclude you have a heart problem?

Patient: I don't understand.

Therapist: How could thinking you had a heart problem cause your chest pains?

Patient: (silent for about a minute) Oh yes, I see it now. It might make me pay close attention to anything going on in my chest, looking for any possible sign that something is wrong. I think I have probably done that. I worry so much about my heart that I get tense, the tension causes chest pains, and then I worry that my chest pain means I have a bad heart.

Therapist: Yes, I think that is a real possibility. And it would explain why you have been worried about your heart since that day in the store. But we still need an explanation as to why you got so tense that day. What happened that day in particular that caused your anxiety?

Patient: I don't know.

Therapist: Do you think there could be any relationship between your chest pains and having to put up with a score of obnoxious customers?

Patient: I don't know. I have had bad customers before.

Therapist: Can you pick a specific time?

Patient: Well…yes. Yesterday, for example.

Therapist: OK. Write down on a piece of paper what you thought, what you felt, and how you acted yesterday, and then on the other side what you felt, thought, and acted that day three months ago.

Patient: (pauses while she writes) OK. Now compare the two lists. What is different about the two situations?

Patient: (pauses) Well, three months ago I was tired, drank five cups of coffee and smoked two packs of cigarettes that morning. *(pause)* Yeah! I get it. I really worked myself up with all that caffeine and nicotine.

Therapist: Looks that way. But we still don't know why you worked yourself up that way. But we do know you have the core belief that you are fragile and inadequate and still need your parents to protect you. Is there any possibility that something happened three months ago that activated that belief?

(Client and therapist explore some related questions)

Patient: I remember now. I was tired that day because the night before I had had another argument with my mom about moving out.

Therapist: How did that activate the core belief?

Patient: I got worried about being alone and unprotected.

(continued)

Box 13-6 continued

Therapist: Good! That fear is the main reason you came to see me and we will continue to work on it. But in the meantime, let's look again at your more immediate fear of getting a heart attack or having lung cancer. You have come up with some other interpretations of this thinking. I think it would be useful to write them down, so that you can use the counters against the thought of having a heart problem.

(With the therapist's help, the client discovered the following counters:)

1. My chest pains mean that I'm tense, not that I'm having a heart attack.
2. I'm tense because three months ago I had an anxiety attack after drinking five cups of coffee and smoking two packs of cigarettes.
3. I misread the cause of my tension and mistakenly called it a heart problem.
4. Since that time I have been hypersensitive to my chest, causing me to feel more tense, causing my chest to hurt more, causing me to get even tenser, and so on, until I am constantly worried about my heart.
5. My tension, then and now, comes from the same golden oldie belief that I can't take care of myself without my parents.
6. When I get scared again, I'll work on my core fear and try not to sidetrack myself into thinking I have heart problems.

From Mc Mullin, 1986, pp. 8–10.

The second intervention category, *perceptual shifting*, provides clients with the opportunity to modify their mistaken perceptions, which usually have their origins in earlier experiences and often cause considerable unhappiness. Perceptual shifting seeks to undo the conceptualizations that have occurred in the past and persist into the present in spite of little or no evidence of their validity. Cognitive therapy seeks to modify these habituated perceptions and replace them with ones that are more appropriate in terms of present reality.

The third intervention category consists of the various *conditioning techniques* that have the potential to modify the emotional reactions that are sometimes attached to experiences. These techniques derive from classical conditioning theory and include cognitive desensitization, which pairs relaxation with anxiety-provoking stimuli in order to inhibit conditioned anxiety responses; extinction procedures, which serve to detach emotional reactions from the original experiences to which they were linked; and cognitive restructur-ing, which can strengthen cognitions by reinforcement or weaken cognitions by punishment.

CONCLUDING COMMENTS

Rational-emotive psychotherapy has proven to be a remarkably durable approach in the treatment of a variety of psychological disorders. In large measure, this durability is a tribute to its originator, Albert Ellis, who has persistently described and underlined its virtues. The singular contribution of Ellis to the world of time-limited psychotherapy is his insistence on the cognitive control that patients have over their own thoughts, feelings, and behavior. Helping clients achieve greater control over their cognitive and emotional life can ultimately allow them to have greater control over their own symptoms. According to Ellis, patients think themselves into psychological disorder and can think themselves out of it—a message that is exceedingly affirming and supportive.

CHAPTER 14

FARRELLY'S PROVOCATIVE THERAPY

Overview

Origins of Provocative Therapy

Assumptions, Hypotheses, and Goals

Therapeutic Techniques

The Therapeutic Process

Becoming a Provocative Therapist

Concluding Comments

Provocative therapy (Farrelly & Brandsma, 1974) is an aptly named form of relatively short-term individual, group, and family therapy (average number of interviews is twenty to twenty-five with a range of two to one hundred) that has been practiced by its originator, Frank Farrelly, since 1963. Jeff Brandsma organized, monitored, criticized, and provided structure for Farrelly's thinking, as well as contributing to the process of putting these ideas down in written form.

Farrelly, a psychiatric social worker, expresses his indebtedness to Carl Rogers, with whom he worked at Mendota State Hospital in Wisconsin in the study of client-centered therapy with chronic schizophrenics, for helping him appreciate the importance of developing an empathic understanding of patients. But Farrelly moved past the role of a client-centered therapist as he slowly realized that the more traditional passive, receptive role of the therapist was not for him.

Farrelly discovered that when he "threw therapy out the window" (1974, p. 19) and began telling patients how he found himself reacting to them, they began to improve. That is, Farrelly had come to the conclusion that empathic understanding, warm caring, and genuine congruence were rarely enough and even when effective as a therapeutic strategy were far too slow. Furthermore, Farrelly found that these conclusions were as valid for private- as for public-sector patients and as appropriate for neurotics as for psychotics. Thus, Farrelly believes that

there are no patients for whom his approach is clearly unsuitable.

ORIGINS OF PROVOCATIVE THERAPY

Farrelly found that another strategy worked well with his patients—he could assist patients to develop stronger egos if he sided with their superegos. Farrelly wrote:

While in the 91st interview with the patient whom I'll call "Bill," I "stumbled" onto what felt like a crystallization of these previous experiences. Because I had not yet integrated my learning experiences and was a member of the project, I felt somewhat constrained to use a client centered approach with this patient. I had been essentially communicating three basic ideas to him: 1) You are worthwhile and of value; 2) You can change; and 3) Your whole life can be different. He, in turn, had been persistently communicating back to me three complementary responses: 1) I am worthless; 2) I'm hopeless and can never change; and 3) My life will always be one long psychotic episode and hospitalization. It was becoming increasingly clear that empathic understanding, feedback, warm caring, and genuine congruence were simply not enough and were getting us nowhere. At this point I "gave up" and said to him, "Okay, I agree. You're hopeless. Now let's try *this* for 91 interviews. Let's try agreeing with you about yourself from here on out. Almost immediately (within a matter of seconds and minutes, not weeks and months), he began to protest that he was not *that* bad, nor *that* hopeless. Easily observable and measurable characteristics of his in-therapy behavior started changing. For example, his rate of speech markedly increased, his voice quality changed from a dull, slow motion, soporific monotone to a more normal tone of voice with inflections and easily noticeable affect. He became less over-controlled and showed humor, embarrassment, irritation, and far more spontaneity. (1974, p. 26)

As an example of how the historical derivatives of the thinking of brief psychotherapists can be traced, Erickson (see Chapter 16) had earlier been reported to have used the same approach in working with patients with particularly low levels of self-esteem. Haley (1973) has described how Erickson, uncommonly skilled as a psychotherapist, reacted to an overweight client who described herself as a "plain, fat slob." Rather than trying to reassure the client by pointing out that the client may be overlooking unusually worthwhile aspects of herself, Erickson agreed with the client, saying, "You are *not* a plain, fat, disgusting slob. You are the fattest, homeliest, most disgustingly horrible bucket of lard I have ever seen, and it is appalling to have to look at you....But you do need help. I'm willing to give you this help. I think you know now that I won't hesitate to tell you the truth" (p. 116; see also Rosenbaum, 1990, p. 355).

Another related example was provided by Watzlawick, Weakland, and Fisch (1974) in a book published the same year as Farrelly and Brandsma's. They wrote:

If one tells a bright thirty-year old schizophrenic who has spent ten years of his life in various hospitals that he should change, that he should free himself from the influence of his family, get a job, start a life of his own, etc., he may agree, but then explain that his voices are confusing him and that he simply is not ready to leave the hospital. He has heard these exhortations often enough and knows how to defeat them. A very different situation arises if one takes the why-should-you-change? approach. Instead of countering nonsense with common sense...the Judo technique of utilizing the other's resistance is the method of choice: "I know I should not tell you this, because what are you going to think of a doctor who says such things; but strictly between you and me I must tell you what I really think of your situation. As far as I am concerned, it is I who should have his head examined, not you. Because you have made it, you have found a way of life which most of us would dearly love to live....You don't even have to

get up if you don't want to, your day is safe and predictable." (pp. 134-135)

ASSUMPTIONS, HYPOTHESES, AND GOALS

In examining provocative therapy retrospectively, Farrelly and Brandsma have been able to identify ten assumptions that govern their behavior as therapists. These assumptions are shown in summary form in Box 14-1.

Two central hypotheses govern the behavior of a therapist practicing provocative therapy. First, "if provoked by the therapist (humorously, perceptively, and within the client's own internal frame of reference), the client will tend to move in the opposite direction from the therapist's definition of the client as a person" (1974, p. 52). Second, "if urged provocatively (humorously and perceptively) by the therapist to continue his self-defeating, deviant behaviors, the client will tend to engage in self- and other-enhancing behaviors which more closely approximate the societal norm" (1974, p. 52). As can be seen, the use of humor is an important therapeutic technique in provocative therapy (see also Furman & Ahola, 1988).

The assumptions and hypotheses invoked by Farrelly are crucial for the achievement of the major goals of provocative therapy—to help the patient: (1) affirm self-worth, (2) be appropriately assertive, (3) defend himself or herself realistically, (4) respond to reality adaptively, and (5) communicate his or her own feelings in personal relationships freely and authentically.

THERAPEUTIC TECHNIQUES

To accomplish the goals of provocative therapy, Farrelly and Brandsma believe in employing virtually any tactic—"obvious lying, denial, rationalization, invention (e.g., of 'instant research'), crying and zany thinking" (1974, p. 57). Farrelly and Brandsma write: "Figuratively therapists are often bound by Marquis of Queensbury type rules while patients use the psychological equivalent of knee to the groin and thumb in the eye. The outcome of such a contest is not often in doubt—to the ultimate detri-

---

Box 14-1: Assumptions of Provocative Therapy

1. People change and grow in response to challenge.
2. Clients can change if they choose to do so.
3. Clients have far more potential for achieving adaptive, productive, and socialized modes of living than they or most clinicians assume.
4. The psychological fragility of clients is vastly overrated both by themselves and others.
5. Clients' maladaptive, unproductive, antisocial attitudes and behaviors can be drastically altered whatever the degree of severity or chronicity.
6. Adult or current experiences are at least, if not more, as significant as childhood or previous experiences in shaping client values, attitudes, and behaviors.
7. Clients' behavior with the therapist is a relatively accurate reflection of their habitual patterns of social and interpersonal relationships.
8. People make sense; the human animal is exquisitely logical and understandable.
9. The more important messages between people are nonverbal.
10. The expression of therapeutic hate and joyful sadism toward clients can markedly benefit them.

From Farrelly and Brandsma, 1974, pp. 36–52.

Box 14-2: Provocative Therapy in Action

Patient: (loudly and furiously) Goddamn you! If you don't stop talking in that snotty, sarcastic way of yours, I'm going to quit therapy and not pay your bill!
Therapist: (with an alarmed, anxious, pleading expression): Please, *don't!* I need the money! *(Slumps dejectedly in chair, holding forehead in hand, in a depressed, choked tone of voice.)* Oh well, I'll just have to tell June and the kids no Christmas again *this* year.
Patient: (A kaleidoscope of emotions crossing his face—anger, laughter, suddenly placating) OK, OK, damn you, I know I need you more than you need me, but damn it, Frank, won't you please just...

From F. Farrelly and J. Brandsma, *Provocative Therapy* (p. 60), Cupertino, CA: Meta Publications, 1974. Reprinted by permission of the author and the publisher.

---

ment of the patient" (1974, p. 57). Box 14-2 gives an example of provocative therapy in action.

The therapist plays devil's advocate; sides with the negative half of the patient's ambivalent conflicts; urges the patient to continue deviant and pathological behavior (for plausible reasons); verbalizes the patient's worst self-doubts, thoughts, and fears; absurdly and ludicrously encourages the patient's symptoms; and lampoons, ridicules, and burlesques the patient's attitudes, always attempting to provoke the patient to give at least equal time to the positive, joyful, and growth-producing experiences in life. This orientation is reminiscent of Watzlawick's assertion that "jokes have a disrespectful ability to make light

of seemingly monolithic world orders and world images. This may help to explain why it is that people who suffer from emotional problems are half over them once they manage to laugh at their predicament" (1978, pp. 55–56).

THE THERAPEUTIC PROCESS

In conceptualizing the process of provocative therapy, Farrelly and Brandsma have identified four stages through which patients typically pass: (1) provocation, (2) reorganization and change, (3) clarification and protest, and (4) consolidation and integration.

Stage One: Provocation

First, "the client is precipitously provoked into a series of experiences that tend to leave him astonished, incredulous, uncertain and even at times outraged. He experiences a marked clash of expectational systems; his expectations of the therapist's role are not only disconfirmed but are almost reversed" (1974, pp. 131–132). Provocation is designed to help patients affirm their own worth, assert themselves appropriately, defend themselves realistically, and engage in risk-taking relationships. The excerpts in Box 14-3 illustrate this first stage; the italicized annotations are Farrelly's.

Stage Two: Reorganization and Change

Farrelly and Brandsma describe the dynamics of the second stage:

The client typically decreases his protestations regarding the therapist's behaviors, begins to recognize that he and not the therapist must change, and starts reorganizing his expectational system toward the therapist....And finally this stage is characterized by a marked diminishing if not total extinction of psychotic defenses if these were initially present. (1974, p. 135).

Box 14-4 provides an example of provocative therapy in stage two.

Stage Three: Clarification and Protest

In the third stage there is considerable clarification and movement. "The hallmark of this state is the client's congruent and increasingly firm protestations that the therapist's definition of him is a skewed, inaccurate one based on a distorted reading

---

Box 14-3: Examples of Provocative Therapy Stage One—Provocation

[A female client was referred to me, her thirteenth therapist.]

Therapist: What's your name again?
Patient: Rachel Levin. *(a pseudonym)*
Therapist: That's Jewish.
Patient: Yeah.
Therapist: Where are you from?
Patient: New Yawk. *[She didn't even have her coat off, nor was she seated yet.]*
Therapist: Oh, my God!...
Patient: I can't believe my ears, do you actually help people this way? I am just continually angry at you.
Therapist: Help? Who's talking about help? Talking you can get, but help is harder to come by. Now you haven't been helped by those twelve other therapists whom you wore out, why demand the impossible of me?

***

Patient: I don't like what you're saying, but I'll say this for you. I don't have to sit around wondering what you're thinking of me like I did with my other therapist.

***

Patient: I found out I could twist other therapists around my little finger, easily embarrass them and make them blush. I can't bully you—and that's good. And when I come in here and try to embarrass you with all that I've done sexually, you don't get embarrassed; you make *me* blush at *your* responses! And you know, that's good—you and Hank *(her boyfriend)* are the only persons I've found that I can't make jump through hoops.

From F. Farrelly and J. Brandsma, *Provocative Therapy* (pp. 132–134), Cupertino, CA: Meta Publications, 1974. Reprinted by permission of the author and the publisher.

Box 14-4: Example of Provocative Therapy Stage Two—Reorganization and Change

[A deeply religious young man entered my private practice with his staunchly Catholic parents. He had a history of a psychotic break, several hospitalizations, and no jobs following a homosexual episode. Convinced that he was immortal, his behavior in traffic was bordering on suicidal. In the first interview it quickly became apparent that his "immortality" was connected in his mind to his homosexual episode. He further averred to the consternation of his appalled parents that anyone who engaged in fellatio with him would also become immortal....]

Therapist: (seriously) I also think it only fair and just that your mother and father here *(gesturing toward parents)*, who are well into middle age and who gave you the gift of Life should, uh, in turn, uh—
Mother: (holding hand up to her mouth as though gagging) I think I'm going to be ill—do we have to talk about these things?
Father: (glaring at his son) God, you have sick patterns of thinking!
Therapist: (trying and failing to keep a straight face but forging ahead) Uh, it's only fitting that Mom and Dad should be the first, uh, I don't quite know how to put this tactfully—
Patient: Dammit, will you quit talking on and on about this crazy shit? I never really believed this stuff for the past year anyhow, even when I was telling people it. It's just crazy, that's all.
Therapist: ("surprised") What? What did you say?
Patient: (forcefully) I said I never really believed all that crazy crap anyway, so why don't you just shut up about it?
Therapist: (with a Pollyanna-like smile, coaxingly) Would you repeat that?
Patient: (laughing) You heard me.
Therapist: (still smiling) I know, but my favorite number is three and some things I like to hear three times. Just once more.
Patient: (noticing his parents are laughing with relief; laughing and smiling himself) Go to hell.
Therapist: (with eyes toward ceiling, hands folded as though in prayer) Don't listen to him, God. You haven't for years. *(to patient, coaxingly)* Aw, come on, just once more for your friendly therapist.
Patient: (smiling, nodding, in a serious tone) OK, OK, I never really believed all that crazy stuff I said about being immortal even when I said it. There. Satisfied?

From F. Farrelly and J. Brandsma, *Provocative Therapy*, (pp. 135–136), Cupertino, CA: Meta Publications, 1974. Reprinted by permission of the author and the publisher.

---

of inadequate samplings" (1974, p. 137). An example of stage three clarification and protest is given in Box 14-5.

Stage Four: Consolidation and Integration

The fourth and final stage is one of consolidation and integration. "The client is now protesting significantly less if at all about the therapist's definition of him as a person. If he does protest, he does it impa-

tiently or humorously and is increasingly confident in his present self's adaptive and coping capacities" (1974, p. 137). Box 14-6 provides an example of stage four consolidation and integration.

BECOMING A PROVOCATIVE THERAPIST

Being a successful provocative therapist requires a good deal of personal learning. Practicing the techniques must involve far more than mechanical imi-

---

Box 14-5: Example of Provocative Therapy Stage Three—Clarification and Protest

Patient: (persuadingly) But it's because I don't like myself that I do these things.
Therapist: (remonstrating) No, no, no! It's because you do these things, that's why you—
Patient: (interjecting) No—
Therapist: (finishing) don't like yourself.
Patient: (louder) No—
Therapist: (overriding her) Oh, you got it all back-asswards.
Patient: (even more loudly and firmly) You're wrong!
Therapist: (matching her tone) What do you mean, I'm wrong?
Patient: (attempting to explain) It's 'cause—
Therapist: (pompously, not waiting for her reply) Hell, you're just a patient and I'm a therapist. Now how the hell do you know, where do you get off telling me I'm wrong?
Patient: (evenly, with assurance) Well, you're not infallible Mr. Frank Farrelly.
Therapist: (laughs) Oh I'm not? And I could be wrong, is that what you mean?
Patient: (with assured firmness) Yes, you're wrong. You're wrong about me. I'm not as, as evil, and not as wicked, and not as—damnable, and not as, as hopeless—*(phone rings, therapist ignoring it)* and not as—*(phone rings again, therapist puts hand on receiver but doesn't lift it, waits for patient to finish)*—inadequate as you contend. *(Patient laughs, nods head abruptly)* There!

From F. Farrelly and J. Brandsma, *Provocative Therapy*, (p. 137), Cupertino, CA: Meta Publications, 1974. Reprinted by permission of the author and the publisher.

---

tation. Farrelly and Brandsma have observed others in the process of being provocative therapists, and they have identified—somewhat impressionistically, they admit—seven stages that seem to appear fairly regularly (Box 14-7).

CONCLUDING COMMENTS

Farrelly and Brandsma's techniques tend to force their patients to prove how healthy they are, if only to prove how wrong their therapist is. It is clear that there is a strong underlying sense of good will that accompanies the provocations in this therapy and that the strategy of helping patients get well by pointing out, tongue in cheek, how wonderful it is to be sick can be effective if undertaken judiciously.

Farrelly stands out dramatically from other cognitive behavioral therapists. He believes that inside many traditional psychotherapists is a provocative therapist "screaming to be let out" (1974, p. 171). Only each individual reader will know whether that hypothesis is true for him or her. But the choice is not one of either "yes" or "no" to provocative therapy; there is much room along that continuum.

Some therapists report that after being exposed to the ideas of provocative therapy they feel differently about their patients—they no longer believe that their patients are as fragile or weak or incapable as they previously thought. They are able to use humor in their psychotherapy more easily than before. Some therapists report that they are more honest and open with patients, that they can work effectively with a wider variety of patients, or that they are far less uneasy about their own reactions to their patients, being now able to use those reactions therapeutically.

This book is designed to provide practicing clinicians with new ways of thinking about their patients and about what they are trying to do to be helpful to them. The ideas expressed in provocative therapy are exactly such new ways of thinking. The ideas add one more arrow to the therapist's technical quiver. How this arrow is used will be an individual matter, of course, but the ideas, as well as the therapeutic techniques, are certainly provocative in more than one sense of the word.

Box 14-6: Example of Provocative Therapy Stage Four—Consolidation and Integration

Patient: (thoughtfully, slowly, as though speaking with himself) You know, I have been getting so much warmth and real love from people lately. I can see that now, now that I'm different. But they really haven't changed that much, they were pretty much like that toward me all along. And yet, I just couldn't see it, or I would explain it away. But it was there all along and I was blind.

Therapist: (pauses, quietly sarcastic) Same old distorted perceptions huh?

Patient: (smiling, assuredly) No, no distorted perceptions this time, Frank. This time it's real, and it's been real for weeks. (pause, thoughtfully) You'd have to travel around with me for a couple of weeks to see the intensity of the warmth that people have toward me. I guess I never really, really noticed it before. But now that I'm more open to them, I can see it.

Therapist: (disgustedly) Aw shit, you're getting grandiose.

Patient: (shakes head, chuckles and grins)

From F. Farrelly and J. Brandsma, *Provocative Therapy*, (p. 138), Cupertino, CA: Meta Publications, 1974. Reprinted by permission of the author and the publisher.

Box 14-7: Stages in the Development of a Provocative Therapist

Stage 1: *Cringing*—"My God! That's no way to talk to these poor people in pain."

Stage 2: *Intrigued fascination*—requests to observe interviews, watch videotapes, or listen to audiotapes.

Stage 3: *Initial attempts at trying provocative therapy*—accompanied by anxiety, considerable tentativeness. Careful supervision is particularly important in this stage.

Stage 4: *Release from traditionally constricted role behaviors*—accompanied by enthusiasm but much questioning.

Stage 5: *Use of whole self as a therapeutic instrument*—increasing ability to catch the nuances, flavors, and sounds of the patient's and the therapist's own experiencing.

Stage 6: *Increasing confidence*—usually combined by two new but easily corrected errors: (1) abrasive and unhelpful confrontations; and (2) the use of humor and provocation to meet the therapist's own needs. In supervision it is important to remind the student that the purpose of the therapy is to help the patient.

Stage 7: *Continued learning, growth, and development*—as a consequence of internalization of the supervisory process and increasing self-monitoring and decreasing need for continuing supervision.

From F. Farrelly and J. Brandsma, *Provocative Therapy*, (p. 139–142), Cupertino, CA: Meta Publications, 1974. Reprinted by permission of the author and the publisher.

CHAPTER 15

BECK'S COGNITIVE RESTRUCTURING THERAPY

Overview

The Cognitive Theory of Depression

Cognitive Therapy

Concluding Comments

Aaron Beck's cognitive therapy, just like Klerman's interpersonal therapy, is identified primarily with the treatment of depression. But, in contrast to Klerman's interpersonal psychodynamic approach, Beck and his colleagues (Beck, 1967, 1976, 1991; Beck, Rush, Shaw, & Emery, 1979; Young & Beck, 1982; see also Phillips, 1985a, pp. 60–63; Weishaar, 1993) believe that depression, regardless of its severity, is the result of cognitive distortions. These distortions are based on errors in thinking, derived from early learning experiences, particularly in drawing inferences about the self, the world, and the future. These inferences result in external events being inaccurately construed to represent loss or deprivation. These chronic logical errors form the basis for a world view or set of assumptions, referred to as *schemas*, that predispose vulnerable persons to repeated bouts of depression. Beck's therapy is designed to modify these cognitive distortions.

Beck (1976), who was himself trained in psychoanalysis, suggests that there are some important similarities between his cognitive approach and traditional psychodynamic psychotherapy, in that both types of therapy require that patients engage in introspection, develop increased appreciation of the meanings they attach to people and events in the world around them, and modify the organization of their cognitions that results in distortions and unrealistic thinking. That is, Beck emphasizes

that psychodynamic psychotherapy has important cognitive components.

On the other hand, there are important differences between his cognitive approach and traditional psychodynamic psychotherapy. Beck focuses on conscious experience, while psychodynamic psychotherapy tends to be more interested in what is unconscious. Cognitive therapy may be more economical in time than psychodynamic psychotherapy and may be more easily researched and taught. Cognitive therapy rests on far fewer and far less complex assumptions than does psychodynamic therapy. Finally, while acknowledging the role of history in determining current behavior, cognitive therapy is less interested in causes than is psychodynamic therapy—it focuses on *how* the patient misinterprets reality, rather than on *why*.

THE COGNITIVE THEORY OF DEPRESSION

While acknowledging that depression involves more than a cognitive disturbance, Beck considers cognitions to be primary, in that they influence motivation, emotion, behavior, and vegetative functions. Cognitions influence feelings that in turn influence cognitions, resulting in the downward spiral of affect called depression. Depression is characterized in part by distorted schemas, which are the cognitive structures that organize experience and behavior and provide the structure for how people view the self, the world, and the future. Research studies that have examined many of the hypotheses generated by the cognitive model of depression have rather uniformly supported these hypotheses (Beck, 1991).

Depressive Schemas

The view of the self is distorted in depression in that people see themselves as inadequate, unworthy, and defective, with the result that they underestimate themselves and are overly self-critical. People who are depressed tend to minimize successes and emphasize failures. Depressed persons tend to attribute socially undesirable traits to themselves and to rate themselves low on socially desirable traits such as self-esteem and optimism.

The view of the world is distorted in that depressives see it as overly demanding, obstructive, rejecting, depriving, defeating, and dependency-producing. In comparison with nondepressed persons, depressed individuals dream of frustration, desertion, injury, and deprivation; recall more negative events in their past; have fewer pleasant memories; and tend to believe that they do not and cannot control their own fate.

Depressives are pessimistic and have a constricted view of the future, which is thought of as negative, without worth, and doomed. As a consequence of these views, all of which suggest that there is little if any hope in trying to overcome inevitable failure, depressed persons display psychomotor inhibition, apathy, and fatigue (Rush & Giles, 1982).

Depression-Inducing Attitudes

Beck (1976) has identified a number of attitudes commonly held by persons who have become depressed. He believes that these attitudes predispose people to excessive sadness. One major aspect of his cognitive therapy is to make these attitudes more explicit, so that they can be reconsidered and modified as seems appropriate. The most common of these depression-inducing attitudes are summarized in Box 15-1. Note that about half of these attitudes are "shoulds."

A perceptive reader will note the similarity between these depression-inducing attitudes and Ellis's list of common irrational beliefs (see Chapter 13, Box 13-2). Ellis has clearly noted this similarity but has identified what he believes to be the fundamental differences between his and Beck's ideas in the following statement:

> Other cognitive-behavior therapies—such as those of Beck...also accept these shoulds and musts as irrational and disturbance-producing, but they do not, as RET does, see them as primary and do not see that the misleading inferences, attributes, and overgeneralizations that also are irrational largely stem from, or are tacitly derived from, disturbed people's musts, and would much less often exist without them. (1993, p. 7)

COGNITIVE THERAPY

According to Beck, cognitive errors, underlying assumptions, and therapeutic interventions are linked. Seven major cognitive errors have been identified, each associated with an inaccurate underlying assumption and an appropriate intervention (see Box 15-2).

Based on their theory of depression, Beck and his colleagues have developed a treatment plan that focuses on detecting, examining, and testing automatic thought processes; developing alternative understandings of day-to-day events; recording dysfunctional thoughts; developing more flexible assumptions about the world; and rehearsing cognitive and behavioral responses based on these new assumptions.

Cognitive therapy is a comprehensive approach that involves therapeutic style as well as therapeutic technique; it requires a new way of viewing patients and their problems. Young and Beck (1982) refer to the therapeutic technique as *collaborative empiricism,* although the approach very much attends to the expression and investigation of maladaptive emotion and to the therapeutic relationship as well.

Beck's cognitive therapy has been evaluated as well or better than most other forms of brief psychotherapy, and the evaluations have generally been positive (Dobson, 1989; Hollon & Najavits, 1988; Rush & Giles, 1982, pp. 165–169). In general, cognitive therapy has been found to be as effective as or more effective than antidepressant medication or other types of psychotherapy such as behavior ther-

---

Box 15-1: Depression-Inducing Attitudes

1. In order to be happy, I have to be successful in whatever I undertake.
2. To be happy, I must be accepted, liked, and admired by all people at all times.
3. If I'm not on top, I'm a flop.
4. It's wonderful to be popular, famous, wealthy; it's terrible to be unpopular, mediocre.
5. If I make a mistake, it means that I'm inept.
6. My value as a person depends on what others think of me.
7. I can't live without love. If my spouse or sweetheart or parent or child doesn't love me, I'm worthless.
8. If somebody disagrees with me, it means he doesn't like me.
9. If I don't take advantage of every opportunity to advance myself, I will regret it later.
10. I should be the utmost of generosity, considerateness, dignity, courage, and unselfishness.
11. I should be the perfect lover, friend, parent, teacher, student, spouse.
12. I should be able to endure any hardship with equanimity.
13. I should be able to find a quick solution to every problem.
14. I should never feel hurt.
15. I should always be happy and serene.
16. I should know, understand, and foresee everything.
17. I should always be spontaneous.
18. I should always control my feelings.
19. I should assert myself.
20. I should never hurt anybody else.
21. I should never be tired or get sick.
22. I should always be at peak efficiency.

Adapted from A.T. Beck, *Cognitive Therapy and Emotional Disorders*, (pp. 255–257) New York: Universities Press, 1976. Used with permission.

---

apy, nondirective therapy, insight therapy, relaxation training, or supportive therapy.

Collaborative Empiricism

The formation of a therapeutic alliance is as important in Beck's cognitive therapy as in any other short-term therapy. Collaboration is important to ensure that the therapist and patient have similar goals, to minimize resistance, and to prevent misunderstandings. The development of such a collaborative relationship requires that the therapist be trustworthy, that communication be open and sincere, and at the same time that the therapist display a degree of confidence that can serve as an antidote to the patient's sense of despair.

Patient and therapist need to agree on a target problem, on the development of an agenda and an overall therapeutic plan, and on the importance of feedback both to the patient and to the therapist. In the process of cognitive therapy itself the therapist and patient need to function as an investigative team, working together to collect information, to develop hypotheses about the patient, and to evaluate these hypotheses by a process of logical examination of the evidence. The process of establishing a productive collaborative relationship is illustrated in the vignette in Box 15-3.

The Process of Cognitive Therapy

Six goals characterize the early sessions of cognitive therapy: (1) defining the focal problems, (2) setting priorities for problem solution, (3) reduction of the feeling of hopelessness, (4) demonstrating the rela-

Box 15-2: Cognitive Errors, Underlying Assumptions, and Appropriate Interventions

Cognitive Error	Assumption	Intervention
1. Overgeneralizing	If it's true in one case, it applies to any case that is even slightly similar.	Expose faulty logic. Establish criteria of which cases are are "similar" and to what degree.
2. Selective abstraction	The only events that matter are failures, deprivation, etc.	Use "log" to identify successes patients forgot.
3. Excessive responsibility (assuming personal causality)	I am responsible for all bad things, failures, etc.	Use disattribution technique.
4. Assuming temporal causality (predicting without sufficient evidence)	If it has been true in the past, then it's always going to be true.	Expose faulty logic. Specify factors that could influence outcome other than past events.
5. Self-references	I am the center of every-one's attention—especially my bad performances. I am the cause of misfortunes.	Establish criteria to determine when patient is the focus of attention and also the probable facts that cause bad experiences.
6. "Catastrophizing"	Always think of the worst—it's most likely to happen to you.	Calculate real probabilities. Focus on evidence that the worst did not happen.
7. Dichotomous thinking	Everything either is one one extreme or another (black or white, good or bad).	Demonstrate that events may be evaluated on a continuum.

From Beck, et al., 1979, p. 261.

Box 15-3: Establishing a Collaborative Relationship

Therapist: Now that you've heard my formulation of the problem, what do you think of it?

Patient: It sounds OK to me.

Therapist: While I was talking, did you have any feeling that there might be some parts that you disagree with?

Patient: I'm not sure.

Therapist: You would tell me if you were uncertain about some of the things I said, wouldn't you? You know, some patients are reluctant to disagree with their doctor.

Patient: Well, I could see that what you said was logical, but I'm not really sure I believe it.

From A.T. Beck, *Cognitive Therapy and Emotional Disorders* (pp. 223–224), New York: Universities Press, 1976. Used with permission.

tionships of cognition and emotion as they appear in the therapeutic sessions, (5) socializing the patient into the world of cognitive therapy, and (6) underlining the importance of self-help homework assignments.

Most sessions begin with agenda setting, which in turn depends on the patient's experiences and homework since the last session. After the agenda for the session has been established, the therapist proceeds to explore the patient's most salient problem, with a view toward identifying thoughts or behaviors to modify. Then the therapist selects and employs the most appropriate techniques to use and explains their rationale. Most sessions end with a request for the patient to summarize (sometimes in writing) the major conclusions that have been derived during the session, evaluate the session, and plan an appropriate homework assignment.

Cognitive Therapy Techniques

Cognitive therapy techniques can be divided into two major categories: (1) locating and investigating automatic thoughts and (2) identifying and analyzing the validity of maladaptive underlying assumptions (Young & Beck, 1982). Automatic thoughts occur, often without awareness, between the time an external event takes place and the person reacts to the event. These thoughts tend not only to be auto-

matic, but also to be repetitive, plausible, and idiosyncratic, and it is crucial to identify them if cognitive therapy is to be successful. The techniques that have been developed for discovering such automatic thoughts include inductive questioning, such as ascertaining the meaning of an event, imagery, role playing, examination of mood shifts during the therapy session, and keeping a daily record.

The use of imagery is illustrated by the vignette in Box 15-4.

Once an automatic thought has been identified, its validity needs to be investigated—a process that requires the patient to be willing to consider the possibility that the thought may be inaccurate. The procedures that can be used to examine the validity of an identified automatic thought include examining available evidence, setting up an experiment, inductive questioning, operationalizing a negative construct, reattribution, and generating alternatives. Box 15-5 provides an example of setting up an experiment.

Behind automatic thoughts are, as we have seen, self-imposed rules, or assumptions, that help determine how people respond to life events. Many of these assumptions are maladaptive, in that they are overly rigid, unrealistic, or absolutist. Maladaptive assumptions are often more difficult to overcome than are automatic thoughts. Young and Beck

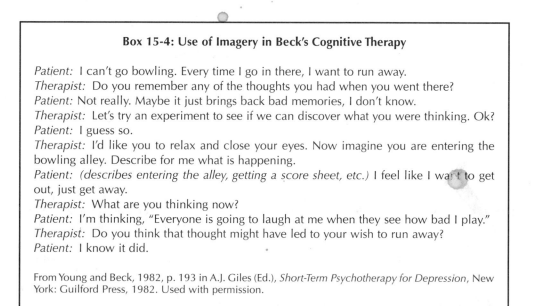

Box 15-4: Use of Imagery in Beck's Cognitive Therapy

Patient: I can't go bowling. Every time I go in there, I want to run away.
Therapist: Do you remember any of the thoughts you had when you went there?
Patient: Not really. Maybe it just brings back bad memories, I don't know.
Therapist: Let's try an experiment to see if we can discover what you were thinking. Ok?
Patient: I guess so.
Therapist: I'd like you to relax and close your eyes. Now imagine you are entering the bowling alley. Describe for me what is happening.
Patient: (describes entering the alley, getting a score sheet, etc.) I feel like I want to get out, just get away.
Therapist: What are you thinking now?
Patient: I'm thinking, "Everyone is going to laugh at me when they see how bad I play."
Therapist: Do you think that thought might have led to your wish to run away?
Patient: I know it did.

From Young and Beck, 1982, p. 193 in A.J. Giles (Ed.), *Short-Term Psychotherapy for Depression*, New York: Guilford Press, 1982. Used with permission.

Box 15-5: Setting Up an Experiment in Beck's Cognitive Therapy

Patient: I can't concentrate on anything anymore.
Therapist: How could you test that out?
Patient: I guess I could try reading something.
Therapist: Here's a newspaper. What section do you usually read?
Patient: I used to enjoy the sports section.
Therapist: Here's an article on the Penn basketball game last night. How long do you think you'll be able to concentrate on it?
Patient: I doubt I could get past the first paragraph.
Therapist: Let's write down the prediction. *(Patient writes, "one paragraph.")* Now, let's test it out. Keep reading until you can't concentrate anymore. This will give us valuable information.
Patient: (reads the entire article) I'm finished.
Therapist: How far did you get?
Patient: I finished it.
Therapist: Let's write down the results of the experiment. *(Patient writes, "eight paragraphs.")* You said before that you couldn't concentrate on anything. Do you still believe that?
Patient: Well, my concentration's not as good as it used to be.
Therapist: That's right. However, you have retained some ability. The next step is to improve your concentration.

From Young and Beck, 1982, pp. 197–198 in A.J. Giles (Eds.), *Short-Term Psychotherapy for Depression,* New York: Guilford Press, 1982. Used with permission.

(1982) tend to think of these maladaptive assumptions as life-guiding aphorisms, such as "In order to be happy, I have to be successful in everything I try to do," or "I should always work up to my potential," or "I can't live without love." The task of the therapist is to help the patient develop evidence against the assumption. In Box 15-6 are two examples of the skillful analysis of the validity of a maladaptive assumption.

Behavioral Therapy Techniques

While cognitive therapy techniques are essentially intrapsychic, a parallel in external behavior exists, in that patients are helped to cope more successfully with situational or interpersonal problems. Behavioral techniques, usually designed to modify dysfunctional cognitions, occur early in the therapy. Thus, a depressed person who believes that "I can't enjoy anything any more" (a dysfunctional cognition), for example, is asked to complete a series of behavioral assignments designed to increase the number and variety of activities that bring pleasure. The behavioral change can then be used to help bring about a cognitive change. Six behavioral techniques that have been specifically identified by Young and Beck (1982) are summarized in Box 15-7.

Use of Questions

According to Beck, most of the comments by the therapist should be in the form of questions. Questions can help make a patient aware of a particular problem area and the significance or meaning of that problem; can provide data to help the therapist assess the patient's reactions to this new awareness, for example, information about coping styles, tolerance for stress, or general level of functioning; can generate possible solutions or alternative approaches to troublesome dilemmas; can elicit automatic thoughts that seem to be generated by the problem; and can raise doubts in the patient's mind about current opinions or actions. Box 15-8 presents some excerpts that demonstrate the use of questioning in cognitive therapy.

Box 15-6: Analyzing the Validity of Maladaptive Assumptions

Patient: I guess I believe that I should always work up to my potential.

Therapist: What is that?

Patient: Otherwise I'd be wasting time.

Therapist: But what is the *long-range* goal in working up to your potential?

Patient: (*long pause*) I've never really thought about that. I've just assumed that I should.

Therapist: Are there any positive things you give up by always having to work up to your potential?

Patient: I suppose it makes it hard to relax or take a vacation.

Therapist: What about "living up to your potential" to enjoy yourself and relax? Is that important at all?

Patient: I've never really thought of it that way.

Therapist: Maybe we can work on giving yourself permission *not* to work up to your potential at all times.

* * *

Patient: I have to give a talk before my class tomorrow and I'm scared stiff.

Therapist: What are you afraid of?

Patient: I think I'll make a fool of myself.

Therapist: Suppose you do make a fool of yourself—why is that so bad?

Patient: I'll never live it down.

Therapist: "Never" is a long time. Now look here, suppose they ridicule you. Can you die from it?

Patient: Of course not.

Therapist: Suppose they decide you're the worst public speaker that ever lived. Will this ruin your future career?

Patient: No, but it would be nice if I could be a good speaker.

Therapist: Sure it would be nice. But if you flubbed it, would your parents or your wife disown you?

Patient: No. They're very sympathetic.

Therapist: Well, what would be so awful about it?

Patient: I would feel pretty bad.

Therapist: For how long?

Patient: For about a day or two.

Therapist: And then what?

Patient: Then I'd be OK.

Therapist: So you're scaring yourself just as though your fate hangs in the balance.

Patient: That's right. It does feel as though my whole future is at stake.

Therapist: Now somewhere along the line, your thinking got fouled up, and you tend to regard any failure as though it's the end of the world. What you have to do is get your failures labeled correctly—as failure to reach a goal, not as disaster. You have to start to challenge your wrong premises.

From Young and Beck, 1982, p. 201 in A.J. Giles (Ed.), *Short-Term Psychotherapy for Depression*, New York: Guilford Press, 1982; and A.T. Beck, *Cognitive Therapy and Emotional Disorders*, (pp. 250–251), New York: Universities Press, 1976. Used with permission.

Homework Assignments

Homework assignments provide an opportunity for patients to try out ideas and concepts in their real lives that they have been exposed to in therapy sessions. Successful completion of these assignments is considered to be extremely important in cognitive therapy. If homework assignments are skillfully selected, they should provide the patient with an opportunity to modify maladaptive behavior without relying on the therapist—by collecting necessary data; testing hypotheses; and, where such hypotheses seem incorrect, generating and testing new, optimally more appropriate, hypotheses.

Box 15-7: Behavioral Techniques Used in Cognitive Therapy

Scheduling Activities: The therapist uses an activity schedule to help the patient plan activities hour by hour during the day. The patient then keeps a record of the activities that were actually engaged in, hour by hour.

Mastery and Pleasure: The patient rates each completed activity for both mastery and pleasure on a scale from 0 to 10. These ratings generally serve to contradict directly patients' beliefs that they cannot enjoy anything and cannot obtain a sense of accomplishment any more.

Graded Task and Assignment: The therapist breaks down an activity into subtasks, ranging from the simplest part of the task to the most complex and taxing. This step-by-step approach permits depressed patients eventually to tackle tasks that originally seemed impossible or overwhelming to them and provides immediate and unambiguous proof to patients that they can succeed.

Self-Reliance Training: The therapist may have to teach some patients to take increasing responsibility for their day-to-day activities. Patients may begin by showering, then may go on to making their own beds, cleaning the house, cooking their own meals, shopping, and so forth. This responsibility also includes gaining control over their emotional reactions.

Role Playing: Role playing may be used to elicit automatic thoughts in specific interpersonal situations, to practice new cognitive responses in social encounters that had previously been problematic for a patient, and to rehearse new behaviors in order for the patient to function more effectively with other people.

Diversion Techniques: Patients can use various forms of diversion of attention to reduce temporarily most forms of painful affect, including dysphoria, anxiety, and anger. Diversion may be accomplished through physical activity, social contact, work, play, or visual imagery.

From Young and Beck, 1982, pp. 203-204 in A.J. Giles (Ed.), *Short-Term Psychotherapy for Depression,* New York: Guilford Press, 1982. Used with permission.

Box 15-8: Examples of the Use of Questions in Cognitive Therapy

Patient: I don't have any self-control at all.
Therapist: On what basis do you say that?
Patient: Somebody offered me candy and I couldn't refuse it.
Therapist: Were you eating candy every day?
Patient: No, I just ate it this once.
Therapist: Did you do anything constructive during the past week to adhere to your diet?
Patient: Well, I didn't give in to the temptation to buy candy every time I saw it at the store....Also, I did not eat any candy except that one time when it was offered to me and I felt I couldn't refuse it.
Therapist: If you counted up the number of times you controlled yourself versus the number of times you gave in, what ratio would you get?
Patient: About 100 to 1.
Therapist: So if you controlled yourself 100 times and did not control yourself just once, would that be a sign that you are weak through and through?

(continued)

Box 15-8 continued

Patient: I guess not—not *through* and *through.* (smiles)

* * *

Patient: I really haven't made any progress in therapy.
Therapist: Didn't you have to improve in order to leave the hospital and go back to college?
Patient: What's the big deal about going to college every day?
Therapist: Why did you say that?
Patient: It's easy to attend these classes because all the people are healthy.
Therapist: How about when you were in group therapy in the hospital. What did you feel then?
Patient: I guess I thought then that it was easy to be with the other people because they were all as crazy as I was.
Therapist: Is it possible that whatever you accomplish you tend to discredit?

* * *

Therapist: Why do you want to end your life?
Patient: Without Raymond, I am nothing. I can't be happy without Raymond. But I can't save our marriage.
Therapist: What has your marriage been like?
Patient: It has been miserable from the very beginning. Raymond has always been unfaithful. I have hardly seen him in the past 5 years.
Therapist: You say that you can't be happy without Raymond. Have you found yourself happy when you are with Raymond?
Patient: No, we fight all the time and I feel worse.
Therapist: You say you are nothing without Raymond. Before you met Raymond, did you feel you were nothing?
Patient: No, I felt I was somebody.
Therapist: If you were somebody before you knew Raymond, why do you need him to be somebody now?
Patient: (puzzled) Hmmm.
Therapist: Did you have male friends before you knew Raymond?
Patient: I was pretty popular then.
Therapist: Why do you think you will be unpopular without Raymond now?
Patient: Because I will not be able to attract any other man.
Therapist: Have any men shown an interest in you since you have been married?
Patient: A lot of men have made passes at me, but I ignore them.
Therapist: If you were free of the marriage, do you think that men might be interested in you, knowing that you were available?
Patient: I guess that maybe they would be.
Therapist: Is it possible that you might find a man who would be more constant than Raymond?
Patient: I don't know. I guess it's possible.
Therapist: You say that you can't stand the idea of losing the marriage. Is it correct that you have hardly seen your husband in the past 5 years?
Patient: That's right. I only see him a couple of times a year.
Therapist: Is there any chance of your getting back together with him?
Patient: No. He has another woman. He doesn't want me.
Therapist: Then what have you actually lost if you break up the marriage?

(continued)

Box 15-8 continued

Patient: I don't know.
Therapist: Is it possible that you'll get along better if you end the marriage?
Patient: There is no guarantee of that.
Therapist: Do you have a *real marriage?*
Patient: I guess not.
Therapist: If you don't have a real marriage, what do you actually lose if you decide to end the marriage?
Patient: (long pause) Nothing, I guess.

From Young and Beck, 1982, pp. 206, 207; in A.J. Giles (Ed.), *Short-Term Psychotherapy for Depression*, New York: Guilford Press, 1982; and A.T. Beck, *Cognitive Therapy and Emotional Disorders* (pp. 289–291), New York: Universities Press, 1976. Used with permission.

To enhance the success of homework assignments, therapists need to provide a persuasive rationale for the specific assignment and should present the task clearly, ideally in written form so that the results of the assignment can be reviewed at the next therapeutic session. Early in therapy the patient plays a relatively small role in designing such assignments but of course plays an important role in reacting to and evaluating them. Later patients can take an active role in helping create homework assignments.

Because the successful completion of homework assignments is so important in cognitive therapy, difficulties in complying with the assignments need to be discussed promptly. It is possible, for example, that the patient does not fully understand the assignment, or does not believe he or she can successfully complete the assignment, or does not really believe that completing the assignment can be helpful, or resents being given homework tasks.

CONCLUDING COMMENTS

Beck's cognitive approach serves as an antidote to the psychodynamic position that psychological difficulties are primarily to be understood as disorders of affect. While Beck's cognitive therapy was designed specifically for treating neurotic depressions, it has far broader implications for the treatment of psychological disorders. Accordingly, it is exciting to note the recent broadening of cognitive therapy to the treatment of personality disorders (Beck & Freeman, 1990), panic disorders (Alford, 1993), anxiety disorders (Butler, Fennell, Robson, & Gelder, 1991), eating disorders (Garner & Bemis, 1982), schizophrenia (Perris, 1988), and substance abuse (Beck, Wright, Newman, & Liese, 1993).

Beck has been single-minded in his examination of cognitive factors in the development and the treatment of psychological disorders. He insists that human beings are first and foremost cognitive animals and that cognitive problems demand cognitive solutions. There seems little doubt that cognitive approaches to treatment can be efficient and effective when cognitive distortions can be implicated in a presenting problem. From this point of view, psychological disorders are thought of as problems of the intellect, for which the optimal solution is a treatment that can be mastered by the intellect.

SECTION IV

STRATEGIC AND SYSTEMIC APPROACHES TO PLANNED SHORT-TERM PSYCHOTHERAPY

Strategic therapy is a directive approach in which both individual and family problems are seen as being the expression of dysfunctional organizational patterns within the family. The therapist begins the therapy by negotiating the goals of therapy with the individual or the family and then "proceeds to develop a *strategy* for achieving these goals" (Simon, Stierlin, & Wynne, 1985, p. 335)—hence the term "strategic."

Throughout this section the importance accorded the therapist as the active director of the therapeutic encounter will become increasingly obvious. Rosenbaum (1993) makes the same observation when he suggests that strategic therapy, rather than being a particular approach to psychotherapy or a particular theory of psychotherapy, can be defined as

> any therapy in which the therapist is willing to take on the responsibility for influencing people and takes an active role in planning a strategy for promoting change....Strategic therapists see clients' problems as being maintained by their attempted solutions. This being the case, strategic therapists usually work briefly, believing that frequently only a small change is necessary to resolve the presenting problem. (p. 109; see also Rosenbaum, 1990)

Systemic psychotherapy also concerns itself with the treatment of families. The term has been used specifically to describe the Milan model of family therapy (Boscolo & Bertrando, 1993; Selvini Palazzoli, Boscolo, Cecchin, & Prata, 1978), but more broadly refers to any therapy that views the client as embedded in a social system (e.g., Epstein, Bishop, Keitner, & Miller, 1990; Fraser, 1986). Rosenbaum (1990) links strategic and systemic psychotherapies by noting that "strategic therapists work with a systemic epistemology" (p. 356).

Both strategic and systemic psychotherapies have their historical and conceptual roots in a concern for family as well as individual dynamics. Thus, in introducing short-term strategic and systemic psychotherapies, we must pay specific attention to the social contexts within which clients function. But because strategic and systemic therapists believe that change can be brought about in a family system by changing a single element in the system, "family therapy" can be undertaken with individuals, and the theories and practices of strategic psychotherapists can be applied to individual as well as to family psychotherapy.

The goals of strategic therapy are to change interpersonal interactions. Even when an individual is being treated, strategic and systemic therapists tend to think about that individual within a family context, that is, as part of a system of interacting individuals.

Strategic and systemic therapists have relatively little interest in the origin of problems (predisposing factors), in how the problems first manifested themselves (precipitating factors), or even in why they are so persistent (perpetuating factors). Rather, the principal interest is with how the problems are to be solved (Held, 1986; O'Hanlon & Weiner-Davis, 1989). Goldsmith (1986) characterizes this orientation in the following statement: "Strategic psychotherapeutic practice is concerned, after all, with getting patients to change rather than getting them to be more aware of themselves" (p. 20). If the psychodynamic psychotherapist can be said to believe that "you are your past," and the cognitive or behavioral psychotherapist can be said to believe that "all that is really important is the present," the strategic or systemic psychotherapist can be said to believe that "we need to concentrate on the future—the present is important only in how it connects with the future."

de Shazer (1985), the founder of solution-focused psychotherapy (see Chapter 18), describes this future orientation as follows:

> For an intervention to successfully fit, it is not necessary to have detailed knowledge of the complaint. It is not necessary even to be able to construct with any rigor how the trouble is maintained in order to prompt solution....Any really different behavior in a problematic situation can be enough to prompt solution and give the client the satisfaction he seeks from therapy. (p. 7)

O'Hanlon and Weiner-Davis (1989), among others, have written about the remarkable differences between the assumptions of past-oriented psychodynamic theories and present- and future-oriented cognitive or strategic theories. They have noted that traditional past-oriented theories tend to subscribe to the belief that: (1) there are deep underlying causes for symptoms, (2) symptoms are functional, (3) insight into the causes of symptoms is necessary for symptom resolution, (4) symptom removal in the absence of insight is useless and may even be dangerous, (5) patients are resistant to psychotherapy and ambivalent about changing, (6) change takes time and brief interventions do not last, and (7) the fundamental task of psychotherapy is to identify and correct psychopathology.

In contrast, present- and future-oriented psychotherapeutic theories are based on a quite different set of beliefs: (1) patients bring with them into therapy the resources that are necessary to resolve their complaints; (2) personal change goes on continuously, with or without therapy; (3) the task of the psychotherapist is to identify and amplify change; (4) resolving symptoms does not require knowing the causes or the functions of the symptoms; (5) small changes are all that is necessary—these changes reverberate throughout the personality and can bring about changes in many areas of functioning; (6) patients define the goals for their own therapy; (7) rapid changes in behavior and problem resolution are possible; (8) there is no single right way to view symptoms; and (9) therapists should focus on what is possible and changeable rather than on what is impossible and intractable.

Important differences can also be identified between cognitive-behavioral and the newer strategic and systemic approaches to psychotherapy, both in terms of theory and technique; and as will be seen, they have very little in common. Small wonder, then, that a major section of this volume is being devoted to these new and exciting ideas. Three historically interconnected approaches to strategic and systemic psychotherapy will be presented: first, the seminal ideas of Milton Erickson; second, the work of the Palo Alto Mental Research Institute Brief Therapy Center; and, finally, the work of de Shazer and the growing group of psychotherapists who have been influenced by him.

CHAPTER 16

ERICKSON'S BRIEF STRATEGIC PSYCHOTHERAPY

Overview

Psychopathology as an
Interpersonal Phenomenon

Therapeutic Techniques

A Case Example

Concluding Comments

Milton Erickson, trained in psychology and psychiatry, was known for many years primarily for his contributions to the field of clinical hypnosis (e.g., Erickson, 1954, 1964). In addition, however, he developed a unique and original style of brief psychotherapy based in large measure on concepts derived from his understanding of hypnosis. Erickson worked in relative anonymity for some years until the 1950s, when other psychotherapists became attracted to his thinking and his methods. He had a highly productive 30-year career as a psychotherapist and died in 1980. Because Erickson's work is based on an interpersonal theory of psychopathology and psychotherapy, it is as pertinent and is employed as often for couples or families as it is for individuals.

Jay Haley, who first met Erickson in 1953, edited a number of Erickson's papers (1967) and described Erickson's work and underlying theories in a volume (1973) that is primarily a casebook. This work, read and approved by Erickson, is based on two decades of collaboration, and its details come from many hours of recorded conversations between Haley and Erickson. It is perhaps unnecessary to add that Haley is a great admirer of Erickson. He has tried Erickson's methods with success and believes that many psychotherapists can adapt these methods to their own styles. A summary of Erickson's clinical work has been prepared by O'Hanlon and Hexum (1990; see also O'Hanlon, 1985).

Erickson has left an extraordinary intellectual and clinical legacy. His ideas spread through Haley to Watzlawick and his associates (Evans, 1989; Haley, 1963, 1973, 1984, 1987; Watzlawick, 1978; Watzlawick, Weakland, & Fisch, 1974) and to Rabkin (1977), among others (see also Zeig, 1982).

In addition to his contributions to psychotherapy in general, Erickson made important specific contributions to the field of brief therapy. Fisch (1982) describes those contributions in the following way:

> In his work, Erickson opened the door for change and in that way had a major impact on brief therapy, as well as on therapy itself....First and, I think, foremost was what he persistently did not do.... Erickson did not ask for lengthy histories before he intervened in the problem....He did not measure the session by the clock, but rather by the task to be performed in that contact....He did not place importance on getting people to "express their feelings."...In this manner of speaking, he cut out a lot of the work of conventional treatment, long-term or "brief." However, in addition to not doing things, Erickson did some intriguing things....He did spend considerable effort in obtaining a rather detailed picture of the symptom, problem, or complaint....He would not interpret resistance to the patient, but would use it to expedite client performance of therapeutic tasks. He simply did not waste time arguing with patients, focusing instead on the task the patient was to perform to resolve his or her problem....In all of these above tactics, important messages are conveyed: that he and the patient are to get down to business, that change is

expected, that there are some simple things to consider and understand and tasks to be undertaken, which, however arduous, can and are to be accomplished. (pp. 157–159)

In addition, Erickson had great respect for the healing power of humor, of surprise, and of the metaphor. He could bring out the child within the adult, the humor within the presenting problem, and the possibilities for change embedded within a story told to the client.

PSYCHOPATHOLOGY AS AN INTERPERSONAL PHENOMENON

A rather direct relationship exists between one's theory of psychopathology and one's approach to psychotherapy. If psychopathology is viewed as learned behavior, therapy is designed to extinguish or unlearn the behavior. If psychopathology is thought of as the consequence of repressed feelings, therapy is designed to help the patient become aware of those feelings. To the extent that Erickson thought of psychopathology, he thought of it in uncompromisingly interpersonal terms—as a way of gaining control of a relationship. As such, his therapy was designed to help the patient develop better ways of dealing with relationships.

Haley (1963) provides an illustration of the relationship of theory to therapy in the case of a woman who sought psychotherapy because of her compulsion to wash her hands and take showers several times each day. From an intrapsychic point of view, the symptom could be viewed as a defense against unacceptable impulses against her husband or her children. The problem would be hers, and there would be no particular need to see her husband in therapy. In this case, however, her husband was seen, and the struggle between the husband and wife regarding the wife's compulsive behavior was quickly evident. The husband was quite tyrannical, and although his wife objected to his behavior, she was unable to oppose him except by her handwashing—a strategy that allowed her to refuse almost any request he made.

A psychodynamic approach toward treating this woman might well view the principal therapeutic task as helping the patient discover the causes of her compulsions in her own intrapsychic history. Such an approach would view the behavior of wife toward the husband as secondary gain. An interpersonal approach toward treating this woman would begin by noting the advantage the symptom gives the patient in gaining control of the relationship with her husband, even though the cost of this advantage in terms of personal distress is considerable. The pathology is not in attempting to gain control of a relationship, but rather in denying that that is what is occurring. Thus, one person's secondary gain can be another person's principal symptom (see also Watzlawick, Weakland, & Fisch, 1974, p. 26).

Erickson's interpersonal approach to brief psychotherapy was to be solely concerned with the patient's present predicament. He was not interested in helping the patient make connections between that predicament and the past, that is, with helping the patient gain insight, and ordinarily would spend no time exploring the patient's childhood or youth. Indeed, the most radical aspect of Erickson's approach was his apparent complete disinterest in helping a client discover the causes of the problem. Erickson did not help people understand their interpersonal difficulties, he did not attend to transference phenomena, he was not concerned with motivation, and he did not attempt to extinguish previously reinforced responses.

Watzlawick, Weakland, and Fisch write: "Everyday, not just clinical, experience shows not only that there can be change without insight, but that very few behavioral or social changes are accompanied, let alone preceded, by insight into the vicissitudes of their genesis" (1974, p. 86; see also Duncan & Solovey, 1989). Erickson's theory of change was based on the interpersonal impact of the therapist outside the patient's awareness. It included providing directives that caused changes of behavior, and it emphasized communicating in metaphor, a figure of speech in which one thing is likened to another. Many of Erickson's interventions were also paradoxical—"the specific tactics and maneuvers which are in apparent opposition to the goals of therapy, but are actually designed to achieve them" (cited in Selvini Palazzoli, Cirillo, Selvini, & Sorrentino, 1989, p. 3).

Erickson did not actually find concepts associated with the fundamental notion of psychopathology to be particularly useful. Fisch (1982) has noted that Erickson's ideas in fact made the very concept of pathology largely irrelevant. He did not view patients' problems as exceptional or unusual. Rather, Erickson dealt with patients as if they were perfectly normal and resilient, simply struggling, as we all are, with the human condition. From this point of view, concepts such as symptoms, defenses, or mental illness made no sense. Not only did he deal with patients as if they were perfectly competent, but he did so with all of his patients, rather than with only some of them.

THERAPEUTIC TECHNIQUES

Haley has used the word *strategic* to describe Erickson's therapeutic style. He writes:

> Therapy can be called strategic if the clinician initiates what happens during therapy and designs a particular approach for each problem. When a therapist and a person with a problem encounter each other, the action that takes place is determined by both of them, but in strategic therapy the initiative is largely taken by the therapist. He must identify solvable problems, set goals, design interventions to achieve those goals, examine the responses he receives to correct his approach, and ultimately examine the outcome of his therapy to see if it has been effective....Strategic therapy is not a particular approach or theory but a name for those types of therapy where the therapist takes responsibility for directly influencing people. (Haley, 1973, p. 17; see also Rabkin, 1977, pp. 5 ff.)

Madanes writes about a strategic approach to psychotherapy as one in which the "therapist takes responsibility for what happens in the therapy room and plans a strategy for each particular case. The main therapeutic tool is the directive, which is to strategic therapy what the interpretation is to psychoanalysis" (1990, p. 18).

Strategic therapy is thus directive and active in character and stands as a logical extension of hypnotherapy, in which the therapist generally initiates all that is to happen. But Erickson thought of hypnosis far more broadly than as a procedure in which a person is "put to sleep" and given suggestions. For Erickson, hypnosis referred to a type of communication between people. Hypnosis shares goals and procedures with other forms of therapy, and in particular includes two types of directives. First, clients are asked to do something they can voluntarily do, for example, sit or lie down, look at a certain spot, or concentrate on a certain image or idea. Second, clients are asked to behave in ways that are not under their voluntary control; that is, certain behaviors are suggested, for example, feel better, free associate, see something that isn't there, or turn off a physiological process. Like all other forms of therapy, hypnosis is based on a relationship that is voluntary, yet tinged with hesitancy and resistance. In this sense, hypnotists, just like other therapists, must deal with resistance, motivate clients to cooperate, and use a certain amount of persuasion (Kline, 1992; LaCrosse, 1994; Mathews, 1988).

Using Paradoxical Psychology

Many of Erickson's specific techniques were unusual, and Haley has singled out several of them for special comment. Erickson was often able to deal with resistance by labeling it as cooperation, that is, by working with rather than against it. If a couple fought continually, in spite of good advice to the contrary, he was likely to direct them to have a fight, but he would specify the place or the time, thus causing a change in their behavior. If Erickson sensed that a patient could not help but withhold information, he might have directed the patient not to tell him everything.

Erickson would often direct a client to engage in one of a large class of behaviors, knowing that the specific suggestion would not be readily accepted. In that case the client would choose to engage in another behavior, but still in the desired class. For example, Erickson might have wanted clients to exercise and would instruct them to engage in a specific exercise that they would not find acceptable. As a consequence, clients would choose another more congenial exercise for themselves. Erickson would sometimes encourage a client to relapse, when the client had been improving "too rapidly." He might say, for example, "I want you to go back and feel as badly as you did when you first came in with the problem, because I want you to see if there is anything from that time that you wish to recover and salvage" (Haley, 1973, p. 31). Such instructions almost always prevented a relapse. Erickson would often encourage a response by inhibiting it, for example, encouraging a silent family member to speak by interrupting him for a period of time whenever he looked like he is about to say something. Erickson frequently communicated in metaphor and by analogy. Haley writes:

> If Erickson is dealing with a married couple who have a conflict over sexual relations and would rather not discuss it directly, he will approach the problem metaphorically. He will choose some aspect of their lives that is analogous to sexual relations and change that as a way of changing the sexual behavior. He might, for example, talk to them about having dinner together and draw them out on their preferences. He will discuss with them how the wife likes appetizers before dinner, while the husband prefers to dive right into the meat and potatoes. Or the wife might prefer a quiet and leisurely dinner, while the husband, who is quick and direct, just wants the meal over with. If the couple begin to connect what they are saying with sexual relations, Erickson will "drift rapidly" away to other topics, and then he will return to the analogy. He might end such a conversation with a directive that the couple arrange a pleasant dinner on a particular evening that is satisfactory to both of them. When successful, this approach shifts the couple from a more pleasant dinner to more pleasant sexual relations without their being aware that he has deliberately set this goal. (1973, p. 27)

Watzlawick (1978) recalls that Erickson might treat a case of frigidity by instructing his patient to

> imagine in the greatest possible detail how she would go about defrosting her refrigerator…how she will approach this task, whether she will begin with the top shelf, or the bottom shelf, or perhaps in the middle. What she will take out first, what next?…How will she go about the actual thawing, and while she is doing this, what forgotten memories or completely unrelated thoughts might perhaps come to her mind? (p. 62)

Erickson's willingness to accept working within metaphors applied not only to verbal interchange but even to persons who live a metaphoric life. Such a style of life is typical of schizophrenics, and Erickson assumed that with a schizophrenic the important message is the metaphor. For example, Haley noted:

> When Erickson was on the staff of Worcester State Hospital, there was a young patient who called himself Jesus. He paraded about as the Messiah, wore a sheet draped around him, and attempted to impose Christianity on people. Erickson approached him on the hospital grounds and said, "I understand you have had experience as a carpenter?" The patient could only reply that he had. Erickson involved the young man in a special project of building a bookcase and shifted him to productive labor. (Haley, 1973, pp. 27–28)

Rabkin (1977) has written about Erickson's therapeutic techniques using the phrase *reverse psychology*. Watzlawick, impressed with both the research and conceptualization regarding the two-brain theory (our left brains being concerned with speech, writing, counting, and reasoning; our right brains being concerned with concepts, totalities, configurations, abstractions, and emotions), has written about Erickson's therapeutic techniques as "blocking the left hemisphere" (see Watzlawick, 1978, pp. 91–126).

Directing the Patient

Brief strategic psychotherapy is inevitably somewhat directive. Patients are told to do something related to their problems. Haley provides an example of a woman who complained to Erickson of incapacitating headaches that lasted for hours. Erickson accepted the headache pain as real and as necessary, but he was able to direct the patient to change the time of occurrence and its duration, so that she then had the headache every Monday morning for 90 seconds. One technique for helping a patient change is to ask the patient when he or she would prefer to have the pain—daytime, evening, weekends, severe pain for a short time or mild pain for a long time (Haley, 1963, pp. 44–45; see also O'Hanlon & Weiner-Davis, 1989, pp. 128–129).

A patient complained to Erickson that he was lonely and had no contact with other people, spending most of his time in his room in idle work. Erickson directed him to go to the public library where he would have to be silent and not have contact with others, and where he could waste his time just as he was doing in his room. But the patient was curious and began reading magazines and then reading about cave exploration. One day someone at the library asked him if he was interested in exploring caves, and soon thereafter the patient became a member of a cave exploration group that led him into a more active social life.

A 17-year-old enuretic was instructed to go for a two-mile walk whenever he awoke during the night after wetting his bed, and then get back into the wet bed. If he slept through an enuretic episode, he was to set the alarm for 2:00 a.m. the next morning and go for the two mile walk and then get back into bed.

A 65-year-old recently widowed man who suffered from insomnia and who had not slept more than two hours a night since his wife died was told that he could be helped if he was willing to give up about eight hours of sleep and if he was willing to do some work. He agreed. He had informed Erickson that he lived with his son in a large house that had hardwood floors. He did most of the cooking and his son polished the floors, because the patient hated the smell of floor wax. Erickson directed the patient to polish the floors all night, quitting at 7:00 a.m. in order to get ready for work. He was to go to work and resume polishing the floors that evening. He was to do this for four nights in a row. The patient polished the floor for three nights after losing six hours of sleep, but on the fourth night lay down to rest before starting the floor polishing and slept until 7:00 in the morning. A year later he informed Erickson that he had been sleeping every night. He would do anything to get out of polishing floors—even sleep (Haley, 1984, pp. 3–5).

Another example of this directive strategy can be found in the work of Bergman (1985). Bergman describes his efforts to help a professor getting ready to go to Paris for several months whose aging mother was telling him that if he went abroad she would probably not be around when he returned, and might even commit suicide. Bergman continues:

I gave the professor the following homework: He was to take his mother out to dinner and at the appropriate moment tell her all the loving thoughts and feelings he has had for her, both presently and in the past. He was also to tell her in what ways she was a good mother to him. If mother asked why he was telling her all these loving, positive things, he was to say something like, "Well, Mother, it sounds like you are probably not going to be around when I return from Paris and if that is the case, I wanted you to know how much I loved you, and I wanted to say these things to you before I no longer had the opportunity." Upon hearing this the professor's mother told him that he was talking nonsense and that there would be lots of opportunities for him to say these things when he returned from Paris. The professor left for Paris with a clear conscience and found his mother alive and well in New York six months later when he returned. (1985, p. 117)

A CASE EXAMPLE

While there are numerous Ericksonian case histories in the literature (e.g., Watzlawick, Weakland, & Fisch, 1974; Zeig, 1982), there are relatively few verbatim transcripts of the strategic therapist at work. The case in Box 16-1 is excerpted from Haley (1987, pp. 179–185) and is a good example of an active initial interview. Parenthetical remarks are summaries of a number of exchanges between the therapist and a married couple who were considering a separation and who had three children age 14 to 22. Bracketed remarks are Haley's comments about the therapeutic process. The therapist is Richard Belson, D.S.W., Professor of Social Work at Adelphi University. The interview was conducted in a one-way mirror room with Haley supervising it from behind the mirror. This initial interview is conducted with enormous skill, good humor, and a light hand. Only the first few minutes of the interview are excerpted here. The entire transcript is well worth examining in detail.

CONCLUDING COMMENTS

The literature on planned short-term therapy demonstrates the extraordinary influence that Erickson has had on both individual and family therapists. Erickson and those he has influenced have remarkably little interest in causes, in the past, in insight, in motivation, or in transference phenomena. Their

---

Box 16-1: Ericksonian Marital Therapy—Initial Session Excerpts

Therapist: Could you tell me a little bit about who you are and what you do? Let me begin with your wife. What kind of work do you do?

Wife: I work as a secretary in the university, and also attend class.

Therapist: Why the class? Are you trying to form a new career, or is it just your own interest in an education?

Wife: Just my own interest.

Therapist: What class are you taking?

Wife: Calculus.

Therapist: (laughing) So you're an advanced mathematician.

Wife: No, only second semester.

Therapist: I was taking some math in my college career, but when I came to calculus, I knew I was in the wrong field.

[The therapist then learned more about where the wife was working and then turned to the husband, who told him he was an electrical engineer and worked for a utility company.]

Therapist: So both of you have this mathematical thing in common. I don't think it's the basis for a happy marriage, but it's rather remarkable. I don't know many people in math, and least of all do I know a couple that both knew anything about math except to fight over the checks.

Husband: Well, she possibly knows more about math than I do.

Therapist: No kidding. So you're being very gracious as a husband that is about to get divorced. Which I want to ask you about. Are you interested in changing your marriage, or what is the change you would like from your wife that we can help you with?

[In this casual way the therapist slides from a social discussion into the issue of why they are there.]

Husband: Well, my wife has, evidently, a great deal of difficulty talking to me. I detect that she doesn't tell me some things. She won't talk to me about some things. She is acting like she's afraid to talk to me, or she's hostile, or something. There's some hostility there. It is uncomfortable and she would like me to move out.

Therapist: Why is she here today? What is it she wants from you?

[When beginning therapy with a couple, one usually finds that they have a list of complaints about each other. Sometimes they have rehearsed in their minds what they will say before they arrive. If a therapist asks each of them to say what the problem is, they can go on at length attacking the other. When that is done, the situation looks hopeless. It is sometimes best not to allow those speeches. One way to do that is to ask the husband, "If I asked your wife what the problem is, what would she say?" Then one does the same with the wife. Each then has to say what the other's complaints are. In this case, the therapist used a modified version of this approach by asking the husband what it is that the wife wants.]

Husband: Well, she said she would like me to come in for a couple of sessions, and I agreed to do this. I personally would like to see the marriage continue, but I think that she's getting very uncomfortable over the past few weeks, and I've become uncomfortable too.

Therapist: Well, when things start to get bad, it's hardly enjoyable. What is it your wife wants you to do that you're not doing? Could you be just a little more specific?

Husband: Well, I have a temper.

(continued)

Box 16-1 continued

Therapist: You, an electrical engineer, have a temper?

Husband: I get mad at the kids sometimes.

Therapist: I see. So she would like you to control your temper with the children. What is it she would like for herself from you?

Husband: Well, other than not yelling at the kids, I don't know exactly what she wants from me. She won't tell me.

Therapist: Well, let's just guess and then we'll ask her. What do you think she would say if I asked her what it is that she wants?

Husband: Well, I think she would want me to control my temper, but other than that, I don't know. I think there are probably other things, but I don't know what they are.

Therapist: Well, we'll find out very soon. Do you hit her?

Husband: I haven't for quite a few years.

Therapist: I see. Did you used to hit her badly?

Husband: Well, I hit her a couple of times.

Therapist: How long ago was that?

Husband: About 12 or 15 years ago.

Therapist: So it was a long time ago. Has she hit you recently?

Husband: No.

[The therapist has easily and quickly learned whether there is abuse in this family. In this approach there is no history taking to begin with, since that biases the therapy in a historical and information-gathering direction rather than one of change. Relevant aspects of the problem are sought and brought up as the first interview is conducted. The information gathered is then in context, not a sociological-historical review.]

(The therapist asked more about what the wife wanted, and the husband said she would like him to read less and get involved in more hobbies.)

Therapist: What are these hobbies that you used to do that she wants you to do? Make love to her?

[Again, in a casual way, the therapist slides in an important issue.]

Husband: Well, that is something she definitely does not want me to do now. She used to not feel that way.

Therapist: Was there a time that was a hobby she liked?

Husband: I would say yes.

Therapist: (when discussing the cost of hobbies)
Is money an issue between you?

Husband: I think it probably is.

Therapist: She thinks you make too much?

Husband: She thinks I don't make enough.

Therapist: How much money do you make?

(A brief discussion of income takes place.)

Therapist: Is it enough to cover your costs? I notice you have three children.

[The therapist has straightforwardly asked about the couple's income, just as he did about sex, as a therapist should with a couple.]

(continued)

Box 16-1 continued

(In the discussion of the children, it turned out that one daughter had just graduated from college at the early age of 19. They had a son who was, as the father put it, "moving along toward getting a degree. Slowly." They agreed he could be doing better, but it turned out the father never saw his grades. The therapist asked why not.)

Husband: Because he doesn't choose to show me.
Therapist: You're the father. Where does he get the nerve to talk that way to you?
Husband: I'm encouraged not to inquire. *(indicating his wife)*.
Therapist: Really. So there is some issue going on there too. Who is paying for your son's education?
Husband: My wife is.
Therapist: How did you make this arrangement between the two of you that the wife pays for the tuition? I mean it's an interesting idea. It's a new idea.

(The husband explained that when he had said he didn't have the money to send the son to college, the wife had gone to work to earn the money to pay his tuition. Apparently this couple quarreled over the years about this particular son. When the wife went to work to help the son, she benefited herself by becoming a more independent woman. Previously the husband had controlled all the money; when she went to work, she had money of her own. A problem for the couple was that the son was about to graduate from college, and they did not have his problems to communicate with each other about. That was when they began to have more trouble in the marriage.)

[This couple could be thought of as at the stage where a child who was an issue between them leaves home; then they must communicate with each other more directly. That situation can cause difficulties or even a separation, which was threatened here.]

Therapist: (turning to the wife) What if I asked your husband what he wants from you, what would he say?
Wife: Someone to wash the clothes and buy the food and prepare it and clean the house and run the errands and quit running up high bills.
Therapist: What about the bills?
Wife: It seems that whenever a bill comes in, there is a confrontation over it. *(mockingly)* You've overspent the clothing category again. You are not to spend any more money for clothing.
Therapist: So what you're saying is that you work together well around the money.
Wife: It's just easier not to say anything to him. We fight less if we don't say anything at all.
Therapist: So you're like passing ships. You wave to each other occasionally that you still exist.
Wife: Nope. Don't even wave.
Therapist: How long has this been going on?
Wife: Years and years.
Therapist: This trouble about money is one of the major issues. Is that it?
Wife: The struggle about money is a power struggle, not a money struggle.
Therapist: Sometimes in marriage people struggle about power. Are there any happy years you had together?

[Often with a couple in severe difficulty it is good to go to a time in the past when they got along well. That marks that period as a baseline and establishes the possibility that

(continued)

Box 16-1 continued

they can get along well again. In this case, the wife did not imply that they had ever got along better.]

Wife: There were years when we fought less.

(The wife described how they had been to several counselors over a period of years, sometimes in relation to their son and sometimes in relation to each other. She found it helpful. Her husband did not.)

Therapist: (to the husband) What didn't you like about them? I don't want to make the same mistakes.

Husband: I didn't see any change in the marriage.

Therapist: So that must make you a little bit cautious about whether or not this therapy is going to be helpful.

Husband: Well, I have serious doubts that it will be helpful. I think her mind is made up and she wants a separation. If that's true, this counseling is not going to prevent that.

Therapist: Do you think your wife has the slightest interest in seeing what could still be done? You know, a lot of things turn around even when they've reached a very bad point.

Husband: Well, that's the reason I agreed to come in at all.

Therapist: Yes. You've had a lot of experience in your life that sometimes when things look very black, they start to get better.

[The therapist emphasizes that a positive change is possible in their marriage, and he also begins to explore their plans for separation. Sometimes one can take a couple through a hypothetical separation and get rid of it. That is, they may find they will still be financially entangled, they will still be parents of the children together, and so on.]

(The husband in this case says he would live nearby if they separated, and he would have to support the wife and children. He would also visit the children.)

Husband: I think it would be a financial hardship on both of us, but I don't contribute much to the house.

Therapist: You mean emotionally, spiritually, sexually, or financially?

Husband: Oh, the tasks I do aren't much—dishes, a little work around the house. My wife would probably find the four-bedroom house too big for the one child left at home.

Therapist: (to the wife) What is your view about the possible future separation?

Wife: The house is too big.

Therapist: Would you stay in touch and speak with your husband?

Wife: Arguing on a false premise, I honestly don't know.

Therapist: A false premise?

Wife: That he is not at home.

[This comment was the first suggestion by the wife that she was not assuming, and perhaps did not want, a separation.]

From J. Haley, *Problem-Solving Therapy* (2d ed.) (pp. 179–185), San Francisco: Jossey-Bass, 1987. Used with permission.

---

interest is exclusively in the present and the future. It is hard to imagine an approach to therapy that shares less with the psychodynamic orientation (Fisch, 1982).

Erickson believed that all brief psychotherapy must be directive. His own approach was in fact extremely directive. It is in that sense that its relationship to hypnosis was emphasized, for in hypnosis, patients are instructed to do exactly what the therapist asks of them, even if they think that the therapist's instructions make no sense or cannot be carried out.

Perhaps the most original aspect of Erickson's work was his use of metaphor and symbol in therapy. Many of the therapeutic techniques he developed have been adopted by brief therapists who subscribe to a wide variety of approaches to psychotherapy. Erickson's creative maneuvers that result in rapid control over symptoms or improvement in previously pathological relationships have become a legitimate part of much brief psychotherapy. Erickson has rightly gained fame by skillfully assessing what change is possible for a patient and building a remarkably subtle therapeutic program around those possibilities.

CHAPTER 17

HALEY AND THE MENTAL RESEARCH INSTITUTE

Overview

Systematizing the Distinguishing Characteristics of Strategic Psychotherapy

Helping Change Take Place

A Case Example

Haley's Problem-Solving Therapy

Criticisms of Strategic Psychotherapy

Concluding Comments

The staff of the Mental Research Institute (MRI) in Palo Alto, California, founded in 1959, began its long-standing interest in brief psychotherapy in 1966. Many of its original staff (Jay Haley, John Weakland, Richard Fisch, Cloé Madanes, and Paul Watzlawick among others) had earlier been influenced by Milton Erickson., Their work was problem-focused and had ten sessions as its initial time limit. Like Erickson, they were interested only in the present and the future and were entirely uninterested in underlying pathology or causes.

In addition, this group continued most of Erickson's therapeutic techniques—the use of directives, metaphor, and reverse psychology. Watzlawick (1978) has described this practice by noting that "instead of engaging in the time-honored but futile exercise of exploring anamnestically *why* a human system came to behave the way it behaves," it would be more important to investigate "*how* it behaves *here and now* and what the consequences of this behavior are" (p. 158). Thus, according to Watzlawick, the intervention must be directed toward the failed solution.

Fisch, Weakland, and Segal (1982) describe the goals of this group as trying to see what could be done in a strictly limited amount of time by focusing on the main presenting complaint, using any active techniques for promoting change that any of them knew of or could borrow from others and looking for the least amount of change that would be required to resolve the presenting problem.

SYSTEMATIZING THE DISTINGUISHING CHARACTERISTICS OF STRATEGIC PSYCHOTHERAPY

The founders of the Mental Research Institute brief psychotherapy project were the first to systematize strategic psychotherapy principles (Fisch, Weakland, & Segal, 1982; Watzlawick, 1983, 1984; Watzlawick, Beavin, & Jackson, 1967; Watzlawick, Weakland, & Fisch, 1974; Weakland, 1990; Weakland & Fisch, 1992; Weakland, Fisch, Watzlawick, & Bodin, 1974; Weakland & Jordan, 1992). These distinguishing characteristics (Rosenbaum, 1990, pp. 354–372), are important enough to describe in some detail.

First, strategic psychotherapists are in the business of influencing people. Indeed, from a system point of view, human interactions are inevitably influential. The strategic task for the therapist is to plan that influence so as to be as beneficial as possible. Thus, there is no question as to who is in control of the treatment—it is the psychotherapist who is responsible for guiding the therapy.

Second, the client's view of the world is as important and as valid as the psychotherapist's. What the strategic psychotherapist offers is a new or different perspective on that world.

Third, strategic psychotherapists work from a systemic as opposed to a linear epistemology. Rather than believing that causality is unidirectional and is the result of the functioning of discrete independent elements, the strategic psychotherapist believes that reality is in relationships, specifically in the therapist–client relationship and that it is recursive—how the therapist construes events acts on the therapist to change how events are construed.

Fourth, strategic psychotherapy focuses on problems and their solutions. The therapeutic task is to transform a presenting problem into a nonproblem through the use of insight, reframing, identifying innovative alternatives to failed solutions, or whatever else might be helpful. Madanes puts this principle into a very brief sentence: "A strategic therapist must have a strategy" (1984, p. 139).

Fifth, clients' problems are maintained, in part, by their attempted solutions. That is, some "solutions" can make problems worse; the solution can be part of the problem.

Sixth, only a small change is necessary since any change can significantly modify a system. The strategic psychotherapist looks for the smallest acceptable change that will create the possibility for new behaviors.

Seventh, strategic psychotherapy is brief psychotherapy. Fisch, Weakland, and Segal (1982), in writing about reversing the vicious circle in which problems are maintained by continuing application of failed solutions, suggest that the therapist's primary aim "need not be to resolve all difficulties, but to initiate such a reversal. This also means that even severe, complex and chronic problems are potentially open to effective resolution by brief and limited treatment" (p. 19). Strategic psychotherapists approach every session assuming that it might be possible to create the context for significant and sufficient change. Clients are encouraged to change as little or as much as seems appropriate to them.

Eighth, strategic psychotherapists try to expand the usefulness of everything the client brings to the therapy. Even the actual presenting problem may be part of the solution.

Ninth, strategic psychotherapists do not use the concept of resistance. All client behavior, compliant or otherwise, is significant and informative. What one therapist views as resistance, another therapist may view as assertiveness.

Tenth, there is no single technique suitable for all clients; strategic psychotherapists design a unique approach for each client. Haley (1987) enunciated this principal in the statement, "A skillful therapist will approach each new person with the idea that a unique procedure might be necessary for this particular person and social situation" (p. 8).

Rosenbaum (1990) summarizes these distinguishing characteristics of strategic psychotherapy in the following statement:

> Strategic therapy is ultimately about freedom ... the freedom to change [or] the freedom not to change....Strategic therapy teaches choice ...the choice of embarking on different roads when you have reached a crossroad....As therapists, we see people who often are so intent on reaching their destination that they get lost in the woods; we also see people who are so lost in the woods they have lost sight of their destination. To some we give a compass; with others, we walk along by their sides; and with yet others, we may urge them to sit down awhile and look around before moving further....The pleasures of strategic therapy are the pleasures of aiding in a birth and wondering at what emerged inevitably. The strategic therapist looks not for finalities but for changes setting off in new directions. The completion of the birth is not an end, but yet another beginning. (p. 401)

Weakland and Fisch (1992) view the MRI approach to doing psychotherapy as interactional and behavioral. That is, problems brought by clients are thought of as an aspect of the social interaction between individuals in some interpersonal system rather than as wholly within a single person, and as consisting of some persistent behavior that is stimulated by the behaviors of other persons. Thus, resolution of problems specifically requires the therapist to facilitate behavioral changes by those who are part of the interpersonal system.

This approach is narrow in that it does not examine the origins of symptoms, it does not examine social systems beyond the requirements of changing the specific behaviors that are deemed undesirable by the client, it makes no particular distinction between what is normal behavior and what might be pathological behavior, and its goals are limited to resolving the original complaint. In addition, the approach is based upon the assumption that behavioral changes in any interpersonal system can be brought about by helping an individual member of the system change his or her behavior. Thus, the person who most appropriately receives therapeutic attention is ordinarily the one who is most interested in changing the behavior of the social system or who has the greatest leverage in that system.

The pertinent material of the therapy consists of some observable and undesirable behavior that persists despite efforts to change it and that provokes sufficient discomfort to lead a prospective client to seek help. Strategic therapists who subscribe to the MRI position usually find that the client's traditional efforts to solve the problem often make it worse; hence the belief that the solution can be the problem. Initially, then, the task of the therapist is to explore "*who* is doing *what* that is seen as a problem, *who* sees it as a problem, and *how* is this behavior seen as a problem" (Weakland & Fisch, 1992, p. 308).

HELPING CHANGE TAKE PLACE

With their principal focus on change, strategic psychotherapists have explored what change is and how it can be enhanced. Watzlawick, Weakland, and Fisch (1974) have written extensively about change, making a special distinction between what they refer to as *first-order change*—"one that occurs within a given system which itself remains unchanged"—and *second-order change*—"one whose occurrence changes the system itself" (p. 10). It is, of course, second-order change that is the key to the successful therapeutic encounter, for it can deal with failed solutions.

Watzlawick, Weakland, and Fisch (1974) provide an edifying example of second-order change in the following anecdote. Note that the intervention is aimed at the solution, not the problem, and that the situation is dealt with in terms of its effects rather than its causes—the critical question is *what* rather than *why*.

> On her first day of kindergarten a four-year-old girl became so upset as her mother prepared to leave that the mother was forced to stay with her until the end of the school day. The same thing happened every day thereafter. The situation soon grew into a considerable stress for all concerned, but all attempts at solving the problem failed. One morning the mother was unable to drive the child to

school, and the father dropped her off on his way to work. The child cried a little, but soon calmed down. When the mother again took her to school on the following morning, there was no relapse; the child remained calm and the problem never recurred. (p. 79)

The likelihood of change taking place can be enhanced by defining the problem in concrete terms; specifying, also in concrete terms, the change to be achieved; identifying solutions that have already been attempted; and, finally, formulating and implementing a plan to produce that change.

The principal way of facilitating second-order change is *reframing,* that is, changing the conceptual or emotional setting within which a situation is experienced and placing it in another interpretive context that fits the facts at least as well while changing its entire meaning. For example, a schoolboy can be helped to complete his homework assignment by forbidding him to work on his homework after the time he initially thought he would have completed the assignment. Enforced nonhomework leisure time is thus reframed as punishment for failure to complete the assignment.

In another case described by Watzlawick, Weakland, and Fisch (1974) a teenage boy was suspended from school because he was selling drugs, but the principal informed him that he would be given credit for any homework he completed. The boy was furious because of his suspension and was absolutely unwilling to complete any homework assignments. When the mother sought help, it was suggested to her that she report to her son that she had discussed the matter with other parents and believed that the principal, who placed great importance on attending class, believed that the boy could not possibly obtain passing grades in his courses since he was forbidden to attend class, and that he would quite probably fail the entire school year. She was to suggest to her son that he should not do too well on his homework assignments in order not to embarrass the principal. Upon hearing this proposal, the boy discovered his revenge—he would do well on his homework assignments in order to get even with the principal. Thus, completing homework assignments was reframed as a form of retaliation.

Fisch, Weakland, and Segal (1982) have divided strategic psychotherapy reframing interventions into two broad categories—general interventions that have broad applicability and can be used in a variety of settings; and specific interventions, formulated after the collection of sufficient data to justify developing a unique plan designed for a specific case (see Box 17-1). The similarity to Erickson's earlier work is clearly evident.

Box 17-1: Examples of Strategic Psychotherapy Reframing Interventions

General Interventions

1. *Urging the client to go slow:* "You need to take it real easy and go real slow, and not try to solve everything right away. Hold back, do very little this week. Make only the minimal changes this week. You need time to recover."

2. *Stressing the dangers of improvement:* "If you improved, it might have a deleterious effect on your husband. You see, if you functioned better, he could no longer boss you around and he might get depressed. I don't know if you want to do that to him."

3. *Proposing a change in direction:* "I had the feeling in the last session that we were stuck and that we were working at cross purposes. So I gave a lot of thought to that session and looked over notes from previous sessions and I realized that I had been missing the boat."

4. *Making the problem worse:* "I don't know what to suggest that will help you, but I can, at least, give you some definite advice on how to make things worse."

Specific Interventions

1. *Helping the client fail to eliminate a troubling symptom:* "If you can plan on being impotent and make sure that nothing interferes with that task, your mind will be more open to grasping what I believe is a fleeting but vital awareness."

2. *Requiring failure in mastering a feared event:* "While you said that you are too preoccupied with the dangers of driving, it seems to me that you have actually treated those dangers rather lightly. If you are to resolve your fear, as a first step you must be more appreciative of the dangers involved in driving. To get you in the mood, I want you to think about these things while you are sitting in your parked car."

3. *Placing the powerful figure in a powerless or unpredictable role:* Instead of insisting that a teenage child obey a specific directive (e.g., "You wear the coat to school. It's freezing cold, and if it gets warm you carry it home and that's it."), which the child rarely does, express uncertainty about what the child should do (e.g., "Is a sweater enough to wear to school today?" "Well, it's awfully cold, Suzie. A coat might be better." "But it might get hot this afternoon; then I'd have to carry it home." "Then probably a sweater would be fine.").

4. *Resolving chronic quarrels by agreeing with the accuser:* Instead of disagreeing with the accusations made by one member of a couple against another, the accused person can agree. A wife had accused her husband for over 30 years of not being any fun and of not earning enough money. The husband had characteristically defended himself by saying that he had done the best he could. He was encouraged by the therapist who saw him alone to make two statements—(1) "You're right. I'm no fun. The doctor helped me to see it." and (2) "They told me that I am too old to change." After a few additional rounds of accusation and agreement the accusations ended.

From R. Fisch, J. H. Weakland, and L. Segal, *The Tactics of Change: Doing Therapy Briefly* (pp. 132–171), San Francisco: Jossey-Bass, 1982. Used with permission.

The strategy that the therapist chooses to help the client change is a function of how much power or influence the therapist has in relation to the client system and how the therapist conceptualizes the problem presented by the client. Power can wax or wane over time, and therapists need to assess how strong or weak their positions are relative to the client system. Certain intervention strategies will be more effective when the therapist has large amounts of influence; when the therapist is in a relatively weak position, other intervention strategies may be more likely to succeed. Madanes (1984) has identified a number of questions that the therapist typically keeps in mind in conceptualizing the problem and thus in choosing the most appropriate intervention strategy (see Box 17-2).

Box 17-2: Questions Employed in Conceptualizing a Problem and in Designing an Intervention

1. Is the problem voluntary or involuntary?
   A young woman was displaying epileptic-like seizures, in large measure as an attention-getting device in relation to her parents. The parents are instructed to request that their daughter pretend to have seizures, and then to comfort and reassure her as they ordinarily did. The seizures thus become voluntary and achieve the same objectives as the involuntary seizures had done earlier.

2. How helpless or powerful are the members of the client system?
   In dealing with a child who was setting fires, the father is required to see that the child sets five different kinds of fires every day and that he put them out correctly and safely. The level of helplessness in both the child and the father is thereby reduced.

3. How egalitarian or hierarchical are the members of the client system?
   If a daughter is suicidal, the mother is asked to pretend to be depressed and the daughter to help the mother. Thus, the positions of family members are reversed with respect to who needs help and who is helped.

4. How loving or hostile are the members of the client system toward each other?
   Children can be put in charge of some aspect of the lives of their parents, such as their happiness. Children can express their love of their parents by taking care of them or by fantasizing how they might take care of them. Under these circumstances, parents can become more responsible and caring and can resolve their own problems. As parents improve, children can develop increased self-esteem and can resolve their own problems.

5. To what extent are the members of the client system motivated by altruism or by personal gain?
   In a family in which a daughter was seriously anorectic and the father was seriously alcoholic, the therapist made a contract with both father and daughter to the effect that if the father drank on any given day, the daughter could starve herself, but that if the father did not drink, the daughter had to eat. Thus, if the father drinks, he is threatening the life of his daughter; if the daughter continues to starve herself, she is threatening the life of her father.

6. Should the presenting problem be thought of in metaphorical or literal terms?
   If the person with the presenting problem is thought of as a metaphor for someone else in the family, other members of the family can be directed to have the problem. A father was asked to take over his daughter's depression for a week so she could be free to engage in other activities. As a consequence, the father's genuine depression was discovered and treated.

7. What is the optimal level of interdependence and freedom among the members of the client system?

(continued)

Box 17-2 continued

In order to disentangle the symptom from its interpersonal conflictual context, the therapist suggests that a special time, place, and manner be arranged for the expression of the symptom. Thus, other family members can no longer trigger the symptom. As the family carries out the instructions, they engage in increased positive communication and interaction.

8. How committed or resistant are the members of the client system to change?
   If there is a strong commitment to change, symptoms can be linked to the very behavior that the symptom is designed to avoid. Thus, if a wife spends excessive time housecleaning in order to avoid being with her husband, the couple can agree: (1) the wife should have a normal work day; (2) if the wife engaged in housecleaning before dinner but beyond the normal work day, the husband would take her out to dinner; and (3) if the wife engaged in housecleaning after dinner, she would be required to lie in bed with her husband and watch television for the remainder of the evening.

Adapted from C. Madanes, *Behind the One-Way Mirror: Advances in the Practice of Strategic Therapy* (pp. 140–147), San Francisco: Jossey-Bass, 1984. Used with permission.

A CASE EXAMPLE

It may be useful at this point to consider an example of strategic psychotherapy as practiced at MRI (see Box 17-3). The boxed example is excerpted from the first two sessions of strategic psychotherapy conducted by Richard Fisch (Weakland & Fisch, 1992, pp. 311–316). While the identified patient is an angry 19-year-old son who has a 21-year-old sister, the treatment began with two interviews with the 47-year-old divorced mother. The son had recently been arrested following an altercation with the police and had a long history of physical aggression.

In commenting on the case example in Box 17-3, Fisch calls the reader's attention to the initial rather vague complaint, to his efforts to make the issue more specific and to reframe the mother's complaint in terms of her trying to be "reasonable," and later to testing out the intervention whereby the mother would describe herself as not as good a mother as she would like to be.

HALEY'S PROBLEM-SOLVING THERAPY

Haley's work (1987; Grove & Haley, 1993) also takes place within a problem-solving framework. His emphasis is on clear initial formulation of the presenting problem and design of an intervention that is sensitive to the social context of the problem and that has the potential for changing the presenting symptoms. Haley (1987) defines a problem as behavior that is "part of a sequence of acts among several persons" (p. 2). Since symptoms are viewed as adaptive to a social situation, therapy needs to focus on changing the social situation in order to change the symptom. That social situation includes not only family members, friends, employers, and so forth, but also the therapist, other professional colleagues, and often the far wider social milieu.

Unless there is some compelling reason to the contrary, interviews usually involve as many of the pertinent members of the social system as possible in addition to the therapist. The first phase of the interaction, often accomplished in the initial interview, typically involves some brief period of initial socialization, inquiry about the presenting problem, conversation among the family members who may be present, goal setting, and the provision of appropriate therapeutic tasks or directives.

Directives

The concept of the directive is a broad one; in a sense, everything the therapist does can be thought of as a directive. Providing directives to individuals

---

Box 17-3: An Illustration of Strategic Psychotherapy

Therapist: What's the problem?

Mother: Well, I don't know what the problem is, but the reason he's here is he's angry.

Therapist: What I mean by "what's the problem?"—I don't mean anything profound by it and I don't mean the whys and wherefores, but just that, assuming you are coming in because you are concerned about him, my lead question would be, "What reason do you have to be concerned...what's the trouble?"

Mother: Well, he has been arrested twice. He did nothing wrong except he couldn't control his temper. He really didn't break the law but he kept hassling the policeman. He hassles me all the time. He used to be delightful and fun and laughing. Now I'm with him two minutes and I'm ready to scream. He's just angry. He gets into fights...that's not like him. I guess you know he's broken his arm five times now, three of them fighting. He's going to kill somebody or get killed. I...he's just not a happy kid. He's miserable and he's making me miserable.

Therapist: Can you give me an example of that or how would that go?

Mother: Well, recently...

Therapist: ...where he was fine, and then he starts to change in his behavior?

Mother: OK. Monday he came home from the hospital and he was fine and we discussed all this and he was so relieved and delighted and he was pleasant and helpful, and we'd laugh, and I said, " Bob, I haven't seen you laugh in so long." Everything was going great. I left for Boston Tuesday morning and I called in Tuesday night. First thing he says is, "Jean *[his sister]* isn't home. She hasn't been around. Nobody's cooked my dinner, nobody's.... I said, "Bob, wait a minute. I'm in Boston....I can't, I can't do anything about this." And I said, "Talk to your sister," and he knew where she was, "and ask her, if you need something, if she could come home. Call me back." This is in Boston. "Jean won't come home." "Well, you're mobile; you can take care of your problems and...." He called me seven times that night complaining. Finally, I said to him, "Bob, you're out of control again. You're, you're....All this good behavior is gone. You're right back to where you were." And then his sister called me there and said, "Mom, he's calmed down, he's OK now." I ...but...he's 19 and he called me that many times...? And I don't deal with it well. I just think, why can't he appreciate that I can't do this? *(long pause)*

Therapist: That's in part because the reasonableness doesn't work.

Mother: I always lose. I always give in first. I always back down. I can't deal with the high velocity thing. I've never liked it. I back off...and he knows that.

Therapist: When you get angry, what kind of thing would you be saying?

Mother: I would be trying to make him hear what he is saying to me; "Now Bob, why are you reacting like this? Why are you doing this to me?"

Therapist: The way you've tried dealing with Bob normally, is to try to be reasonable?

Mother: Uh huh, and I give in a lot. That's also a way of dealing with it.

Therapist: OK, but that's in part because the reasonableness doesn't work. He needs to come to terms...

Mother: Yes.

Therapist: ...he needs to grow up.

Mother: And he knows that too.

Therapist: Well, he knows and he doesn't know it.

Mother: I think he knows the difference...and what it's going to entail.

Therapist: And I'm saying that, in particular, I think a good part of your helping him would be avoiding, as much as you can, legitimizing his stuff, his comments when he's coming on abrasively, rudely, demanding, being unrealistic about it.

(continued)

Box 17-3 continued

Mother: I do what?

Therapist: Well, if you're not going to be reasonable, then, I guess, it would be some form or forms of being unreasonable. It would be any form that, mainly, would convey, without argument, there's no room for discussion on this. This is not a legitimate thing to discuss, any more than what should you pack to go to Mars. That would be in general. Let me show you how tricky it is, because to say, "Look, there's no point in discussing this" is to be reasonable.

Mother: Yes…"And why can't we discuss it? And just give me three reasons why we can't discuss this."

Therapist: Right.

Mother: "Well…because…" and then I'm into discussing it.

Therapist: That's right. It's tricky.

Mother: He's demanding. What do I do then?

Therapist: Well, as I said, it is how to respond to that in a way that delegitimizes his unreasonableness, because it needs to be for his own benefit, in a way, that just cuts it short, no discussion. It's not worth discussion and, also, where it doesn't lead to further polemics—that is, doesn't get his back up.

Mother: That's the problem.

Therapist: I'd say a part of it may depend on your willingness to be a bit arbitrary for his sake, because arbitrariness is a way of cutting short things, like "Go fight City Hall." I'm not saying to say that, but just everyday arbitrariness.

Mother: So I just have to be firm in the… "I can't handle this, I can't deal, I can't answer your problems; you're going to have to do this. That's it!"

Therapist: Well, it would have to be something that is just unarguable, no point.

Mother: I haven't found one of those.

Therapist: Well, if you don't mind the onus, since you've said, looking back, there are a number of things I've done, a lot of things I've done that I don't think have been for the best….

Mother: Of course.

Therapist: Okay. So to that extent, it would be quite true, you could say that you haven't been as good a mother as you would have liked.

Mother: Uh huh.

Therapist: And that if you don't mind the onus, you might be willing to say, "That's wrong." That after talking with me, you've come to realize that you haven't been "as good a mother as I had hoped."

Mother: And?

Therapist: Period. Then, when he calls and says, "I want you to take care of this," you can say, "No, I won't. If I were a better mother, I would."

Mother: How interesting! *(laughs)* This is so good because I would have come at it from the other side: "I am being a good mother now, by not solving all your…" and I would have gone into this long dissertation making me look OK because I wasn't doing what I *knew* I shouldn't be doing. That's wonderful!…Oh, it may not always work, but it certainly…it will stop him for a while.

From J.H. Weakland and R. Fisch, pp. 311–316 in S.H. Budman, M.F. Hoyt, and S. Friedman (Eds.), *The First Session in Brief Therapy*, New York: Guilford Press, 1992. Used with permission.

or to families has three purposes—to help clients behave differently and, as a consequence, to have new subjective experiences; to intensify the relationship between the clients and the therapist; and to gather important information by examining the behavioral consequences of the task prescription.

Whether dealing with a family or with an individual, directives should involve all or most members of the family. Directives may be quite straight-forward, particularly when the therapist has enforcement power, or may be indirect when the therapist has less authority. Directives may be designed to stop an individual, or a family doing something that they are doing or may be designed to get an individual or a family to start doing something that they are not doing. Therapists have to judge how much authority they have, have to make sure that their directives fit not only the problems but also the characteristics of the client or the family, and have to be clear and precise in prescribing tasks. In all cases, therapists should be expected to ask for a report from the clients at the next therapy session. With increasing skill and experience, therapists should be able to identify appropriate tasks more and more easily.

Directives may be quite transparent, as in the case of a husband who is asked to do something pleasant and unexpected for his wife that he has never done before, or may be quite metaphorical or paradoxical, as was the case in much of Erickson's work. Interest in the metaphoric aspects of behavior is not merely abstract; rather, it is quite practical. Madanes writes:

> When a family presents a problem, it is useful to think: If the problem is a metaphor for another behavior, for what does it stand? Who else in the family has a similar problem? What interaction is not possible because this interaction is taking place? To what interaction does this situation lead? What is the situation that is replacing another situation? To answer these questions, one must understand metaphors. (1984, p. 2)

Haley illustrates the way he uses the concept of metaphor by describing the treatment of a boy who had been adopted and who also was afraid of dogs. The boy did not know he was adopted because his adoptive parents were unwilling to tell him. The therapist used a metaphoric approach to the boy's treatment by discussing the possibility of his adopting a frightened puppy. Thus, whatever concerns the boy had about himself or his adoptive parents had about him were discussed in metaphoric terms in the context of the proposed adoption of the puppy. A metaphoric approach can involve action as well as words. In treating families, for example, when therapists act toward a child the way they would like the

parents to act, they can be said to be acting metaphorically. By making it clear what course of action is approved of by the therapist (adopting the puppy or behaving in a certain way in interactions with the child), the therapist creates the possibility that clients may emulate the therapist.

Paradoxical interventions are those that encourage clients to change by asking them not to change. For example, if a couple enters therapy because they chronically quarrel with each other, the therapist might direct them to enter into quarrels at specified times and for specified durations—often for longer than they typically quarrel. If the therapist has already established a productive relationship with the client or clients, if the problem is clearly defined, and if the goal of treatment is explicit and unambiguous, paradoxical interventions can often be quite effective.

Ordeal Therapy

A special type of directive, identified primarily with the work of Haley, deliberately creates some sort of ordeal for the patient but, at the same time, keeps the control of the problem in the patient's hands. Haley (1984) described the ordeal as a task imposed on a patient, that is appropriate to the problem but more severe than the problem (see also Goldsmith, 1986, pp. 69 ff.; Rosenbaum, 1990, p. 391–392). Furthermore, the ordeal should cause distress that is equal to or greater than the distress caused by the problem; should be good for the patient, such as doing exercise, eating a healthy diet, or making a sacrifice for others; should be something the person can do; should be something that the person cannot object to doing on moral or ethical grounds; and should not cause harm to the person or to anyone else. Usually successful ordeals have significant effects not only on the patient but also on the social contexts within which the patient functions.

Ordeals can be straightforward, as, for example, doing fairly strenuous exercises in the middle of the night if the symptom occurred during the previous day, or reading in the middle of the night from books that the patient should have read long ago but put off reading; or they can be paradoxical, as, for example, scheduling a depression at a certain time in the day for a person who came for psychotherapy because of a depression, or overeating or avoiding eating if those are the symptoms. What is important about these ordeals is that they put the symptoms under the control of the patient (see also Watzlawick, 1978, pp. 101 ff.).

In order for ordeal therapy to be effective, four criteria must be met: (1) The problem must be clearly defined, (2) The person must want to overcome the problem, (3) the ordeal must have an explicit rationale, and (4) the ordeal must continue until the problem is resolved (see also Watzlawick, Weakland, & Fisch, 1974, pp. 110 ff.).

CRITICISMS OF STRATEGIC PSYCHOTHERAPY

In describing the MRI brief therapy model, Weakland and Fisch (1992) have noted that "a number of people who have read our publications and then come to see our actual practice say, with some surprise, 'You really do what you say you do!'" (pp. 306–307). Because this therapeutic approach emphasizes the deliberate, active, but quite opaque use of influence by the therapist, a number of clinicians have expressed a certain amount of discomfort with it. Zeig (1985) has acknowledged that strategic psychotherapies utilize concealed techniques such as indirect suggestion, paradoxical techniques, confusion, allusion, alogical communication, and metaphor, and Booth (1988) has characterized strategic psychotherapies as having a kind of manipulativeness or trickiness and as misrepresenting the truth (see also Duncan, Solovey, & Rusk, 1992, pp. 220 ff.).

Fisch (1990) is quite aware of this possibility and has provided a useful discussion of the ethical issues that may arise in the practice of strategic therapy. Fisch writes: "When therapists are faced with getting clients to *do* things, they are faced with the task of persuasion. With the increasing interest in, and use of, strategic therapies, it is to be expected that more questions of ethical practice will come to the fore" (p. 429).

The issues raised in this debate are complex and their full discussion is beyond the scope of this volume. Indeed, it is not at all clear whether the issues that have been raised are really "ethical" or, more

accurately, "technical." But, as the previous paragraphs indicate, issues have been raised by some of its critics about the manipulative aspect of strategic psychotherapy, not as much in the case of Erickson as in the case of some of those who have been influenced by him, and it is appropriate to examine these concerns. Consider the excerpt in Box 17-4.

Fisch, Weakland, and Segal comment:

> Telling a depressed woman not to feel better and to deliberately mar her appearance does not make common sense. Neither does it fit with commonly held ideas about psychopathology and therapy—for instance, that patients need support and encouragement. Therefore, this therapist's behavior is likely to be considered simply illogical and quixotic, and to be dismissed out of hand—if not censured. (1982, p. 3)

But now consider the start of the next interview two weeks later (see Box 17-5).

Again, to turn to the comments of the authors, Fisch, Weakland, and Segal (1982) suggest, quite appropriately, that "what the therapist said in the previous interview appeared to have a positive effect, despite its strangeness" (p. 5).

Fisch (1990) has argued that: (1) manipulativeness is unavoidable in any therapy, (2) outcome measures should be the principal way of judging the value of any therapeutic approach, and (3) manipulation should be judged by the extent to which therapists are aware of its use. Zeig (1985) has made a distinction between more traditional linear psychotherapies, in which the client's understanding of the therapeutic process is overt, and "modern" approaches to psychotherapy, in which interventions may be quite indirect and not at all obvious to the client. He believes that admonitions requiring clients' informed consent, at least in the traditional ways in which that concept is employed, may be contrary to clients' best interests, or, to use his words, that "direct concrete communication may be antithetical to constructive influence" (p. 466).

CONCLUDING COMMENTS

The staff of the Mental Research Institute represent the first generation of psychotherapists whose work extended the extraordinary insights of Milton

---

Box 17-4: An Excerpt from the Second Interview with a Professional Woman

Therapist: You say depression is your main problem. Anything else?

Patient: Yes—I don't have any lasting relationships with men. They are all brief and unsatisfying.

Therapist: Could you describe that a bit more specifically?

Patient: Well, when I'm feeling relatively OK, I'll take some action to find somebody. I may go to a bar and meet a man there.

Therapist: Then what?

Patient: After we get acquainted, we may go home together. But it never lasts long. After a few days or a week—a couple of weeks at most—I don't hear from him anymore. And if I call him, he puts me off. Then I wonder what's the matter with me, and I get depressed again. This happens over and over.

Therapist: Are you depressed right now?

Patient: Yes—and I'd like to feel better.

Therapist: I can understand that. But I have to tell you that it really would not be a good thing for you to start feeling better, less depressed, right away. Let me explain why, since I know this may seem contradictory to you because you came here to get over your depression. You see, you have another problem: In some way—it's not yet clear just how—at this point, you don't know how to handle your relationships with men so that they work out to your satisfaction. In that particular area, you must lack some social skill you need. So, if your depression were to get better right away—before you have time to find out what you need to handle things better—then you would be in serious danger of getting involved with another man, only to have it end badly soon. And then you'd feel even more depressed.

Patient: Well, I can sort of see that, even though I'd like to feel better.

Therapist: Of course you would, but right now it's too big a danger for you. In fact, I'm concerned that if you got to feeling even a little better, you might be tempted to go out looking, and fall into a bad relationship despite what I've explained to you. So let me suggest a way to prevent that. If you should feel an urge or need to go out, OK, you may have to. But you definitely should do something to make yourself less attractive, so as to prevent or at least slow down this quick involvement in relationships—until we can get an idea of what you need to have them work out better. You don't have to do very much. If you do go out, you could just make a black mark somewhere on your face—as a sort of blemish.

From R. Fisch, J. H. Weakland, and L. Segal, *The Tactics of Change: Doing Therapy Briefly* (pp. 2–3), San Francisco: Jossey-Bass, 1982. Used with permission.

Erickson (see Chapter 16). Strategic psychotherapy may, however, underplay the importance of helping clients manage their own lives after the current treatment episode has been completed. This approach may run the risk of failing to make clients any wiser about themselves or developing enhanced general coping skills.

As a reexamination of the brief excerpt in Box 17-5 will indicate, the client is quite uncertain about the reasons for the obvious improvement in her condition. The interventions employed by strategic psychother-apists may result in rapid improvement in the case of the current predicament without providing a foundation for generalizing to other predicaments that may arise in the future. A similar observation has been made by Selvini Palazzoli, Cirillo, Selvini, and Sorrentino (1989) whose family therapy was initially significantly influenced by members of the MRI group: "Years of experience with so-called paradoxical interventions have taught us that we must restore to the patient the dignity of carrying out voluntary, comprehensible actions. We never consider the

---

Box 17-5: Excerpt of Interview Two Weeks Later

Therapist: Maybe you'd just kind of fill me in on where you are at this point.

Patient: OK. Well *(in a bright voice)*, I don't know whether I was at the end of my depression or what, but the suggestion given two weeks ago that I be very cautious about relationships because I really didn't know what I was doing, and so to—if necessary—even do something to enforce the fact that I shouldn't go into them too quickly. Well, I didn't see myself as needing a special kind of blemish, or whatever you could call it, to keep me out of relationships, because I don't see myself as really having to do that in order to keep people away. I see myself as doing a good job without intentionally setting anything up. Maybe that wasn't the purpose of it, but that's the way I interpreted it. Anyway, just that thought—that I really didn't know what I was doing, and maybe I should be cautious—uh—made me feel really good—and I kind of went around thinking, "I don't have to *(laughs)*, you know, meet someone; I don't have to have this wonderful relationship; I can just take care of myself," and—uh—it's like doctor's orders that I should stay away from this—this thing. And so I've been feeling pretty good for the past couple of weeks. And that was kind of a surprise to me; I didn't know that it would have that effect. But, as I say, I don't know; could be that I was at the tail end of what—maybe I was at the tail end of the depression. But I know when I thought about that, you know, "Beware of…"—it somehow lightened me, rather than making me feel deprived.

From R. Fisch, J. H. Weakland, and L. Segal, *The Tactics of Change: Doing Therapy Briefly* (pp. 3–4), San Francisco: Jossey-Bass, 1982. Used with permission.

---

patient's behavior compulsory, uncontrollable, or incomprehensible" (1989, p. 223; see also Cade & O'Hanlon, 1993, pp. xiii ff., and Chapter 22).

By concentrating on the here and now, however, strategic psychotherapists have learned much about human behavior and about ways of successfully modifying it. As a consequence, their writings have made enormous contributions to furthering the effectiveness of brief episodes of care. As will be seen in the following chapter, their work is, in turn, having an influence on a new generation of psychotherapists.

CHAPTER 18

DE SHAZER'S SOLUTION-BASED BRIEF THERAPY

Overview

The Ecosystemic Approach

The Solution-Focused Model

Concluding Comments

Solution-focused psychotherapy, developed in the mid-1970s by Steve de Shazer and his colleagues, originated as a promising approach to brief marriage and family therapy averaging five or six sessions per treatment episode. de Shazer (1982, 1985, 1988, 1990, 1991, 1994; de Shazer & Molnar, 1984; Nunnally, de Shazer, Lipchik, & Berg, 1986), who had been studying brief psychotherapy since the late 1960s, was one of the founders of the Brief Family Therapy Center in Milwaukee, Wisconsin when it began in 1978. He describes his therapeutic lineage as deriving from Erickson (1977; Haley, 1967, 1973; see also Chapter 16); Bateson, Watzlawick, and others at the Mental Research Institute in Palo Alto, California (Bateson, 1972, 1979; de Shazer, 1979; Watzlawick, Weakland, & Fisch, 1974; see also Chapter 17); and to a lesser extent from the work of the Milan Group (Selvini Palazzoli, Boscolo, Cecchin, & Prata, 1978; see also Chapter 22). In Milwaukee he joined with other family therapists who began to work together in the hopes of combining clinical practice, clinical research, training, and theory building into a synergistic whole.

de Shazer identified a small group of creative and enthusiastic family therapists who shared the view that a family should be thought of as a system of interdependent individuals and who worked together to learn as much as they could from their clients and from each other. The ideas being developed by this group of therapists and by others who have been

influenced by them continue to undergo change and are being conscientiously described in a remarkable number of books and journal articles (e.g., Berg & Miller, 1992; Furman & Ahola, 1992; McFarland, 1995; Nunnally, 1993; O'Hanlon & Weiner-Davis, 1989; Selekman, 1993; Walter & Peller, 1992; Washburn, 1994). These ideas appear to have enough generality so that they can be applied in individual as well as family psychotherapy and to working with children and adolescents as well as with adults (e.g., Klar & Coleman, 1995). Indeed, most of the more recent publications of these therapists include considerable attention to individual psychotherapy (Ahlers, 1992; Eisenberg & Wahrman, 1994; Kral, 1992; Neumann & Hudson, 1994; Rhodes, 1993; Tuyn, 1992).

THE ECOSYSTEMIC APPROACH

Because de Shazer's thinking has gone through a number of phases, it seems most appropriate to present his ideas in a historical sequence. Prior to the development of solution-focused psychotherapy, de Shazer (1982) was essentially problem-focused and defined brief family therapy as an attempt to help people change their *frames*, that is, their viewpoints or customs that cause trouble in the family. The therapy was intended to change, that is, to *reframe* the ways in which family customs develop, so that the meaning of the same concrete situation would be modified by being viewed and reacted to differently. de Shazer wrote:

> The effects of reframing are confirmed by the appearance of a new set of beliefs, or perceptions, *and* behavior modifications that can be described as a logical consequence of the shift in perception....The result is that the family can look at things from a different angle. Once they "see things differently," they can behave differently. (1982, p. 25; see also Cade & O'Hanlon, 1993)

The practices that set de Shazer's initial work apart from that of most others included systematic observation of the family sessions by colleagues and a consulting break midway through each session that allowed the therapist to meet with the observers to discuss the therapy session (see also Berg & Miller, 1992; pp. 95–95; Chapter 9) and plan the intervention that would constitute the concluding phase of the session.

Each brief family therapy session was divided into six sections: (1) presession planning, (2) the prelude, (3) data collection, (4) the consulting break, (5) intervention, and (6) postsession assessment. The therapy was conducted by a team, one member of which (called the *conductor*) interacted with the family while the others observed the process through a one-way mirror and provided advice and consultation to the therapist during the consulting break. Because there was a family group with its interdependencies and multiple points of potential intervention as well as a therapist group involved in the family therapy, de Shazer has called attention to the complex ecosystem that makes up the therapeutic environment—hence the adjective *ecosystemic* in his initial description of his brief family therapy.

Before the family's arrival, during the presession planning, the team members briefly discussed the family situation as they understood it and worked out a light-handed temporary guide for the benefit of the conductor. The guide was not thought of as a rigid formula to be followed, but rather as a set of provisional ideas about the family, derived from a number of different points of view.

The prelude usually took up the first 10 minutes of each hour-long session. During the prelude the conductor focused on the social context of the family in a way that might have seemed like small talk.

The conductor avoided discussion of the complaints that brought the family into therapy, trying rather to develop a helpful relationship with the whole family and to learn something about the specific world of this family.

The next half hour or so made up the main part of the session, in which the family as a whole was asked to consider which specific problem they hoped the therapeutic group would be able to be most helpful about, or what they hoped to accomplish in their work in therapy. In this data collection phase the conductor was accepting and noncritical and helped the family be as specific as possible about their complaints. One particular approach used by the conductor was to ask family members about their observations of other family members. According to de Shazer, it seemed easier for a person to describe the interactions between two other people than between himself or herself and another person.

The conductor helped the family formulate therapeutic goals. In this process the conductor might ask how the family would know that progress had been made toward their goal or how one family member would know that another family member thought that a start had been made in solving the problem. The conductor helped clients establish goals that were salient to them, achievable even though difficult, concrete, positive, and a step toward some distant objective. Meanwhile, the team observed the family and the interactions between the conductor and the family, seeking to identify and outline frequently observed family interaction patterns.

At the conclusion of the data collection period the meeting with the family was adjourned briefly while the conductor met with the other team members. The purpose of this meeting was to design an intervention. (A number of solution-focused psychotherapists have reported adjourning the session for a brief period of time even if there were no observers, since a break gives the therapist an opportunity to think through the session thus far in order to design an appropriate intervention.) The intervention always involved two components—paying the family a compliment and giving the family a homework assignment along with its rationale (see also Berg & Miller, 1992, pp. 101–102; O'Hanlon & Weiner-Davis, 1989, pp. 104–106). The purposes of the compliment were to provide a positive context for the therapeutic intervention, highlight the constructive moves already being made by the client by focusing on what seemed to be working, alleviate anxieties that the client may have had about the therapy experience or the therapist, underline the normal components of what the client was reporting, give credit to the client for efforts being made to change, and frame statements with which the client or family could agree so that they would be more likely to accept suggestions or assignments that followed (Walter & Peller, 1992, p. 114). For example:

First of all, we are impressed with all the fine details you've given us about your situation. Most families we've met are nowhere near as observant of these details. Your descriptions have been very helpful to us. It's clear to us that you are both loving and dedicated parents who've been resourceful in trying to find ways to solve the problem. Another unusual thing struck us: You each seem to care a lot about how the other parent treats the boy. Many parents would be only interested in the boy's difficulties....Between now and next time we meet, the team would like you each to observe what happens when you are alone with Jimmie and

he misbehaves like this. And we would like to know some other details: When during the week— which days and what time—does Jim most frequently misbehave while both of you are there. (de Shazer, 1982, pp. 44–45)

The team noted how the family reacted to the compliment and the assignment. The conductor gave the family a little time to clarify the suggestions and to react to the entire message and then moved to conclude the session quickly. Finally, after the family left, the team met to make its assessment of the entire session and to make its best guesses as to what was likely to take place with this family before the next session.

A CASE EXAMPLE

Box 18-1 contains an excerpt from the first session of a de Shazer case that illustrates some of the principles of ecosystemic family therapy in working with a married couple. The annotations are de Shazer's (1982, pp. 73–75).

Box 18-1: de Shazer's Ecosystemic Family Therapy—A Case Example

Therapist: What would you like to see changed?
Wife [Barbara]: Get rid of a lot of shame that I seem to be carrying around with me. Get more self-confidence developed and become more, have more spontaneity and less tension. Get the tension out of me. *[Peter—husband—is watching closely, nodding.]* And, in our relationship, I'd like to get more freed up in my sexual expression with you *[Peter]*, ah, my mind's gone blank.
Therapist: Ah, OK.
Wife: I've got a lot thought up I'd really like to work on.
Therapist: Obviously, we won't get it all in tonight anyway. So, when it comes back, that's the time to bring it up.
Wife: Sexual expression. I have a thing: I try to parent everybody, and I would like to be less of a parent to Peter...be more communicative than we have been. We've had some training, and that's improved everything, but I need to work on it more than I have been. And I really want to get out of this to be a better listener, particularly of Peter. That just goes across the board I think.
Therapist: Ah, that's a pretty good picture. How about you Peter?
Husband [Peter]: Well, for me it's increasing my confidence level to kind of develop or heighten my ability to accept responsibility for myself and behaviors. I tend to pass the buck, or blame situations on other people for my inactivity, or my lack of response. I think that is one of the real big hang-ups. I think—what Barbara said, sexual expression—freeing myself up to allow myself the pleasures, or to be in the here and now versus thinking about situations before they occur, or setting things up in rigid analytical thinking. Kind of putting aside my ego. Just accepting myself.

(continued)

Box 18-1 continued

Therapist: OK.

Wife: (overlapping) Are you done? A very big one for me is accepting self-responsibility.

Therapist: Well, what prompted you to call last week? Why then and not, say, six weeks ago?

Wife: Well, it's been put off. Procrastination. I keep thinking—each of us thinking—well, if we just work at it, use our communication skills, we should be able to handle it. I don't know what happened last week. I really got down in the pits again.

Husband: I think it was, for me, increased irritability. Just kind of heightening to the point of being fed up with the way things were going. Our conversation being irritable to each other. My losing patience and kind of pulling out. And, Barb getting down in the pits and depressed. To me, that was kind of the height, and I said, "Maybe we should."

Wife: I just kind of got pretty scared of, ah, just how I feel? Which feels pretty hopeless. *(Tears)*

Therapist: What's so hopeless? *(Scratching his head)*

Wife: Just me, and that I'm a worthwhile human being?

Husband: When Barb's like that, I find myself backing out of the relationship.

Therapist: (looking puzzled) After you back out, how do you get back in?

Husband: At times like that, I get a hold of myself, realize what I'm doing. Or, sometimes when Barb breaks down and cries, or says she needs some closeness, or whatever....

(The conductor then attempted to clarify some of [their] above statements about the problem and tried to get some specific information that was buried in [their] above descriptions. However, these efforts met with little success. The couple's responses to these questions were similar to the [previous] dialogue. Eventually, from watching the tapes (of this session and the next) the team learned some of the sequence: For some unknown reason Barbara would get "depressed"; then Peter would try to cheer her up in a playful manner. She did not like what she called his "little boy act," and so his attempt would further depress her, and then she would "back out."

The only concrete material to come out...was that Peter was rebuilding a valuable antique. Through very careful questions it was discovered that Peter had been working on this project for years. Lately he did very little work on it. This "gnawed" at Barbara because it was their plan to sell the antique to finance a move to another part of the country. So, periodically, she would nag about it, but he still would not do anything. Barbara saw this as a big worry since she really did want to move. In fact, she was afraid Peter would never finish it and, therefore, they would never move. Peter said he did not work on it because he was afraid the move would not live up to their expectations, even though he saw the move as probably helping him reach his real "potential." Therefore, it was safe for him not to work on the project and face the possibility of losing this dream.

At this point in the first session the team took its consulting break. The data around the antique were the only specific material developed in the first 40 minutes of the session. This type of systemic confusion paralyzed Barbara and Peter and left both of them to wonder about what it is that is going on. But finishing the antique was the only concrete item they both agreed about that the team could think of as a goal. However, the team decided not to pursue the matter actively because it wished to avoid seeming to be on "her side" by picking this as a formal goal. Although Barbara and Peter both said they wanted to move, when and where was very vague. Again, this seemed more "her goal" than his. The team decided to make further attempts at goal definition.

When the conductor returned to the session, he asked the couple to think about how they would know for sure that therapy had been successful. They thought this a good idea, and the session ended.)

From S. de Shazer, *Patterns of Brief Family Therapy: An Ecosystemic Approach* (pp. 73–75), New York: Guilford Press, 1982. Used with permission.

THE SOLUTION-FOCUSED MODEL

Continued clinical and theoretical work by de Shazer and his colleagues has resulted in the development of a most significant additional component to their theory and practice—what they call the *solution-focused* model of family therapy (de Shazer, 1985, 1988; de Shazer, Berg, Lipchik, Nunnally, Molnar, Gingerich, & Weiner-Davis, 1986; O'Hanlon & Weiner-Davis, 1989). This model, first described in 1985, represents a shift from a focus on problems to a focus on solutions.

Hoyt (1994b) has used the phrase "competency-based future-oriented therapy" to characterize psychotherapies that are concerned with solutions. O'Hanlon and Weiner-Davis (1989) have suggested that there is a growing interest in solutions among psychotherapists of many different persuasions—a trend "away from explanations, problems, and pathology, and toward solutions, competence, and capabilities" (p. 6).

In the case of treating alcoholics, for example, Berg and Miller (1992) have suggested that "instead of putting emphasis on stopping the problematic drinking, the more effective, economical, and efficient treatment approach is to elicit and enlarge upon the existing successful solutions that the client has generated" (p. 95).

The focus on solutions presupposes that there are solutions (usually more than one) that can be constructed by the client and the therapist working together. Constructing solutions requires that the client's goals be clearly identified; that the client do more of what seems to be working in achieving his or her goal; and that if nothing seems to be working, the client be helped to do something different. Furthermore, solutions are thought of as occurring in the relatively near future rather than in the more distant future. Thus, in response to client who says, "I want to make a decision whether to stay married or get a divorce," the therapist, realizing that this decision may be aimed too far in the future, might ask, "So if you were now on track toward making a decision, what would you be doing differently?" (Walter & Peller, 1992, p. 55).

Solution-focused psychotherapy has three objectives: (1) helping clients change how they perceive the problem that brings them to therapy, (2) helping clients change what they are doing, and (3) helping clients develop greater access to their strengths in order to bring them to bear on how they perceive their difficulties and what they are doing. The therapist can intervene to modify the presenting complaint by requiring the client to modify some aspect of the symptom—changing its frequency, or its timing, or its duration, or its location, or its context, or its sequence of component parts (O'Hanlon & Weiner-Davis, 1989).

Assumptions of a Solution-Focused Approach

Both Berg and Miller (1992) and Walter and Peller (1992) have identified the assumptions that form the foundation of a solution-focused approach. These assumptions are meant to be comprehensive and are presented in somewhat reworded form in Box 18-2. Since these assumptions guide the thinking and the behavior of solution-focused therapists, many of them will be discussed throughout this chapter.

Exceptions to the Presenting Problem

As part of the growing interest in solutions, de Shazer has taken special note of what he calls *exceptions*, that is, those occasions when the presenting problem does not occur. de Shazer (1991) comments, "For the client, the problem is seen as primary (and the exceptions, if seen at all, are seen as secondary), while for therapists the exceptions are seen as primary; interventions are meant to help clients make a similar inversion, which will lead to the development of a solution" (p. 58).

Nunnally (1993) exemplifies this interest as follows:

A couple who complain that they quarrel too much about money matters will be asked if they sometimes discuss money without quarreling. If the answer is yes, the next step is to explore the conditions under which they peacefully discuss money and examine with them how these conditions differ from the times when they quarrel. After identifying those elements that seem to make a difference between quarreling and not quarreling, clients are encouraged to expand upon these and report back in subsequent sessions on progress achieved in reducing the degree and/or frequency of quarreling. (1993, p. 272; see also O'Hanlon & Weiner-Davis, 1989, pp. 82 ff.)

Box 18-2: Basic Assumptions of Solution-Focused Psychotherapy

1. Focus on the positive, on the solution, and on the future. Emphasize clients' strengths, resources, and healthy attributes rather than their deficits and disabilities.
2. Exceptions to every problem can be identified by the therapist and client. These exceptions can be used to build solutions using the general principle that if you know what works, help the client do more of it, and if you know what doesn't work, help the client do something different.
3. Change is inevitable and is occurring all the time.
4. Small changes lead to larger changes. Minimal interventions can result in dramatic changes. Thus, therapists can be quite parsimonious in their interventions.
5. Clients are always cooperating and have all they need to solve their problems. They are showing us how they think change takes place. As we understand their thinking and act accordingly, cooperation is inevitable.
6. Look to the individual's particular complaint and attempt to find a solution for that individual rather than searching for a universal solution to a universal problem.
7. The client rather than the therapist is the expert. The therapist should accept and work within the client's frame of reference with the goal of helping the client discover his or her own problem solutions.

From Berg and Miller, 1992, pp. 1–17 and Walter and Peller, 1992, pp. 10–35.

Exceptions are thought of in four categories—*new* exceptions, which have only recently begun to happen, including changes that have taken place between the establishment of the initial appointment and the first session; *recurrent* exceptions, which occur regularly; *past* exceptions, which have occurred in the past but no longer occur; and *future exceptions*, essentially a time in the future when the complaints will have disappeared or be substantially reduced.

Solution-focused therapy, then, has three components—discussion of complaints or symptoms, specific attention to exception behaviors, and interventions. In the search for exceptions, questions may focus on the presenting complaints or on possible solutions and may focus on the individual or on the family system. In addition to the search for exceptions, interventions include provision of positive feedback and educative comments designed to create or encourage exceptions.

Goals in solution-focused therapy are narrowly defined in terms of the presenting complaint, and therapy is terminated either when the client's goals have been reached or when the client feels that the goals can be reached without additional formal contact with the therapist. Because specification of goals is so important, clients are frequently asked how they will know when their goals have been achieved and how they expect to be better off having reached their goals.

According to de Shazer, family therapists need to pay at least as much attention to solutions as to problems, since solutions involve someone doing something different and therapists are in the business of helping family members do something different. While most initial therapy sessions typically devote a large proportion of time to describing the problem that led the patient to seek help, de Shazer suggests that, with growing interest in solutions, less and less time is now spent in exploring the presenting problem. Rather, more time is spent in looking for exceptions to the problem—that is, for times when the problem does not occur.

Exceptions can often be identified by asking the patients (usually at the first session) to observe and describe at the next session what happens in their family that they want to continue to have happen (de Shazer & Molnar, 1984). This specific request is usually called the "first session task" in the solution-focused literature. Indeed, the same task can be assigned when the appointment is made for the initial interview; "Between now and the time you come for your first appointment, I would like you to keep track of all the things that go well in your life and that you would like to have continue" (see also Cade & O'Hanlon, 1993; Talmon, 1990). Note that successful completion of this task does not require the description of a presenting complaint.

In the subsequent description of things that go well in the family, the client will often report having done something different or having had something different happen—the observational data for solution-focused therapy. Since exceptions to the presenting complaint can nearly always be identified, psychotherapy is designed to help change continue rather than to initiate change. In Box 18-3 is an example of how the therapist can identify exceptions.

Box 18-3: Identification of Exceptions in Solution-Focused Psychotherapy

Therapist: You mean you did not drink for two years? How did you do that, with all those hassles going on in your life?

Client: It was no big deal. I just decided I was tired of it.

Therapist: How do you suppose you did that, I mean, not drinking?

Client: It wasn't that hard. I had to test myself whether I could do it or not. And I found out that I can do it.

Therapist: If I were to ask your wife, what do you suppose she would say it took for you to stop drinking in those days?

Client: I suppose she would say it wasn't easy. I was a mess. She helped a lot. I just kept busy, stayed away from my drinking buddies, worked out a lot. Actually, I got pretty healthy. I liked working out and really getting into the healthy life. I ate better and even quit smoking for a while.

Therapist: What do you suppose your wife would say was different about you in those days?

Client: She probably would say I was calmer. Maybe even more sure of myself. I spent more time with the kids.

Therapist: What do you suppose she would say was different about your relationship with her during that time?

Client: She would say that she was not as angry in those days. Actually, we got along much better.

Therapist: What do you suppose she would say it will take for you to get back into doing that again?

Client: Actually nothing. I just have to want to do it. I did it for two years.

Therapist: What do you suppose your wife would say it will take you to get back into doing it again?

Client: I will just have to get up early tomorrow morning and go jogging. If I tell my kids that I will be home by a certain hour, I will do it. I hated it when my father disappointed me, and I promised myself when the kids were born I would always keep my promises to them.

Therapist: Being a good father means a great deal to you, doesn't it?

Client: Yeah, they need me. They are so small and helpless. I'm their hero right now. I know it won't last, but by golly, I'm going to enjoy it while I can.

Therapist: So, I know that your children will not be able to put it into words, but if they could, what do you suppose they would say was different about you during those two years when you stopped drinking?

From Berg and Miller, 1992, pp. 112–113.

The Miracle Question

By 1988, de Shazer had added a new strategy for working toward solutions—posing the so-called "miracle question," nearly always in the first therapy session. This question, generally considered the most important question in the solution-focused psychotherapy model, takes the form of "Suppose that one night, while you were asleep, there was a miracle and this problem was solved. How would you know that a miracle had occurred?" Focusing this question provides an opportunity for the client to describe specific and concrete behaviors that help define what the solution would look like. Another aspect of the miracle question that aims precisely at the future is the question "What will your life be like when this misery is over?"

Client responses to the miracle question and to the request to imagine a future without the current problem help clarify the precise nature of the presenting problem by describing a world in which it doesn't exist. By concentrating on such a world, changes in behavior are encouraged, cooperation on the part of the client is enhanced, and the therapist can help the behavior change become significant in the client's life.

de Shazer writes, "Solutions to problems are frequently missed because they often look like mere preliminaries; we end up searching for explanations believing that without explanation a solution is irrational, not recognizing that the solution itself is its own best explanation" (1988, p. 10).

What is perhaps most interesting about the miracle question is that it creates an opportunity to develop a therapeutic encounter without paying much attention either to the past or to the present. That is, it is quite possible to work toward eliminating a presenting problem without knowing anything about the problem per se. Specifically, it is quite possible to resolve a presenting problem without understanding its origins or what perpetuates it. de Shazer (1988) describes this process as follows:

> No matter how much the client tells the therapist about the complaint, the conversation will be brought back to when it is that the complaint does not happen. Then the therapist will switch to working with the client to describe a vision of the future when the complaint is resolved. This is done with-

out getting a full description of the problem and/or its etiology and, surprisingly, it is sometimes done without discussing what steps might be necessary to resolve the complaint. (p. 51)

Concentration on future solutions can have a significant impact on how one views the past and the present. As Furman and Ahola (1992) note, people with traumatic past histories often have dim views of the future. Dim views of the future often cast a backward shadow on the past and the present. At the same time, however, a sense of hope in the future can help people cope with a difficult past and a stressful present. The potential usefulness of the miracle question is that it directs the attention of the client to a hopeful future. Box 18-4 provides an excellent example of how the miracle question can be used, even in the absence of significant exploration of either past history or the present predicament.

Here is an example of how the request to predict the future can be used in solution-focused psychotherapy (Box 18-5). Until the question is posed, this brief interview excerpt doesn't seem any different than any other exploratory early interview. But the question transforms the interview into one that is focused on solutions.

Influencing the Client's Language

Another strategy for working toward solutions is for the therapist to use solution-focused words and phrases as potential replacements for client's words and phrases that emphasize pathology and chronicity. For example, the therapist can refer to a clients' symptoms as a "transitional period," such as in the statement "It is obvious to me that you already have done several things to help yourself through this transitional period," or can respond to a parent who refers to his child as "immature" by referring to the child as a "late bloomer" (O'Hanlon & Weiner-Davis, 1989, p. 68).

It is equally important for the therapist to pay special attention to the tenses used by the client and to use a therapeutically more appropriate tense. Thus, in responding to a client who reports that "I binge and vomit every day," the therapist can say, "So you've binged and vomited every day for some time now" (O'Hanlon & Weiner-Davis, 1989, p. 69).

Box 18-4: Use of the Miracle Question

(Sirkka, who was a psychiatric nurse, participated in one of our training groups. She brought to the session Emma, a middle-aged unmarried woman who was a patient on her ward at the local psychiatric hospital. She had also invited several members of the staff, a physician, a social worker, the head nurse of the ward, and the patient's designated nurse to join the session.

We learned that Emma had been in various psychiatric hospitals for most of the past six years because of what had been diagnosed as major depression. The current problem, from the staff's point of view, was that she complained all the time and refused to talk about anything but her misfortune and her misery. I invited Emma to think about her future by asking:)

Therapist: What will your life be like when this misery is over?
Emma: Oh, it'll never be over.
Therapist: Let's imagine that it will. How would your life look then?
Emma: I can't even imagine such a thing.
Therapist: I understand that. But let's imagine that a miracle takes place one night and that you wake up in the morning and the problems are gone. How would you know that a miracle had occurred?
Emma: (after a short pause) This awful anguish in my chest would be gone.
Therapist: You'd wake up in the morning, you'd notice that the anguish is gone, then what would you do next?
Emma: I don't know. I guess I'd go to the hairdresser.

(This statement opened a discussion about her future. We imagined that after her recovery she would soon return home. When she was asked about what she would do when she was back at home, Emma said she might consider taking up the job she used to have. The group was curious to know what she had done before her "illness." It emerged that she used to have her own small catering business and that she had been so well respected that when the former president visited her town she had been asked to take charge of the catering arrangements. The excellence of her former reputation was confirmed by several members of the staff.

The group joined the discussion and questioned Emma about her past. She took pride in her answers, and the discussion about the subject of "life before the illness" had a remarkable effect on her appearance. She no longer looked like a chronically depressed patient from a psychiatric hospital, but like a dignified and capable woman.

At the end of the session I asked all present whether they thought that talking about future visions and past successes were subjects worth further discussion on the ward. Both Emma and the staff agreed with the recommendation. When everyone was getting ready to leave, one of the male psychologists in the group politely helped Emma to put on her coat and she was more than pleased.

A year later I was once again teaching a course in the same town. One of the participants was a nurse in the same hospital where Emma had been in treatment. She reported that soon after the session Emma had moved into a house of her own and had not returned to the hospital. In addition, the nurse had heard that Emma had helped in the recovery of another patient. She said she had been wondering about what had happened at the consultation. She had been on duty on the evening of the session, and when Emma returned to the ward she had spoken about nothing else but the fact that a psychologist had helped her with her coat.)

From Furman & Ahola, 1992, pp. 99–101.

Box 18-5: Requesting a Prediction of the Future

Therapist: So you were saying that you want to do something about your weight?
Client: Yes, I am just too overweight, and I hate myself for it. Actually, I think I overeat because I hate myself. I just eat out of control, you know, as if I just do not care how I look. I am trying to work the Overeaters Anonymous program, but I just get so discouraged.
Therapist: So you think that your being overweight is due to how you feel about yourself and you have been feeling discouraged and down on yourself, is that right? And when this is no longer a problem for you, what will you be doing differently?...
Client: I will be turning this all over to my higher power.
Therapist: So, you will be turning this over, and how will you be doing that?
Client: I am not sure. I have a difficult time seeing myself without this problem or weighing what I want.
Therapist: So it is not clear to you yet...So if it were clearer to you, what would you guess you would say?
Client: I think I would be eating and doing things in a "slow busy" way.
Therapist: "Slow busy"—what will that be like?
Client: I will still be busy because I like to accomplish things, but I won't think it all has to be done yesterday.

From J. L. Walter and J. E. Peller, *Becoming Solution-Focused in Brief Therapy* (pp. 43–44), New York: Brunner/Mazel, 1992. Reprinted with permission from Brunner/Mazel, Inc.

An excerpt from an initial interview illustrates how the therapist's attention to the tense used by the client can help induce a solution-focused orientation to the psychotherapy (Box 18-6).

Avoiding Traps

Therapists who have written about solution-focused psychotherapy have been particularly helpful in identifying difficulties that less experienced solution-focused therapists are prone to fall into. According to O'Hanlon and Weiner-Davis (1989) these traps can be grouped into four categories: (1) not knowing where you are heading, (2) persisting in doing what hasn't worked in the past, (3) not attending to clients' responses, and (4) reifying pathology.

Relatively inexperienced solution-focused therapists sometimes pursue their own goals rather than their clients' goals. They sometimes begin a therapeutic episode without a clear picture of a client's goals. They may lose sight of the goal, or be diverted by an impulse to go sightseeing.

The importance of trying something different in solution-focused psychotherapy has been mentioned

several times in this chapter. Persisting in doing what has not been effective in the past is another common error. Inexperienced therapists may repeat past therapists' ineffective approaches. They may try to do exactly what the client has tried in the past without effect. They may repeat well-meaning advice and suggestions of friends or family members that have not been effective.

Inexperienced therapists can forget to test out their interventions by observing how their clients react. They may fail to notice when clients are using solution-focused strategies. They may fail to interrupt their clients when clients are making unhelpful statements or posing unhelpful questions. They can look for resistance when they ought to be accentuating the positive and cooperative.

CONCLUDING COMMENTS

In its short history, solution-focused psychotherapy has gone through several developmental phases. With its focus on reframing and on the near future rather than on the distant future, with its concern for what works as well as what doesn't

---

Box 18-6: Attention to Tense in a Solution-Focused Interview

(The client is a woman who is married and has an eight-year-old son.)

Client: Jack and I lead very stressful...well, all America does, I guess. But we lead very busy lives. We both have supervisor positions. We're very busy and stressed. But I couldn't really figure out why...I figured out that I was mad at both of them and I couldn't really figure out why. So, I finally, after a lot of thinking, I decided that I was really resenting Jack because his life is, was, so stress-free and I...I'd constantly worry if the dishes were done, if the laundry was done. It's not his fault—Jack helps very much. It was carrying the responsibility around in my mind.

Therapist: He does help you?

Client: (Emphatically) Oh yes, very much. I do initiate a lot of things but...

Therapist: He pitches in.

Client: Oh, oh yeah. I told him when I married him he would have to do his half or I would move out. *(laughs)* So I was really resenting him for that fact and I was really resenting my son. He's a very manipulative kid and he can manipulate me without me even knowing it. Basically what I was resenting was that he was outsmarting me and I really didn't like that. Plus I realized that at home I make decisions based on guilt. I feel responsible if Jack isn't happy or if something happened. I feel responsible if Bill's *[her son]* life isn't wonderful and complete and I feel responsible....I just felt totally responsible for the things done...

Therapist: Let me interrupt you for a second. You, when you're talking about all this, you're talking in the past tense. Have you since put some of this together?

Client: Yes, well I have to some degree and it was really interesting. When I made the phone call and made the appointment it was kind of like...We came to counseling before and it triggered something in us that we needed to really talk. And...

Therapist: And you did that.

Client: We are doing that. I don't think we are done...

Therapist: You are never done.

Client: No, but I mean, we are doing that.

Therapist: Good.

Client: I've made conscious...

Therapist: How did you get that to happen?

Client: Just by saying to myself that I am not going to live like this...So, we are talking.

Therapist: Okay. Are you feeling like you are starting to...

Client: I feel a lot better today. I mean, last night. We got into a point where we were both so tired from our jobs that we weren't having enough sex, which is enough for us. We kind of got ourselves into a vicious cycle. And I think we have kind of gotten ourselves out. Last night we made wonderful love and it was nice and we both felt better.

Therapist: Great. How did you get that to happen?

From O'Hanlon and Weiner-Davis, 1989, pp. 70–71.

---

work for the client, and, most importantly, with its specific interest in solutions, it has enormous appeal as a *strategy* for psychotherapy, regardless of the clinical orientation of the therapist. As a consequence, it is attracting a growing number of

adherents and is having a significant impact on the entire field of psychotherapy.

Contemporary solution-focused approaches to psychotherapy represent a profound departure from most prior ways of thinking about psychopathology and psychotherapy. The theoretical foundation for solution-focused psychotherapy dispenses with most complex propositions, retaining a small number of rather straightforward assertions that do not appear to be difficult to master.

As for the practice of planned short-term psychotherapy, solution-focused approaches have under-lined a number of specific clinical intervention techniques that have very wide applicability. Searching for exceptions to problem behavior, encouraging a vision of a life without the troubling problem behavior, and even attending to the grammar of clients' statements all are useful enhancements to the therapeutic encounter.

CLINICAL SETTINGS FOR PLANNED SHORT-TERM PSYCHOTHERAPY

In the past 15 years or so, while original theoretical and technical contributions to individually oriented planned short-term psychotherapy have continued to be published, a very large number of contributions that are associated with specific clinical settings and clinical tasks have also appeared. The most important of these varied settings are: (1) crisis intervention programs, (2) planned short-term psychotherapy with patients who are medically ill, (3) brief contact therapy, (4) planned short-term group and family psychotherapy, and (5) planned short-term psychotherapy in inpatient psychiatric units.

In this section we shall examine these five areas of practice. In every case the chapters will identify contributors whose names have not appeared earlier in the book—such is the current nature of specialization within the already specialized field of planned short-term psychotherapy.

CHAPTER 19

CRISIS INTERVENTION

Overview

Origin of Crisis Theory

General Principles of Crisis Theory

Clinical Crisis Intervention Techniques

Combining Crisis Intervention and Brief Psychotherapy

Concluding Comments

A crisis is a "perception of an event or situation as an intolerable difficulty that exceeds the resources and coping mechanisms of the person" (Gilliland & James, 1993, p, 3; see also Janosik, 1994; Parad & Parad, 1990). Crises are thought of as having a maximum duration of six to eight weeks and are characterized by symptoms of stress, a sense of panic or defeat, preoccupation with obtaining relief, and lowered efficiency.

According to Caplan (1961), a crisis is provoked

> when a person faces an obstacle to important life goals that is, for a time, insurmountable through the utilization of customary methods of problem-solving. A period of disorganization ensues, a period of upset, during which many different abortive attempts at solution are made. Eventually, some kind of adaptation is achieved, which may or may not be in the best interests of that person and his fellows. (p. 18)

The management of personal crises has become of great interest to mental health professionals because crisis resolution often has implications for our emotional well-being, and because during a crisis a person is believed to be unusually receptive to clinical intervention. Straker (1980) put it well when he wrote, "The temporary state of heightened susceptibility presents an unparalleled opportunity for internal boundary realignments. It is an opportunity for better—or for worse" (p. 226).

If brief contacts during crises are at least as effective as longer therapy after a time on a waiting list, developing a crisis intervention strategy will enable mental health professionals to reach greater numbers of clients with greater impact and less time, possibly increasing their ability to meet the mental health needs of a community without significant increases in cost (see Phillips, 1985a; Wells, 1994).

There is also a growing interest in crisis intervention because of its implication for prevention. For example, initial adverse reactions to crises are rarely true psychiatric disorders, but if such reactions persist, they may become disabling. Hence, effective crisis intervention services may reduce the incidence of psychiatric disability. A crisis presents an opportunity for growth as well as a possibility for regression. Successful resolution of a traumatic crisis may make a person stronger and healthier, better able to deal with future crises. By this line of reasoning, psychological well-being may be thought of as the result of a history of successful crisis resolutions. That is, mental health may, at any particular moment, be fully defined as the summation of crisis resolutions in a person's life—analogous to a kind of batting average based on the success of crisis resolutions to date.

ORIGIN OF CRISIS THEORY

Virtually all reviews of the field of crisis intervention (e.g., Bloom, 1984; Butcher, Stelmachers, & Maudal, 1983; Davanloo, 1980d; Ewing, 1978; Flegenheimer, 1982; Straker, 1980) date the beginning of mental health professionals' interest in personal crises to a paper by Erich Lindemann (1944) that has been one of the most influential clinical studies in mental health in the past half century.

Lindemann, then affiliated with the Department of Psychiatry at Harvard Medical School and with the Massachusetts General Hospital, was active in providing psychiatric help to families of victims of an extraordinary disaster. On the evening of November 28, 1942 a fire swept through a large crowded nightclub in Boston—the Cocoanut Grove—and 493 people perished. In this kind of emergency situation, only the briefest kind of psychotherapy was possible. Yet Lindemann was able to help the survivors and at the same time study the process of acute grief and conceptualize how his efforts were or were not helpful to people in the management of their grief. His paper is a model of superb clinical reporting and analysis.

In addition to describing the remarkably uniform immediate reactions to grief as well as the course of events that normally followed the initial grief reaction, Lindemann developed some ideas about how a mental health professional could assist in the management of grief—by helping people express their grief; by attending to underreactions as well as overreactions; by helping the survivor find new patterns of rewarding interaction, review his or her relationship with the deceased, and verbalize feelings of guilt; and by prescribing appropriate medication. All these interventions went far beyond the more traditional responses practiced since time immemorial—comforting the survivor, invoking divine will, and offering the promise of a later reunion with the deceased.

Lindemann reinforced earlier psychoanalytic ideas (Freud, 1917/1953) about how normal and pathological mourning differ from each other. Normal mourning can include a variety of complex emotions—guilt, anger, anxiety, and hostility and feelings of helplessness, denial, or detachment; as well as a number of somatic symptoms (Davanloo, 1980d; see also Chapters 10 and 11). Mourning takes on pathological proportions when it is prolonged, delayed, or distorted. In such cases it is often found that the relationship of the patient to the deceased was highly ambivalent, the death was sudden and unanticipated, and in some way the patient felt personally responsible for the death.

Lindemann felt that unsuccessful crisis resolution could precipitate significant psychiatric problems and that all mental health practitioners, as well as members of the clergy and workers in social welfare agencies, could assist in crisis resolution by offering psychological first aid following any crisis. The fundamental purpose of crisis intervention is to convert maladaptive responses to adaptive ones.

GENERAL PRINCIPLES OF CRISIS THEORY

Crises are generally divided into two types—(1) *accidental, situational, or unanticipated crises,* such as death of a family member, illness, accident, loss or change of jobs, or marital disruption; and (2) *normative, maturational, or developmental crises* such as entering kindergarten, high school, or college, becoming engaged, marrying, becoming a parent, or retiring. The first type of crisis is often characterized by periods of acute disorganization of behavior or affect precipitated by the stressful, somewhat unpredictable life experience and is more pertinent to the clinician's work. The second type is precipitated by a transition from one developmental phase to another; because these crises are more predictable they lend themselves to the development of preventively oriented interventions within social institutions such as schools, hospitals, or work settings.

Baldwin (1979) has identified a set of principles that emerge from a careful analysis of basic crisis theory and have useful implications for clinical practice. These principles are listed in Box 19-1.

The crucial aspects of crisis intervention are its situational quality and its call for a quick response by the mental health professional. A number of basic principles of crisis intervention that derive from these two characteristics of crisis seem to be generally affirmed in the literature, for both individual and group crisis intervention (see Donovan, Bennett, & McElroy, 1981). The best way to use professional time and effort is to schedule frequent contacts with the client during the brief period of the crisis rather than infrequent interviews over an extended period of time. Crisis intervention should support the integrity of the family and prevent its fragmentation, so as to preserve its capacity to

---

Box 19-1: Baldwin's Principles of Crisis Theory

1. Because each individual's tolerance for stress is idiosyncratic and finite, emotional crises have no per se relationship to psychopathology and occur even among the well-adjusted.
2. Emotional crises are self-limiting events in which crisis resolution, either adaptive or maladaptive, takes place within an average of four to six weeks.
3. During a crisis state, psychological defenses are weakened or absent and the individual has cognitive and/or affective awareness of material previously well-defended and less accessible.
4. During a crisis state the individual has enhanced capacity for both cognitive and affective learning because of the vulnerability of this state and the motivation produced by emotional disequilibrium.
5. Adaptive crisis resolution is frequently a vehicle for resolving underlying conflicts that have in part determined the emotional crisis and/or that interfere with the crisis resolution process.
6. A small external influence during a crisis state can produce disproportionate change in a short period of time when compared to therapeutic change that occurs during noncrisis states.
7. The resolution of an emotional crisis is not necessarily determined by previous experience or character structure, but rather is shaped by current and perhaps unique socio-psychological influences operating in the present.
8. Inherent in every emotional crisis is an actual or anticipated loss to the individual that must be reconciled as part of the crisis resolution process.
9. Every emotional crisis is an interpersonal event involving at least one significant other person who is represented in the crisis situation directly, indirectly, or symbolically.
10. Effective crisis resolution prevents future crises of a similar nature by removing vulnerabilities from the past and by increasing the individual's repertoire of available coping skills that can be used in such situations.

From B.A. Baldwin, "Crisis Intervention: An Overview of Theory and Practice," *Counseling Psychology 8*, pp. 45–47, copyright © 1979. Reprinted by permission of Sage Publications, Inc.

---

assist the family member in crisis. Undue dependence on the mental health professional should be prevented, by dealing with current realities as well as with pertinent historical antecedents of the problem. The goal should be to facilitate the client's mastery of the problem by giving information and hope, which in turn will help the client in confronting and dealing with the crisis. Outside supports should be sought and provided wherever possible. Finally, the goal of crisis intervention should be to help the client deal affirmatively with the current situation, regardless of his or her prior history of success or failure in crisis resolution (see also Davanloo, 1980d).

Ewing (1990) has suggested a number of important general principles in the clinical practice of crisis intervention. Crisis intervention should be readily available and brief. Crisis intervention can deal not only with individuals but also with families and other social networks. It is suitable for dealing with a wide range of contemporary human problems. Crisis intervention aspires not only to resolve the present difficulty but also to help clients develop more effective ways of coping with future difficulties. The intervention is reality oriented and may require psychotherapists to assume nontraditional roles. Finally, crisis intervention services may help prepare the client for additional treatment.

CLINICAL CRISIS INTERVENTION TECHNIQUES

Ewing (1978; see also Straker, 1980) postulates six essential and overlapping stages in the process of crisis intervention: (1) problem delineation, (2) evaluation, (3) contracting, (4) intervening, (5) termination; and (6) follow-up. The goal of problem delineation is to "define a fairly specific problem area toward which the intervention may be directed" (p. 95). To achieve this objective, the therapist has to develop a trusting relationship with the client. Clients often have multiple difficulties and may only be dimly aware of some of them. Accordingly, the therapist may need to review the major dimensions of the client's life history and identify any recent life changes or stresses.

The stage of evaluation involves an assessment of the client and of the current life situation that should include the basic demographic facts, previous and current psychotherapeutic history and involvement, accessibility to intervention, psychological functioning, motivation, and a general assessment of precrisis adjustment. The process of contracting includes specification of the problem focus, time limits for the intervention, whether other persons should be involved in the process, and the individual responsibilities of the client and the therapist. Since initial contracting already includes the issue of length of treatment, the process of termination starts when the treatment starts. As for follow-up, Ewing suggests that some type of follow-up be instituted to determine the client's condition and progress, even if only by telephone. It can take place a month or two after the termination and can serve important evaluative, educational, and clinical functions.

As for clinical techniques that should be kept in mind during the intervention itself, Ewing suggests nine specific tactics: (1) listening and encouraging verbalization, (2) identifying and using the support of friends and family, (3) using other institutional and agency supports and services, (4) advocacy on the client's behalf, (5) sensitive yet pointed confrontation, (6) providing factual information, (7) exploring alternative coping mechanisms, (8) judicious advice and suggestion, and (9) assigning carefully selected homework tasks.

These views are unusually important because they underline a special point rarely stressed enough. All mental health professionals provide a certain amount of crisis intervention. Yet it is not uncommon for mental health professionals to believe, sometimes implicitly, that psychotherapy can begin only after the crisis is over. Ewing urges the clinical practitioner to look to crisis intervention itself as a golden opportunity to do significant short-term psychotherapy (see also Flegenheimer, 1982, pp. 180–184; Wolberg, 1980).

Puryear (1979) has spelled out eight basic guidelines that the mental health professional should keep in mind when working with clients in crisis. These guidelines (see Box 19-2) are a useful companion to Ewing's (1990) clinical techniques already enumerated and to Baldwin's (1979) set of principles (see Box 19-1) that summarize crisis theory.

The psychotherapeutic techniques that Puryear (1979) recommends with people undergoing crises reinforce those already identified by Ewing (1978)—establishing communication and rapport; assessing the client's problems, resources, and strengths; formulating a plan; mobilizing the client; terminating the episode; and following up.

Greenstone and Leviton (1993) suggest that there are six major components in effective crisis intervention: immediacy, control, assessment, disposition, referral, and follow-up. The intervener must act immediately to relieve anxiety, prevent further psychological deterioration, and ensure that no harm comes to the person in crisis or to others. The intervener must take control of the situation and be clear about who is the client and what can be done. The intervener must determine what is troubling the client and which problems are of immediate concern. The intervener must be able to decide how to handle the situation after it has been assessed. The intervener must know the local community well enough to be able to make appropriate referrals and should arrange to follow up the case to make sure that referral agencies have been contacted and that the situation is in hand.

Roberts (1990, 1991, 1995a) has outlined a similar set of steps in the process of crisis intervention: (1) making psychological contact and establishing a working relationship, (2) examining the dimensions of the problem, including the assessment of lethali-

---

Box 19-2: Puryear's Crisis Intervention Guidelines

1. *Immediate Intervention.* A crisis is a time of danger and a time-limited opportunity for intervention. When someone asks for help, you try to decide if there is a crisis. If there is, you should see them right away.
2. *Action.* In crisis intervention the worker very actively participates in and directs the process of assessing the situation and, together with the client, formulates a plan of action for the client to pursue.
3. *Limited Goal.* The minimal goal of crisis intervention is to avert catastrophe. The basic overall goal is to restore the client to his equilibrium state, optimally with some growth also occurring.
4. *Hope and Expectation.* The worker must initially instill hope into the situation. He does this through his whole approach, including his attitude and his expectations of the client and about the situation.
5. *Support.* The worker must provide a great deal of support to the client, primarily by being "with him," available to go through the process with him. The support must be carefully given so that it is sufficient without being excessive.
6. *Focused Problem Solving.* This is the backbone of crisis intervention; it provides the structure that shapes and supports the whole process. Basically, we try to determine the problem—the basic unresolved problem that led to the crisis—and then assist the client in planning and putting into action steps aimed at resolving it. We keep our own and the client's attention focused on that problem and on the problem-solving process, and we avoid being distracted and sidetracked.
7. *Self-Image.* Efforts must be made to assess and understand the client's self-image, to consider carefully the effect that any of the intervention maneuvers might have upon it, and to protect and enhance it. These efforts will pay off in many ways, including increased rapport, decreased defensiveness, and mobilization of the client's energies.
8. *Self-Reliance.* From the very onset, attention must be paid to fostering self-reliance and combating dependency. This need must be carefully balanced with the need for support.

From D.A. Puryear, *Helping People in Crisis* (pp. 20–21), San Francisco: Jossey-Bass, 1979. Used with permission.

---

ty, (3) encouraging an exploration of feelings and emotions, (4) assessing past coping attempts, (5) generating and exploring alternatives and specific solutions, restoring cognitive functioning through the development and implementation of an action plan, and (6) follow-up (see also Mc Mullin, 1986, pp. 269–271; Roberts & Dziegielewski, 1995).

Establishing Communication and Rapport

Most people who write about crisis intervention are strong advocates of what is called "active listening"—listening for and responding to the latent, underlying, sometimes coded message and then checking to see if you've heard it right. Puryear, for

example, considers active listening as perhaps the most basic component of the psychotherapeutic relationship, in part because it allows emotions to be expressed in a controlled way. Box 19-3 provides an example taken from an interview with a mother and her son.

In addition to active listening as a general therapeutic strategy, Puryear identifies two specific techniques, plussing and paradox, that are used throughout the crisis intervention. These two techniques help to establish and maintain rapport, avoid power struggles between the therapist and the client, raise self-esteem, and leave the responsibility for problem solving with the client.

Plussing assumes an attitude that people are basically good and that all actions have some positive

---

Box 19-3: Using Active Listening During an Initial Interview

Mother: He is a terrible boy.

Therapist: You don't see much good in him.

Mother: It's not that. He's got some good points, but he won't use them. He hangs out with that crowd, he comes in late, he smokes and I know he's drinking, and …

Therapist: (interrupting) You worry about him a lot, and about what he's doing.

Son: Yeah, she worries all the time. She's always on my back about something.

Therapist: Just a minute, Johnny. You think your mother overdoes the worrying, and we want to hear how it looks to you in a minute, but right now let me hear what your mother's saying. *(to mother)* You were saying you do worry a lot.

Mother: Yes, I do. I've talked and talked to him till I'm blue in the face, and it does no good. He just ignores me.

Therapist: Your efforts just don't seem to get you anywhere.

Mother: No. Sometimes I wonder where I went wrong.

Therapist: When you think of all these things that worry you, you even wonder if you're failing as a mother.

Mother: Yes. I've tried, but I must be doing something wrong. Maybe there's some other way.

From D. A. Puryear, *Helping People in Crisis* (pp. 58–59), San Francisco: Jossey-Bass, 1979. Used with permission.

---

motivation. In the early therapeutic sessions, plussing enhances communication and helps build rapport. Examples of plussing are such statements as: "I see, Mr. Jones, you're so angry at Tom because you worry about him so much" or "I see, Mrs. Jones, you hit Sally because you just exploded when you thought she might be getting herself into serious trouble, and you felt absolutely helpless to stop her" or "So, Mr. Jones, after the car wreck you knew your wife was going to be worrying about you, and when you went into the bar your intention was to call her" (Puryear, 1979, p. 87).

Paradox refers to techniques by which clients, especially families, are maneuvered into conflicting positions that force them to change for the better. These techniques include the following practices:

- Reversal—arguing against a client's doing what you want him or her to do;
- Speaking past the point—saying something and then continuing by focusing on another point;
- Speaking to the wrong person—talking to one person but referring to another person;
- Yes-and—disagreeing by agreeing and then countering the position just expressed;

- Being wrong—deliberately making an statement that is inaccurate, in order to have the client make a less extreme statement in response;
- You don't mean—a maneuver that confronts someone's behavior by suggesting that the person doesn't really mean what has just been said;
- Requesting the symptom—asking a client to display a symptom as a strategy for reducing its frequency;
- Exaggeration—suggesting that a problem is worse than it is in order to have the client respond by saying that it is less severe than it is

Examples of paradox techniques given by Puryear are shown in Box 19-4.

Assessing Problems, Resources, and Strengths

Assessment begins at the time of the first contact with the client. During the assessment process the therapist needs to achieve some understanding of the immediate situation, develop an idea about the chain of events that brought the situation about, and identify the problem that started that chain of events. The initial focus is usually on the presenting problem.

Box 19-4: Examples of Puryear's Paradox Maneuvers

Reversal

Therapist: (to father) I know how concerned you are and how much you want to help. But look, you're working hard, you might have trouble getting more time off from the boss, or if we meet in the evening you'll be pretty tired out. Don't you think it's putting a little too much on you for you to try to attend?

Speaking Past the Point

Therapist: Mr. Jones, you've just heard your wife's concerns about your drinking, and I expect you've worried about it yourself from time to time, but do you think there are other areas in your marriage that could maybe become more satisfying for the two of you?

Speaking to the Wrong Person

Therapist: So, Mrs. Jones, you're concerned about your husband's drinking, and although he'd probably deny it, of course, haven't you ever thought he's probably concerned about it sometimes too?

Yes-And

Patient: All psychiatrists are quacks who are only out to soak their patients.
Therapist: Yes, and have you been aware of how helpful they are and that they're usually very concerned about their patients' welfare?

Being Wrong

Therapist: What'd your father do then, John?
Patient: Nuthin' much.
Therapist: He probably hit you alongside the head with a two by four, right?
Patient: Naw, he just slapped me around a little.

You Don't Mean

Therapist: (to mother) You certainly don't mean to make Johnny feel guilty; you're trying to clarify how much he means to you.

Requesting the Symptom

Therapist: Mr. Jones, can we try a little experiment? This may not make good sense, but I want to try something and see how it goes. OK? For the next five minutes, I'll time it, would you interrupt your wife every time she starts to say something?

Exaggeration

Therapist: My God! I don't see how you've stood six months of this. You must be about to collapse.
Patient: Well, Doc, it hasn't been quite that bad.

From D. A. Puryear, *Helping People in Crisis* (pp. 96–103), San Francisco: Jossey-Bass, 1979. Used with permission.

Puryear suggests that it is important for the therapist to assess such questions as: Is this a crisis? If so, for whom? Is crisis intervention appropriate? Who is in the most distress? Who seems motivated for the work? Who seems calm, who verbal, who intelligent? Where are the alliances and strains within the family system? Where are the most likely obstacles to the work? Why did they come here? What do they want and expect? Why did they come now?

The therapist tries to identify the chain of events that ended in the presenting problem, using techniques described in the previous section, seeking additional information as needed until the fundamental problem can be put into words that are acceptable to the patient. Gathering information about other crises the patient has coped with provides information on strengths and resources available to the patient. In addition, the therapist would be wise to be familiar with community strengths and resources.

Formulating a Plan and Mobilizing the Client

Assessing the problem and the available resources merges into planning and mobilizing the client. Puryear thinks of plans as being either short-term or long-term. If, for example, the long-term goal is improved communication between a husband and wife, a short-term goal might be to have the wife agree to tell the husband what she learned when she called the school to find out what the situation is with their son who is having difficulty there. Plans ought to unfold naturally and collaboratively, and Puryear suggests that the therapist ought to incorporate any ideas offered by the client, as long as the ideas are not

doomed to failure. Box 19-5 provides an example of planning and mobilization in action

Puryear (1979) suggests that assessing, planning, and mobilizing are all part of the same process. He writes:

> In the course of evaluating the problem and unfolding the chain of events, a plan of action naturally evolves; with a plan, the clients begin to be mobilized. The problem and the plan suggest a task, which is then used to further the mobilization and to ensure that it is carried on beyond the session. (p. 135)

Termination and Follow-up

In brief crisis intervention a start is made at dealing with termination at the first interview, in the sense that the entire intervention is defined as lasting only "a few times." Termination is most useful when it involves a review of where the clients were at the beginning of the intervention and what took place during the sessions, that is, a review of what was accomplished by the clients. In addition, Puryear obtains permission to check in with the clients by phone in a couple of months. Box 19-6 shows an excerpt of a termination session.

Box 19-5: Formulating a Plan and Mobilizing the Client

Therapist: Well, Mr. Jones, you were pretty upset about your mother, and then when you learned your wife had a tumor you thought she'd die right away, like the worst thing that could happen, and then you didn't know of anywhere you could get help with the kids. That's when it just seemed too much, and you left for a while. Then, of course, your wife was furious when you got back and things really fell apart between you and got even worse after you hit her.

Mr. Jones: Yeah. I knew I couldn't help her and work and take care of the kids, too, and then when I got back we couldn't even talk any more. And I don't really even know what's really wrong with her.

Therapist: Yeah, Mrs. Jones, when the doctor talked to you, you got so scared, and you weren't sure what he was saying after you heard "tumor."

Mrs. Jones: Uh huh. He was talking so fast. If only he could explain it to my husband. Jim always understands things quicker than I do anyway.

Mr. Jones: Well, he explained pretty good when she had that hyster-thing operation. Maybe I could call him.

Therapist: That sounds like an idea. Do you think he'd really sit down and talk to both of you together like that? *[Implying that going to see the doctor together was Jim's idea]*

From D. A. Puryear, *Helping People in Crisis* (p. 127), San Francisco: Jossey-Bass, 1979. Used with permission.

Box 19-6: Excerpt from Terminating the Brief Crisis Intervention

Mr. Jones: I think we got a handle on it now, Doc. I don't see why we need to come here any more.

Therapist: Yeah, you seem to be on top of it. This has really been a rough time for both of you.

Mr. and Mrs. Jones: Yeah.

Therapist: You can look ahead and see some pretty rough things still coming up.

Mr. Jones: Yeah, sure, but you know, like they say, the Lord will provide a way.

Therapist: Yeah, and you've planned things out a bit too; like you said, right now you're worried about if Mrs. Haskins doesn't work out with the kids.

Mr. Jones: Yeah, but you know, I called my sister, and I think she'd help a while, and that's like a backup.

Therapist: Uh huh. You remember, you two were pretty upset when you first came here.

Mr. Jones: Right. My wife was all torn up over what happened and all. We just don't like to think about it now.

Therapist: Sure. Well, you'd really been in a spot. You know, Mrs. Jones, your mother-in-law had died *[speaking to the wrong person, following Mr. Jones' lead]*, which left your husband pretty upset, and with no help around, and you got the bad news from your doctor.

Mrs. Jones: And we didn't really know what it meant.

Therapist: Sure, and you didn't know, and your husband was so worried about you and the kids.

Mr. Jones: I just couldn't think straight.

Therapist: Right—and things just built up, with your leaving, and both of you feeling bad about that, too, so there was such a row when you came back.

Mrs. Jones: I was just so upset about the cancer, and he'd never hit me before.

Therapist: Yeah—really, all of this was so totally new for both of you *[giving a reason for lacking an adequate coping mechanism]*; you'd had no experience.

Mr. Jones: Uh huh.

Therapist: I was wondering. You're both really on the tracks now, handling all the problems coming up; if you look back, what did you do that helped you, how did you get yourself back on the track?

Mr. Jones: I don't know. Things just worked out, you know.

Mrs. Jones: Yeah, it's funny, but you know, I think when we went back to the doctor, and Jim went with me Mr. Jones: Yeah, that was so upsetting, I mean for my wife, you know, but at least we knew what the deal was.

Therapist: You knew then what was really going on, what you had to deal with.

Mr. Jones: Right.

Therapist: And was it then, like that helped you start making plans, knowing what the deal was?

Mr. Jones: Right, yeah, I talked to the neighbor then, and all, and called that cancer society, and—

Mrs. Jones: Yes, and you were a big help, too, doctor.

Therapist: Sure, sometimes it helps to have someone to talk to, to get your ideas out in the open, you know, and then you start making plans, like you two started working on these things.

Mr. Jones: Right, that was good.

Therapist: You mean the talking.

Mr. Jones: Yeah, it helped me think, and then I could make plans.

From D. A. Puryear, *Helping People in Crisis* (pp. 152–155), San Francisco: Jossey-Bass, 1979. Used with permission.

Follow-up telephone calls are designed to find out how things are going and to check on any particular question that was left unresolved at termination. The follow-up call extends the support of the therapist beyond the formal termination of the crisis intervention and helps create the sense that the intervention and its effects continue beyond the end of the therapy. Information collected at the follow-up helps the therapist prepare a summary of the case and evaluate the outcome and allows the therapist to make referrals to other community agencies if needed.

COMBINING CRISIS INTERVENTION AND BRIEF PSYCHOTHERAPY

Because the techniques employed in crisis intervention and planned short-term psychotherapy differ somewhat from each other, a number of writers have examined the similarities between crisis intervention and brief psychotherapy both in terms of theory and clinical implications. Stuart and Mackey (1977) distinguish among the three clinical concepts: crisis intervention, emergency psychotherapy, and short-term psychotherapy, using the equation *Person* plus *Stress* yields *Reaction.* These concepts are not always distinguished when clinicians face the need to design appropriate interventions. In Stuart and Mackey's formulation, if the focal issue is the person (demographic information, family background, previous coping mechanisms, developmental history, value systems, and beliefs), the treatment of choice is planned short-term psychotherapy. If the focal issue is the stress (the situation that is being experienced), the treatment of choice is crisis intervention. If the focal issue is the reaction (the response to the stress), the treatment of choice is emergency psychotherapy.

Marmor (1979) believes that the differences between crisis intervention and short-term psychotherapy are primarily in terms of emphasis. He writes:

The primary goal of crisis intervention is the restoration of homeostasis. The secondary goal is to improve the patient's adaptive capacity when necessary. The basic goal of short-term dynamic psychotherapy is to improve the patient's coping abilities. The termination point of crisis intervention is when the crisis is resolved. The termination point of short-term dynamic therapy is not dictated

by the resolution of the crisis. Crisis intervention involves a more supportive approach than does short-term dynamic psychotherapy. It can also be more directive. In short-term dynamic therapy, the approach is active but nondirective. Crisis intervention deals only with the here and now; short-term dynamic psychotherapy includes the exploration of the past to illuminate the present. Finally, crisis intervention may involve a variety of other techniques (e.g., family therapy, group therapy, and dealing with the social network), but short-term dynamic psychotherapy is essentially a one-to-one approach. (p. 154)

In contrast, many writers believe that there are profound and significant differences between crisis intervention and brief psychotherapy. Greenstone and Leviton (1993), for example, suggest that:

Ordinary upsets can be handled with day-to-day skills. Crises happen suddenly and unexpectedly and seem arbitrary. Inexplicable events raise stress to a critical level. Crisis intervention is a timely and skillful intrusion into a personal crisis in order to defuse a potentially disastrous situation before physical or emotional destruction occurs....Crisis intervention is not therapy. It is the skilled attempt to stop the emotional bleeding in a way that will allow the individual to continue life effectively....Successful crisis intervention achieves problem management, not problem resolution. The intervener who has helped the victim of a crisis regain pre-crisis stability has met the goals of crisis intervention. (p. vii)

Shiang and Bongar (1995) distinguish crisis intervention and brief psychotherapy in terms of both their core principles and clinical techniques. Regarding their core principles, brief psychotherapy assumes that: (1) clients are capable of changing throughout their life-span, (2) time to achieve therapeutic goals is limited, and (3) a constructive working alliance between the therapist and the client is required to achieve therapeutic goals. Crisis intervention shares in particular the first two core principles, but in addition includes the need to define the nature and impact of the crisis and to provide immediate intervention in order to restore the client to the precrisis level of functioning.

As for clinical techniques that distinguish brief psychotherapy from crisis intervention, Shiang and Bongar (1995) suggest that brief psychotherapy principles lead to (1) the careful selection and exclusion of clients, (2) rapid and early assessment, and (3) therapist interventions that include such techniques as maintenance of a focus, high therapist activity, therapist flexibility, and promptness of intervention. In contrast, crisis intervention principles suggest that the therapist, in addition to needing to make a rapid and early assessment of the client's predicament, should provide a reality-based approach to the treatment and to the social system within which the client functions and should be able to play multiple roles—educator, advisor, facilitator—as well as therapist. Thus, crisis intervention techniques bring into play a somewhat different and perhaps broader set of therapist skills than those associated with brief psychotherapy.

Whereas the principal goal of crisis intervention is to restore the precrisis level of functioning, planned short-term therapy aims at the more ambitious goal of increasing the level of psychological functioning and adjustment and promoting more adaptive coping mechanisms. In addition, while there is considerable debate about the selection criteria that should be used in identifying patients suitable for brief psychotherapy (see Chapter 24), the only selection criterion that is appropriate for crisis intervention is that the patient be in a crisis.

Matching these differences in selection and in goal are, of course, important differences in the structure and techniques of therapy, in the use of the therapeutic relationship, and in the concepts that govern how the therapy is terminated. Because of these differences, Flegenheimer (1982, p. 177; see also Davanloo, 1980c), among others, has suggested that crisis intervention and planned short-term psychotherapy have less in common, except for their brevity, than might initially be thought.

Flegenheimer (1982) believes that there is little difficulty in deciding whether crisis intervention or brief psychotherapy is most appropriate in a given situation. He believes that the term *crisis intervention* should be thought of in a relatively restrictive way and that the two modalities are rarely indicated for the same individual at the same time. If the two forms of intervention are confused, a proper evaluation of the patient may not be made before the therapy begins. According to Flegenheimer, people in crisis cannot usually profit from brief psychotherapy; conversely,

people who appear suitable for brief psychotherapy are rarely in crisis. What is common, however, is that a person is seen for crisis intervention, and then, when the crisis has abated, it becomes clear that the patient is now suitable for brief psychotherapy.

Furthermore, according to Flegenheimer, it is important to make sure that the crisis is fully resolved before brief psychotherapy is discussed. Likewise, since strong positive and sometimes dependent attachments can form between the patient and the therapist during a period of crisis intervention, it is important to make sure that these transference relationships are put into proper perspective before undertaking brief psychotherapy. It may also be appropriate to allow some period of time to elapse between the end of the crisis intervention and the beginning of the brief psychotherapy or to assign a different therapist for each type of intervention.

On the other hand, since so many people enter psychotherapy because of a crisis in their lives (see Kovacs, 1982, pp 146 ff.), it is important for brief psychotherapists to examine crisis intervention techniques very carefully. Wolberg (1980) has suggested that the goal of crisis intervention is rapid emotional relief. But, he notes, this does not mean that we neglect opportunities to bring about personality change when such change is possible. Much of the time it is possible for a patient in crisis to learn something about the relationship of previously existing problems to the crisis situation and the discomfort that has been produced by it.

CONCLUDING COMMENTS

The enormous appeal of crisis intervention theory and practice lies in the hope that, by following its principles, mental health professionals can significantly increase their impact in the community. There seems little question that a very small number of interviews, skillfully conducted during a time of crisis, can have profound and long-lasting effects, at least with patients who are otherwise reasonably intact. Crisis intervention techniques are fairly well developed. The basic theoretical and conceptual foundations for crisis intervention are being extended, and a number of publications oriented toward training crisis counselors have appeared (e.g., Atlas, 1994; Tidwell, 1992) Evaluation studies have generally found that brief crisis intervention has significantly positive effects on adjustment (e.g., Auerbach & Kilmann, 1977; True & Benway, 1992).

The basic ideas associated with the concept of the psychological crisis resulted in including the provision of crisis and emergency services as part of the mandate of community mental health centers when the federal government began its support of such centers in 1963 (Bloom, 1984). Chapter 1). Crisis services were thought of originally as particularly pertinent to people in the community who found themselves unable to cope with a specific life stress that overtaxed their adaptive capacities. In recent years, however, such crisis services have been used increasingly by the chronically mentally ill who reside in the community and who make full use of the community mental health center to maintain their equilibrium. Relatively little has yet been written about how to make such readily available services most helpful to patients with chronic stressful life circumstances (Roberts, 1995b).

It is difficult to evaluate the significance of the writings distinguishing between crisis intervention and brief psychotherapy. The principles of brief crisis intervention appear to be somewhat different from most general principles of brief psychotherapy, but it should be appropriate for most brief therapists to provide crisis intervention services, keeping in mind the differences between the two modalities in terms of selection criteria, goals, therapeutic techniques, and transference phenomena.

CHAPTER 20

PLANNED SHORT-TERM THERAPY IN MEDICAL SETTINGS

Overview

Medical Cost-Offset Studies

Psychodynamic Psychotherapy in
Medical Settings

Rational-Emotive Psychotherapy in
Medical Settings

Strategic Psychotherapy in
Medical Settings

Concluding Comments

The planned short-term psychotherapy literature of the past decade includes a substantial body of work illustrating the use of time-limited psychotherapy in working with people who are medically ill. In this and the next chapter we shall examine the clinical approaches that have been suggested for providing brief psychotherapy to medically ill patients whose illnesses are complicated by the presence of some form of psychological disorder. In many cases the psychological disorder can be thought of as part of the causal complex related to the medical illness. In perhaps more cases the psychological disorder can be the consequence of the stress induced by the illness.

The scope of such approaches is remarkably broad and includes efforts to be of help to patients with general somatization disorders, or with such specific disorders as chronic pain, excessive weight gain, migraine and tension headaches, tics, myocardial infarctions, cancer, diabetes, and herpes (e.g., Casanueva, Legarreta, Diaz-Barriga, Soberanis, Cárdenas, Iturriaga, Lartigue, & Vives, 1994; Compton & Purviance, 1992; Croake & Myers, 1989; Klerman, Budman, Berwick, Weissman, Damico-White, Demby, & Feldstein, 1987; Liberzon, Goldman, & Hendrickson, 1992; Margo & Margo, 1994; Nielsen, Barth, Haver, Havik, Mølstad, Rogge, & Skåtun, 1988; Stern, 1987; Teitelbaum & Kettl, 1988). In addition, psychother-

apeutic efforts have been reported to be of help to mothers whose preschool children are undergoing uncomfortable or painful medical procedures (e.g., Campbell, Kirkpatrick, Berry, Penn, Waldman, & Mathewson, 1992).

Reports of the use of planned short-term psychotherapy in working with the physically ill are remarkably uniform in their positive findings. Mumford, Schlesinger, and Glass (1982), for example, reported that a brief psychological intervention with patients hospitalized following heart attacks reduced the average duration of hospitalization by approximately two days when contrasted with control groups for whom no psychological intervention was provided. Needless to say, reducing length of hospitalization in an intensive care unit by two days represents an extraordinary reduction in the cost of medical care.

The literature on planned short-term psychotherapy with medically ill patients is divided into two very discrete domains. This chapter will deal with time-limited psychotherapy provided by mental health professionals to patients who are medically ill. Such patients are generally referred to mental health professionals by primary care physicians, who continue to manage their patients' medical problems.

The next chapter will examine the literature concerned with psychotherapy provided to medically ill patients by their own primary care physicians. Since most primary care physicians are scheduled to see three or four patients every hour, often twenty or thirty patients in a single day, a type of time-limited psychotherapy called *brief contact therapy* has been developed. Brief contact therapy limits the duration of individual treatment sessions to 15 to 20 minutes. The works that have been published on this topic are designed to train primary care physicians to help their medically ill patients cope with the emotional components and emotional consequences of their illnesses, working in blocks of time that match the physician's typical busy working schedule.

MEDICAL COST-OFFSET STUDIES

Some planned short-term psychotherapy evaluation studies have searched for evidence of what has come to be called *medical cost-offset*. These studies, such as the Mumford, Schlesinger, and Glass (1982) study already cited, typically take place in medical settings and seek to determine whether time-limited psychotherapy can significantly reduce the use of medical care. That is, these studies examine whether the cost of psychotherapy can be more than offset by savings in the cost of other aspects of medical care (e.g., Budman, Demby, & Feldstein, 1984). As the cost of medical care rises, the possibility that time-limited psychotherapy may save substantially more than it costs has become increasingly attractive to persons interested in the financial aspects of health care.

Mumford, Schlesinger, Glass, Patrick, and Cuerdon (1984; see also Mumford & Schlesinger, 1987), examined a number of published studies of health insurance claims in order to determine whether outpatient mental health services could be shown to reduce subsequent use of other medical services. These investigators found significant cost-offset in the form of reduced inpatient care, particularly among patients over age 55. These authors suggest that the commonly observed underutilization of outpatient mental health services among the older population may not only result in needless suffering but also in unnecessary expenditures for inpatient care.

Perhaps the most provocative findings reported in the literature are those linking a single therapeutic interview with subsequent reductions in the use of medical care. There is already a substantial body of literature showing that brief psychotherapy can have this effect (e.g., Goldberg, Krantz, & Locke, 1970; Jameson, Shuman, & Young, 1978; Jones & Vischi, 1979; Rosen & Wiens, 1979), but to demonstrate it following a single interview is startling indeed.

Cummings and Follette (Cummings, 1977a, 1977b; Cummings & Follette, 1968, 1976; Cummings & VandenBos, 1979; Follette & Cummings, 1967) undertook a series of studies investigating the role of psychotherapy in reducing medical care utilization in a prepaid health plan setting. They found that patients in such settings could easily somatize emotional problems and thus overutilize medical facilities. They estimated that "60% or more of the physicians visits are made by patients who demonstrate an emotional, rather than an organic, etiology for their physical symptoms" (Cummings, 1977a, p. 711).

Among the groups they studied was a sample of eighty emotionally distressed patients who were assigned to receive a single psychotherapeutic interview. They found, quite unexpectedly, that one therapeutic interview reduced medical utilization by 60 percent over the following five years, and that this reduction appeared to be the consequence of resolving the emotional distress that was being reflected in physical symptoms.

In another study, Rosen and Wiens (1979) examined the same issue at the University of Oregon Health Sciences Center. Comparisons were made between four groups of patients: (1) those who received medical services but were not referred for psychological services, (2) those who were referred for services in the Medical Psychology Outpatient Clinic but never kept their scheduled appointments, (3) those who were referred for psychological services but received only an evaluation, and (4) those who were referred and who received both an evaluation and subsequent brief psychotherapy. Groups 1 and 2—that is, those who were either not referred or who were referred but did not keep their appointments—showed no subsequent reduction in the utilization of medical care, including number of outpatient visits, emergency room visits, days of hospitalization, diagnostic procedures, and pharmaceutical prescriptions. Groups 3 and 4, those receiving only an evaluation or an evaluation and brief psychotherapy (averaging seven interviews), showed significant subsequent reduction in the utilization of medical care, but the group receiving only the evaluation demonstrated the most consistent reduction in, among other things, medical outpatient visits, pharmaceutical prescriptions, emergency room visits, and diagnostic services (see also Brown, 1984; Gask, 1986; Goldberg, Krantz, & Locke, 1970).

The one fact that links the findings of all these studies is that a single contact, virtually regardless of the purpose of that contact, appears to have salutary consequences for medically ill patients. That is, it appears to make no demonstrable difference whether the contact is designed to serve a primarily evaluative function or whether its purpose is primarily therapeutic in intent. Hoyt (1994b) has noted that the finding that a very brief episode of psychotherapy can result in a significant reduction of the cost of medical care has been replicated sixty times and that it is one of the most robust findings in the clinical research literature. It is findings such as these that have attracted mental health professionals to examine the consequences of single-session episodes of psychotherapy (see Chapter 8).

Bearing in mind this consistent evidence of the usefulness of brief psychotherapy in the context of medical illness, three very different approaches to working with medically ill patients will be examined—psychodynamic, rational-emotive, and strategic.

PSYCHODYNAMIC PSYCHOTHERAPY IN MEDICAL SETTINGS

Bellak and Siegel (1983; see also Chapter 3) suggest that brief psychotherapy may be necessary at the point where a physical illness or reaction to its proposed or past treatment becomes a psychiatrically incapacitating disorder. Such an event can occur, for example, when a patient is informed about the gravity of a disorder or the necessity for treatment procedures that are risky or painful, or postoperatively when the patient is in the midst of reacting to procedures already completed.

Bellak and Siegel believe that in order for the mental health professional to be helpful to the phys-

ically ill patient, it is essential to understand the nature of patients' reactions to their illnesses in terms of their prior life history. That is, the illness or surgery, for example, likely has specific meanings for the patient, and these meanings can be explored and clarified with considerable benefit.

Frightening experiences such as having to confront a serious physical illness can result in denial, depression, anxiety, or severe changes in the image of the self. In a case of impending surgery, for example, the mental health professional should carefully explore both the general and the specific fears associated with the impending event and how these fears can be understood in the context of the patient's life.

Bellak and Siegel have suggested a number of specific techniques that can be useful in the psychotherapeutic management of patients with severe physical illnesses. These include: (1) exploring the patient's concept of the illness or impending treatment, as well as the personal meaning and role of the illness; (2) educating the patient (see Bloom, 1988), (3) establishing contact with the treating physician or surgeon in order to enhance the mental health professional's effectiveness and to avoid being at cross purposes with the medical treatment plan; (4) exploring the meaning of anesthesia to the patient and the patient's attitudes and specific fears of death; and (5) exploring the patient's fantasies and attitudes about the specific illness and specific proposed treatment, paying particular attention to illnesses associated with organs of sexual significance, to malignancies, and to diseases of the heart.

Bellak and Siegel have suggested that "specific kinds of surgery to sexual organs stimulate rather standard reactions. A prostate operation will usually arouse fears of impotence and reawaken old castration anxieties. Breast operations, on the other hand, are often perceived as threats to a patient's femininity" (1983, p. 100). Regarding malignancies, Bellak and Siegel write: "For some cancer patients, the oral aggressive features of the patient's personality may find exaggeration in the disease so that they perceive the cancer as an eating, boring, destroying phenomenon. With others in whom the sado-masochistic features are predominant, the cancer may be perceived as a brutal, sadistic, attacking introject" (p. 101).

The heart has not only a vital physical significance but a special symbolic one. In the case of heart disease, postdischarge issues are often the most important. Bellak and Siegel have noted that "the therapist must anticipate the patient's feeling of depression following discharge from the hospital, and be prepared to take a supportive role in the follow-up treatment" (1983, p. 101). The mental health professional can help the patient cope with excessive fear and passivity and thus avoid becoming a chronic and fearful invalid. Because the cardiovascular system reacts so quickly to stress of any kind, the mental health professional has the opportunity to help cardiac patients cope with their increased sensitivity to their illness and to their reactions to stress.

Patients who have had heart attacks often are afraid that any exertion may shorten their lives, and as a consequence they may view work as far more of a hazard to their health than is actually the case. Bellak and Siegel also have suggested that physicians may be themselves uneasy about heart disease (in part because heart disease is so common among physicians) and may transmit some of that anxiety to their patients.

RATIONAL-EMOTIVE PSYCHOTHERAPY IN MEDICAL SETTINGS

Ellis and Abrahms (1978) have coined a number of terms to describe neurotic reactions of medically ill patients to their illnesses. Among them are "awfulizing," "musturbation," "self-downing," and "I-can't-stand-it-itis." All these terms describe a kind of whining that chronically characterizes the behavior of medically ill people who are not dealing with their illnesses in a healthy way. *Awfulizing,* as its name suggests, is the term used to label the person who says, "It's *awful* that I have such a horrible ailment, and it would be absolutely *terrible* if I suffered greatly or died of it." *I-can't-stand-it-itis* describes the patient who says, "I *can't stand* this utterly abominable condition and the uncertainty that I have about it." *Self-downing* is the term used to describe the person who says, "Since I could have watched myself more carefully and gone for regular medical examinations, and I did not do this well enough, that is rotten behavior and I am an exceptionally stupid, rotten person for behaving in this way."

These three forms of inadequate coping are all derivatives of thinking in *musts* rather than in preferences or desires. Thinking in musts is represented by the belief that patients *absolutely* have to do the right thing by themselves or by others. Such people nearly always conclude that they absolutely should have done everything they could have to ward off the disease, that they absolutely must not have the disease, and that since they have it, it absolutely must be their fault. Ellis would like medically ill patients to think "Tough luck"—that is, the philosophy that makes it possible for a patient to say, "Tough luck—it is truly unfortunate that I have this…problem. But that's the way it is. I damned well *can* stand the inconvenience, though I'll never like it. The problem likely won't mean the end of my life, and I can still live happily in spite of it."

Ellis and Abrahms (1978) recommend a kind of positive thinking that can be represented by "I can succeed and am therefore a pretty good individual." Contrast this with the negative thinking implicit in the statement "I can't succeed and am therefore a crummy person." They also recommend helping medically ill patients develop an unconditional self-acceptance by accepting the proposition that they have not done everything they could have done to prevent becoming ill, but that doesn't mean that they are contemptible people. Primary care physicians should help their patients think of their illnesses as representing problems to be solved and medical regimens to be followed and should communicate their support and affection for their patients with all their failings, and the sense that they can do more to help themselves than they realize.

Specific techniques of rational-emotive therapy can help patients dissipate the sense of shame that is often associated with physical illness; talk about and disclose things about themselves in ways they have never previously dared to; and become appropriately emotional, rather than under- or overemotional.

STRATEGIC PSYCHOTHERAPY IN MEDICAL SETTINGS

Goldsmith (1986) predicates his strategic approach to psychotherapy with medically ill patients on his assessment of their likely responses to psychotherapeutic intervention. Response tendencies to therapeutic interventions are grouped into three categories—straightforward compliance, defensive compliance, and opposition.

Assessment of likely responses to psychotherapy is particularly important in the case of medically ill patients because many such patients are opposed to psychological approaches to their difficulties. For these patients the only pertinent reality is their physical symptoms, and their only interest is in ameliorating those symptoms. For these patients, according to Goldsmith, a paradoxical intervention is required in which therapists ally themselves with the symptomatic side of the patient's ambivalence, allowing the patient to concentrate on the other side of the ambivalence, the side that wants to get rid of the symptom. Goldsmith calls this paradoxical intervention the position of the devil's advocate, and often it manifests itself in the therapist suggesting that the patient continue symptomatic behavior (see Boettcher & Dowd, 1988; Kovacs, 1982).

Goldsmith uses the patient's response to a restatement of the problem or to an empathic statement during the initial interview or to a homework assignment as part of the assessment procedure. For example, if the therapist repeats a remark that the patient has previously made and the patient rejects the comment as being inaccurate, or if a patient denies the validity of a carefully crafted empathic remark, or if a patient does not correctly or fully complete a homework assignment, these are all indications that paradoxical interventions may be the most effective in helping the patient.

Many medically ill patients resent being referred to a mental health professional for a consultation. They resent what they think of as not being taken seriously by the primary care physician, or the implication that their symptoms are thought of as imaginary or as malingering. Goldsmith (1986) writes:

> A patient suffering from a physical symptom interrelated with life stresses, who is unaware of the influence of these stresses, will experience the physical symptom as the only valid subjective reality. An investigation or explanation of non-physical causes of these symptoms will indicate to such patients, consciously and unconsciously, a lack of understanding and empathy on the part of the clinician....Even patients who...are aware...of such... influences on their symptoms will always be ambivalent about fully accepting the fact of an

> "emotional" causation. If this were not the case, they would probably no longer have their physical symptoms. (pp. 18–19)

Typically mental health professionals cope with such resentment by some combination of empathy, reassurance, the promise that mental health assistance will help patients cope with their symptoms, and education about the role of stress in precipitating physical illness. These mental health consultations sometimes fail to accomplish their objectives because consultants underappreciate why patients express their distress through physical symptoms and try to force the patients into thinking of the problem as *either* physical *or* psychological.

Goldsmith identifies two specific therapeutic techniques, the use of the therapeutic metaphor and reframing, as particularly helpful in working with medically ill patients. The therapeutic metaphor is a form of story telling, and its advantages lie in the fact that it can bypass a patient's resistance because the therapist talks about other people; its telling can induce a kind of hypnotic trance; and it can stimulate an individual's mental associative to help find a creative solution to the presenting problem. Goldsmith provides an interesting case example illustrating the use of the therapeutic (see Box 20-1). This case involved a 58-year-old electrician who had been promoted to a supervisory position three months earlier and who had been suffering with tension, nausea, and vomiting and "jumpiness" in his abdominal region since his wife had died eight years earlier and whose symptoms had become more severe since his promotion. He wanted to be free of vomiting and to have his nausea reduced to manageable proportions. He felt he could take care of the tension and the jumpiness himself. At the third session, Goldsmith induced a hypnotic trance and told him the story of another patient he had seen who had had a similar problem.

Reframing, the second of Goldsmith's special therapeutic techniques for working with medically ill patients, consists of changing the context of some behavior, event, or emotion so that its meaning changes. Vomiting is labeled as a sign of strength rather than weakness. A patient who derives pleasure from baffling physicians is told that if her symptoms disappear, that would really baffle her physicians because it would prevent them from ever discovering

Box 20-1: Use of the Therapeutic Metaphor

I said that I told the other patient that the stomach was a marvelous organ of complex capabilities. I described in great detail the stomach's sensory and secretory abilities, as well as its ability to adjust its size, shape, and the dimensions of its openings to the esophagus and small intestine by means of adjustments in the degree of muscular contraction at these openings. I told him how the walls of the stomach were lined with secretory cells and with powerful slabs of muscle, which contracted in order to break down food and pass it through to the small intestine. These wall muscles very capably and strongly broke down food, but their contractions could also produce vomiting. Vomiting was brought about by the contractions of these and other muscle groups, which produced a reversed flow of food up through the esophagus. Vomiting was a sign of great muscle strength and capability. The wall muscles of his stomach had quite sufficiently demonstrated their capability in that regard already, and why not just let them show their power in ways that could produce greater comfort for him, by their pulverizing food fully and propelling it properly and comfortably on to the small intestine, where it could really be enjoyed by the rest of the body.

In that way, he could be pleased and proud of the activity of these muscles. In addition, I said that I told this other patient that the human nervous system was really a marvelous set of intertwining electrical circuits. Nerves could be seen as electrical wires and cables. Junctions between nerves could be seen as switches and electrical junction boxes. The junctions of nerves and various parts of the body could be seen as outlets and electrical fixtures of various types. The brain could be imagined as a wonderfully capable electric service panel or else as an electrical box with a variety of switches, rheostats, and other mechanisms attached. Electrical information would be transmitted along the wires to the box in the brain, and the brain would send information to the various parts and organs of the body to govern the functioning of these organs. I described how such flow of information was as true of the stomach as of any other part of the body. I invited him to see and even feel how he could construct his own electrical circuits in his mind that would regulate the functioning of his stomach and would regulate the flow of information from his stomach to his brain.

He was to construct such circuits in detail. Such circuits could prevent the occurrence of vomiting in the stomach when such an occurrence was no longer necessary, and, I added, it no longer did appear necessary. Such circuits could also prevent the experience of any unnecessary degree of nausea. Such circuits could still allow the experience of tension and jumpiness in his stomach area, should the continuing experience of these sensations still be necessary. I was then silent for a minute or two in order to allow this unconscious activity to take place. I proceeded to give the patient posthypnotic instructions to the effect that these circuits could operate for his benefit any time he wished in the future....Upon awakening, he was able to describe to me a series of electrical circuits he had designed in a detailed and sophisticated manner. He was clearly pleased with the degree of expertise and prowess that went into that design, which he subsequently used successfully. Three months later, Goldsmith learned that the patient was free of vomiting, had only occasional nausea that was mild and tolerable, and that he continued to have tension and jumpiness. The patient had no idea why he still had these symptoms or why the vomiting had disappeared. He was fully satisfied with the results of the therapy.

From S. Goldsmith, *Psychotherapy of People with Physical Symptoms: Brief Strategic Approaches* (pp. 22-24), Lanham, MD: University Press of America, 1986. Used with permission.

the cause of her symptoms. A patient's symptoms are redefined as a noble sacrifice for the sake of helping his parents become more comfortable with their own lives. Communication difficulties between a husband and his terminally ill wife are reframed as evidence of his great concern for her and as evidence of her own inner strength in keeping feelings to herself when she wanted to. Willingness of a woman to tolerate her boyfriend's behavior (even though it included giving her gonorrhea) is reframed as evidence of great loyalty to him and as a wish to protect him from being alone (see also Kovacs, 1982, pp. 152–153).

Goldsmith has noted that reframing is as old as the human race, particularly in the context of illness and death. Sick people gain the ability to appreciate life more fully or are grateful that their illnesses give them an opportunity to learn about courage and compassion. Adversity is said to build character. Death is a blessing. Soldiers die for their country. Mourners find meaning in seemingly senseless deaths of loved ones. Such reframing, whether it occurs naturally or is stimulated by the work of a therapist, can help people gain new perspectives on their lives and can decrease personal distress.

CONCLUDING COMMENTS

Once again, the evidence of effectiveness of planned short-term psychotherapy is virtually unequivocal, including cases of patients who are medically ill. Furthermore, the evidence seems persuasive that the cost of providing psychological treatment is more than offset by the savings in the cost of subsequent medical care. Thus, efforts to study the role of psychological intervention in the treatment of medical illness seem entirely justified, and we can expect increasing application of planned short-term psychotherapy in the medical setting.

The three approaches to brief psychological intervention could not be more different from each other, but, as has been mentioned from time to time in this book, there is no evidence of any superiority of one approach over another. Each of the three approaches is faithful to its fundamental theories. Accordingly, it is important to be aware of a variety of approaches, if only to make a better match between the patient's difficulties and the therapist's clinical treatment preferences.

The psychodynamic approach, exemplified by the work of Bellak and Siegel, begins with the assumption that there are both rational and irrational aspects to patients' reactions to their illnesses and that attention to both aspects is necessary in order for the patient to receive optimal relief of distress. The rational-emotive approach, exemplified by the work of Ellis, treats patients' distresses essentially as neurotic thinking disorders and seeks to help patients think more positively about themselves in relation to their illnesses. These approaches are designed to reduce the sense of shame and guilt so often associated with physical illness and at the same time to promote a greater sense of self-acceptance. The strategic approach attempts to reframe or reconceptualize the symptom or the discomfort rather than removing it, creating the opportunity for patients to think about their distress using an entirely different metaphor from the one that characterized their pretreatment adaptation.

What is clear from these approaches and from the evaluation studies that confirm their effectiveness is that we should expect a significant increase in the reports of psychological intervention in an even wider variety of physical disorders, especially in the case of the elderly, in the near future (e.g., Kirshner, 1988; Lazarus, 1988).

CHAPTER 21

BRIEF CONTACT THERAPY

Overview

Brief Contact Therapy in Psychiatric Settings

Brief Contact Therapy in Medical Settings

Concluding Comments

Planned short-term psychotherapy can be brief not only in terms of the number of sessions, but also in that each contact may be brief. In brief contact therapy the length of the interview is never more than half an hour and frequently less (Koegler, 1966). As was indicated at the start of the previous chapter, brief contact therapy is identified primarily with the psychological treatment of medically ill patients by their own primary care physicians, ordinarily after they have received specialized training in that modality (e.g., Eshet, Margalit, & Almagor, 1993; Mohl, 1988; Sperry, 1987; Williamson, 1987; Zabarenko, Merenstein, & Zabarenko, 1971).

BRIEF CONTACT THERAPY IN PSYCHIATRIC SETTINGS

More than two decades ago Koegler (1966) proposed the use of brief contact therapy by mental health professionals in outpatient treatment settings, because he considered the greatest benefit of a psychotherapeutic interview to occur in the first few minutes, certainly within the first 30 minutes.

In proposing brief contact therapy, Koegler noted that:

> Psychiatry is the only medical specialty in which the patient sees the doctor for a fixed period of time, regardless of the patient's needs. The patient is stretched or shortened to fit the psychiatrist's procrustean time-couch. Psychiatric patients arrive and leave at fixed times; and a psychiatrist whose patients are permitted to overstay their allotted time

is thought to have "guilt about money" by his colleagues. Patients soon become accustomed to the system, too, and woe be it to the therapist who stops the session two minutes short! (1966, pp. 141–142)

Koegler cited several potential advantages of shorter therapy sessions. Greater numbers of clients could be accommodated, and psychiatric service would thus be made more economical and therefore more accessible. In addition, Koegler felt that briefer interviews would be more appropriate for certain clients—those who are seeing the therapist in conjunction with a medication evaluation and those with low verbal ability or who are psychotic or prepsychotic.

In perhaps the first evaluation of brief contact therapy in psychiatric settings, Zirkle (1961), struck by the positive responses of chronic schizophrenics to brief informal contacts with staff, developed a simple rating scale that could be used by ward staff to contrast the levels of improvement of thirty patients who had been divided into three groups. One group served as a control; the second group was seen for 25 minutes once a week in a private contact by a consulting psychologist; and the third group consisted of patients who were seen informally but privately for five minutes for five days each week. Two of the three judges who used the rating scale were blind to group assignment. The treated groups appeared to exhibit greater improvement than the control group, and, of the two treated groups, the patients who were seen five minutes daily improved significantly more than either the group of patients seen in one 25-minute session every week or the control group.

This work was extended four years later by Dreiblatt and Weatherley (1965), who conducted two studies examining the effect of very brief contacts with hospitalized psychiatric patients. In their first study a group of forty-four new patients in a Veterans Administration hospital was divided into three subgroups after an initial evaluation of their self-esteem and anxiety level. One group received regular ward care; the second group received three 5- to 10-minute contacts per week for two weeks in addition to normal ward care; the third group received six 5- to 10-minute contacts per week for two weeks in addition to normal ward care. Self-esteem and anxiety measures were repeated at the end of the two-week program. There were no significant differences among the three groups on initial test scores. Contacts were made at various times of day and were quite informal. They usually began with an open-ended question and were carried out in a friendly, chatty manner. Not only did the two brief contact groups show a significant increase in self-esteem, but they both had significantly shorter periods of hospitalization than the control group. In addition, the group receiving the six brief contacts per week demonstrated a significant reduction in anxiety.

In a second study these authors organized the brief contacts so that they were provided by four different staff members. In addition, they systematically examined the effect of the nature of the brief contact by arranging for one experimental group to talk about their symptoms, a second group to talk about social matters unrelated to symptomatology, and a third group to be contacted to help with a contrived ward task. All experimental groups received six contacts per week. Again, there was a control group that was treated with the normal ward routine. In total, seventy-four new patients were involved in the second study.

The general usefulness of the brief contacts was confirmed. Among the brief contacts, those patients who discussed issues unrelated to their symptoms seemed to gain most, and those who were contacted to help with a ward task gained least. The authors concluded that

brief contact therapy can have a markedly beneficial effect upon hospitalized psychiatric patients.... The beneficial effects of brief contacts are best understood as a product of an implicit message which they convey to the patient. The message is an ego-enhancing, supportive one; it tells the patient that he is accepted as a person. (1965, p. 518)

BRIEF CONTACT THERAPY IN MEDICAL SETTINGS

Most of the writing about brief contact therapy is directed toward primary care physicians, in an effort to persuade them to think about their 15- or 20-minute appointments as representing opportunities to deal with emotional as well as physical symptoms (e.g., Eisendrath, 1993; King, Broster, Lloyd, & Horder, 1994). In addition, there is some interest in brief contact therapy as practiced by mental health professionals in working with medically ill patients (e.g., Goldsmith, 1986, p. 66).

The importance of the primary care physician's role in the treatment of the mentally ill can hardly be overestimated. Regier, Goldberg, and Taube (1978) analyzed some major characteristics of the mental health service delivery system in the United States and found that primary care physicians provide about two-thirds of all mental health services delivered to the mentally ill (see also Gonzales, Magruder, & Keith, 1994). Thus, the effort to help primary care physicians provide more effective services to their patients with significant emotional difficulties within the reality constraints imposed by their modes of practice is not a trivial enterprise.

We shall examine five examples of the brief contact literature. As will be seen, these examples share many similarities, but they are far from identical. Each approach emphasizes special possibilities of brief contact therapy, and together these approaches display the rich opportunities that primary care physicians have to be of help in treating the emotional needs of their patients.

The Work of the Balints

The first systematic study of brief contact therapy with medically ill patients took place between 1966 and 1971 at University College Hospital in London under the direction of Michael and Enid Balint. Michael Balint, whose work was mentioned earlier in this book (see chapters 4 and 8), had been examining the doctor–patient relationship in general medicine for the preceding decade (see Balint, 1957) and had been struck by the enormous psychotherapeutic potential of that relationship. After his unexpected death in 1970 the London study was continued by his widow, under whose direction the report of the project was published (Balint & Norell, 1973). The Balints and their colleagues spent six years studying the six-minute interview—the average length of time a patient was found to spend with a primary care physician. Contacts between patients and primary care physicians rarely lasted longer than 15 minutes.

The Balints found that a meaningful and therapeutic relationship—a "brief, intense and close contact" (1973, p. xi)—could develop between patients and their primary care physicians even when only a few minutes were available for the contact. What was necessary was that the physician choose, in addition to trying to pinpoint the physical problem, to provide patients with an opportunity to talk about whatever they wanted to, and to focus on what their patients were trying to say. Under these circumstances a positive therapeutic moment often occurred—Enid Balint called it a "flash." That therapeutic moment, the research group believed, was intensity-dependent rather than time-dependent and thus could occur even in a contact that was very brief. It only required that the physician make one genuinely insightful or empathic comment during each treatment contact with the patient.

No one has competed with the Balints for the world's record for the shortest time required to conduct a meaningful therapeutic interview with a medically ill patient, but the general idea of brief contact therapy has resulted in one book called *The Twenty-Minute Hour* (Castelnuovo-Tedesco, 1965), and, more recently, another called *The Fifteen Minute Hour* (Stuart & Lieberman, 1986).

Castelnuovo-Tedesco's Twenty Minute Hour

Castelnuovo-Tedesco (1967, 1970, 1971) has experimented with a maximum of ten 20-minute interviews in the context of training primary care physicians, who are often interested in learning how to incorporate a psychotherapeutic orientation into their relatively busy medical practices. Castelnuovo-Tedesco suggests that, in addition to being concerned about the problem of time, primary care physicians hesitate to enter into psychotherapeutic relationships with their patients because of their lack of familiarity and training in short-term therapeutic techniques and because of the complexity of their attitudes toward psychotherapy. These attitudes often simultaneously consider psychotherapy to be virtually inert (since the psychotherapist does not really *do* anything) and magically powerful (since one false step can release dark forces that can engulf both patient and doctor).

Physicians' attitudes toward psychotherapy can also be complicated by some discomfort about being emotionally close to a patient, about thinking of a patient as a human being rather than as an object, and about the fear that patients will become too dependent on them. All this means that primary care physicians will consider undertaking brief contact psychotherapy only if convinced that they will not need to transform themselves into someone different, that they can practice psychotherapy within the usual constraints of their busy schedules, that the concepts and principles of psychotherapy are rooted in empirical investigation, and that by undertaking brief contact therapy they can in many cases enhance their ability to understand and to heal.

The "20-minute hour" is designed for the primary care physician who is not a specialist in psychiatry. Its goals are circumscribed and essentially supportive. Thus, its usefulness may be limited to patients with relatively simple neurotic disorders and might be contraindicated for patients whose neurotic disorders are disabling, who have gross disturbances in their thought processes or behavior, whose ability to deal with ordinary realities of life is significantly impaired, who are severely depressed, whose disorders appear to include organic pathology of the central nervous system, who have not been able to establish a stable pattern of living, who are abusers of alcohol or other drugs, whose problems include sexual perversions, who suffer from severe "psychosomatic" disorders, or who are unmotivated for any form of self-exploration.

On the other hand, brief contact therapy is appropriate for patients who suffer from neurotic or psychosomatic disorders that are annoying, uncomfortable, or limiting but not seriously incapacitating or who are mildly depressed or anxious. Medical patients who are suitable for brief contact therapy generally have a stable life situation and the capacity for satisfying and long-lasting social relationships and can point to some stressful life event or other precipitating factor that helps them understand their symptoms. Such patients are thought to be suitable for brief contact therapy because they are motivated to deal verbally with their difficulties.

Castelnuovo-Tedesco describes the two major steps in brief contact therapy as: (1) identifying the patient's major difficulties and selecting the goals of treatment and (2) engaging in therapeutic maneuvers to help patients label their current problems in a useful way and come to some decisions about what can be done to alter their current situation so that it is more satisfying to them. Note the almost total focus on the present and future, a strategy that is identified with a strategic approach to psychotherapy, even though Castelnuovo-Tedesco is psychoanalytically trained.

Helping patients identify their major problems starts with the initial history that is taken when the patient first appears, and it requires that patients focus on those aspects of their current predicament that are creating difficulties for them. This requirement is often difficult for some patients to meet because they have become accustomed to neglecting or ignoring problems that they think of as being both painful and seemingly hopeless. Castelnuovo-Tedesco reports that many patients show dramatic improvement just from successfully identifying and talking about their current difficulties.

In describing the general stance of the primary care physician, Castelnuovo-Tedesco suggests that the physician is a catalyst, a guide, a friendly mentor who keeps the patient on track and helps the patient avoid useless digressions by being facilitative, reflective, and questioning. The principal therapeutic techniques that are appropriate in achieving these goals are, according to Castelnuovo-Tedesco, confrontation, clarification, interpretation, education, advice giving, and reassurance.

Dubovsky's Primary Care Psychotherapeutics

Dubovsky (1981) also believes that psychiatric components of medical problems that are not severe or pervasive are best treated by the primary care physician, although he seems to think of the physician as someone with significantly developed psychotherapeutic skills and a high level of self-awareness. The milder problems that are amenable to primary care psychotherapy generally can be traced to some specific precipitating event and generally leave the patient fairly intact in most areas of functioning. From Dubovsky's point of view, psychotherapeutic sessions with medical patients can last from 15 to 50 minutes depending on the nature of the problem and of the physician's practice. As for the number of interviews, they too depend on the same variables—with acute problems, meetings may be scheduled once or twice a week; for supportive care, appointments may be scheduled as infrequently as twice a year.

Even with mildly distraught patients, however, Dubovsky believes that patients and their physicians need to make sure that they start out with shared common goals for the psychotherapy. But more often than not, according to Dubovsky, goals are not overtly discussed. The physician may believe that the patient needs to examine why he or she is unable to maintain a relationship, while all the patient wants is to get out of a terrible marriage. Another patient may want never again to be depressed, while the physician may think that helping the patient recover from this depression is all that can realistically be hoped for.

Dubovsky provides a number of informative case studies showing how primary care physicians can work with the emotional difficulties of their patients. In Box 21-1 are some excerpts from his description of the treatment of an acutely depressed patient. Only the first two interviews are excerpted here. This case is particularly pertinent because depression is probably the most common psychiatric problem brought to the attention of the primary care physician. More than 10 percent of depressed adults commit suicide, and suicidal patients far more often visit primary care physicians than psychiatrists.

Box 21-1: An Acutely Depressed Patient Treated by
the Primary Care Physician

(Emmelia Eckhart, a 30-year-old businesswoman, has been a patient of Dr. Durant's for the past few years. Conflicts over her involvement in her work resulted in divorce four years ago. Since then she has had little time for dating, and most of her spare time has been devoted to furthering her career. Emmelia is an interesting person, and during routine office visits she usually involves Dr. Durant in brief but animated discussions about everything from politics to art. Although Dr. Durant likes his patient, he feels that he really knows little about her. She has never discussed personal problems, and it has seemed appropriate to respect her apparent wish for privacy. Today, however, Emmelia seems preoccupied and unhappy. She does not engage her physician in the usual banter and seems in no hurry to be on her way. She seems to be saying "something is bothering me" without stating it openly, and Dr. Durant decides to use the time he would ordinarily spend chatting with her to find out what is wrong. Dr. Durant's thoughts are shown in brackets.)

Doctor: Emmelia, you seem upset today.
Patient: No, not really. I just haven't been feeling well. [*She seems more upset than she says she is.*]
Doctor: Care to tell me about it?
Patient: Oh, you're much too busy. I don't want to bother you. [*She's right. I am busy.*]
Doctor: It's true that I'm busy, but I have about 15 minutes in my schedule right now, and I can make more time later today or tomorrow if necessary. Now, tell me what's been bothering you.
Patient: I don't know whether to talk about it or not.
Doctor: Go on.
Patient: Well, I have been feeling kind of bad lately.

[*Something about the way she says this makes her feelings sound more than "kind of bad."*]

Doctor: How bad have you been feeling?
Patient: I get sad from time to time.
Doctor: You seem very sad.
Patient: I guess I do wonder from time to time if it's worth it.
Doctor: If what's worth it?
Patient: You know...life.
Doctor: Have you had thoughts of dying?
Patient: I guess sometimes. [*She can't be talking about killing herself.*]
Doctor: Have you been having thoughts of killing yourself?
Patient: Yes...[*What do I do now?*] Lately I've been thinking about how easy it would be to take the rest of the sleeping pills I have left from the prescription you gave me last year. [*Kill herself with my pills? How could she do that! I don't think I could stop her.*] I don't know...sometimes I think I'd be better off dead. Nobody would miss me anyway. People are so busy in this world, no one really cares. [*What is she talking about? She's got everything to live for!*]
Doctor: Emmelia, you must be feeling desperate to have thought about killing yourself. [*Although this seems obvious to me, it may help her to know that I see how bad she's been feeling.*]

(continued)

Box 21-1 continued

Patient: I guess I have been. I just haven't seen any other solution. *[She sounds hopeless. I hope I can help her.]*

Doctor: I'm sure that we can work together and find out why you've been feeling the way you have. *[I want to sound confident without making promises I can't keep.]*

Patient: You seem awfully sure. *[This is an invitation to say more.]*

Doctor: Depression is a problem that usually gets better with treatment. I'm reasonably certain that we can work together to understand what went wrong and find a better solution.

Patient: Well, if you really think it will help, I'm willing to try. *[She seems to be responding to my confidence.]*

Doctor: I'd like us to meet regularly for a while. For starters, how would it be if we met once a week for about a half-hour?

Patient: Do you think that's often enough? *[She may be telling me that she wants to meet more often. How can I help her to say this a little more directly?]*

Doctor: Do *you* think it's often enough?

Patient: Well, I wouldn't want to take up a lot of your time. *[I may feel like I'm giving up a lot of my time, but it's important that I respond to her need for more contact with me. For some reason, she seems unable to be more direct in stating her needs, at least at this time.]*

Doctor: Nevertheless, why don't we start by meeting twice a week and see how it goes?

Patient: If you think that's best, it's OK with me. *[She got me to take responsibility for this decision. She seems to have trouble asking for what she wants.]*

Doctor: Now, I'd like to talk about how we'll work together.

(A few days later)

Patient: I felt a little better after we talked. I don't know why. *[That's a relief.]* I don't know where to go from here. What do I talk about? *[I don't know either. What should I tell her?]*

Doctor: Why don't we start with whatever seems most important to you.

Patient: OK...I haven't told you about Jack, have I? *(With some encouragement from the physician, the patient describes her relationship with Jack, a married co-worker. She did not mention him earlier because of her shame at dating a married man, something she thought she would never do....Eventually Jack told the patient that he planned to leave his wife and marry her. Although she was happy at first, when a year went by without him taking any action, she began to realize that the plan was just a dream. She finally demanded that he decide whom he wanted. When he remained reluctant to commit himself, she discontinued the relationship.)*

Doctor: It must have really hurt when you realized that Jack wouldn't marry you.

Patient: I was crushed. I didn't know what to do. He's such a wonderful person. And his wife is so nice, I don't blame him for staying with her. *[How can she not blame him? He sounds awful!]*

Doctor: You don't sound very angry at Jack.

Patient: How could I be angry at him? He treated me so well! I just wish him the best. It was wrong of me to get involved with him anyway. *[She must be putting me on. She must hate him!]*

Doctor: We'll have to stop for now. Let's pick up again at our next visit.

Patient: OK. Is it Thursday?

From S. L. Dubovsky, *Psychotherapeutics in Primary Care* (pp. 86–96), New York: Grune & Stratton, 1981. Used with permission from W. B. Saunders Company.

Stuart and Lieberman's Fifteen-Minute Hour

Stuart and Lieberman (1986) are concerned with the same issue that was of interest to Castelnuovo-Tedesco 20 years earlier—how to persuade primary care physicians that they can incorporate a psychotherapeutic orientation into their medical practice to increase their effectiveness in dealing with the emotional components of the problems that their patients bring to them. Stuart and Lieberman have proposed a flexible, practical approach that consists of relatively simple techniques that are easily learned and that are effective without requiring lengthy therapy sessions, that is, without the necessity for physicians to modify their ordinary mode of practice.

The primary care physician has several advantages in working with patients that a psychiatrist does not have. Being diagnosed as having a psychological problem may be considered stigmatizing, and the primary care physician can treat the emotional problems of patients without labeling them as mental patients. Second, treatment of the emotional component of a physical illness can be incorporated into the normal medical treatment of the patient. The physician ordinarily sees the patient far earlier in the history of the problem than does the mental health professional, and under these conditions, small amounts of psychologically oriented treatment over a long period of time can sometimes be much more effective than a large amount of treatment concentrated in a short time period. Third, because referrals to a mental health professional may be viewed by the patient as rejecting, if primary care physicians are willing to incorporate psychotherapeutic techniques into their everyday work with their patients, they can come to be viewed as unusually accepting of patients regardless of the nature of their difficulties. Fourth, being that the body and mind are interdependent, the primary care physician is in a unique position to understand and treat the whole patient.

Stuart and Lieberman are clearly interested in persuading the primary care physician that treating the whole patient can be the best way of practicing medicine. While they acknowledge that in some cases a referral to a mental health professional may be necessary, they note that a high proportion of patients can have their emotional issues dealt with quite effectively within the physician's time constraints. They do not think of brief contact therapy as consisting of a certain number of short sessions devoted only to the consideration of the psychological elements of an illness, but, rather, that every contact between a physician and a patient should include attention to the emotional components of the problems that the patient presents. To be sure, emotional problems may be of sufficient severity so that additional appointments may be necessary to help patients cope with their difficulties. But even these additional twice-weekly, weekly, or bi-weekly appointments should deal with the whole patient.

Trying to be of help to a patient within the context of the 15-minute appointment requires much self-discipline on the part of the primary care physician. The physician must begin with the realizations that the problem belongs to the patient, that the physician can help the patient identify and become fully aware of an emotional problem that is contributing to physical symptoms, and that the physician can encourage the patient to explore potential solutions for the problem. But the physician is not responsible for determining the etiology of the problem, or its full impact on others, or for solving the problem. Stuart and Lieberman write:

> When the physician communicates to the patient that there is the expectation that the patient, having identified the problem, is expected to find some constructive resolution, a positive message is conveyed. The physician agrees to be part of the process, to make suggestions for strategies that can be employed, but it is clear to both parties that the patient has the responsibility to deal with the problem—which by definition is expected to yield to resolution. (1986, p. 89)

In order to keep the objectives of the brief therapeutic contact within realistic limits, Stuart and Lieberman suggest that the focus should be on the here and now and on the patient's strengths and that, when possible, the patient's family should be involved in trying to help the patient. The therapeutic approach they advocate includes, first and foremost, empathic concern for the patient, and, secondarily, the use of a variety of therapeutic techniques such as exploring options, encouraging new behavior, and providing explanations and anticipatory guidance.

When there are only a few minutes available to examine the psychological components of a medical problem, and when the patient is fortunate enough to have a primary care physician who allocates those few minutes for that purpose, the patient quickly learns to put emotional difficulties in some priority order. And because so little time is available, it is necessary for the patient to do some therapeutic work as a form of homework, the results of which can be discussed at the next appointment. Patients may be asked to keep track of their periods of upset, sleep patterns, instances of successful or unsuccessful coping, options, wishes, advantages or disadvantages of some particular potential course of action, arguments, or accomplishments.

Stuart and Lieberman conceptualize how the limited amount of time in a normal appointment with a patient can be put to best use by the acronym

BATHE—background, that is, what is the context of the difficulty; affect, that is, how does the patient feel about the problem; trouble, that is, what about the situation is most troubling; handling, that is, how is the patient coping with the problem; and empathy, that is, legitimizing the patient's feelings. Box 21-2 provides an example of the use of these five components of the brief contact therapy.

Stuart and Lieberman are fully cognizant of the fact that undertaking the treatment of the emotional components of a physical illness adds significantly to the stress under which the primary care physician operates. Accordingly, they have proposed a dozen rules for physician survival, that is, rules that help ensure personal psychological well-being for physicians who seek to engage in brief contact therapy with their patients. The rules are well worth excerpting (see Box 21-3).

Box 21-2: Stuart and Lieberman's BATHEing the Patient

(A 34-year-old woman, who had been a patient at the family practice center for about a year, presented in the office complaining about a vaginal discharge. She appeared to be quite agitated. The physician inquired about what was going on in her life. The patient started to cry.)

Patient: I just found out that my husband has been having an affair with my oldest sister for the past year and a half.
Therapist: How do you feel about that? [The physician felt a little foolish. It seemed like this was an inane question to ask under the circumstances, but he really didn't know what else to ask.]
Patient: I feel angry. I have mood swings. I go up and down. I also feel depressed.
Therapist: What about the situation troubles you the most?
Patient: I have two children. They are two and five, and I really don't want to be a single parent. [The physician was surprised. He would have expected her to be most troubled because of the familial involvement or the time frame.]
Therapist: How are you handling it?
Patient: I feel I am handling things very badly. I am angry and do a lot of shouting at my husband. I am afraid that the children are starting to be affected, and I don't want that.
Therapist: [taken aback] That sounds like a horrendous situation.
Patient: Yes it is. *(visibly relaxed)*
Therapist: Why don't we examine you now, and find out what we can do about your vaginal discomfort, and then we'll talk some more.

From M. R. Stuart and J. A. Lieberman, *The Fifteen Minute Hour: Applied Psychotherapy for the Primary Care Physician* (p. 103), reprinted with permission of Greenwood Publishing Group, Inc., Westport, CT. Copyright © 1986 by Praeger Publishing.

Box 21-3: Stuart and Lieberman's Rules for Physician Survival

Rule 1: Do not take responsibility for things you cannot control.

Rule 2: Take care of yourself or you can't take care of anyone else.

Rule 3: Trouble is easier to prevent than to fix.

Rule 4: When you get upset, tune into what is going on with you and go through the three-step process—1. What am I feeling? 2. What do I want? 3. What can I do about it?

Rule 5: If the answer to Step 3, Rule 4 is "Nothing," apply Rule 1.

Rule 6: Ask for support when you need it; give people permission to feel what they feel.

Rule 7: In a bad situation you have four options—1. Leave it, 2. Change it, 3. Accept it, 4. Reframe it.

Rule 8: If you never make mistakes, you're not learning anything.

Rule 9: When a situation turns out badly, look at where the choice points were, then decide what you would do differently next time.

Rule 10: At any given time you can only make decisions based on the information you have.

Rule 11: Life is not fair—or a contest.

Rule 12: You have to start where the patient is.

From M. R. Stuart and J. A. Lieberman, The Fifteen Minute Hour: Applied Psychotherapy for the Primary Care Physician (pp. 167–171), reprinted with permission of Greenwood Publishing Group, Inc. Westport, CT. Copyright © 1986 by Praeger Publishing.

Eshet, Margalit, and Almagor's Ambulatory Medicine

Eshet, Margalit, and Almagor (1993; see also Eshet, Margalit, Shalom, & Almagor, 1993) have described their approach to family-oriented ambulatory medicine that takes place in 10- to 15-minute encounters in a primary medical care clinic. Their work has been influenced by a number of theoretical domains—biopsychosocial concepts and a variety of individual and family counseling approaches, as well as the recognition that medical difficulties can often be best understood in the context of a search for meaning in life. Their report has been based on a collaborative relationship between physicians and psychologists with about a hundred cases seen over a three-year period.

In the basic meeting, which averages about 11 minutes in duration, Eshet, Margalit, and Almagor attempt to create a socially sensitive relationship with the patient, inquire about the problem and its biopsychosocial context, conduct an appropriate physical examination, formulate an accurate and helpful diagnosis and treatment plan, provide a significant intervention, and evaluate the encounter both from the point of view of the patient as well as the physician. For example, the physician can

> offer a written prescription to a woman who suffers from headaches during summer, in order to reduce the pain. He can suggest that she drink larger amounts of water and take evening walks with her husband whom she longs to be with....During the walk the older son should take responsibility of the younger sister and in return, the father will help him with his homework when they return from the walk....The prescription will accompany cognitive intervention and include an explanation about the connection between lack of fluids plus workload and headaches. (Eshet, Margalit, & Almagor, 1993, pp. 183–184)

Subsequent meetings can be planned that focus on more specific objectives—follow-up of treatment recommendations, practice and instruction, short meetings for minor issues, or somewhat longer family meetings. Whatever the specific purpose of the meeting, this general approach is based on a patient-centered and family-centered orientation.

CONCLUDING COMMENTS

The writings in the field of brief contact therapy have an important message for mental health professionals, quite apart from what they say about primary care medicine. That message is that every minute counts. If the mental health professional has 15 minutes to spend with a patient, as is often the case when monitoring psychopharmacologic regimens, for example, or when doing so-called routine follow-up interviews, those minutes are golden. What can take place during that brief period of time has the potential for significant impact on the patient. Mental health professionals who start from the premise that because they have only a short appointment with a patient they can't realistically expect to get any therapeutic work done need to rethink that point of view.

We have examined five approaches to brief contact therapy in the primary care setting. All share a set of assumptions: that only mildly disturbed patients are suitable for this therapeutic modality; that goals must be sharply limited; that the focus must be on the present and on the future; that it is patients and not the physician who have the responsibility for making changes in their lives; that the principal contribution of the primary care physician is to provide an opportunity for the patient to talk in a setting that is supportive, empathic, and affirmative; and, of course, that the time allotted to the therapeutic contact must conform to the normal working schedule of the physician. While these assumptions

seem to create constricting limits on who may be helped, in fact these limits are more apparent than real, and, as we have seen, there are some special advantages to patient and physician alike if the primary care physician offers to be helpful to the patient in dealing with psychological difficulties.

The writings on brief contact therapy illustrate two different approaches to the task. On the one hand, as in the work of the Balints and of Stuart and Lieberman, primary care physicians are urged to incorporate a consistent interest in the psychological components of physical symptoms during every appointment with every patient. The other approach, as in the work of Castelnuovo-Tedesco and of Dubovsky, is to teach primary care physicians the elements of psychotherapeutic intervention so that they can emulate mental health professionals. From this vantage point, primary care physicians can schedule one interview or a series of brief psychotherapeutic appointments in order to help patients cope with their emotional problems. Both approaches can be valid, depending on the nature of the situation, and the wise mental health professional may be able to ascertain which approach may be most appealing to each specific primary care physician—for it must be recognized that not all primary care physicians are interested in or temperamentally capable of dealing with the mental health needs of their patients. For those primary care physicians who are interested, however, the mental health professional has much to contribute to enhancing their skill and effectiveness.

CHAPTER 22

TIME-LIMITED GROUP AND FAMILY PSYCHOTHERAPY

Overview

Historical Roots of Short-Term Group Psychotherapy

Brief Approaches to Group Psychotherapy

Brief Marital and Family Psychotherapy

Concluding Comments

While the majority of the literature on planned short-term psychotherapy concerns itself with individual therapy, there is a substantial and growing body of work dealing with the clinical aspects of time-limited group, marital, and family psychotherapy. The principles that appear to be useful in time-limited group and family psychotherapy bear a significant relationship both to those of time-unlimited group and family psychotherapy and to time-limited individual therapy.

Since group therapy tends in general to be longer than individual therapy, brief group therapy tends to be longer than brief individual therapy (Sabin, 1981). According to Budman and Gurman (1988), time-limited group psychotherapy is usually conducted in weekly 90-minute sessions and lasts anywhere from eight to 60 weeks. Groups that focus on a specific circumscribed issue, such as the loss of a relationship or a recent geographic move or illness, may last as little as eight or ten weeks (e.g., Garvin, 1990; Goldberg, Schuyler, Bransfield, & Savino, 1983; Oppenheimer, 1984; Rempel, Hazelwood, & McElheran, 1993; Trad, 1991). Recently, however, there have been reports of eight-session groups for far more severe conditions, such as schizophrenia (O'Shea, Bicknell, & Wheatley, 1991 and sexual abuse (Isely, 1992); and for holocaust survivors and their children (Fogelman, 1992).

Groups that deal with a significant developmental issue or life transition typically last from twelve

to twenty sessions (e.g., Kemp, Corgiat, & Gill, 1991/1992; Lieberman & Yalom, 1992; Pavan & Mangini, 1992). Groups that aspire to make significant characterological changes or that are concerned with helping clients cope with ongoing developmental difficulties may last a year or even longer (e.g., Vardi & Buchholz, 1994). Membership in time-limited therapy groups may be open, with new members being admitted from time to time, or closed, with no new members admitted once the group has begun, and the time limit may be predetermined for the group as a whole or for each individual group member.

A special form of group therapy that has attracted the attention of a number of short-term psychotherapists is clinical work with couples and families. Paralleling the variety of approaches to short-term individual therapy, short-term marital therapy approaches have been developed from psychodynamic, cognitive-behavioral, and systemic perspectives (Gurman, 1981). As indicated in the discussion of Milton Erickson's work in Chapter 16, strategic approaches associated with his work with individuals have been carried over to marital and family therapy, where they are playing an unusually important role in influencing marital and family therapists. Gurman (1981) writes:

> In the structural-strategic view, the symptoms of individual family members are both system maintained and system maintaining, and all individual

problems are seen as manifestations of marital-famil-ial disturbance. Marital conflict is viewed as the result of interaction, largely unaffected by intrapsy-chic (especially unconscious) forces. The psycholog-ical symptoms of a husband or wife are assumed always to have interpersonal meaning and, in fact, to function as communicative acts, so that a sympto-matic individual cannot be expected to change unless his or her family system changes. (p. 427)

Family and marital psychotherapies appear to be reasonably effective, certainly in contrast with out-comes for untreated clients. Differing approaches do not appear to yield different outcomes, and marital and family approaches to psychotherapy appear to be indistinguishable from individual approaches in terms of their effects (Shadish, Montgomery, Wilson, Wilson, Bright, & Okwumabua, 1993).

HISTORICAL ROOTS OF SHORT-TERM GROUP PSYCHOTHERAPY

According to Sabin (1981), present-day short-term group psychotherapy can be traced directly to the early work of Kurt Lewin. Lewin, a social psychol-ogist, left Nazi Germany and came to the United States prior to World War II, bringing with him an abiding interest in how groups have an impact on individual behavior, feelings, and perceptions. Lewin believed that groups have enormous power to affect individuals, for better or worse, and that deci-sions made in a group setting have far more viabili-ty and power than do individual decisions, regardless of the nature of the decisions. Lewin's early action research included helping factory work-ers work together more productively and helping train community leaders to learn to combat racial and religious prejudice.

Lewin and his colleagues chanced upon a strate-gy that transformed the working groups into training groups, or T-groups, as they were later called,—a strategy that included having observers in atten-dance at the meetings who later presented and dis-cussed their observations with the group members. This discussion, now called feedback, turned out to have an enormous impact on the group members and became the basis of training in group dynamics.

Experience with these T-groups subsequently led to a strategy for organizational consultation, on the one hand, and for a newly developing type of sensi-tivity training that had a frankly personal therapeutic objective. It is these sensitivity training groups, or, as they were later called, encounter groups that served as the direct predecessor of short-term group therapy.

BRIEF APPROACHES TO GROUP PSYCHOTHERAPY

In this chapter, we shall examine a number of quite different approaches to short-term group, marital, and family psychotherapy. Each approach seems to have its special virtues and possibilities. While mari-tal and family therapy involve couples or families, group psychotherapy typically brings people togeth-er who do not, at least initially, know each other. Members of therapy groups tend to be brought together because they share a common predicament, for example, a contemporary crisis that they are unable to manage on their own, or the residual effects of childhood physical or sexual abuse, or recent mar-ital disruption, or being newly admitted into a mental health treatment facility. Some therapy groups are formed because members are thought to need the opportunity to develop increased interpersonal sensi-tivity or because they are socially isolated.

Budman's Short-Term Experiential Group Psychotherapy

Budman and his colleagues (Budman, Bennett, & Wisneski, 1980, 1981; Budman & Clifford, 1979; Budman, Demby, & Randall, 1980; Budman & Gurman, 1988) have for a number of years been thoughtfully describing their work at the Harvard Community Health Plan, a health maintenance orga-nization located in the Boston area.

Budman uses the term experiential to describe his general approach to group psychotherapy because the model is "more than simply an economical way to treat several unrelated individual patients or cou-ples simultaneously. Rather, the emphasis is upon those interpersonal factors (e.g., cohesion, group development, feedback, self-disclosure, etc.) that are believed to be pivotal elements of any experiential group treatment" (Budman & Gurman, 1988, p. 247).

Four principles govern Budman's approach to time-limited group psychotherapy: (1) pregroup preparation and screening; (2) establishing and maintaining a focus in the group; (3) developing group cohesion; and (4) establishing a time limit and coping therapeutically with its reality. Pregroup screening and preparation in both individual and workshop formats are taken very seriously. Individual sessions are designed to help prospective patients determine if their problems can be conceptualized in the context of what is likely to be the focus of the group.

Pregroup workshop sessions are used to develop skills in desirable group behaviors, to improve patient selection, to provide an opportunity for prospective patients to make an informed decision about the appropriateness of their participation in the envisioned group, and to help reduce subsequent dropout rate. The workshop takes place in a single 90-minute session with 8 to 12 prospective members and includes an opportunity for small group and large group experiences that are analogues of what is likely to take place in the therapy group. Following the pregroup individual meetings and workshop, prospective patients are in a position to decide whether they would like to become part of the time-limited therapy group.

Once the group itself begins, the fundamental initial task of the therapist is to establish a thematic focus. Budman distinguishes between what he calls the working focus and the emergent focus. The working focus represents the therapist's preliminary idea of what the group is to be about—a definition that can help, for example, in recruiting members, in planning time limits, and in deciding whether the group is to be open or closed. A working focus might be to deal with difficulties young adults have in establishing intimate relationships or to help a number of married men and women deal with the breakdown of their marriages. Once the therapy group begins, a refined, more specific emergent focus develops, one that takes into account the unique pattern of needs and characteristics of the group members.

Much of the therapeutic value of groups comes from the sense of cohesion that develops among its members—the psychosocial forces that cause members to choose to remain part of the group. Budman and his colleagues have developed a broad concept of cohesion that includes six dimensions: (1) withdrawal and self-absorption versus interest and involvement, (2) mistrust versus trust, (3) disruption versus cooperation, (4) being unfocused versus being focused, (5) abusiveness versus expressed caring; and (6) global fragmentation versus global cohesiveness. Cohesive groups are those in which members express interest and involvement, trust, cooperation, focus, and caring. These attributes help create a setting in which individual group members can learn and profit from each other's experiences and struggles to cope with the stresses in their lives.

Budman and his colleagues believe that each short-term therapy group must have a clear and definite time limit. Their concept is reminiscent of Mann's beliefs (see Chapter 6) and can be illustrated by the following statement:

> When group members are able to explore the issues raised by the time limit, the fact that is often brought into focus is that the time available in one's life is also limited. Often, this realization helps to 'get members moving' who have previously been too fearful or too stuck to attempt even minimal changes. (Budman & Gurman, 1988, p. 268)

Budman also includes a follow-up group meeting in his planning. A group reunion takes place 6 to 12 months after the group has terminated. It provides an opportunity for group members to learn what has happened in each of their lives and for the therapist to develop a useful appreciation of the outcome of the group psychotherapy. Budman and Gurman (1988) conclude a description of time-limited group psychotherapy by noting:

> Time-limited groups are an important therapeutic modality for the brief therapist. Such groups can, for some patients, be at least as effective as individual treatment....For the therapist who is concerned about issues of time, efficiency, and organizational or financial constraints, time-limited groups may offer a significant opportunity for treating homogeneous populations of patients. Although it still remains unclear who will profit the most from group as opposed to individual therapy, we believe that with many people this "either-or" choice does not need to be made. Since a patient's group therapy, in our model, can be perceived of as part of an

overall course of treatment, it is only one element in the broad array of tools available to the brief therapist. (p. 282)

The Crisis Group

Donovan, Bennett, and McElroy (1981) describe the rationale for a special type of group treatment designed to help patients troubled by life crises. They hypothesize that a timely but brief intervention can ameliorate symptoms of the crisis (see also Imber & Evanczuk, 1990; Prazoff, Joyce, & Azim, 1986) and that such a group would fit naturally into any organization that values rapid access, rapid assessment, and rapid treatment.

In the program organized by Donovan, Bennett, and McElroy, patients are referred via the medical triage department where patients in acute distress are first seen. Referrals to the crisis group are made when a patient reports acute onset of significant symptoms following an identifiable precipitating stressful life event, provided that the patient does not seem psychotic, homicidal, or suicidal and that he or she is interested in participating in a group. Seven or eight such patients meet twice a week for 90 minutes for four weeks. The group is led by two co-therapists, a triage nurse and a mental health professional.

The crisis group focuses on the present, particularly on the problem that precipitated the crisis. Patients take turns telling their stories; the other group members listen and sometimes comment. When a story has been completed, the therapists and other patients raise questions, try to clarify issues, and provide advice. The general tone of the group is supportive, friendly, and task oriented. Members of the group see its purpose as to help each member with a specific problem. The therapists are active and confrontive about both group and individual issues as seems appropriate—"What does this long silence in the group mean when this woman tells us she will be terminating the group early?" or "You're hanging onto this man who has been continually unfaithful. How come?" As group members learn how to be of help to each other, the therapists tend to become less active in promoting problem-solving behavior. There is a general effort to help patients help themselves, although supportive behavior by other group members is also encouraged.

Nearly half of the patients who start the crisis group participate in fewer than four sessions, indicating that the crisis group may not be optimal for everyone. On the other hand, social relationships among group members often continue after the group has terminated. About half of the patients seek additional therapy after the crisis group is over, and Donovan and colleagues report that patients who remain with the group virtually always report that they benefited from the experience.

More formal evaluation conducted with a sample of forty-three patients who completed the crisis group yielded highly favorable results both at the conclusion of the group and one year later in terms of reduction of anxiety and depression and increase in ego strength. The most common reasons given by these former patients for the helpfulness of the crisis group were: (1) the support from other group members, (2) knowing that other people had similar problems, and (3) the opportunity the group gave them to talk about their difficulties.

Treating Loss Through Short-Term Group Psychotherapy

Traditionally, group methods of intervention in the case of loss have not been developed to work with newly grieving persons. Rather, such interventions have been limited to providing help to people who, after the initial shock of the loss has subsided, have failed to adjust to an environment that does not include the missing person and also to people who are unable or unwilling to invest psychological energies into forming new relationships—that is, to people who are experiencing pathological grief reactions.

Piper, McCallum, and Azim (1992) have developed a short-term group psychotherapy treatment program for clients who have not adapted well to the loss, either through death, divorce or separation, or a geographical move, of significant persons in their lives. The general orientation of this group psychotherapy program is psychodynamic in that it works toward the identification of internal conflicts that impede normal mourning. Major techniques employed in working with these clients include interpretation and clarification as well as facilitating improved adaptation to loss. Evaluation studies built into the clinical program suggest that the treatment has a significant positive effect.

The group psychotherapy program developed by Piper and his colleagues consists of twelve 90-minute weekly sessions with groups composed of seven or eight individuals who are expected to attend all of the sessions. Clients are required to be open, sober, and honest and to work toward learning more about themselves and about others in the group. Finally, clients have to agree to hold in confidence whatever they hear from other group members.

A number of common themes have been found in many of the groups, including questions of trust, dependence versus independence, and privacy versus intimacy. In addition, a number of common roles have been identified among the clients in many of the groups: the "apparition," a client whose attendance is unpredictable; the "monk," a silent but attentive client; the "professor," a client who speaks in generalities and who seems to deal with loss in an intellectualized way; the "nurturer," who provides support and encouragement to other group members, often at the cost of monopolizing the meetings; the "emotional conductor," who seems to take over the expression of emotions for the entire group; and the "cruise director," whose joking and sarcasm divert the group from its principal tasks.

Therapists, in following a psychodynamic approach to their work, encourage, if only passively, a regressive process within the clients; maintain a generally neutral stance regarding whatever is disclosed during the sessions; and use transference analysis and interpretation as the main therapeutic technique. Therapists tend to be confrontive rather than supportive, and, as a result, their role is a demanding and stressful one. Therapists tend to focus on common characteristics that patients share and to keep in mind the structural limitations of the group, notably its short-term character. The time limited nature may be particularly pertinent, in that these patients who have all dealt poorly with loss enter the group knowing that they will shortly lose the relationships that may develop during the group meetings. In a sense, then, helping clients cope with the impending loss of their group plays a therapeutic role in helping clients cope with the loss that led them to join the group.

Group Treatment of Children and Adolescents

This book makes virtually no mention of individual short-term psychotherapy with children and adolescents except, as will occur shortly, in the context of children being treated along with their families. When one considers the amount of individual short-term psychotherapy that goes on with children and adolescents just within the public school system alone, it is astonishing that so little has been written about short-term individual psychotherapy with young people (e.g., Shapiro, 1984; Sloves & Peterlin, 1986).

Virtually all therapeutic contact with school-age children is short-term, and it is unfortunate that school personnel who have such rich experiences working with young people do not often share their experiences with others through the written word. Perhaps school counselors and special education teachers are uneasy about describing their contacts with school children as "therapy."

There is, however, an interesting literature on brief group treatment of children and adolescents that is worthy of review and assessment. Scheidlinger (1984) has prepared an overview of approaches to short-term group therapy with children and finds it useful to distinguish between those groups that are conducted by professional, specially trained group practitioners and those that are not. The professional therapeutic groups are designed to help repair pathology; the nonprofessional groups have, according to Scheidlinger, goals that involve preventive intervention, remediation, or enhancement of optimum functioning. Scheidlinger insists that the two types of groups are not to be differentiated in terms of actual or alleged superiority, although the distinction he makes may help explain why school personnel may be reluctant to write about their experiences working as therapists with school-age children.

Examples of nonprofessionally organized groups include discussion groups for children who share a common experience such as divorcing parents, summer therapeutic camping groups, groups of children of mentally ill parents, or groups of children facing a common transitional crisis such as moving from an elementary school into a junior high or middle school. Such groups are often located in school settings. Professional short-term therapy groups for children tend, on the other hand, to be located in traditional mental health settings, either inpatient or outpatient, and may include play therapy; activity therapy; and, among older children, groups that focus on verbal interaction as the principal therapeutic modality and deal directly with a variety of developmental issues.

According to Scheidlinger, short-term group psychotherapy with children and adolescents should focus on current issues rather than on the resolution of unconscious conflicts. Its emphasis should be on encouraging corrective emotional experiences and on active participation in the change effort. Because children's character structure is more flexible than adults' and because children appear to be more resilient than had previously been assumed, Scheidlinger believes that short-term group treatment should be increasingly accepted as a treatment of choice for children.

Bornstein, Bornstein, and Walters (1984) have described a six-session group experience designed for children ages 7 to 12 whose parents have recently undergone a divorce. The primary objective of the sessions is to enhance communication between parents and children. The group meets for 90 minutes on six consecutive weeks with male and female cotherapists. While rules are kept to a minimum, the therapists provide a carefully thought-out structure to each of the sessions. Thus, at the first session, after a snack and general introductions, group members are asked to discuss a number of relatively safe topics, including why people get married, what makes a good marriage, how their parents met, why their parents got married, why some marriages fail, and why there are more divorces now. After this discussion the therapists help the group members discuss why divorce is hard on children, what are the benefits of divorce, how the members found out that their parents were divorcing, and what happened when they talked with their parents about the impending divorce.

The second session is given over to a review of the previous session and a discussion of communication problems in a divorced family. Exercises are provided by the co-therapists that allow group members to try out ways of communicating with their

parents under a variety of circumstances. Group discussion follows the exercises. The third session is devoted to a discussion of feelings, again with the use of a number of exercises. The fourth session is devoted to problem-solving techniques, and the fifth session to the control of anger. Parents are invited to take part in the final session, and, with the use of videotapes, children and parents are provided an opportunity to discuss a number of issues pertinent to being part of a divorced family.

Another short-term group program, this time with behaviorally disturbed young adolescents, has been described by Rauch, Brack, and Orr (1987). This program, consisting of five one-hour meetings held after school, is offered as an alternative to suspension for boys in grades six through eight (ages 11 to 14) whose behavior would under normal circumstances have resulted in their being suspended from school.

A behavior management system using both group rewards and group consequences is used. A point system is negotiated, and at the end of the five sessions, group members can pool their remaining points for rewards—food from a neighboring fast food restaurant or free-time use of the school gymnasium.

Rauch, Brack, and Orr (1987) have described their therapeutic orientation as follows:

> The group leader used an approach in group sessions which stressed here and now, responsibility for and consequences of behavior, and exploration of feelings. The sessions allowed participants to examine their behavior and how it affected themselves and others. They were encouraged to consider the consequences of their actions as well as to identify alternate ways to obtain the response their negative behavior sought. Role playing the alternatives was used to help the participants use the alternative. (pp. 20–21)

During the five weeks of the group therapy, referrals to school officials for disciplinary action dropped dramatically, but the improvement was short-lived. Three months after the treatment program ended, referrals for disciplinary problems had returned to pretreatment levels. The authors have suggested that lengthening the period of group treatment might extend its effectiveness. Even without extended effectiveness, the group treatment would be an inexpensive and useful alternative to school suspension.

One other finding deserves mention. In comparison with boys matched for age and school grade who did not present behavior problems, the boys in this group treatment program were significantly more sexually mature. If this observation is replicated in other studies, it would suggest that the group program might be modified by attention to the issues raised by this accelerated maturation.

Clinical studies of short-term groups with sexually abused boys and girls have appeared in the literature (e.g., Damon, Todd, & MacFarlane, 1987; Friedrich, Berliner, Urquiza, & Beilke, 1988), and a review of short-term group therapy with depressed adolescent outpatients has recently been prepared by Fine, Gilbert, Schmidt, Haley, Maxwell, and Forth (1989). Their review suggests that brief group therapy has been remarkably helpful with emotionally disordered adolescents in general.

Fine and his colleagues (1989; Fine & Gilbert, 1993) examined two different twelve-session approaches to the brief group treatment of depressed adolescents—a social skills training program and a therapeutic discussion group. The social skills program made use of a previously prepared manual that dealt with seven specific social skills: (1) recognizing feelings in oneself and others, (2) assertiveness, (3) conversational skills, (4) giving and receiving positive feedback, (5) giving and receiving negative feedback, (6) social problem-solving, and (7) social conflict negotiation. The therapeutic discussion group provided an opportunity for group members to share ideas and gain an improved understanding of common concerns, as well as to provide mutual support. The therapist provided an atmosphere in which these opportunities could be maximized. As time went on, group leaders became less active as group members began taking greater responsibility for what was discussed in the sessions. Fine and his colleagues concluded that if therapists are skillful, particularly in recruiting new members for the group experience, the discussion group approach can be unusually rewarding and successful because adolescents seem to respond so much to their peers.

BRIEF MARITAL AND FAMILY PSYCHOTHERAPY

Interest in brief marital and family psychotherapy has paralleled the growing interest in brief individual psychotherapy, in part because this area too has been affected by reduced public funding and the limitations on reimbursement from third-party insurance, but also because there are some advantages to keeping family psychotherapy as brief as possible (Hurley & Fisher, 1993). In addition, however, brief family or marital therapy has been found useful in making significant changes in family interactions and relationships (Popchak & Wells, 1993; Snyder & Guerney, 1993).

Haley (1987) has observed that all clinicians must deal with marriages in some way, because every adult "is either married, planning to be married, or avoiding marriage" (p. 161). He has made a number of important observations about marital therapy and marital therapists that bear repetition. Haley cautions that marital therapists should avoid minimizing problems; that they should avoid abstractions such as debating about life in general, but rather focus on specific behaviors; that they should avoid being in a consistent coalition with either spouse; and that they should avoid the past and focus on a fresh start. For example, Haley suggests that in discussing a past quarrel, rather than just going over the event in detail, it might be better to think of it in terms of how the incident should have been dealt with so that the couple could have been pleased with each other.

Haley also suggests that that the therapist should allow for complexities in interactions. Instead of suggesting that a wife ask her husband for what she wants, it might be more useful for the therapist to suggest, "I want you to ask for what you want in such a way that it takes your spouse a while to understand what you mean." Finally, he suggests that the therapist should avoid allowing irreversible positions. In summary, Haley (1987) suggests that the therapist must

> take problems seriously, focus on specific issues, form deliberate coalitions to tip balances, not allow free expression of ideas that might cause irreversible harm, formulate goals, not always require

that couples talk explicitly about problems [and] not assume that one couple or one problem is identical with another (p. 179)

These admonitions have wide clinical applicability and are sufficiently general to be subscribed to by any therapist undertaking marital therapy.

Dysfunctional families are frequently characterized by impaired parenting, placing children in the role of parents, boundary violations, chronic rejection, traumatic experiences, disordered cognitions, and disordered communications. When these conditions are present in a family, particularly in combination, the development of strong self-esteem, adaptive coping skills, and mature relationship patterns is far more difficult for children (Bedrosian & Bozicas, 1994; Trad, 1993).

Impaired parenting can be a multigenerational phenomenon. Children who find themselves in the role of parents to their own parents are vulnerable to low self-esteem, anxiety, and feelings of guilt, even when they are reasonably successful at the task. Boundary violations include such phenomena as recurrent physical abuse, inappropriate seductive behavior, intrusions into the child's privacy, and inappropriate coalitions between parents and children. Chronic rejection may include scapegoating, inappropriate blaming, or verbal abuse. Disordered cognitions can include superstitions, distorted perceptions of the self or others, or invalid ideas about marriage or the family. Distorted communications can include lack of assertive skills, double-binding, avoidance of discussion of topics that should be openly considered, or other forms of interpersonal withdrawal.

Friedman, Budman, and Hoyt (1992) have suggested that treating couples and families is particularly challenging because negotiating a focus with the clients is very difficult. In treating couples or families, there are two or more clients who may not always agree with each other about why they are seeing the therapist. On the other hand, having several members of the same family in the same room at the same time does provide the therapist with an unparalleled opportunity to view the interpersonal relationships among the family members.

Perhaps the single most informative general description of a time-limited child and family treatment program is that written by Kreilkamp (1989). Kreilkamp works in a mental health department of a comprehensive health maintenance organization in which the fundamental responsibility is to provide care—psychological as well as medical—to all members who ask for it. Referrals to the mental health department come mainly from pediatricians; thus, while the entire family is usually seen, a child is ordinarily the identified patient.

While appointments are necessary, access to all forms of care is easy in this comprehensive setting. Families have a generally positive attitude toward the entire health care system, each patient has a single integrated medical record, and communication between mental health and physical health professionals is excellent. But clinicians are very busy and there is a premium placed on prompt clinical action designed to produce significant change in the client. There is relatively little time for leisurely information collection and diagnostic assessment.

The average number of sessions that a family is seen is five, but there is no limit on the total number of sessions that a client may be seen in any particular time period. Patients are encouraged to identify and work on a limited problem with a therapist and then to continue working on the problem on their own. Clients are told that they can always return for additional appointments when necessary.

The key concept in the therapeutic program is what Kreilkamp calls "action." Action is relatively easy to observe and to alter. Observing actions can often yield clues as to underlying feelings. Efforts to modify actions can often result in changes in these underlying feelings and may be easier to accomplish than focusing direction on the feelings. Family members can influence each other's actions. Parents can provide security so that children can try new actions and under the best of circumstances can evaluate their children's actions to help them profit from their experiences and refine their actions.

In therapy the therapist can act so as to help family members modify their actions. Therapist actions include observing, listening, questioning, hypothesizing, and suggesting. The intensity of these actions distinguishes the short-term psychotherapist from one who is less concerned with time and, accordingly, less active. The importance of action cannot be overestimated in understanding the fundamental character of brief psychotherapy. If there is one therapist attribute that all brief therapists share, it is likely to be their emphasis on action in therapy. This concept is so important that we shall return to it at the end of this volume.

Weiss and Jacobson's Brief Behavioral Marital Therapy

Behavioral marital therapy is, as its name suggests, essentially cognitive in character. Weiss and Jacobson (1981; see also Jacobson & Margolin, 1979) have developed this form of marital therapy on the assumption that problem behaviors have both maladaptive as well as adaptive qualities. Their therapeutic approach is particularly appropriate in the case of couples who are still involved enough with each other to work actively toward problem resolution.

Behavioral marital therapy seeks to make changes in four target areas—responses, skills, competencies, and contexts. By *responses,* Weiss and Jacobson refer to behaviors that one or both marital partners make that are seen as destructive to the relationship. Thus, couples can be admonished not to engage in certain behaviors, such as discussing whether or not to move or whether or not to separate, for a specified period of time, often until after the next meeting with the therapist. By *skills,* Weiss and Jacobson mean specific proficiencies such as good listening or encouraging elaboration of something just said by the partner, that is, behaviors that can enhance communication and generalize to settings outside the therapeutic relationship.

Weiss and Jacobson use the *competencies* to refer to more generic skills that apply to any content area. Examples of competencies include the ability to discriminate among and within different environments as opposed to thinking that all environments are the same, the ability to be supportive and understanding in interactions with the partner, the ability to problem solve in order to achieve mutually shared objectives, and the ability to effect change in oneself and one's partner. Finally, by *contexts,* Weiss and Jacobson refer to specific areas of marital interaction, such as child care or communication processes, and to how responses, skills, and competencies can be targeted to especially identified aspects of the marital relationship.

According to its proponents, behavioral marital therapy has the potential to help couples exercise better control over their context-specific behavior, their patterns of mutual reinforcement, their generation of alternatives when in conflict situations, their problem-solving skills, and their abilities to step back from their immediate conflicts in order in discern patterns to their own behavioral histories.

Marital therapy, say Weiss and Jacobson, requires a master plan that comprises a number of specific techniques designed to accomplish a specific set of objectives that are established on the basis of a careful pretreatment assessment followed by the development of a treatment contract. This contract focuses on the purposes of the sessions and their likely duration (usually 8 to 10 sessions). Behavioral marital therapy is far more concerned with the future than with the past and is far more concerned with problem solving than with rehashing old problems. That is, behavioral marital therapy shares much in terms of theory and technique with individually oriented cognitive or behavior therapy.

Behavioral marital therapy is brief by design— that is, brief because it is believed that shorter is better. The therapist has the specific responsibility of moving the therapy along, making sure that time is used wisely and is not wasted. This built-in brevity represents a special difficulty in marital therapy because it often requires that the couple temporarily sacrifice the little positive that they have in the present for the promise of increased rewards in the future. For example, Weiss and Jacobson comment:

> Consider the directive that each spouse increase the frequency of pleasing behaviors during the ensuing week. The assignment requires effort; each spouse must concentrate on pinpointing behaviors in his or her repertoire that the other spouse finds pleasing and then generate these behaviors at a higher frequency. Neither spouse can be sure that the other will reciprocate; in other words, the overall consequences of compliance with the assignment are uncertain. Therefore, one would expect spouses to be ambivalent and behavioral resistance to be a rather common occurrence. (1981, p. 411)

The very brevity of the treatment creates a compelling focus on compliance with therapist directives, on overt verifiable behavior, and on attention to change. Weiss and Jacobson's position is that brief behavioral marital therapy can therefore accomplish certain objectives that cannot be achieved in longer, time-unlimited therapy.

Weiss and Jacobson (1981) have undertaken a number of controlled experiments designed to evaluate their work. In fact, they indicate that their emphasis on empirical validation of their concepts and practices may be behavioral marital therapy's greatest strength. They report that their treatment techniques, when applied conscientiously, appear to be very effective.

Hudson and O'Hanlon's Brief Marital Therapy

Hudson and O'Hanlon (1991) describe their brief marital therapy as being solution-oriented rather than explanation-oriented. Thus, while they see some similarities between their work and many other approaches to marital therapy, they identify primarily with the earlier work of de Shazer (Cade & O'Hanlon, 1993; also see Chapter 18). They describe their ideas as simple without being oversimplified; their approach is brief, yet it is designed to bring about permanent improvement in the spouses' relationship with each other.

Hudson and O'Hanlon believe change is always possible. They believe relationships can change rapidly and that the most changeable aspects of a couple's relationship are in what each of them does and how each of them views what the other member of the couple does. In working toward change, they believe it is fundamental to validate each person's experience in the relationship actively and articulately. They avoid blaming, avoid labeling, and avoid explaining. In their opinion, these actions discourage change.

Their approach is built on the importance of distinguishing between observable facts, interpretations of these facts, and inner reactions to these interpretations. More often than not, this distinction results in asking couples to move from discussion of their interpretations or reactions to describing facts, that is, to what any observer who was in the vicinity might also have seen. According to them, it is, the interpretations and reactions—the labeling, the blaming, and the explaining—that get couples into trouble.

The focus of attention is typically the person who can effect change, rather than who is thought to have caused the problem. Either partner can bring about changes in the behavior pattern, regardless of who might have been responsible for bringing about the undesired behavior.

Hudson and O'Hanlon routinely supplement their psychotherapy sessions with task assignments that are to be undertaken between sessions. Such assignments are designed to bring about behavior change outside the therapy sessions, and are typically developed jointly between the therapist and the couple. The interview excerpt in Box 22-1 illustrates the process of developing a task assignment.

Task assignments can involve deliberately changing some repetitive counterproductive behavior, providing an opportunity for the couple to practice some underdeveloped interpersonal skill, or suggesting that the couple try to notice something about each other's behavior that they had not previously recognized. Developing effective task assignments is often facilitated by inviting the couple to identify objections they might have or difficulties they might foresee in carrying out specific tasks; by suggesting that the couple try something out as an experiment; or by discussing the assignment as if it will be carried out, as in, "After you do this, I want you to tell me…." Task assignments are always put into writing, with a duplicate given to the couple.

Hudson and O'Hanlon pay particular attention to rituals, restoring stabilizing ones that have somehow been lost by the couple as well as creating new ones to help them move on with their lives. Thus, rituals can maintain continuity with the valued past as well as mark discontinuity with a past that must be left behind. In addition, Hudson and O'Hanlon encourage the use of humor and playfulness in the relationship, suggesting that a lasting relationship requires four factors—interpersonal skills, a sense of ethical behavior, commitment to the relationship, and a good sense of humor.

Bergman's Systemic Family Psychotherapy

Bergman (1985) thinks of his brief systemic psychotherapy with and about families as emergency road service, designed to get families who are stuck

> **Box 22-1: Developing a Task Assignment**
>
> *Wife:* You know, one of the big things that led to a lot of our troubles is that he wasn't telling me how he feels. A lot of times, like last weekend are very stressful. We moved into our apartment, we were all sick with colds and everything, and he just kind of phased out on me. He was just like kinda not there, and I said, "What's going on? How are you feeling? What are you doing?" "OK, I'm all right, OK." And it's like, if it's just the stress of moving in together, just tell me what you're feeling and a lot of times he doesn't do that, he doesn't deal with that.
> *Husband:* I'm usually the last to know how I feel!
> *Therapist: (laughs)* It's like, "I wonder how I do feel." And so during those recent conversations that you've had, when you've been sitting down together every night, have you been able to say a little more about what you're feeling?
> *Husband:* Sometimes.
> *Therapist:* Sometimes. OK, so it takes a little practice to tune in to what you are feeling.
> *Husband:* I need some kind of an exercise or something that would help me do that.
> *Therapist:* OK.
> *Husband:* I could sit down and write. I'm able to do that much better than talking.
> *Therapist:* Good, OK. So how about keeping a journal in preparation for your nightly talks, sort of like Olympic trials? You write out what's going on with you or what's been going on with you in the last day or so. It's funny that you mentioned writing, because sometimes when I have couples that get into these real blocked or stuck places in communication, I just tell 'em, "Okay, get a pad of paper. Now you write out what's going on with you or what you want to say and you've got five minutes to do it…and then you pass the pad of paper to her and she'll write out what's going on with her and then you pass it back and forth." So sometimes because she's maybe a little better with expressing it in words and you may be a little better expressing in writing, you may want to switch back and forth between those…
> *Wife:* We kind of, we kind of did that, just to see if we were on the same wavelength, when we were getting back together. We sat down at one point, before he had moved back in, and we wrote down what our short-term goals were and our long-term goals, just to see if we were on the same wavelength.
>
> From Hudson and O'Hanlon, 1991, pp. 71–73.

somewhere back on the road as quickly as possible. While Bergman works with a wide variety of individuals and families, always about family issues, he has a special interest in resistant families, those who have previously been unable to profit from contacts with mental health professionals. Bergman has provided an informative description of his therapeutic interventions and their rationale and of his particular use of homework assignments and of what he calls *rituals* (Bergman, 1990)—a term he uses somewhat differently from the way Hudson and O'Hanlon do.

Bergman is careful in selecting families for his therapy to make sure that their motivation for help is genuine and that their level of resistance is not so high as to preclude their being helped. After concluding that the family is suitable for therapy, Bergman's task is to "capture" them—that is, to create a truly therapeutic relationship as quickly as possible. His job is to join with the family in word (by being appropriately self-disclosing) and manner, while remaining sufficiently uninvolved so as not to become entangled in it. With such a therapeutic relationship in place, Bergman next formulates clinical hypotheses about the family, if only tentatively, and sets out to help them change the nature of their interrelationships.

Three assumptions guide the process of hypothesis formulation: "(1) All children's symptoms reflect some marital dysfunction; (2) the more serious the child's symptoms, the more intense and resistant the marital conflict; and (3) the more covert the marital conflict, the more resistant the family system will be to change" (Bergman, 1985, pp. 64–65). Critical questions that Bergman raises in the process of hypothesis formulation may include: "Who has the problem?" "Why is the symptom a problem?" "Does anyone in the family not consider the symptom a problem?" "Who in the family is most upset about the problem?" Another set of questions deals with the symptom itself: "How often does it occur?" "When?" "Where?" "Who reacts to it?" "In what way?" "When did the symptom begin?" "How does the family account for the problem?" "Why has the family come into treatment now?"

As for attempted solutions, Bergman asks, "What has been tried, by whom, and for how long?" "Is there anything the family tried that they feel could have been done more?" "Do the parents agree or disagree about the solutions?" "How do family members react to each other's solutions?" "What would happen if the symptom got better or worse?" Finally, questions can be framed to deal with treatment goals: "What do the family members hope will happen by coming here?" "What is their ideal goal?" "What will they settle for?" "How optimistic are they about improvement?"

Bergman sees identified patients as taking the position of "victims"—people who place other people's needs before their own; who are vulnerable, overly sensitive, and in need of approval from others; who feel angry, impotent, afraid, frustrated, helpless, and deprived; and who are usually unable to express their feelings directly. Other family members may be "killers"—who are equally vulnerable but who hide this vulnerability behind a cold, tough, aggressive, snobbish, omniscient, inexpressive, selfish exterior. Or they may be "snipers"—who lash out against vulnerable family members when they themselves become frustrated or angry. Family members of all three types are in fact victims, but killers and snipers have the ability to cause victims considerable pain. Bergman's principal task in therapy is to help victims change, by helping them handle killers or snipers.

Victims can profit by being told that they are acting as victims, which, because victims are sufficiently reactive, can mobilize them out of the victim role. In addition, asserting that the patient is assuming the role of victim and demonstrating how that role assumption manifests itself are fundamentally hopeful stances, implying that the patient can assume a different role.

Depending on the specific situation, Bergman might point out to victims that they are spending much more time avoiding what they do not want than trying to obtain what they do want. Bergman might point out how a patient's adherence to the role of victim demonstrates protective loyalty to parents, by making them feel needed or by showing that they are more unhappy than their parents. Deliberately demanding that the patient continue this practice can sometimes be therapeutic. For example,

> I sometimes give a resistant victim a powerful ritual to perform. I tell him to find photographs (preferably enlargements) of his mother and father and each night to "tell" these photos what he did (or did not do) that particular day to ensure that he remained unhappy or less happy than his parents. Then he is to say that he did these things for his parents and that he wanted them to know this. (Bergman, 1985, p. 105)

Bergman's strategies for helping victims deal with killers are designed to reverse or reframe their typical ways of dealing with them.

> If, for example, a victim becomes anxious because the killer is perceived as cold, I would encourage the victim to be affectionate, warm, or embracing....The reversal...transfers the anxiety from the victim to the killer. After the reversal, the coldness no longer produces anxiety, and the victim no longer feels in a one-down position. At this point, the killer might become anxious because the level of affection (closeness) is now being controlled by the former victim....Another reversal I find effective is used for victims who see their killers as aggressive, angry, attacking, or blaming. I encourage the victim, after he receives a shot from an attacker, to convert the killer into a mental patient with earnest sympathetic questions such as: "Are you all right?" "Is everything OK?" "Is something wrong?" When the killer responds with, "Of course everything is OK. Why do you ask?" the victim gently and sympathetically says, "You seem so upset, unhappy, and I thought that maybe something was wrong." (1985, pp. 109–110, 111–112)

Since snipers strike irregularly, they are harder to identify in a family context and thus are harder for the victim to deal with. The first task, therefore, is for the victim to identify the possible sniper. The next step is to help the victim respond to the sniper with shorter periods of delay and in ways that neutralize the snipes. For example, Bergman writes:

> My personal preference for responding to snipers is to use confusion and humor....What I do after being sniped, and what my patients have done with considerable success, is to kiss the sniper on the nose, giving no explanation. People know immediately when they are being sniped, and although they cannot react fast enough to think, they can react fast enough to kiss a sniper on the nose. The kiss does several things. First, it provides an immediate (and therefore powerful) reaction to the sniper. Second, it probably confuses the sniper, since the last reaction to the snipe he expects is affection. Third, responding to a snipe with affection has a "forgiving"...quality about it. Thus, both the confusion induced in the sniper and the forgiving posture move the victim from a potential one-down position to an almost double one-up position. (1985, pp. 112–113)

Guerney's Family Relationship Enhancement

Guerney (1990; Guerney & Guerney, 1985) has developed an approach to brief family psychotherapy that focuses on relationship enhancement, an approach that has shown unusually significant results. Based on an educational model, relationship enhancement psychotherapy appears to be well accepted by clients, in part because it teaches interpersonal skills that have impact not only on the family itself but also on relationships with friends and with colleagues at work.

In contrast to many other approaches to family therapy, relationship enhancement has a format that encourages clients to speak only to the therapist, that is, not to each other, and to learn a set of communication techniques from the therapist that are highly specialized. These techniques help clients learn to become both Expressers (expressing one's own thoughts and feelings) and Empathizers (expressing others' thoughts and feelings).

One of these techniques is called *Becoming*—a technique that is invoked toward the end of an interview designed to teach clients how to listen to each other and remember what has been said, how to make sure that they understand the other person, and to be honest about their own feelings without putting the other person on the defensive. In using this technique, the therapist tries to become each of the clients in turn and speak as though he or she were that client. An example of this technique can be found in Box 22-2. The clients are a married couple, Stan and Amy, who have been married for four years and have arrived at a point in their marriage when they think divorce may be inevitable. Stan has been married before and has a high school–aged daughter who spends every other weekend with Stan and Amy. This episode of psychotherapy was completed in five two-hour sessions, after which the couple reported significant improvement in their relationships with each other. Follow-up telephone contacts confirmed the continuing improvement.

The Becoming technique follows five guidelines that allow the therapist to accomplish the goals set out for it. These guidelines are: (1) speaking subjectively, (2) expressing deep positive as well as negative feelings, (3) referring to specific events and behaviors rather than speaking in general terms, (4) expressing positive feelings that underlie negative feelings, and (5) asserting exactly what each person wants from the other person and the benefits that might occur if these wants were met.

Homework assignments are made that include listening to relationship enhancement demonstration audiotapes, reading from a relationship enhancement manual, and completing relationship enhancement questionnaires. Specific relationship skills are taught and the clients are given opportunities to practice their skills both inside and outside of the therapeutic sessions. Clients are asked to audiotape their interactions at home when they are practicing their new skills, and the therapist provides supervision based on listening to these audiotapes.

Other techniques that are used by the therapist and taught to the clients, in addition to Becoming, include Laundering (alternately becoming both parties in a dialogue while also receiving input from both parties), Modeling (expressing the exact words that clients can use to express their thoughts and

---

Box 22-2: "Becoming" in Relationship Enhancement Therapy

Therapist: Before I explain more about the nature of the therapy I will be doing with you, I would like to be you, Stan, talking to Amy. And then I would like to be you, Amy, talking to Stan....After I'm finished being you, Stan, I'll check with you so you can add or change anything that I don't get quite right; you can also interrupt me if I get off base. And I'll also check with you, Amy, about whether you felt at all defensive listening to me as Stan. Then I'll switch and be you talking to Stan....

Therapist: (to Amy as Stan) Well, first and most important, I don't want to lose you. This last year, and even before, have really been painful for me, even though I've been the one to leave you the first two times, and I'm usually the one to threaten it. I do that because I get really scared that you don't care about me the way I want you to. And I get really angry, too. You know, I lived alone for 5 years, and I took care of our daughter on alternate weekends, and I did OK, but what I longed for was someone to really share my life with, to talk everything over with, and to lean on when I needed to. And when we got married 4 years ago, it seemed to me that you were that person....

Therapist: (to Stan as Amy) You know, I really like it that you love me, but sometimes I feel so strongly that I have to pick between you and me! Sometimes I feel like I can hardly breathe in this relationship. And then I want to make room for myself, to be really free—not divorced, not unfaithful—just free. For instance, I love my job, and my second job, too, and I love being active in company activities. And I love traveling to conferences. And I love seeing friends. And, although I love your daughter—and I do love you—I lived alone for 13 years before I met you, and I got really used to being independent, and I know I don't want to give that up.

From M. Snyder and B. G. Guerney, pp. 224–225 in R.A. Wells and V. J. Giannetti (Eds.), *Casebook of the Brief Psychotherapies*, New York: Plenum Publishing Corporation, 1993. Used with permission.

---

feelings if they choose to do so), Prompting (suggesting ideas or types of responses as opposed to exact wordings), Facilitation (coaching each other at home); Generalization (extending newly learned relationship skills to different settings) and Maintenance (practicing relationship enhancement skills). In Box 22-3 is an example from the fourth session with this couple of how a therapy session can use many of these techniques.

The Family Therapy of the Milan Group

Mara Selvini Palazzoli and her colleagues (1978, 1989; see also Gustafson, 1986, pp. 215 ff.; Tomm, 1984a, 1984b), working in Milan, Italy, have described their family therapy approach as having initially been influenced by the ideas of the staff of the Mental Research Institute in Palo Alto (see Chapter 17). Their work was directed at understanding how family processes influenced child behavior, particularly in cases of severe psychopathology.

Using many of the ideas regarding paradoxical interventions developed by the MRI group, the Milan therapists initially had a number of remarkable successes in working with families. But they subsequently found that these interventions were of limited usefulness and that relapses frequently occurred. In particular, they noted that paradoxical interventions were helpful primarily early in treatment, that is, during the first or second session; if such strategies failed to produce significant family change quickly, the therapists were at a loss as to how to proceed. In their views, "further recourse to paradoxical intervention was of no avail and sometimes even grotesque" (1989, p. 11; see also Roberts, 1986). Accordingly, they extended their investigations by searching for other innovative theories and therapeutic strategies to supplement the MRI approach.

Box 22-3: Relationship Enhancement in Action

Amy: (as Expresser) I tried to think about what I could have done differently. Like maybe I could have apologized sooner. But when you picked up your boots and left the room, that was really hard. I mean, I thought if you were just going to go to the other room, you would have left your boots. To me that was like, "I'm leaving."

Stan: (as Empathic Responder) It was like implying to you that I was going away. You thought maybe you could have apologized sooner. But in any event, when I picked up my boots, you got upset because you thought I might be leaving.

Amy: Yeah.

Therapist: (to Stan, Modeling for the Empathic Responder) Try adding something like this to your own words: "It means a great deal to you that I've made a promise to myself and to you not to leave. It's a tremendous relief to you to know that when I'm upset or scared or angry, I'm not leaving it as an option to walk out. It helps you to feel safe and feel like you're not going to get abandoned or treated like you're bad....

Therapist: (to Stan, Prompting for the Expresser) I'm wondering if, when you picked up your boots, you were thinking for a moment that you might leave the house, like an old habit that you're changing, just like Amy is changing her old habit of not apologizing after she's been grumpy with you. Or whether maybe it was just a way of showing Amy what was going on with you. Could you talk to her about that?

Stan: (to Amy) I was feeling really disempowered by what was going on between us, and I got up out of the bed maybe feeling "pouty." I felt, like really—in my bare feet—I felt disempowered, and I grabbed my boots to feel empowered. I guess, I think I knew what it would do. I didn't have any intention of leaving the house.

From M. Snyder and B. G. Guerney, p. 229 in R. A. Wells and V. J. Giannetti (Eds.), *Casebook of the Brief Psychotherapies,* New York: Plenum Publishing Corporation, 1993. Used with permission.

Undertaking clinical work with one particular family was especially influential in that it resulted in the development of a prescription to the parents that has since, in somewhat revised form, become a standard part of their clinical intervention. The couple had had a serious marital conflict for a number of years. Their eldest daughter was a chronic anorectic and her problem severely affected the family, especially since she had made several dramatic attempts at suicide. The most remarkable aspect of the first three sessions was the highly aggressive way the three daughters, all of them in their teens, interfered in and controlled their parents' daily lives. At the end of the fifth session the team members, feeling that they had made little progress, decided to summon only the parents to the following session. Their hope was to find a nonverbal way to prevent the girls from intruding themselves into their parents' problems. Selvini

Palazzoli has described the subsequent history of this case as follows:

We came up with the following prescription, which we handed to the parents during the session that followed: Keep everything that has been said during this session absolutely secret from everyone. Should your daughters ask questions about it, say that the therapist has ordered everything to be kept only between her and the two of you. On at least two occasions between now and your next scheduled appointment, you are to "disappear" from home before dinner without any forewarning. Leave a note worded as follows: "We shall not be in tonight." Each time you go out, pick some place to meet where you are reasonably sure no one will recognize you. If, when you get back home, your daughters ask you where on earth you've been, simply smile and say: "That concerns only the two of us." Each of you is also to keep a sheet of paper, well out of everyone's sight, on which to jot down personal observations on how each of your daughters has reacted to her parents' unusual behavior. At our next meeting, which will again be with only the two of you, each of you will read your notes out loud. (1989, p. 16)

Treatment of the family ended after three additional sessions with the parents. Within a month significant positive results had been obtained both in terms of the eldest daughter and the entire family. Follow-up a year later indicated that the results had remained stable. Three years later the parents reported that their eldest daughter was happily married.

Selvini Palazzoli has reported that this intervention has been used with more than twenty families with generally excellent results. Her explanation of these encouraging findings is that the prescription interrupts what she calls "the ongoing family game" by awarding preeminence to the parental couple, by making an explicit alliance with the parents against the other subsystems of the family, and by keeping in focus the importance of the disturbed child's recovery. This prescription started out as invariant—that is, it was employed with every family.

The secrecy aspect of the alliance with the parents has become particularly important in their work. Generally the initial session includes the entire family as well as appropriate members of the extended family. The second session is usually limited to the immediate family, and the third session, when adequate progress is being made, is limited to just the parents, with the secrecy prescription presented at the end of that session. Subsequent sessions are used to lengthen the periods of family subsystem independence and also involve only the parents, who are appointed to serve in "co-therapist" roles.

Sessions are generally limited to a maximum of ten and are held approximately one month apart. Sessions, which may last as long as three hours, and are often interrupted for team members to discuss what they have learned from the family and how best to proceed. More recently the invariant prescription has been replaced by a somewhat more flexible approach that is specifically designed for each family. It is clear in reading the reports prepared by the Milan group that their family therapy approaches are undergoing continuing modification as they learn more about how families interact and how children are impacted by their parents.

CONCLUDING COMMENTS

The variety of approaches to group and family therapy is well exemplified in this chapter. Strategic-systemic theories come into their own in group and family therapy, while psychodynamic and cognitive-behavioral approaches, even though they originated in the context of work with individuals, have found favor among numerous clinicians who are also involved in working with groups.

Two potential virtues of group and family therapy seem particularly evident in the writings just reviewed. First, group treatment seems especially suitable for dealing with clients who share some life experience or life issue, for example, a crisis, a stressful life event, or a developmental transition. That is, a theme of some kind can serve as an organizing principle for group treatment. Second, treatment of more than one patient at a time allows for the possibility that the therapist may not be the only person in the room who is therapeutic. Patients can and do help each other, often in ways that are not easy for the therapist to emulate, such as by providing and receiving mutual support. Third, writings in the field suggest very strongly that therapeutic work with couples concerned with relationship issues may present unusual promise—perhaps far more than working with them one at a time.

There is probably far less planned short-term group and family therapy going on in the mental health field than individual therapy, and this may account for the fact that planned short-term group and family therapy theory is not as well elaborated as are the theories of planned short-term individual therapy. Because there is more than one patient in the room at the same time, an additional level of complexity is introduced into the clinical setting, one that is not welcomed by all clinicians. Many clinicians find planned short-term individual therapy sufficiently challenging.

But some practitioners seem to be drawn to working with couples, families, or other groups, and it will only be a matter of time before short-term group therapy theory will have the same richness and variety as does short-term individual therapy. The critical issue may well be to determine whether the group setting will allow certain necessary therapeutic processes to take place that cannot take place in individual therapy. In addition, there is reason to believe that group or family therapy may be only one of what may be more general strategies for being of help to groups or families. Such strategies could include serving as a family consultant or even larger systems consultant (see Kreilkamp, 1989; Wynne, McDaniel, & Weber, 1987). These activities, in a sense alternatives to family or group thera-py, may under certain circumstances offer a better way of being helpful to families and other groups. Family consultation, for example, may provide a family the opportunity to examine a variety of alter-natives that might be open to them in dealing with a family issue, to identify poorly used family compe-tencies, or to take stock when a complex family sit-uation arises.

CHAPTER 23

PLANNED SHORT-TERM PSYCHOTHERAPY IN INPATIENT PSYCHIATRIC SETTINGS

Overview

Characterizing Time-Limited Inpatient Psychiatric Treatment Programs

Evaluation of Time-Limited Inpatient Programs

General Principles of Time-Limited Inpatient Care

Time-Limited Inpatient Programs in Action—A Case Example

Concluding Comments

There was a time when virtually all psychiatric hospitalizations took place in publicly funded state and county mental hospitals and when treatment was routinely thought of as requiring years if not a lifetime. But that has not been true for many decades, certainly not since the advent of the community mental health movement in the early 1960s. In the last twenty years, private psychiatric hospitals and psychiatric units in community general hospitals have begun to play an increasingly important role in the care of psychiatric patients thought to require hospitalization. With their emergence has come a complex change in the ways in which mental health professionals make use of inpatient facilities as well as in the nature of inpatient psychiatric facility therapeutic programs.

In the early days of the community mental health movement (in the 1960s and early 1970s) there was a growing belief that hospitalization could and should be avoided at all costs and that outpatient care should always be the treatment of choice. Directors of public mental hospitals found themselves in a friendly competition to see who could empty out public mental hospitals most quickly. Program planners at the federal and state levels envisioned a time when state mental hospitals would be converted into community mental health facilities, chronic care hospitals, or perhaps vocational training schools (see Bloom, 1984).

But a few authors cautioned against excessively rapid abandonment of the psychiatric inpatient facility. Mendel (1967), for example, noted that hospitalization might be the treatment of choice under certain conditions, for persons: (1) who are so disturbed that they cannot maintain useful relationships with therapists as outpatients, (2) whose impulse control is so poor that they frighten members of their families who must care for them, (3) whose psychopathology has alienated them from family and friends who now refuse to care for them, (4) who are malnourished or who make excessive use of drugs, (5) who need to be protected against self-destructive impulses, (6) from whom regularly available supportive resources in the community need a brief vacation, and (7) who must be removed from a pathological environment (see also Gruenberg, 1974).

Since the 1960s there have been complex changes in admissions rates and length of hospitalization in public and private inpatient facilities. Between the 1960s and the 1970s the number of admissions into public inpatient psychiatric facilities and the length of hospitalization associated with these admissions decreased. At the same time, however, admissions into both the long-established as well as the newly developing private inpatient psychiatric facilities increased dramatically. Length of hospitalization was generally shorter in private hospitals than in tax-supported state and county mental hospitals, however.

During the 1970s the average length of hospitalization in public mental hospitals decreased from 41 to 23 days (Taube & Barrett, 1985; see also Meyer & Taube, 1973; Faden & Taube, 1977) but in the 1980s length of hospitalization in public mental hospitals began to increase, reaching 28 days in 1986 (Manderscheid & Sonnenschein, 1990).

During the 1980s, while the number of private inpatient facilities and number of admissions into these facilities continued to increase, length of hospitalization also began to increase. While the average length of hospitalization in private psychiatric facilities was about 20 days from 1970 through 1980, by 1986 it had increased to 24 days, and by 1988 to nearly 31 days. Thus, in the mid-1980s, length of hospitalization in private psychiatric hospitals actually exceeded that of public psychiatric hospitals.

In 1990 the average length of stay in private psychiatric hospitals began to decrease, dropping to 24.8 days and by 1993 to 17.8 days (Brown, 1994). Only in the case of psychiatric units in general hospitals has the average length of hospitalization remained steady, averaging about 10 days during this entire time period (Graves & Lovato, 1981; Manderscheid & Sonnenschein, 1990; National Center for Health Statistics, 1989).

These changes in admission rates and length of hospitalization in public and private psychiatric hospitals tell an interesting tale of inpatient psychiatric care and the health insurance systems. In the case of public mental hospitals the increase in number of admissions and the recent increase in length of hospitalization are probably due to the fact that private facilities are now siphoning off the less disturbed patients while those who are more seriously disabled, and who disproportionately do not have health insurance, are being admitted to tax-supported inpatient facilities (Glover & Petrila, 1994).

In the case of private psychiatric hospitals the recent increase and then decrease in length of hospitalization are probably due to the changing nature of third-party health insurance reimbursement policies. Until recently, third-party insurance programs appeared to be far more willing to reimburse inpatient care than outpatient services, seemingly regardless of programmatic emphasis, cost, duration, or effectiveness. Some years ago, for example, third-party insurance programs began reimbursing a variety of new, often month-long inpatient programs that were being developed. As a consequence, the number of private psychiatric hospitals and the length of hospitalization began to increase. As third-party insurance programs subsequently stopped supporting these relatively long-term hospitalizations, length of hospitalization began to decrease.

Indeed, since the late 1980s, private psychiatric hospitals have experienced a continuing crisis as insurance companies and other third-party payers have attempted to further reduce the cost of inpatient psychiatric treatment (Dorwart, Schlesinger, Davidson, Epstein, & Hoover, 1991; Freeman & Trabin, 1994; Glover & Petrila, 1994). Occupancy rates and lengths of stay in private inpatient settings have dropped dramatically as studies have shown that many patients who would ordinarily have been treated in inpatient facilities could be treated just as successfully in outpatient settings (Lieberman, McPhetres, Elliott, Egerter, & Wiitala, 1993; Lutz, 1991; Sharfstein, 1991) or in alternative residential programs (e.g., Budson, 1994; Glick, 1994; Mikkelsen, Bereika, & McKenzie, 1993; Nehls, 1994). With this diminished demand for inpatient psychiatric care a number of private psychiatric hospitals have closed and plans to build new ones have been put on hold. Private psychiatric hospitals that are still open have begun to expand their treatment programs to include partial hospitalization and outpatient services—program elements that are far less expensive than traditional inpatient care.

Once again, just as was the case a generation ago, there is a growing interest in shortening the duration of psychotherapeutic programs, in this case, psychiatric inpatient care.

CHARACTERIZING TIME-LIMITED INPATIENT PSYCHIATRIC TREATMENT PROGRAMS

To some extent the interest in shorter inpatient psychiatric care is part of the same phenomenon that is characterizing outpatient care. It is attributable, first, to a growing concern about reducing the cost of psychiatric care and, second, to the accumulating evidence (see Chapter 1) that shortening the duration of inpatient care does not appear to reduce its effectiveness.

At the same time remarkable changes in the nature of psychiatric inpatient care undoubtedly have had an impact on its increasing efficacy. Among these changes has been the recognition that social processes in the inpatient environment, or, as it is frequently called, the milieu, can have a significant impact on the therapeutic experiences of hospitalized patients.

Many psychiatric inpatient units now provide treatment programs that take advantage of the therapeutic potential of the milieu, and it is interesting to compare them with the older, more traditional inpatient programs. These earlier programs, according to Oldham and Russakoff (1987) were characterized by:

1. Little or no selection of patients for admission
2. A hierarchical system of administration and decision making with the physician as the most expert, the other staff next, and the patient least
3. A high degree of confidentiality among staff, with no general sharing of information with patients
4. No patient government
5. Little use of group therapy or of patients in therapeutic roles for other patients
6. Medical uniforms
7. Emphasis on disease and its diagnosis, on individual psychotherapy, and on biological treatments such as psychopharmacology and electroconvulsive therapy
8. Security precautions such as locked doors, restraints, and use of seclusion rooms

In contrast, the more contemporary therapeutic community model of inpatient psychiatric treatment emphasizes (see also Tasman, 1993):

1. General exclusion of certain patients, such as involuntary admissions, in order to maintain the therapeutic potential of the milieu
2. Shared responsibility among staff and patients for administration and clinical decision making
3. Frequent and open information sharing among all patients and staff
4. Creation of patient government with specific but broad responsibilities
5. Emphasis on groups for therapeutic purposes

6. No uniforms for staff
7. Deemphasis of diagnosis and of medication or other forms of biological treatment
8. Unlocked doors, no seclusion, and little use of restraints

EVALUATION OF TIME-LIMITED INPATIENT PROGRAMS

Research evaluations of time-limited inpatient psychiatric treatment programs indicate that such planned short-term hospitalizations have significant treatment effects. The larger context for viewing these studies is the startling general observation that inpatient care of seriously ill psychiatric patients is, in general, no more effective than any of a variety of alternative inpatient or outpatient treatment programs (Caffey, Galbrecht, & Klett, 1971; Endicott, Herz, & Gibbon, 1978; Glick, Hargreaves, & Goldfield, 1974; Glick, Hargreaves, Raskin, & Kutner, 1975; Hargreaves, Glick, Drues, Shaustack, & Feigenbaum, 1977; Herz, Endicott, & Spitzer, 1975, 1976; Mattes, Rosen, & Klein, 1977; Mattes, Rosen, Klein, & Millan, 1977; Rosen, Katzoff, Carrillo, & Klein, 1976; Swartzburg & Schwartz, 1976).

Riessman, Rabkin, and Struening (1977) reviewed a group of studies that contrasted the efficacy of brief and standard psychiatric hospitalizations. They concluded:

> Evidence from the studies that we have reviewed provides support for the null hypothesis that the effects of brief hospitalization are essentially equivalent to those of standard hospitalization....These investigations cumulatively indicate that groups of patients hospitalized for an average of 3 to 60 days do not significantly differ from those with longer average hospitalizations with respect to symptoms, social functioning, global adjustment, or the risk of rehospitalization either at discharge or within the next 2 years. These findings appear to be consistent across diagnostic groups and across hospitals characterized by marked differences in treatment philosophy, patient-staff ratio, and other factors. (1977, pp. 8–9)

Five years later Kiesler (1982) reviewed reports of experimental studies that randomly assigned patients to either inpatient care or to some outpatient alternative. These studies included an impressive array of outcome measures, including psychiatric status, subsequent employment, school performance, and independent living arrangements.

As in the case of Reissman, Rabkin, and Struening's earlier review, Kiesler's conclusions are worthy of quotation:

> For the vast majority of patients now being assigned to inpatient units in mental institutions, care of at least equal impact could be otherwise provided. There is not an instance in this array of studies in which hospitalization had any positive impact on the average patient which exceeded that of the alternative care investigated in the study. In almost every case, the alternative care had more positive outcomes. (1982, pp. 357–358)

GENERAL PRINCIPLES OF TIME-LIMITED INPATIENT CARE

Peake, Borduin, and Archer (1988) have provided a useful set of recommendations for planning effective brief inpatient psychiatric treatment. These proposals have come from their own clinical experiences in inpatient settings, comparison with other psychiatric inpatient programs, and an examination of the inpatient treatment literature. Their recommendations are as follows:

1. Employ therapeutic goals and treatment objectives that are realistic within a time-limited environment
2. Strengthen and improve discharge planning and aftercare services
3. Reduce or eliminate the amount of "dead time" in inpatient services
4. Form utilization review or efficiency groups at the unit level
5. Provide unit leadership with individuals who have experience with short-term treatment modalities
6. Modify the view of the role of the hospital to include the concept of intermittent or episodic care
7. Base treatment intervention on a rapid operational assessment of what is needed to return the patient to the community
8. Reduce the discrepancy between patient and staff treatment goals by mutually derived treatment contracts
9. Don't be afraid to try something different, and do it early in the treatment process.

Closer examination of these recommendations reveals that they can be grouped into four categories. First are proposals that can result in setting more realistic treatment goals, keeping in mind the special role of the inpatient facility in the entire treatment spectrum and developing treatment goals through a process that involves the patient as well as the staff. Second are proposals that increase the efficiency of the treatment—reducing down time, forming utilization review groups, and rapid assessment and inauguration of treatment. Third are proposals that have the specific potential for improving treatment effectiveness—inaugurating discharge and outpatient follow-up planning virtually from the beginning of inpatient treatment, including the possibility of intermittent care in treatment planning, and trying new and different treatment approaches. Finally, Peake, Borduin, and Archer recognize the necessity of identifying clinical program directors who have a high level of competence and a strong commitment to time-limited inpatient care. This set of recommendations is unusually important not only because it may apply across a broad spectrum of inpatient treatment facilities, but also because it is very likely that similar recommendations would improve the efficacy of time-limited outpatient care.

Inpatient Group Psychotherapy Programs

The fact that inpatient facilities bring a substantial number of psychiatric patients together virtually 24 hours a day for several days or longer has resulted in a high level of interest in establishing and evaluating group psychotherapy programs (Wayne, 1966). Brabender and Fallon (1993) have identified and characterized several different models of inpatient group psychotherapy. These models differ from each other as a function of the underlying assumptions about psychopathology and its treatment, the treatment environment, and the population being served. The models that they have identified include the educative model, the interpersonal model, the object relations model, the developmental model, the cognitive-behavioral model, the problem-solving model, and the social skills training model. A number of parallels to differing in approaches to brief individual psychotherapy can be noted in this analysis.

Each of these models can be viewed from a number of different perspectives—the clinical mission of the care setting (its goals, values, and theoretical orientation), the context of the group (its importance in the treatment program); temporal variables (duration, frequency of meetings, etc.) the size and composition of the group; and characteristics of the therapists. While differences among inpatient group therapy models are emphasized in this analysis, the groups usually share a number of common elements, including a warm, active therapist with a moderate level of transparency, the establishment of specific goals; the provision of some cognitive framework for understanding emotional expression and psychopathology; an insistence on establishing clear boundaries both within the group and between the group and the rest of the institutional program; and concentration on the here and now rather than on the outside and the past.

For example, Kanas (1990) has described the use of short-term inpatient groups in the treatment of schizophrenics. Regarding selection of the most appropriate candidates, Kanas suggests that because group psychotherapy is interpersonal in nature, those patients who are able to sit in a room and interact with others will benefit more than those who are withdrawn and isolated. In addition, patients are particularly suitable for group psychotherapy if they are motivated to explore the nature of their problems by means of a discussion-oriented approach.

Two specific goals of the group treatment seem most pertinent. First, the group experience should help patients improve their interpersonal relationships and contacts with others by learning how to discuss their difficulties and by practicing social skills. Second, the therapy group should help patients cope more successfully with their psychotic experiences, by helping them understand that hallucinations and delusions are not typical of most people and then by developing specific effective coping skills.

Kanas suggests that short-term inpatient groups for schizophrenics can be held three or more times per week but that the group meetings should not last longer than one hour. Therapists should be active, open, supportive, and consistent. Because patients may become difficult to manage, groups conducted by co-therapists appear to be particularly successful. Issues that appear particularly important to discuss include relationships with others; feelings of loneliness and despair; coping with the symptoms of schizophrenia; better organization of thought processes; and such practical problems as dealing with the side effects of medications, exploring job opportunities, and finding places to live in the community.

Because of the importance of group treatment in contemporary inpatient programs that emphasize the therapeutic community model of treatment, there has been a growing literature on the use of short-term group therapy within the inpatient setting (e.g., Beeber, 1988; Brabender, 1985, 1988; Dacey, 1989; Lefkovitz, 1988; Lettieri-Marks, 1987; McGuire, 1988; Rosegrant, 1988; and Starr & Weisz, 1989). Leibenluft and Goldberg (1987) have provided useful guidelines for conceptualizing the group therapy process in inpatient settings. They suggest that short-term inpatient groups go through three phases. In the first phase, when the patient is usually the most distressed, a therapeutic alliance must be established, goals of treatment must be set, a treatment contract must be developed and agreed to, and limits must be set on unacceptable acting-out behaviors. In the second phase, when the patient has begun to see the hospital environment as supportive and therapeutic and has begun to improve, the therapist must stay focused on the goals defined during the first phase while also keeping the issue of discharge from the hospital consistently near the top of the day-to-day agenda. In the third and final phase, issues of separation from the hospital are addressed, and the therapist has to help the patient disengage from the environment that has been so helpful. Leibenluft and Goldberg (1987) write: "An unfortunate reality of inpatient treatment is that the therapist spends half his time engaging the patient in inpatient treatment and the other half disengaging him" (p. 42; see also Leibenluft, Tasman, & Green, 1993).

As can be noted, patients have far more active roles to play in the therapeutic community model than in the more traditional medical model. But duration of treatment has traditionally been longer in the therapeutic community model than in the medical model of ward organization and programming. Thus, efforts to shorten inpatient treatment programs while still making use of the milieu are all the more remarkable.

TIME-LIMITED INPATIENT PROGRAMS IN ACTION—A CASE EXAMPLE

A number of comprehensive time-limited psychiatric inpatient programs have been described in the literature. Oldham and Russakoff's (1987) unusually thoughtful description of their time-limited inpatient psychiatric treatment program places it as nearer to older medical model inpatient programs than to newer therapeutic community programs. Their program does, however, contain several modifications of the medical model program. Information is shared with staff and patients based on each patient's estimated needs. A patient government is created, but its functions are limited to a liaison and advisory role. Group therapy is available for selected patients. Community meetings are held, but they have a carefully structured agenda and are always chaired by a staff member. Staff personnel wear name tags but do not wear uniforms. Aside from these exceptions, the Oldham and Russakoff program follows the medical model.

Their program is located in a twenty-five–bed unit in a university-based training hospital. Median length of stay is about 26 days. Each patient is assigned to one of three multidisciplinary teams and, within each team, to a primary therapist as well as to a social worker, a nursing staff member, and a medical student. Each day begins either with team-based group therapy or with a ward-based community meeting. Following this meeting, patients participate in a variety of supervised therapeutic activities while team staff members meet to discuss patient progress, medical and psychiatric evaluations, and treatment planning. Each patient is seen in individual therapy by his or her primary therapist and meets regularly with the nursing staff member assigned to the case. The theoretical orientation of the ward is based on an object relations framework that is unusually applicable to severely disturbed patients, whose problems usually predate the oedipal period (Oldham & Russakoff, 1987, pp. 35 ff.).

Individual psychotherapy is critically important to the patient because it helps counter the sense of failure and anger occasioned by the hospitalization itself. Individual psychotherapy can thus help build or maintain self-esteem at the same time that it enhances self-understanding (Oldham & Russakoff, 1987, pp. 51-68). Group psychotherapy provides an opportunity for patients to examine interpersonal aspects of their psychopathology through experiencing their effects upon other people, to increase their social skills, and to learn to behave interdependently (Oldham & Russakoff, 1987, pp. 69-84).

The community meeting, designed to provide a formal opportunity for interaction among the entire patient and staff membership of the ward, provides a vehicle for input into important ward- and patient-related decision making. On a twenty-five–bed unit there may be as many as forty or forty-five people present at the community meeting. Oldham and Russakoff (1987), noting that relatively little information about such meetings is available in the literature, provide a clear rationale and considerable insight into how their community meetings are organized and conducted. They have found that 45 minutes provides adequate time for significant work to be done without taxing the tolerance of the most severely disturbed patients. Staff members and patients sit together, with staff members deliberately assigned to sit alongside particularly disturbed patients An excerpt from such a community meeting can be found in Box 23-1. The importance and therapeutic potential of such meetings is clearly illustrated in this excerpt.

Oldham and Russakoff (1987) have found six techniques useful in conducting community meetings:

1. At the beginning of each meeting, roll call of patients and staff is taken with careful explanation given to account for any missing patient or staff member, and new members of the community, whether patients or staff, are introduced.
2. The agenda for the meeting is created by open discussion.
3. Information pertinent to carrying out the agenda is gathered openly, without recourse to knowledge not available to the entire community.
4. Each agenda issue is brought to a close before the next item on the agenda is introduced.
5. Impending departures from the community, whether of patients or staff, are formally noted.
6. Every effort is made to ensure that meetings begin and end on a positive and supportive note.

Box 23-1: Excerpt from an Inpatient Community Meeting

(This meeting is held in the living room area adjacent to the nursing station. Patients and staff begin to congregate a few minutes before 8:30 a.m. Chairs are set up in rows facing the front of the room where the leader sits; other chairs are arranged along the sides of the room, also facing the leader.)

Dr. Clark (Team Leader): It's now 8:30 and time to begin. I'm Dr. Clark. I don't believe that all the patients are here. Mr. Lewis, who are we missing?

Mr. Lewis (Mental Health Worker): Misses Jackson, Kane, and Lee are still in the ladies' room. Misters Baker, Campbell, Daniels, and Edwards said they are coming. Mr. Walsh is in his room per his nursing care plan. *(Misses Jackson and Lane arrive and take seats, as do Misters Baker, Campbell, and Daniels.)*

Miss Farrell (Patient): Is Mr. Walsh dying? Why were there so many doctors in his room yesterday? What are you doing to him?

Miss Gardner (Patient): Yeah! What's happening to him? Why doesn't he talk?

Dr. Clark: Hold on for a moment. In this meeting if you'd like to speak, please raise your hand and wait to be recognized by me. Now, Mr. Walsh is OK. His illness interferes with his ability to communicate well with others or to take nourishment. He is receiving fluids by vein because he is not able to drink or take food right now. He is receiving medications, and we expect that he'll do all right. Why don't we finish with the other people who are supposed to be here, and, since Mr. Walsh's condition is a concern, we can put it on the agenda. Now that accounts for all the patients. What about the staff? Miss Anderson?

Ms. Anderson (Head Nurse): Dr. Diamond called and said that she would be in late this morning. We can expect her after the Team Meeting.

Mr. Hall (Patient): Did I hurt Dr. Diamond? I mean I asked her a question yesterday.

Dr. Clark: No, Dr. Diamond called and said she would be in late. She's OK; you did not hurt her. She won't be at this meeting today.

Mr. Hall (Patient): Oh, I see.

Dr. Clark: Are there other staff not present, not accounted for?

Ms. Anderson (Head Nurse): No, I think that covers everyone.

Dr. Clark: OK, before I proceed, let me tell the new members of the community that this is our community meeting where we discuss issues of concerns to the entire community. I'm Dr. Clark. We meet Tuesday and Thursday mornings in the living room here, from 8:30 a.m. until 9:15 a.m. Because we have so many people in this meeting, we don't permit smoking. We use an agenda that is developed during the meeting; we'll be doing that in a moment....Let's see, we have three new patients. When I call your name, perhaps you could raise your hand—Miss Smith and Mr. Thomas *(The patients raise their hands as their names are announced.)* Mr. Walsh was admitted yesterday, and we have already said a few words about him. Let me welcome both of you. I hope that your stays here are comfortable and useful. We have four patients about to be discharged—Miss Martin, Mr. Edwards, Mrs. Grant, and Miss Nelson. We'll get back to you in a moment. Let's collect the rest of the agenda items. Can I hear from the President of the Patient Committee?

Mr. London (Patient and President of the Patient Committee): We just have a few items: We need more diet soda, especially Diet Coke; there aren't enough towels; we'd like a change in the snacks; and the stereo is broken.

Dr. Clark: OK. Other items besides the discharges? Mr. Thomas?

Mr. Thomas (New Patient): I want to be discharged. I don't need to be here.

Dr. Clark: Mr. Thomas, that sounds like an issue you should discuss with your individual therapist. We discuss items here that concern all of the community. When you are to be

(continued)

Box 23-1 continued

discharged is a personal issue, to be worked out between you and your treatment team. We discuss the impact of people's discharges here, but don't decide them. Other items? Miss Becker?

Ms. Becker (Charge Nurse): No one has mentioned that Miss Lane had some problems last night. We need to talk about it—she submitted a 72-hour notice *(written request to leave the hospital which must be responded to within 72 hours by state law)*. Also, there was an incident last night involving Miss Jackson and Mr. Reid.

Dr. Clark: OK. Anything else? *(pause)* We have the item from before about Mr. Walsh. *(pause)* All right. The first item is the discharge of Miss Martin. Could you tell the community what your experience in the hospital was like and what your plans are for the future?

Ms. Martin (Patient): This morning I'll be leaving after 3 weeks of therapy and medication. I'll be going to the day hospital near my home and seeing a therapist there. This hospitalization has helped me more than any of the three others I've had. I think that I can accept the need to take my medications better, even though I still don't like the side effects. If the day hospital works out all right, I'll look for a job. I'd like to thank my doctor, Dr. Evans, who helped me through some rough times, as well as Miss David who always seemed to listen and really care. My social worker, Mrs. Harris, was a big help to me and my family. I want to thank the other patients, especially my roommate Nancy *(Marks)*.

Ms. Marks (Patient): You have been a great roommate. Good luck!

Dr. Clark: Miss Able?

Ms. Able (Patient): I'll miss you. Hope things go well.

Dr. Clark: Dr. Evans?

Dr. Evans (Psychiatric Resident): Miss Martin, your stay in the hospital was not smooth. Initially you had a lot of questions about whether or not the stay would be useful. In fact, you submitted a notice to leave early on. However, I think that your perseverance in your treatment has paid off for you. I believe that you have a better appreciation of your need for medication and continued treatment. I think that the discharge plans are good, and I wish you well.

Ms. Martin (Patient): Thanks, Dr. Evans.

Dr. Clark: Other comments or reactions? Miss David?

Ms. David (Staff Nurse): I've worked closely with you during this stay, Miss Martin. I know that you've struggled and worked hard. Hope all goes well for you. Good luck.

Ms. Martin: Thanks.

Dr. Clark: Mrs. Harris?

Mrs. Harris (Social Worker): I really can't add to what's been said—best wishes.

Ms. Martin: Thanks.

Dr. Clark: Any other comments or reactions? *(silence)* OK, let's move on…. Let's go to the incident last night with Miss Lane. Can we hear about what people observed? Miss Able?

Ms. Able (Patient): At about 9 p.m. last night, Kathy *[Lane]* was on the phone with her boyfriend, and they had a fight. After that I talked to her for at least an hour. She was pretty shaken up—crying, feeling that she had made a big mistake in coming into the hospital. She talked a little about putting in her 72-hour notice, but I thought that she was feeling a bit better after we had talked. The next I knew, people were rushing down the hall. I didn't know that she actually submitted her notice.

Dr. Clark: Miss Martin?

Ms. Martin (Patient): She said to me that she was feeling okay, but I was a little worried and told Mary *(David)* that Kathy seemed to be pretty upset by the phone call. That must have been after you *(Miss Able)* had spoken to her. Mary spoke to her after that.

(continued)

Box 23-1 continued

Dr. Clark: Miss David?

Ms. David (Staff Nurse): I spoke with her for a short while. She said that she and her boyfriend had broken up. She felt it was because she had come into the hospital, that she should sign out. I told her that didn't seem like such a good idea, that perhaps she should talk to her therapist today about it. She said that that was a good idea. At that point, she didn't seem especially upset. She ended the meeting without protest. I went back to the nursing station after that.

Dr. Clark: Miss Ingram?

Ms. Ingram (Patient): I went into the bathroom at a little after midnight. I saw the blood on the floor in her stall. I asked who was in there. No one answered, and I ran to tell the staff. They pushed the buzzer, and in a minute or two there were a whole bunch of people here.

Dr. Clark: Miss Anderson?

Ms. Anderson (Head Nurse): She was found in the stall with cuts on both her wrists. The doctor on call examined her and determined that she needed to be sutured. There were pieces of a light bulb next to her. She was alert and could move her fingers. She was escorted to the local Emergency Room where her wrists were sutured. On return to our hospital, she submitted a 72-hour notice. She is currently on CS *(constant supervision)* status.

Dr. Clark: Maybe we could hear from Miss Lane about her experience of it?

Ms. Lane (Patient): I don't have anything to say. I don't want people to talk about it! It's my private business.

Dr. Clark: Dr. Adams?

Dr. Adams (Unit Chief): When someone does something like this it affects the entire community, and we must talk about it; it no longer is a private affair. Cutting one's wrists in the unit bathroom and submitting a 72-hour notice is of community concern!

Dr. Clark: Comments or reactions regarding Miss Lane's cutting her wrists or her 72-hour notice?

Mr. Hall (Patient): I didn't cut her!

Dr. Clark: We know that, Mr. Hall....Miss Martin?

Ms. Martin (Patient): I was pretty upset last night. I thought that Kathy was doing OK. It was pretty scary with all those people on the unit last night. They did a great job, although I thought she had died at first.

Dr. Clark: Other comments? Mr. Oliver?

Mr. Oliver (Patient): I don't understand why the bathroom is unlocked at night. Shouldn't it be locked at midnight? How do you know what's going to happen?

Dr. Clark: Others feel that way? Miss Marks?

Ms. Marks (Patient): Yeah, what's going to stop someone from cutting themselves in the bathroom? You can't see what goes on in there. It's unsafe.

Dr. Clark: What about others? How do others feel? Miss Martin?

Ms. Martin (Patient): I don't know. The staff can't watch every move we make. Some of it is up to us.

Dr. Clark: (gestures to Miss Able)

Ms. Able (Patient): I agree. I was pretty upset by what Kathy did, but I think that we need to talk straight to people about our problems.

Dr. Clark: (gestures to Miss Martin)

Ms. Martin: Kathy, when I first came here I couldn't stand it. I thought that my biggest problem was that I was hospitalized here and forgot all the troubles I had had before. With

(continued)

Box 23-1 continued

a lot of encouragement, I decided to stay, and I think that was a tough but good decision. You really should take out your notice.

Dr. Clark: Mr. Daniels?

Mr. Daniels (Patient): I want to know what you're going to do about the bathrooms. I think that the staff should check them every ten minutes.

Dr. Clark: Dr. Adams?

Dr. Adams (Unit Chief): It sounds like people are concerned about their safety here in the hospital. Some wish that all responsibility be taken over by the hospital, guaranteeing that they will be safe and secure. However, an environment that would be that safe would be pretty restricted and uncomfortable. There is a limit to how much the staff can do for people; we are dependent upon patients to let us know how they are feeling and to clue us in as to when to provide more supervision. It certainly is uncomfortable for me as a staff member to hear of what occurred with Miss Lane. Patients need to tell us directly of their needs, and even then we may not hear the requests as well as we ought. Repeated messages may be necessary, but will hopefully result in a reasonable response.

Dr. Clark: Comments or reactions?

From J. M. Oldham and L. M. Russakoff, *Dynamic Therapy in Brief Hospitalization* (pp. 197–208), Northdale, NJ: Jason Aronson. Used with permission.

CONCLUDING COMMENTS

Evaluation studies of planned short-term inpatient psychotherapy have regularly come to the same conclusion as have evaluation studies of planned short-term outpatient psychotherapy: Short-term inpatient treatment is indistinguishable from time-unlimited inpatient treatment in its effects.

As we have seen, hospitalization is believed to be the treatment of choice under a number of circumstances. But to ensure that health insurance programs will be able to provide that inpatient care when it is needed, it is increasingly evident that hospitalization should be avoided when it is not necessary. The reasons for this avoidance are clinical as well as fiscal, for hospitalization inevitably induces a form of regression that may feed on itself. For example, in the case of a psychiatric emergency, particularly during the night when mental health personnel are not readily available, it is easy to decide to hospitalize the patient until morning, at which time the patient's condition can be reevaluated. But even by the next morning many patients have already come to the conclusion that they should be hospitalized, that they can only be treated successfully if their hospitalization is continued.

There is thus a kind of tension between administrators responsible for maintaining the viability of psychiatric hospitals, by making sure that all beds are filled, and those responsible for maintaining the viability of health insurance programs—a tension between clinicians and fiscal agents that parallels that found in general medical hospitals. In the case of medical disorders the results of that tension are increasingly evident. Many medical procedures that used to be performed in hospitals are now routinely done in outpatient surgical and diagnostic facilities, with an attendant reduction in cost and sense of disability to the patient. Health insurance companies are well aware of evaluation studies such as those described in this chapter, and policies encouraging the reduced use of psychiatric inpatient units are following those regarding reduced use of general medical inpatient facilities. These developments are creating high levels of tension for medical administrators, particularly in communities where there may already be a surplus of medical or psychiatric beds.

Because reducing the duration of inpatient care plays such a significant role in reducing the cost of mental health services, alternatives to traditional psychiatric inpatient care should be sought with greater vigor. Many health care providers have instituted round-the-clock crisis intervention services so that patients being considered for hospitalization can be seen before being admitted. Fiscal agents typically require prior authorization for inpatient admission, a policy that helps reduce the unnecessary use of inpatient facilities. Another alternative to traditional hospitalization worthy of exploration is the use of hotel-type facilities in lieu of traditional inpatient settings. Such facilities are substantially less expensive than general hospital beds and may in fact be more therapeutic than being admitted into a general hospital psychiatric unit or a traditional private psychiatric hospital.

At the same time that issues of cost need to be considered, there is evidence that clinicians are increasingly interested in organizing inpatient treatment programs that take advantage of everything that is healthy in both patients and staff. As this chapter has indicated, both individual and group approaches to brief inpatient psychotherapy are being explored. The value of pluralism in inpatient treatment approaches is being increasingly recognized.

Contemporary inpatient treatment programs are a far cry from the programs of a generation ago, in large measure because individual and psychosocial approaches are being included in the treatment program alongside improved pharmacological approaches. Thus, inpatient psychiatric programs may shortly begin to diminish in number and in duration, while increasing in quality and effectiveness.

SECTION VI

GENERAL ISSUES AND OVERVIEW

This final section discusses two topics that transcend the individualized views of theory or practice of planned short-term psychotherapy. The first is the question of selection of clients for planned short-term psychotherapy, a topic that has been of interest to virtually every writer in the field. Second, in the final chapter the overall field of planned short-term psychotherapy will be considered, both in terms of its present status and its future potential. We shall discuss issues regarding sufficiency of treatment, try to identify some general principles of planned short-term psychotherapy, and suggest some factors to keep in mind in enhancing its continued development.

CHAPTER 24

SELECTING PATIENTS FOR PLANNED SHORT-TERM PSYCHOTHERAPY

Overview

Approaches to Selection Criteria

Type of Therapy by Type of Patient

Contraindications for Planned Short-Term Psychotherapy

Concluding Comments

The literature dealing with selection criteria for identifying patients suitable for planned short-term psychotherapy is voluminous, with strongly held opinions ranging completely across the logical spectrum. At one extreme are assertions that no specific selection criteria have been reliably identified for selecting potential short-term therapy patients and none should be used. That is, every patient is at least as suitable for time-limited psychotherapy as for time-unlimited psychotherapy. At the other extreme are writings that propose quite specific criteria for establishing the appropriateness of potential clients for time-limited psychotherapy.

There is some evidence that selection criteria have become less stringent in recent years, perhaps as a consequence of the growing confidence of clinicians in the general effectiveness of planned short-term psychotherapy with a wide variety of patients (Budman & Stone, 1983). Furthermore, there is a growing realization that as long as one begins with the belief that certain people are unsuitable for planned short-term psychotherapy, the full utility of time-limited therapy will never be explored. We are left with clinical impressions of suitability—not to be dismissed out of hand, to be sure, but subject to the problems of interpretation that characterize all anecdotal assertions. In this chapter we shall try to review and evaluate the assertions and evidence that

bear on the issue of patient selection criteria and come to some kind of judgment as to the state of the knowledge base.

APPROACHES TO SELECTION CRITERIA

As has just been suggested, statements about selection criteria for planned short-term psychotherapy range from those that are extremely broad and inclusive to those that are quite narrow and exclusive.

Broad Selection Criteria

Broad criteria are of two types. First, some writers take the position that there are no criteria whereby prospective patients can be confidently excluded from time-limited psychotherapy, and, therefore, the most appropriate clinical decision to make about selection is to start with every patient in a time-limited mode e.g., Curtis & Silberschatz, 1986; Gillman, 1965; Kreilkamp, 1989; Krupnick & Horowitz, 1985; Manaster, 1989; Propst, Paris, & Rosberger, 1994). This is the *accept everyone* approach. As will be noted, an impressive group of scholars subscribes to this position.

For example, Wolberg (1965c), taking an inclusionary but conservative point of view, writes:

The best strategy, in my opinion, is to assume that every patient, irrespective of diagnosis, will respond to short-term treatment unless he proves himself to be refractory to it. If the therapist approaches each patient with the idea of doing as much as he can for him, within the span of say up to twenty treatment sessions, he will give the patient an opportunity to take advantage of short-term treatment to the limit of his potential. If this expediency fails, he can always then resort to prolonged therapy. (p. 140)

Wolberg equivocates, however. He elaborates this last sentence by noting that short-term psychotherapy will turn out to be sufficient in the case of three categories of patients: patients who have a history of adequate adjustment prior to current difficulty; patients who display disturbing symptoms and maladaptive behavior patterns, such as phobias; and patients whose symptoms are related to deep-seated intrapsychic problems and who suffer from personality disturbances with a prior history of marginal functioning. In the first case the goal is to return the patient to that prior level of adjustment, typically by using a crisis intervention model, usually of not more than six sessions. In the second case the goals are symptom relief, modification of destructive habits, and help in the development of more adaptive behavioral practices—goals that can generally be achieved in eight to twenty sessions using a supportive-educational model of psychotherapy. In the third case the goal is some form of personality reconstruction plus symptomatic and behavioral improvement, requiring somewhat longer treatment than is currently encompassed within the concept of short-term therapy.

As for those patient characteristics that make the necessity for prolonged psychotherapy more likely, Wolberg (1980) identifies two categories of patients. In the first category are chronic psychotics, patients whose psychoses are in remission, alcoholics, drug addicts, persons with acting-out tendencies, persons fixated at infantile and childish levels or with excessive dependency needs, intractable obsessive-compulsives, paranoid personalities, persons with psychosomatic and hypochondriacal conditions, and depressives. For this group, Wolberg believes that prolonged management will be needed after an initial course of short-term psychotherapy. Finally, Wolberg includes a second group for whom prolonged psychotherapy might be needed persons who require extensive reconstructive personality changes and who have the financial ability, time, forebearance, and ego strength to tolerate long-term psychoanalysis or psychoanalytically oriented psychotherapy; and highly disturbed children and adolescents. Wolberg estimates that more than three-quarters of the typical patient load carried by the average mental health professional comprises patients who may be adequately managed by short-term approaches.

This elaboration, one that would be congenial to many of Wolberg's psychoanalytic colleagues, assumes that long-term psychotherapy is unquestionably more helpful than short-term psychotherapy and that dynamic short-term psychotherapy is more effective than supportive-educational psychotherapy, which is in turn more effective than crisis intervention. In fact, however, none of these assertions has any compelling empirical evidence to support it, and, thus, for the moment these elaborations constitute hypotheses in need of verification. Let us not lose sight, however, of Wolberg's initial, perhaps fundamental, assertion, namely, that the wise clinician will begin psychotherapy by assuming that every patient will respond favorably to planned short-term psychotherapy, even if the prediction is that some patients will respond more favorably than others.

Cummings and VandenBos (1979), writing 15 years after Wolberg, described their conclusions of 20 years of research on the effectiveness of psychotherapy of varying durations in the following assertions:

The treatment of choice for all persons presenting themselves with emotional complaints and problems in living is active short-term psychological intervention without preselection criteria. For 85% of these unselected persons, such treatment is more effective than long-term psychotherapy, and for another 5% of patients, intensive long-term psychotherapy may actually be deleterious. (p. 432)

Budman and Stone (1983) have come to the same conclusion, based on their own clinical experience and review of the literature—namely, that "it is unwarranted to exclude patients from brief therapy on the basis of diagnosis, symptoms, or apparent motivation" (p. 941; see also Propst, Paris, & Rosberger, 1994). Manaster (1989) writes: "Brief therapy should be the treatment, the approach, and the intent in all cases" (p. 247). Garfield (1989) asserts that "with the exception of the very seriously disturbed…brief therapy can be considered for most patients who are in touch with reality, are experiencing some discomfort, and have made the effort to seek help for their difficulties" (p. 13).

Bellak discusses his broad approach to patient selection in an interesting autobiographic account in which he contrasts his approach with that of Malan. He writes:

> My method has some similarities to Malan's (1963), who published his first book shortly before Small and I, unaware of his, published our own….We both had a psychoanalytic background, and eventually Malan came to share my willingness to take on virtually all comers….Malan's technique, however, was developed in the relative tranquility of the Tavistock Clinic. Thus, not only could Malan offer more time to his patients than I had available in my original settings, but he was also probably dealing with patients who were not as sick as mine. (1984, p. 12)

More recently Binder, Strupp, and Henry (1995) have concluded that many of the selection criteria that have been suggested

> are quite abstract, and clinicians have a difficult time agreeing on their precise meanings and behavioral referents. More important, there is no convincing evidence that clinicians can utilize these criteria to predict usefully what will happen in an individual treatment….Relatively better predictions are based on the quality of the patient's involvement in the early sessions of treatment….Therefore, it seems advisable to offer therapy to all patients who are motivated to accept it and who seem at all suitable for the type of treatment being considered. (pp. 54-55)

The second type of broad selection criterion asserts that there are no characteristics that distinguish patients suitable for long-term psychotherapy from those who are suitable for time-limited psychotherapy. This is the *accept everyone you would accept for long-term psychotherapy* approach. Strupp (1980d; see also Binder, Henry, & Strupp, 1987) asserts, for example, that only patients whose "criteria are essentially identical to those traditionally considered crucial in assessing a patient's suitability for psychoanalysis" (p. 953) are also good candidates for short-term therapy.

Similarly, Migone (1985) suggests that "we cannot even argue that the two techniques [psychoanalysis and short-term dynamic psychotherapy] are to be used for different indications, because the patients that are not considered good candidates for STDP are the same ones that have always been considered not suitable for psychoanalysis and for whom psychopharmacological treatments or support therapies have been preferred" (p. 615).

Budman and Gurman (1988) make an equivalent point:

> Many of the attributes recommended in the past for patient selection have excluded those individuals who are most difficult and problematic in *any* form of psychotherapy. The vast array of selection criteria for brief psychotherapy have developed over the years despite a lack of empirical data to support the contention that some types of patients are better suited to brief treatment than are others. (p. 22)

Narrow Selection Criteria

Narrow selection criteria specify patient characteristics that are required in order to be confident that planned short-term psychotherapy will be significantly helpful. Such criteria are relatively exclusive. In spite of the fact that there is little empirical evidence substantiating these selection criteria, there is a cumulative weight to these assertions (Lambert, 1979). Such conservative approaches to patient selection often emphasize the importance of careful initial assessment of the client and of the client's problems (Barber & Crits-Christoph, 1991, pp. 324 ff.).

Early reports in this historical review tend to be based primarily on clinical experience. Later reports are also based on clinical experience but make ready reference to corroborative earlier reports, which in the meantime have developed a certain cachet largely as a function of their age.

Balint's (Balint, Ornstein, & Balint, 1972) impressions about what factors to keep in mind in selecting patients for brief focal psychotherapy (see Chapter 21), as he readily acknowledged, were based on clinical rather than statistical evidence. First, Balint believed that prospective patients should give the impression that they can develop a workable alliance with their therapist, an alliance that can withstand the interpersonal strains that therapy inevitably will cause. Second, the therapist should have the impression that patients see their symptoms as ego-dystonic and that they have the motivation to try to change. Third, patients have to appear capable of accepting interpretations, however tentatively, and doing some constructive work with them. Fourth, two people who interview a prospective patient independently of each other should come to the same general conclusions as to the nature of the difficulties the patient is facing. Finally, it should be possible to identify a focus for the envisioned therapy around which the work can take place (see also Malan, 1976, 1978a; Malan & Osimo, 1992, pp. 298 ff.).

Sifneos (1978, 1979, pp. 22–39, 1980, 1981a, 1981b, 1987, 1992) believes that in order to profit from his short-term anxiety-provoking psychotherapy a patient should have: (1) the ability to circumscribe a chief complaint, (2) above average intelligence and psychological-mindedness, (3) a history of at least one meaningful give and take relationship during early childhood, (4) motivation for change and not simply for symptom relief, and (5) an ability to relate to the therapist and to express feelings freely. Again, the overlap in selection criteria is clear.

Concerning motivation for change, Sifneos includes a number of subcriteria—evidence that the prospective client has the ability to recognize that the symptoms are psychological in origin; appears to be introspective and honest; seems willing to be an active participant in the therapeutic situation; is actively curious and willing to understand the self; is willing to explore, experiment, and change; has realistic expectations regarding psychotherapeutic outcome; and is willing to make reasonable sacrifices in the service of psychotherapy. Indeed, Goldberg and Green (1986) suggest that Sifneos's selection criteria for anxiety-provoking short-term psychotherapy are so rigid as to restrict treatment to the "almost psychologically healthy" (p. 79).

The narrowness of selection criteria for anxiety-*provoking* short-term psychotherapy can be seen when they are contrasted with the shorter list of criteria by which selection can be made for anxiety-*suppressive* short-term therapy. Sifneos suggests that suitability for this more supportive therapy might be judged simply by: (1) the ability to maintain a job,

(2) a strong appeal for help to overcome an emotional difficulty, (3) the recognition that the symptoms are psychological in origin, and (4) willingness to cooperate with psychotherapy.

Davanloo's (1978b, 1980b, 1980e) criteria for selection of patients for time-limited psychotherapy are somewhat more complex. They include the ability of the prospective patient to enter into an emotional interaction with the therapist, evidence that such interactions have occurred in the past, the ability to tolerate affect, a high level of motivation and psychological-mindedness, the ability to tolerate and respond to interpretations, above-average intelligence, and adequate flexibility of ego defenses.

Davanloo has formulated his selection criteria as a series of questions to be posed at the conclusion of the initial interview. (Davanloo, 1980b, 1980e; see also Nahmias, 1991; Ursano & Hales, 1986, p. 1511).

1. Is the patient's problem a circumscribed one?
2. Is there a crisis?
3. Has a psychotherapeutic focus been established?
4. Is the psychotherapeutic focus related to a disturbance in interpersonal relationships?
5. How adequate have prior human relationships been?
6. How accessible are feelings to this patient?
7. What is the motivation to change?
8. Is the patient of above-average intelligence?
9. Does the patient display a high level of psychological mindedness?
10. How adequate is the patient's ability to respond to interpretation?

Bauer and Kobos (1987; see also Fuhriman, Paul & Burlingame, 1993; MacKenzie, 1988)) have integrated selection criteria by six patient characteristics that appear to be repeatedly identified as important in short-term psychodynamic psychotherapy assessment:

1. *Motivation for change:* acceptance of the need to change maladaptive coping strategies and an inclination to become actively involved in the change process
2. *Psychological-mindedness:* the ability to attend to and verbally communicate thoughts, feelings, and fantasies; a willingness to reflect on the functioning of inner psychic processes and to be introspective and think in psychological terms

3. *Ego strength:* adequate intelligence, academic and vocational achievements, stability of interpersonal relationships, persistent and successful goal-directed behavior, and ability to tolerate frustration and painful affects through the flexible use of a variety of ego defenses and coping strategies and to tolerate the stresses of therapy and to use this experience constructively toward further growth
4. *Ability to interact with the therapist:* ability to develop a sense of basic trust and to believe in the basic benevolence of others
5. *Response to trial interpretations:* evidence of being able to work with early interpretations, to collaborate with the therapist in examining thoughts, feelings, and reactions, even though such work elicits painful affect (e.g., guilt, anxiety, dysphoria); to accept and elaborate on therapist interpretation; to explore
6. *Establishment of treatment focus:* ability to identify a central area of conflict to be focused on in treatment

The various recommendations listed here include high motivation for change, the ability to establish a productive working relationship with the therapist, a history of meaningful relationships with others, psychological-mindedness, and an identifiable and compelling focal issue of concern. It is hard to argue with the assertion made by a number of writers that these are also the most commonly mentioned criteria for selecting patients for long-term psychotherapy.

Patient Selection Case Examples

Sifneos (1987) has provided a number of interesting examples of patient selection at work in the initial clinical interview, examples that illustrate both success and failure in meeting one or another of his criteria for acceptance into planned short-term psychotherapy. Boxes 24-1 and 24-2 illustrate the extent to which two patients meet the criterion of having had a meaningful interpersonal relationship in the past. The rationale for Sifneos's decisions regarding success or failure in meeting this criterion will become self-evident when one reads the examples. If these examples are at all typical, it seems that judging the presence or absence of specific selection criteria is not a difficult task for the experienced clinician.

Empirical Studies of Selection Criteria Validity

Assuming that therapists' judgments regarding individual selection criteria are valid, the next question is whether presence or absence of the criteria accurately predicts therapeutic outcome. While there is a substantial literature on the prediction of outcome in the case of time-unlimited psychotherapy (e.g., Luborsky, Crits-Christoph, Mintz, & Auerbach, 1988), studies of the validity of selection criteria in the case of planned short-term psychotherapy are far fewer in number.

In one of the earliest studies of the accuracy of outcome predictions, a study that had both clinical and empirical elements, Gelso and Johnson (1983) examined patient characteristics associated with good outcomes in time-limited psychotherapy (eight to fifteen sessions) in a university counseling center. The sample consisted of thirty-eight students who had completed time-limited psychotherapy an average of 12 months prior to the follow-up. The therapists included nine senior clinical or counseling psychologists, six predoctoral counseling psychology interns, and six advanced practicum students who had received at least one year of time-limited therapy supervision prior to the study. In their summary, Gelso and Johnson (1983) somewhat freely combined their empirical findings with their clinical impressions and with other literature already in the field and concluded that the effectiveness of time-limited psychotherapy might be associated with three specific client characteristics: having a relatively mild disturbance of short duration, high motivation to change, and a good fit with the therapist and with the therapy. Their more specific conclusions are summarized in Box 24-3.

A number of more recent studies that were entirely empirical have attempted to evaluate the various patient selection criteria that have been clinically identified. These studies do not provide consistent support for any of these clinical criteria (e.g., Høglend, 1993; Høglend, Sørbye, Sørlie, Fossum, & Engelstad, 1992; Horowitz, Rosenberg, & Bartholomew, 1993; Horowitz, Rosenberg, & Kalehzan, 1992; Piper, Azim, McCallum, & Joyce, 1990; see also Bloom, 1992a), and, taken as a whole, suggest that in spite of the clinical impressions of

---

Box 24-1: Success in Meeting the Meaningful Relationship Criterion

Therapist: Did you have one good friend in your childhood?

Patient (a 21-year-old male college student): Oh, yes. When I was 7 years old John and I were inseparable. He lived very close by and many times he would come and spend the weekend with me. My mother was very fond of him and felt sorry for him.

Therapist: Why?

Patient: You see, his father was an alcoholic or drank too much. He had a violent temper. They never invited me to their house because of his father. John was very apologetic about it. His mother, on the other hand, was very nice.

Therapist: So, what was your friendship like?

Patient: Well, we used to play soccer. John was poor. He had no toys. When we played soccer it was always with my soccer ball or one of the other kids'. I remember how happy John was when he had received a soccer ball as a Christmas present from his uncle. He showed it to me with great pride and he was planning to use it the next time that we were planning to play the following week. But when the time came John came to my house early. He was crying. When I asked him what was the matter, he said that he had accidentally broken his father's favorite beer mug—one that his father had brought back from Germany after World War II. It seems that his father was furious. He had been drinking, so as a punishment he took a kitchen knife and tore John's soccer ball to ribbons. John was very upset about it and he felt humiliated when he was thinking of how to explain all this to the other kids that afternoon. He wanted me to tell them that he was sick just as an excuse. I said to him, "No, John, you are taking the easy way out if you don't show up. But I am going to help you." So I went up to my room, where I had two soccer balls—one was also brand-new and the other an old one. I said to myself, Well, I'll give John the old one, but I thought that the other kids would have expected John to have a new one, so I took my own new one and gave it to John. He didn't want to accept it but I convinced him. He was very happy. I was a bit sad to give it up but his happiness made me happy.

From P. E. Sifneos, *Short-Term Dynamic Psychotherapy: Evaluation and Technique* (2d ed.) (pp. 35–36), New York: Plenum Publishing Corporation, 1987. Used with permission.

Box 24-2: Failure to Meet the Meaningful Relationship Criterion

Patient (a 24-year-old single female model who complained of asthmatic attacks): My grandmother loved me. She took care of me. She gave me everything I wanted. You will say as others do that she spoiled me, but this is not true, because I was also very good to her.

Therapist: What do you mean?

Patient: I did exactly what she wanted.

Therapist: Can you give me an example?

Patient: Of course. You see, I was a good child. I never gave my grandmother cause for concern. I never spoke back to her. I never crossed her. I—

Therapist: (interrupting) Did you enjoy doing all these things?

Patient: Oh, yes!

Therapist: Well, if this is the case, did you do anything to please your grandmother which you did not enjoy doing?

Patient: Oh, no, no, no. I always enjoyed it.

Therapist: Let me put it differently. Did you do anything that you disliked in order to make your grandmother happy, just to please her?

(continued)

Box 24-2 continued

Patient: Of course not! You don't understand. My grandmother never wanted me to do anything that I disliked doing. She called me her "little princess." She used to say, "My little adorable child should never raise her little finger. She should never do anything for anyone else." It was good advice! I never did anything for someone else and I never felt such a need. Actually, on second thought, by modeling I give pleasure to a lot of people.

Therapist: I see. Tell me, does that make you happy?

Patient: Yes, it does. I love to wear beautiful new clothes. I look good in them. My grandmother always admires me. I work hard but I like my work.

Therapist: Well, that is not exactly what I had in mind. Let me ask you a question. Would you do anything to please someone else?

Patient: (reflecting) To be perfectly honest with you doctor—the answer is no.

Therapist: Not even your grandmother?

Patient: Oh, I see. You don't seem to understand. My grandmother would not want me to sacrifice anything for her. It's against her teachings. She wants me to be happy, and I'm perfectly happy. These attacks of asthma, I'm sure, are due to allergies, although the doctor who referred me to your clinic thinks that they are due to an emotional upset. I am unaware of any such upset.

Therapist: Let me ask you one last question. Do you have or have you ever had a steady boyfriend or a close girlfriend?

Patient: That's a funny question. Steady, of course not. Boyfriends? Yes, many. I'm going out with three fellows right now. I like them all. They amuse me, they entertain me, they take me out to nice places. They don't ask for anything in return. Oh, a little sex here and there, but I enjoy that too. I know that you'll say I'm spoiled. Everyone says that. Whatever you want to call it is your business. Any more questions?

Therapist: No, thank you.

From P. E. Sifneos, *Short-Term Dynamic Psychotherapy: Evaluation and Technique* (2d ed.) (pp. 33–34), New York: Plenum Publishing Corporation, 1987. Used with permission.

Box 24-3: Initial Client Characteristics Associated with Successful Short-Term Therapy

1. Client comes to the agency seeking help with troubling behaviors or feelings.
2. Client's difficulties are relatively recent in onset.
3. Client's difficulties are not ego-syntonic.
4. Client's behavior does not appear very disturbed to others.
5. Client believes that needed changes can be made.
6. Client sees the time as ripe for change.
7. Client has good self-concept.
8. Client's ideal self is not vastly different from real self.
9. Client can make good emotional contact with therapist.
10. Client and therapist hit it off well from the beginning.
11. Client is willing and able to be active in the therapy sessions.
12. Client may have some unresolved dependency desires but is not afraid of intimacy.
13. Client is able to see the psychological aspects of presenting problems.
14. Client is able to see the necessity for a time limit on psychotherapy.
15. Client views therapy as having started some new ways of thinking.
16. Client believes improvement will continue after termination of therapy.

Adapted from Gelso and Johnson, 1983, pp. 205–206.

many psychotherapists, client characteristics are not very useful in identifying who will be especially suitable for short-term psychotherapy. A review of this literature recently prepared by Crits-Christoph and Connolly (1993) led to the conclusion that "the level of prediction outcome achieved by the studies…, however, is not yet high enough to apply to the individual case in clinical practice" (pp. 185–186).

TYPE OF THERAPY BY TYPE OF PATIENT

As we have seen, different therapists have very different approaches to short-term psychotherapy. Accordingly, it should not be surprising that efforts have been made to identify patient characteristics that are thought to bode well for the success of different approaches to brief therapy. Few empirical studies have been undertaken, however.

Reviewing the chapters in the earlier sections of this book, one can note that writers have taken one of two positions on selection criteria—either that their approach is equally suitable for all patients or, alternatively, that it is suitable for specific types of patients. Writers in the first category, that is, those who are generalists regarding issues of patient selection, include Wolberg, Bloom, Phillips and Wiener, Ellis, Farrelly, Erickson, members of the Palo Alto Mental Research Institute, and de Shazer and his colleagues.

The other theoreticians believe that their techniques of planned short-term psychotherapy are particularly suitable for specific types of patients. As has already been mentioned, Bellak (see Chapter 3) has specifically suggested for a wide variety of diagnostic categories. Davanloo and Sifneos have developed an approach to short-term psychotherapy of particular pertinence to high-functioning patients with unresolved oedipal issues, although Davanloo also asserts that his approach can be used profitably with more regressed neurotic patients. Mann's approach seems unusually useful in helping patients cope with pre-oedipal issues. Gustafson and Horowitz see their approaches as specifically useful for treating relatively well-functioning patients who are having difficulties with a current stressful life event or circumstance. Lewin, Gustafson, and Horowitz all view their approaches as useful with

character or personality disorders. Lewin suggests that his approach is particularly useful with masochistic personalities; Horowitz has commented on the use of his approach in the case of hysterical, compulsive, narcissistic, and borderline personalities. Klerman and Beck have developed short-term psychotherapies specifically to be of help to patients who are suffering from neurotic depressions. Horowitz suggests that his approach is specifically pertinent in working with patients who are coping with posttraumatic stress disorders.

Burke, White, and Havens (1979), while urging caution in the degree of specificity that therapists should employ in selecting patients, have contrasted a number of differing approaches to planned short-term psychotherapy in terms of the implications of these differences for optimal patient selection. They suggest, for example, that Sifneos, who deals primarily with oedipal patients (see Chapter 5), looks for patients who are relatively healthy—curious, highly motivated, and able to withstand high levels of anxiety and establish a rational alliance with the therapist. Mann, on the other hand (see Chapter 6), who works with patients at earlier developmental levels who are more passive and dependent on nurturant figures, looks for patients who are aware of and can express their chronic sense of suffering and who establish an irrational alliance with an imagined omnipotent therapist. For these patients the inevitable separation brings with it the opportunity for significant growth (see also Clarkin & Frances, 1982).

CONTRAINDICATIONS FOR PLANNED SHORT-TERM PSYCHOTHERAPY

Except for the finding that lower social class patients have higher dropout rates, no other demographic variables such as age, sex, level of intelligence, have been shown to be significantly related to therapeutic outcome (MacKenzie, 1988). Thus, contraindications to planned short-term psychotherapy are rarely found in demographic characteristics. Rather, the contraindications that have been suggested are mainly found in characterological and symptomatic domains.

Malan and his group (1976) have gone to considerable lengths to specify the criteria for rejection of applicants. First, a potential client with any of the following clinical characteristics is rejected because these conditions are often severe and disabling: (1) serious depression or gross destructive or self-destructive acting out, (2) drug addiction, (3) a history of long-term hospitalization or other signs of latent or actual psychosis, (4) more than one course of electroconvulsive therapy, (5) chronic alcoholism, (6) incapacitating chronic obsessional symptoms, and (7) incapacitating chronic phobic symptoms.

Second, clients are rejected using Malan's approach if it is judged that any of the following events has a strong likelihood of taking place in therapy: (1) inability to make contact, (2) necessity for prolonged work in order to generate motivation for treatment, (3) necessity for prolonged work in order to penetrate rigid defenses, (4) inevitable involvement in complex or deep-seated issues that there seems no hope of working through in a short time, (5) severe dependence or other forms of unfavorable intense transference, and (6) intensification of depressive or psychotic disturbance. The first three of these predicted events would result in an inability to start effective therapeutic work within the limits of time imposed by the nature of the therapy; the next two events would result in an inability to terminate; and the last predicted event would result in a depressive or psychotic breakdown.

Mann (1973) has minimized selection as a central issue for brief psychotherapy, but he has proposed a number of exclusionary criteria—serious depression, acute psychosis, borderline personality organization, and the inability to identify a central issue. In their later publication, Mann and Goldman (1982) expanded their list of contraindications. Patients who may have difficulty engaging and disengaging rapidly from treatment are excluded. This group includes schizoid patients, certain obsessional and narcissistic patients, patients with strong dependency needs, depressive patients who are not able to form a rapid therapeutic alliance, and patients with psychosomatic disorders who do not tolerate loss well. Mann has suggested that "obsessional characters with major and almost exclusive defenses of isolation and intellectualization have a limited capacity for affective experience, although they may appear otherwise....Working with them is like writing on water" (1991, p. 21; also see Davanloo, 1978b; Ursano & Hales, 1986).

Sifneos has suggested that his form of brief psychotherapy would not be suitable for patients with psychotic symptoms; major affective disorders; alcoholism or heavy drug abuse; suicidal tendencies and acting out; or severe schizoid, borderline, or narcissistic personality disorders (Sifneos, 1987; see also Nielsen & Barth, 1991).

Three relative contraindications for planned short-term psychotherapy have been proposed by Reich and Neenan (1986). These include: (1) psychosis or major thought disorder; (2) multiple severe psychiatric problems; and (3) character disorder, if patients lack a specific focus for treatment. As for exclusion criteria, among those most commonly mentioned in the approaches examined by Burlingame and Fuhriman (1987) are the presence of psychosis and inadequate ego strength (see also Barber & Crits-Christoph, 1991; Fuhriman, Paul, & Burlingame, 1993; MacKenzie, 1988).

Just as the criteria for acceptance into planned short-term psychotherapy seem remarkably similar to those for long-term psychotherapy, so do the criteria for rejection. These criteria—chronic severe psychopathology, history of previous failure of psychotherapy to be helpful, lack of adequate reality testing, and insufficient motivation—certainly describe patients who would be difficult to treat in any form of psychotherapy.

CONCLUDING COMMENTS

As we take stock of the ideas and the empirical studies described in this chapter, two alternatives to selecting patients for planned short-term psychotherapy recommend themselves. First, if you use the same criteria as are used for time-unlimited therapy, you won't go far wrong. On the other hand, you won't learn very much about patient selection. Second, if you want to take a risk, don't use any selection criteria. Put everyone in time-limited psychotherapy and work on the assumption that if they don't do as well as you thought they should, it may be your fault, not your patients'.

The easiest hypotheses that suggest themselves if a patient doesn't show sufficient improvement are either that the patient simply isn't suitable for your therapy, or that the patient would have shown more improvement if the therapy had gone on longer.

Harder to assert, but much more challenging, is the hypothesis that if you had only been wiser or more experienced or more alert or had used a more suitable approach, your patient would have shown more improvement. This second alternative is the more intellectually exciting and if used systematically can lead to a significant increase in knowledge about how different kinds of patients can profit from planned short-term psychotherapy.

As for the narrow selection criteria identified by a number of writers in the field, it seems likely that they are not independent of each other—that is, patients who meet one of those criteria probably meet others. Thus, for example, the presence of high motivation for change, the ability to establish a productive working relationship with the therapist, a history of meaningful relationships with others, psychological-mindedness, and an identifiable and compelling focal issue of concern are likely to be significantly correlated with each other; if one of these criteria is present, the others will probably be present as well.

In the next chapter we shall examine the relationship between therapy outcome and therapist characteristics. But including therapist and therapy characteristics as well as client characteristics in the selection process will make such an examination geometrically more complex without guaranteeing compensatory gains in knowledge. All forms of planned short-term psychotherapy have been found to be essentially equally effective, so it is not likely that we shall find that significant differences in outcome will occur simply on the basis of therapy or therapist characteristics. Furthermore, it is not yet clear how one is to group short-term therapies so as to divide them into meaningfully different categories. For the moment, then, there is no appreciable downside to starting patients of all types in time-limited psychotherapy. We have the chance to be pleasantly surprised by our results.

CHAPTER 25

THE CURRENT STATUS OF PLANNED SHORT-TERM PSYCHOTHERAPY

Overview

The Impact of Planned Short-Term Psychotherapy on General Psychotherapeutic Practice

Psychotherapeutic Flexibility

The Concept of Sufficiency

General Principles of Planned Short-Term Psychotherapy

Planned Short-Term Psychotherapy and Managed Care

Concluding Comments

The principal purpose of this book has been to identify individual approaches to planned short-term psychotherapy, describe and illustrate them, and show how they differ from one another. There is little critical comparative literature regarding these specific approaches. Indeed, the field appears to be encouraging, perhaps wisely, the unlimited development of different orientations to brief psychotherapy. We are probably some years away from any comparative evaluative literature in the field of planned short-term psychotherapy.

It is now time to step back from the detailed views of various orientations to planned short-term psychotherapy in order to make some general observations about the field. The general impact of planned short-term psychotherapy on the entire psychotherapeutic enterprise will be examined. Special attention will be devoted to the concept of sufficiency—how one is to know when enough psychotherapy has been provided. Then, some important general principles of all psychotherapies will be examined and similarities that can be discerned across the different approaches to time-limited psychotherapy will be identified. Finally, we shall turn our attention to the rapidly developing move in the United States

toward "managing" the organization and cost of both physical and mental health services.

The field of planned short-term psychotherapy is quickly achieving all the hallmarks of an independent profession. About 150 English language books and edited collections of papers exclusively devoted to the topic have been published in the past 30 years. Nearly two thousand articles on the topic have appeared in journals.

Courses on short-term therapy are increasingly available in graduate and continuing education programs. The field now has its own journals—the *Journal of Systemic Therapies,* founded in 1981; *International Journal of Short-Term Psychotherapy,* founded in 1986; *Crisis Intervention and Time-Limited Treatment,* founded in 1993.

What is clear in the literature is that planned short-term psychotherapy is thought of as being applicable to a very wide variety of psychiatric disorders and to both acute and chronic stressful life circumstances. In the case of specific psychiatric disorders, both clinical and research papers have discussed short-term psychotherapy in the treatment of alcoholism, anxiety disorders, chemical dependence, child sexual abuse, chronic pain, depression and other mood disorders, eating disorders, encopresis, panic disorders, personality disorders, phobic and obsessive-compulsive disorders, posttraumatic stress disorders, schizophrenia, and sexual dysfunctions (e.g., such recent reports as Alfonso, 1992; American Psychiatric Association, 1993; Beck, Sokol, Clark, Berchick, & Wright, 1992; Berg & Miller, 1992; Duckert, Amundsen, & Johnsen, 1992; Durham, Murphy, Allan, Richard, Treliving, & Fenton, 1994; Eglau, 1992; Foa, Rothbaum, Riggs, & Murdock, 1991; Jones, Peveler, Hope, & Fairburn, 1993; Lerner, Sigal, Bacalu, & Gelkopf, 1992; Loar, 1994; Magnavita, 1993b, 1993c; McDuff & Solounias, 1992; McKay, Murphy, & Longabaugh, 1991; Richmond, Heather, Wodak, Kehoe, & Webster, 1995; Saunders, Wilkinson, & Phillips, 1995; Shapiro & Henderson, 1992; Sprang, 1992; Werner, 1995; Whale, 1992; Winston, Laikin, Pollack, Samstag, McCullough, & Muran, 1994; Winston, Pollack, McCullough, Flegenheimer, Kenterbaum, & Trujillo, 1991; see also Bloom, 1992a).

Clinical studies have appeared discussing the role of planned short-term psychotherapy in helping clients cope with such acute as well as chronic stressful life circumstances as aging, bereavement, gay and lesbian issues, hostility, imprisonment, job-related stress, low self-esteem, military service, parent–infant issues, physical impairment, retirement, sexual abuse, single-parent families, and stress of university life (e.g., such recent reports as Ahlers, 1992; Day, Maddicks, & McMahon, 1993; Gluth & Kiselica, 1994; Knight, 1992; Lavoritano & Segal, 1992; Lieberman & Yalom, 1992; Lohnes & Kalter, 1994; McConkey, 1992; Silberschatz & Curtis, 1991; Trad, 1993; see also Bloom, 1992a). It is almost impossible to identify a disorder that has not been found to be responsive to one or another form of time-limited psychotherapy—again, an indication of its remarkable effectiveness.

THE IMPACT OF PLANNED SHORT-TERM PSYCHOTHERAPY ON GENERAL PSYCHOTHERAPEUTIC PRACTICE

The overwhelming research evidence documenting the effectiveness of short-term psychotherapy, the interest on the part of most consumers to be done with their therapy and get on with their lives, and the financial drain to society of long-term psychotherapy have combined to raise serious questions about the continued application of time-unlimited approaches (Cochrane, 1972; MacKenzie, 1988). Most people who write about the future of psychotherapy believe that it will include vastly increased use of short-term interventions (e.g., Luborsky, Docherty, Miller, & Barber, 1993; Magnavita, 1993a; Norcross & Freedheim, 1992).

In fact, Goldin and Winston (1985) believe that short-term dynamic psychotherapy has already had a significant impact on traditional psychoanalytic psychotherapy, particularly regarding general therapeutic approach and the specific handling of resistance and transference reactions. Regarding their general approach, traditional psychoanalytic psychotherapists who observe the work of time-limited psychodynamic psychotherapists tend to "become more active, more courageous in pursuing feelings, appreciably more specific and concrete in delineating chief complaints, and generally more in control of the interview" (p. 69). In handling resistance, traditional psychodynamic psychotherapists appear to ask more detailed questions and to be more assertive in thwarting regression. Finally, regarding dealing with transference reactions, traditional psychodynamic psychotherapists have tended to interpret the transference relationship earlier and to decrease their encouragement of the regressive transference neurosis.

Rogawski (1982), himself a psychoanalyst, has thoughtfully considered three crucial questions that have arisen as a consequence of the increasing evidence of the effectiveness of planned short-term psychotherapy. First, in view of the fact that planned short-term psychotherapy and long-term therapy appear to be equally effective, are there any specific indications for long-term therapy? Rogawski suggests that patients suffering from character disorders or borderline syndromes whose core problems cannot be identified need supportive long-term psychotherapy. In addition, Rogawski believes that the intensive psychoanalytic method remains a unique instrument for the study of human psychology as well as for the education of psychotherapists.

Second, Rogawski asks how the demonstrated effectiveness of planned short-term psychotherapy will affect clinical practice. He suggests that these demonstrations will put pressure on mental health professionals to treat patients more efficiently, if they are to survive economically, and will put pressure on professional training facilities to teach short-term therapeutic techniques. Finally, Rogawski asks why psychodynamic approaches to short-term psychotherapy should continue to be advocated, given the evidence that they have not been shown to be superior to other approaches. His reply is that the psychodynamic approach provides a unique conceptual framework for understanding human behavior; that it is reestablishing links with other scientific disciplines, such as neurophysiology, psychopharmacology, and information theory; and that it has the potential to become a basic element of a general scientific psychology. This loyal defense of psychodynamic theory and the long-term psychotherapy associated with it is sobering in its modesty.

PSYCHOTHERAPEUTIC FLEXIBILITY

The last two decades have witnessed a significant loosening of the rigid definitions of psychotherapeutic approaches. This increasing flexibility in attitudes about the conduct of psychotherapy may well be part of a generally growing diversity of attitudes toward human service delivery. In the case of psychotherapy in particular, this increasing flexibility can be seen in attitudes toward the therapeutic approach, toward the concept of cure, and toward the length and frequency of appointments.

Flexibility in Therapeutic Approach

Increasing liberalization of approaches toward psychotherapy can be seen in a growing eclecticism—increasing recognition, even by therapists who are themselves very doctrinaire, of the important and necessary contributions of therapists with different theoretical persuasions. This eclecticism can be seen in the review of time-limited psychotherapy prepared by Budman and Stone (1983):

> It seems to us inevitable that brief therapy will increasingly become pragmatic eclectic therapy. As we have noted, the movement toward eclecticism is already affecting many therapists, regardless of whether they view themselves as doing brief treatment. Because psychotherapists heavily engaged in

short-term treatment activities begin such endeavors with an interest in time, effectiveness, and innovation, they are individuals who will be (and already have been) open to creative intervention strategies. Such intervention strategies will undoubtedly draw widely from psychoanalytic, behavioral, and humanistic psychotherapy. (pp. 944–945)

Eclecticism in theoretical approach can be seen in the shift from intrapsychic to interpersonal approaches (Horowitz & Vitkus, 1986) and in the growing integration of psychodynamic and strategic psychotherapy (Cummings & Sayama, 1995), strategic and cognitive psychotherapy (Feldman, 1994), and psychodynamic and cognitive-behavioral psychotherapy. MacKenzie (1988), for example, has noted:

> Brief psychotherapy has also incorporated a number of strategies from behavior modification, particularly the emphasis on establishing a contract to work on a restricted interpersonal focus. Application of principles learned in therapy to current outside relationships frequently takes the form of specific homework assignments. Patients' use of diaries to identify social reinforcers and to monitor application of tasks is not uncommon. Relaxation techniques may help the patient attain a sense of personal mastery, and assertiveness training techniques may complement psychodynamic approaches. (p. 750)

Just as a number of studies have examined how client characteristics may be related to therapeutic outcome in the case of planned short-term psychotherapy (see Chapter 24), the relationship of therapist characteristics, most of which transcend specific therapeutic approaches, to therapeutic outcome has also been studied. Sound research in this area is difficult to design. In a review of the literature examining the role of therapist characteristics to psychotherapy process and outcome, Lambert (1989) concluded that while some studies have found that some therapists (paraprofessionals as well as professionals) appear to be more effective than others, failure to randomize assignment of clients to therapists, small sample sizes, and a variety of other confounding variables make it impossible to come to any confident conclusions about how therapist characteristics affect therapy outcome. In spite of these methodological difficulties, some tentative assertions can be made regarding these relationships.

The most useful predictor of clinical outcome in brief psychotherapy appears to be interactional, namely, the nature of the alliance between client and therapist. The therapeutic alliance is generally defined as the ability of the client and therapist to work together collaboratively and with high levels of complementarity and is usually assessed very early in the therapeutic episode. A strong therapeutic alliance provides the safety and security to clients that permits them to tolerate the anxiety often associated with clinical intervention. In general, good clinical outcomes seem to be more frequent when there is a productive alliance between client and therapist (Krupnick, Elkins, Collings, Simmens, Sotsky, Pilkonis, & Watkins,1994; Mallinckrodt, 1993; Marmar, Weiss, & Gaston, 1989; Marziali, 1984; Marziali Marmar, & Krupnick, 1981; Svartberg & Stiles, 1992). One therapist characteristic that is often a determinant of the therapeutic alliance is therapist empathy, and Free, Green, Grace, Chernus, and Whitman (1985) found that clients' ratings of therapist empathy were significantly positively correlated with a number of outcome measures.

Other therapist variables offer intriguing clues to therapeutic effectiveness. Hill, Helms, Tichenor, Spiegel, O'Grady, and Perry (1988) examined verbatim transcripts of 127 sessions of eight cases of brief psychotherapy with anxious-depressed patients and found that experienced therapists had better immediate results when their behavior was characterized by relatively high levels of self-disclosure, interpretation, approval, paraphrasing, and asking open questions. Least helpful were confrontations, provision of information, and closed questions (see also Hill, 1992).

A number of studies have specifically examined the role of transference interpretations in therapeutic outcome. These studies report somewhat mixed results (Hill, 1992; Høglend, Heyerdahl, Amlo, Engelstad, Fossum, Sørbye, & Sørlie, 1993; Joyce & Piper, 1993; Piper, Joyce, McCalluym, & Azim, 1993). Silberschatz, Fretter, and Curtis (1986) found that validity of interpretations, as assessed by their relationship to the dynamic case formulation, was significantly positively associated with therapeutic outcome. In another study, Cox, Rutter, and Holbrook (1988) found that when the therapist

employed a more feeling-oriented therapeutic style, particularly when clients' spontaneous levels of expressed feelings were low, expression of feelings by clients significantly increased. Clinical outcome appears to be better when therapist interventions are clearly related to goals that have been mutually established between therapist and client (Messer, Tishby, & Spillman, 1992; Rudolph, Datz-Weems, Marrie, Cusack, Beerup, & Kiel, 1993; Silberschatz & Curtis, 1993).

In an especially useful study, Jones, Cumming, and Horowitz (1988) found that with severely troubled patients, outcome was most positive when therapists gave explicit advice and guidance, when physical symptoms and body functions were discussed, when dialogue had a specific focus, and when the therapist was reassuring.

In the case of patients whose difficulties were milder and less disabling, outcome was best when therapists explained the nature of psychotherapy and the rationale of their particular approach, when interpersonal relationships were a major theme of the sessions, when the patients' feelings and behavior in the present were linked to past situations, and when therapists drew attention to the connections between the therapeutic relationship and other relationships. Thus, more traditional psychodynamic therapists appeared to be more effective for patients who were only mildly disturbed, while for patients who were more seriously disturbed a more supportive and directive therapist seemed more likely to be helpful.

But, as we have mentioned, few of these hypotheses have been evaluated in well-designed empirical studies. The foundation for such studies is in place, however, in the assertions regarding the special clinical strengths of various approaches to planned short-term psychotherapy that have just been reviewed.

While empirical evidence is still sparse, the literature examining therapist characteristics that appear to be associated with positive therapeutic outcome has suggested a number of other variables that deserve further study. The first of these is therapist expertise. Clinical consensus is that planned short-term psychotherapy requires a greater level of experience and sophistication than does time-unlimited psychotherapy. In particular, such experience brings with it the knowledge of what kinds of interventions have the potential to be helpful to the client.

Gelso and Johnson (1983) in their research studies in a university counseling center identified a number of other therapist characteristics that appear to be related to patient outcome. These characteristics are listed in Box 25-1.

As these studies indicate, certain therapist behaviors may be associated with unusually high levels of improvement. These studies need to be replicated and extended, but what seems clear is that, under potentially specifiable conditions certain varieties of therapist behavior can result in significant increases in the likelihood of patient improvement, regardless of the theoretical approach to the therapy.

The fact that the list of specific therapist characteristics that are significantly associated with outcome measures is relatively short, however, may underline the remarkable general effectiveness of planned short-term psychotherapy that was described in the initial chapter in this volume. To put it differently, the best explanation for the fact that empirical studies of the relationship between clinician characteristics and clinical outcome yield such equivocal results may be that planned short-term psychotherapy generally has a positive outcome almost regardless of how the therapist conducts the psychotherapy.

Flexibility Regarding the Concept of Cure

Mental health professionals in sharply increasing numbers are beginning to reconsider their earlier views of the goals of psychotherapy. That traditional perspective on the psychotherapeutic process, virtually unknown in the rest of the healing arts, is that, first, getting better will take a long time, and, sec-

ond, once you are better, you probably will never need to come back. Budman (1981, pp. 464–465) traces these beliefs to early Freudian thinking that Freud himself later repudiated, but not before the beliefs became firmly fixed as part of psychoanalytic folklore (see also Donovan, 1987).

Cummings and VandenBos (1979) describe this belief system well:

> Any recontact with a former mental health patient is labeled a "relapse" and is viewed as evidence that the earlier intervention was either unsuccessful or incomplete. We usually act as if contact with a professional psychologist is for a single, simple, unified problem, and that six sessions will solve everything forever. No other field of health care holds this conceptualization of treatment outcome. (p. 433)

Watzlawick (1978) describes this unrealistic fantasy in the following words:

> In virtually no other, comparable realm of human endeavor is it postulated and accepted that changes must be final and complete. Everywhere, except in classical psychotherapy, it is considered a simple fact of life that there are no perfect solutions, to be reached once and for all, that problems can recur and that existence is a life-long process of perhaps optimal, but certainly never perfect adaptation...because the scenario of life constantly changes. In therapy, however, we talk about such wondrous states as full genital organization, individuation, and self-actualization, and we consider a treatment to have been successful only if the difficulty or the symptom *never* occurs again. (p. 159)

A number of other writers have commented on other aspects of this somewhat utopian view of psychotherapy. Budman and Gurman (1988) have noted:

Box 25-1: Therapist Characteristics Associated with Successful Short-Term Therapy

1. Therapist's behavior reflects confidence that short-term therapy can be effective.
2. Therapist establishes challenging but limited therapeutic goals.
3. Therapist works toward insight but not to the exclusion of behavior change.
4. Therapist's goal is to start a therapeutic process that can continue after termination.
5. Therapist follows up terminated patients to explore the consolidation of changes that has taken place.

Adapted from Gelso and Johnson, 1983, p. 206.

Patients return to therapy at various points in their lives. Assuming that as a therapist one can (or should) provide a patient with a "definitive" treatment is like assuming that a teacher should provide the definitive class, that a physician should provide the definitive antibiotic, or that a travel agent should provide the definitive vacation. What one hopes is that the ...therapy provided has had sufficient impact to alleviate some of the problems with which the patient presented upon entry into therapy, and that the patient takes with himself or herself some useful tools for dealing with similar problems in the future. (p. 248; see also Wilson, 1981, p 143; Phillips, 1985, p. ix)

Most general human service providers—and mental health professionals in increasing numbers—hold an alternative point of view about cure, one that seems more persuasive in the context of planned short-term psychotherapy: First, let us try to help you as quickly as possible; and, second, something might very well go wrong in the future, in which case we shall try to help you once again as quickly as possible.

In addition, many mental health professionals have yet to learn the lesson that most primary health care providers seem to understand instinctively: Patients have their own restitutive potential, and if therapists can help patients draw on that potential, patients can do a great deal without additional direct help from the caregiver.

Increasing numbers of mental health professionals believe they can better meet their clients' needs by practicing what has been called "brief, intermittent psychotherapy throughout the life cycle" (Cummings, 1988, p. 314, 1990; Cummings & Sayama, 1995), an orientation to mental health and substance abuse services that is entirely consistent with the goals of psychotherapy just discussed. Kupers (1988) calls this kind of psychotherapy "therapy in pieces." He writes:

More and more, clients enter therapy wishing to work through one or another circumscribed issue, end the therapy when they feel satisfied with the immediate results, and then return to be in therapy again when another crisis arises. It is hard to say which came first, the brief therapy or the pattern whereby more and more people begin to utilize therapy in pieces over a lifetime. (p. 106)

As this discussion suggests, the medical concept of cure has largely been abandoned. The treatment relationship is interrupted when presenting problems are resolved, but it is never terminated (Hoyt & Austad, 1992; Siddall, Haffey, & Feinman, 1988). With this orientation, commitment to the client can be seen from a new point of view, as Rabkin (1977) has described:

Under the best of conditions, relationships with professionals other than psychotherapists are not regarded as terminating at all. They are seen as intermittent. For example, the accountant, lawyer, family doctor, or barber may have permanent relationships with clients and perhaps their families, although the actual face-to-face contacts occur only for specific tasks or problems. Particularly in relationships of confidence, as in the case of the accountant and the physician, the tie may last a lifetime. (p. 211)

Flexibility in Length and Frequency of Appointments

Two aspects of the growing flexibility in how one determines the length and frequency of clinical appointments and the duration of episodes of psychotherapy deserve special note. First, there is increasing evidence that therapists are moving away from routinely scheduling 50 minute once-weekly interviews. And, second, attention is beginning to be directed to what may be the most profound question generated by the concept of short-term therapy, namely, how one is to know when enough psychotherapy has been provided.

Time-limited psychotherapy can be scheduled, as we have seen, in many different time frames—appointments generated one at a time; weekly one-hour sessions; half-hour sessions; meetings every two, three, or four weeks or even twice a year; as well as longer sessions of 90 minutes' duration. Barkham (1989a, 1989b; Barkham & Shapiro, 1990; Day, 1993) has developed an interesting scheduling practice in which clients are regularly seen for two sessions one week apart followed by a third session three months later.

Budman (1983) has suggested, just as Barkham has, that it may be most effective to see patients initially on a weekly basis and then to move toward longer intervals between sessions. In addition, Budman proposes planned follow-up and periodic return visits. Such proposals "may be more in line with reality than the now-prevalent therapeutic cure model, where no provision is made for follow-up and maintenance of change by the patient often is not considered" (p. 943). Similarly, Goldsmith (1986) has noted:

> It is not unusual, either in my work or in the work of other strategic therapists, for intervals between sessions to be irregular, or to be every two to four weeks. The longer intervals provide more time for a consolidation of the therapeutic gains within the context of the patient's outside life. Longer intervals can also indicate to a patient that the most important problem-solving efforts will be going on outside the therapeutic sessions. The irregularity of intervals between sessions, the variability in the length of the actual sessions, and the relatively lengthy time that can occur between sessions are all consistent with the belief that change is discontinuous. That is, the rate of therapeutic change that individuals manifest cannot be represented by a single sloping line on a graph. (p. 60)

THE CONCEPT OF SUFFICIENCY

There is perhaps no question of greater current importance in the field of short-term psychotherapy than how to know when enough psychotherapy has been done. Indeed, attention to this issue transforms the entire debate in short-term psychotherapy from one in which time is the central concept to one in which sufficiency and the avoidance of both undertreatment and overtreatment are the central concepts.

Kane (1991) has suggested that:

> Unlike surgery or the treatment of infectious disease, the end point in the treatment of mental illness is often not clear-cut. In some cases, improvement can be viewed on a continuum, whereas in others it may be focused on a particular symptom or symptom pattern. It is the responsibility of the clinician to establish and continually reevaluate goals and objectives in treatment, and the patient should be informed of these assessments. Transference issues and unrealistic expectations of the therapist are important foci of treatment, and the good therapist knows how to manage them. (pp. 16–17)

In spite of the importance of the issue of psychotherapy optimal duration, suggestions about how to know when enough psychotherapy has been done are still uncommon. As was noted at the start of this volume, most psychotherapists believe that clients cannot make significant clinical progress except in the presence of the therapist. Accumulating evidence suggests that therapists need to develop a greater appreciation of how and how much clinical improvement can take place simply as a consequence of a therapeutic process that is started by the therapist.

The greatest objection raised by traditional psychotherapists to the ideas promulgated by short-term therapists is usually what they see as an arbitrary, inflexible, and often capricious ceiling set by their agency or their clients' insurance coverage on the total number of psychotherapy sessions that will be permitted. If a mental health service delivery system functions on the basis of sufficiency instead of time, then it is possible to circumvent the issue of what constitutes the upper limit of short-term therapy, thus bypassing a profoundly refractory clinical objection to short-term psychotherapy. In place of an endless debate regarding how many interviews the agency should permit as its maximum the issue becomes how to know when the therapy that has already been provided is sufficient to meet the patient's needs without running the risk of overutilization. Schlesinger (1994) has commented that if the therapist "would like to keep psychotherapy efficient by assuring that it takes no longer than it has to, the therapist must be able to determine when the patient has accomplished enough to permit him to continue on his own" (p. 15).

Issues of treatment termination are particularly salient in the case of brief psychotherapy, in which concerns about termination are, virtually by definition, always present. Indeed, Hoyt (1979, 1994a) has suggested that in brief psychotherapy, termination may very well be *the* issue. In a sense, of course, therapeutic work is never completely finished, but our question asks when and for how long the therapist can step out of the picture to let clients continue the productive work of therapy on their own. There is relatively little in the published literature that can help in answering our question about when treatment can be terminated.

Termination criteria that derive from psychoanalytically based theories are, to say the least, difficult to operationalize and to evaluate. In their review of the literature regarding the process of termination in psychoanalysis and psychotherapy, Blanck and Blanck (1988) have reminded us of these somewhat imprecise traditional criteria: an optimal level of ego functioning, relative independence of the ego from drives on the one hand and from the superego on the other hand, relative differentiation of self representations from object representations, genital primacy, the unconscious becoming conscious, diminished need of the external object, resumption of phase-appropriate development, and so on. Each of these concepts poses daunting problems for the empirically-oriented scholar-clinician (see also Budman, 1990).

In the psychoanalytic literature, termination is usually thought of as a sign of acting out by the client, a narcissistic blow to the therapist, or a kind of mourning, a painful loss to therapist and client alike (de Bosset & Styrsky, 1986; Perry, 1987; Pekarik & Wierzbicki, 1986). The adjective that is most commonly used to modify the noun "termination" is "premature." That is, termination is often thought of in essentially negative terms.

Quintana (1993) has recently labeled this view the "termination-as-loss" model and has suggested that this model, one with a 40-year history, is in need of revision. One aspect of his proposed modernization is to understand the termination-as-loss model as consisting of two components, "termination-as-crisis" and "termination-as-development." According to Quintana, the crisis component of termination has been greatly overemphasized, while the developmental opportunities inherent in termination of psychotherapy have been underappreciated. A more appropriate model of termination, particularly in the context of brief psychotherapy, would be to think of it as "termination-as-transformation"—transformation of how clients view themselves, their therapy, their therapists, and the client-therapist relationship.

Kupers (1988) seems to have this termination-as-transformation idea in mind when he summarizes his criteria for termination—"the amelioration of most of the symptoms, the resolution of the transference, the likelihood of continued psychological growth, and the therapist's confidence that longer therapy would not add anything to the client's potential in life"—to which he adds, in the context of planned short-term psychotherapy, evidence that the client has become attuned to the psychological sphere, and that "the client has internalized the therapeutic message suffi-

ciently well to be likely to return for another course of therapy when the need arises" (p. 120). de Shazer (1994) seems to have share this idea when he describes the purposes of interviews after the first one:

> In general, the purposes of the second interview, or any interview after the first one, include …(1) constructing the interval between sessions as having included some improvement; (2) checking on whether or not what the therapist and client did in the previous session is seen by the client as having been useful, i.e., leading or allowing the client to perceive things as having improved; (3) helping the client figure out what he or she is doing and/or what has happened that led to improvements so that the client can figure out what he or she should do more of; (4) figuring out whether or not improvements have led to things being "good enough" so that further therapy is not necessary; and finally, (5) when the client does not describe any improvements, preventing both therapist and client from doing more of something that did not work and, therefore, prompting both therapist and client to do something different. (1994, p. 135)

Traditional criteria for termination stand in opposition to the growing realization that we all face repeated challenges to our equilibrium and that a psychoanalysis followed by life-long psychic bliss is, sadly, the exception rather than the rule. With increasing frequency we read that psychotherapy has to be seen as an ongoing process independent of treatment duration that "conflicts, anxieties, losses, and changes are inevitably part of the human condition" that create the "potential for new conflicts to be activated…and…old ones reactivated" (Shectman, 1986, p. 521).

Budman (1990) has added another useful dimension to this growing realization:

> Patients in their actual behaviors generally do not conform to the "cure" model of how therapy ends. They are in many cases pleased to stop therapy. Perhaps this is because regardless of what they are told by their clinician, they realize that they can always get more help as needed. And this they most certainly do. (p. 211)

At the professional system level there is an interesting tension between the attitudes of therapists and the attitudes of clients regarding the issue of termination. de Bosset and Styrsky (1986), for example, have reported that among their second-year psychiatric residents, who spend an average of 50 sessions with their patients, and fifth-year residents, who spend an average of 163 sessions with their patients, only 16 percent felt that their patients were ready to terminate treatment when they did. Out of these beliefs comes the ten-year psychoanalysis.

Other studies have shown, as a kind of counterpoint, that patients anticipate that their treatment will be substantially shorter than their therapists think (Pekarik & Wierzbicki, 1986). While no significant correlation exists between therapy duration and outcome as judged by patients, there is a significant positive correlation between therapy duration and outcome as judged by therapists. In comparison with patients' evaluations of therapeutic outcome, therapists tend to underestimate the effectiveness of brief episodes of care and overestimate the effectiveness of long episodes of care (Bloom, 1992b; O'Leary, 1995).

Termination can indicate not that all conflict has been fully and permanently resolved, but that a significant piece of psychological work has been accomplished that permits clients to manage on their own. From this point of view, psychotherapy, particularly brief psychotherapy, can be seen as an encounter that starts a growth process that will continue long after the formal therapy has been concluded.

Termination has begun to refer not to psychotherapy but to this episode of psychotherapy. This point of view leads to a distinction between the treatment episode and the treatment relationship. It is the relationship that endures over time. Productive treatment episodes of varying lengths may occur on occasion within this enduring treatment relationship (Edbril, 1994; Shectman, 1986). Thus, sufficiency of psychotherapy means sufficiency for now, not sufficiency forever. Walen, DiGiuseppe, and Dryden (1991) make a similar cognitively oriented point in the context of rational-emotive therapy when they note that "if therapy ends before behavior change is stabilized, the outcome may be less than desirable, although not terrible. Clients can always return to therapy for booster shots and further practice if needed" (p. 313).

Another aspect of the question of sufficiency of psychotherapy lies in the fact that both clinical and research studies suggest that the therapeutic gain associated with a single treatment session tends to diminish, and diminish rather sharply, as the number of sessions increases. While no precise computational formula exists for plotting session effect against number of previous sessions, data that have been reported (e.g., Howard, Kopta, Krause, & Orlinsky, 1986; Seligman, 1995) suggest that after the first session each additional session may only have about half of the therapeutic effect of the previous one. Thus, it does not take long before additional treatment sessions have little discernible additive effectiveness. Accordingly, shorter but multiple episodes of care seem to have a far greater potential for significant clinical improvement than longer but fewer episodes of care.

Returning directly to the issue of sufficiency, Fisch (1994) has suggested that:

> How long or short therapy is also depends on whether the therapist knows when to stop. It may be trite to say, but if one has no idea of when something is done one runs the risk of going on interminably. Therapy, therefore, can be briefer if the therapist has some rather clear idea of what needs to occur to mark an endpoint of therapy. (p. 131)

What makes Fisch's comment particularly useful is its message that the therapist has an important role to play in deciding when psychotherapy can be ended. It isn't simply a matter of continuing psychotherapy because the client wants it to continue. As was noted in the first chapter of this volume, such a practice guarantees only that the cost of psychotherapy will be increased. Whether the result will be any better is clearly in doubt.

There are both positive and negative criteria for knowing when enough therapy has been done. On the positive side, enough therapy has been done when patients seem to have learned something important about themselves that they can chew on, and when they have a course of action or strategy that they can view within the context of an explicitly articulated ongoing therapeutic relationship (see O'Hanlon, 1990).

On the negative side, not enough therapy has been done when the client has not finished his or her story, if for some reason the therapist is uneasy about terminating the therapy or has failed to define and communicate something the client needs to know, or if no coherent plan of action has been developed.

Wise therapists will make sure that their psychotherapy is not terminated too soon just as they will make sure that they do not provide more psychotherapy than is needed.

GENERAL PRINCIPLES OF PLANNED SHORT-TERM PSYCHOTHERAPY

A number of authors have identified the common characteristics of planned short-term psychotherapies. These characteristics—the limitation on time, the limitation on goals, the establishment of a focal issue, and a more active and flexible therapeutic approach—have been repeatedly referred to already, and little new can be added here.

The general principles of planned short-term psychotherapy can also be viewed as a subset of the identified general principles of all psychotherapies. Frank (1984), has searched for the general principles that help account for the fact that psychotherapies appear to be equally effective and for the components of all psychotherapies that transcend specific assertions regarding specific techniques or theories:

> One way to identify some of these components would be to ask yourself what qualities you would seek in a guide if you were a tenderfoot about to embark on an exploration into unknown territory with various unknown dangers. Two qualities you would certainly want in a guide would be trustworthiness and competence. You would expect to be able to rely fully on the guide's concern about your welfare....you would want the guide to be thoroughly familiar with the terrain and how to cope with the hardships and dangers you might meet. (p. 422)

These attributes, according to Frank, form the cornerstones of the general psychotherapeutic effort. Regarding trustworthiness, Frank suggests that therapists must be able to convey that they have the patient's interest at heart and that they care about and are concerned about the patient's welfare. In addition, they must be able to create a sense of personal security for the patient, a sense that the patient is accepted and the therapist can be counted on. As for competence, Frank believes that therapists must have mastered the therapeutic procedures they practice and that, regardless of what these techniques are, they must be able to carry out the procedures common to them all—listening, understanding their patients, and conveying that understanding in a useful way.

Frank believes that trustworthiness, caring, and competence set the stage for effective psychotherapy—therapy that is emotionally arousing and that reinforces the sense of self-efficacy that has so often been lost or lowered. With emotional arousal comes increased motivation. With the increased sense of self-efficacy comes a greater willingness to explore issues formerly unexplored. From this perspective, we can immediately see one therapeutic virtue to time-limited psychotherapy, for its fundamental message is very affirming—most patients need only a little help to get back on track and to manage their affairs on their own.

Short-term psychotherapies may be equivalent in their effectiveness because everything inside the patient is connected to everything else. Whatever a caring, competent, and trustworthy therapist does, regardless of what specific techniques and theories are espoused, has the potential for being helpful. In fact, it may be that a workable and congenial theory of psychopathology and of psychotherapy serves its primary purpose by keeping therapists' attention focused during their interviews with patients.

If therapists simply ask patients to think more deeply about themselves, as virtually all psychotherapists do, such requests may have significant therapeutic potential. The request provides an opportunity for patients that is rarely present in normal social interactions. Exploration of the self can lead to discoveries that can clarify and demystify. A single discovery about the self can lead to significant change in how individuals think about themselves and others and in how they carry out their interpersonal interactions.

Freud made this point very clearly in his insistence that psychotherapy served the patient by helping make conscious the unconscious, that is, by increasing self-awareness. Describing his view of the difference between the conscious and the unconscious, Freud noted that everything conscious is subject to a process of wearing away, while what is unconscious is relatively unchangeable. Freud (1909/1953) once reconstructed his comments to a patient to whom he was pointing out the antiques standing about in his office as follows: "They were, in fact, I said, only objects found in a tomb, and their burial had been their preservation: the destruction of Pompeii was only beginning now that it had been dug up" (p. 313; see also Malcolm, 1987; Straker, 1986). Wearing away might not be good for the unburied treasures of Pompeii, but it is exactly what mental health professionals hope will happen in psychotherapy.

Shared Beliefs Among Short-Term Psychotherapists

A somewhat more empirical approach to the identification of general principles of planned short-term psychotherapy would be to look for specific shared beliefs among short-term psychotherapists, that is, principles or therapeutic techniques that many or most psychotherapists seem to subscribe to regardless of their particular approach to planned short-term psychotherapy. Our examination of the literature suggests that a number of shared beliefs probably do exist. A list of these shared beliefs, arranged from the more general to the more specific, is presented in Box 25-2.

Box 25-2: Shared Beliefs among Short-Term Psychotherapists

1. Where there is life there is change—with or without psychotherapy. The job of the therapist is to guide and accelerate that change.
2. Time-limited psychotherapy is hard work for the psychotherapist—intellectually and emotionally demanding and requiring a high level of skill.
3. Available time should be encumbered wisely. When their schedules do not permit them to take on a new client, therapists cease being a resource to the community.
4. Virtually all clients can be helped and can be helped relatively quickly, regardless of diagnosis or problem severity.
5. Psychotherapy is better than no psychotherapy; planned short-term outpatient psychotherapy is equal in effect to time-unlimited outpatient psychotherapy and, except in relatively rare instances, to either time-limited or time-unlimited inpatient psychotherapy
6. There is no evidence that any particular approach to planned short-term psychotherapy is significantly better than any other approach.
7. Planned short-term psychotherapy requires a collaboration between client and therapist for establishing therapeutic goals, for the conduct of the therapeutic episode, and for bringing it to an agreed-upon conclusion.
8. Special training in planned short-term psychotherapy enhances clinical effectiveness.
9. The most critical question facing psychotherapists is how to know when enough psychotherapy has been done. Often that time tends to come sooner rather than later.
10. Psychotherapists significantly underestimate how helpful they can be to people in brief periods of time.
11. A successful episode of brief psychotherapy, however focused, can have a spreading effect throughout the personality of the client. Only small changes may be required to start a process that will lead to significant clinical improvement.
12. The effects of psychotherapy continue long after the therapeutic episode has been concluded.
13. Clients have strengths as well as weaknesses and have the capacity to make quite major changes in their lives both during an episode of psychotherapy as well as after an episode has been completed.
14. The leverage of the therapist, initially very high, decreases rapidly. Therapeutic efficiency and effectiveness can be maximized by keeping episodes as short as possible.
15. Psychotherapy should be thought of as a series of brief therapeutic episodes each of which becomes an opportunity to accomplish some explicit set of objectives.

(continued)

Box 25-2 continued

16. Think of psychotherapy as intermittent—many individual brief treatment episodes within an ongoing therapeutic relationship. Clients should always feel that they are welcome to return for another therapeutic episode.
17. Therapists maintain an optimal level of flexibility regarding the frequency and duration of appointments.
18. It is as important to avoid premature termination of the therapeutic episode as it is to avoid overtreatment.
19. Planned short-term therapists are not uneasy about being teachers at the same time that they are psychotherapists.
20. Short-term psychotherapists look to the time between sessions as a potentially valuable occasion for work to be done by the client. Homework can include keeping a log or a diary, establishing a schedule, having a conversation with a specific person on a specific topic, writing, reading, or rewarding oneself. They urge clients to keep track of, to think about, to try out, to follow up.
21. Once a focal issue is identified, detours should be avoided.
22. Empathic remarks, reassurance, and sympathetic listening facilitate therapeutic progress.
23. The psychological climax of every interview is a skillful intervention—a well-timed interpretation, an educational statement or two, a carefully considered activity plan designed to modify undesired behavior, or a proposal whose goal is to change interpersonal interaction.
24. Planned short-term psychotherapists believe that building a follow-up contact into the therapeutic episode creates the opportunity for them to evaluate the consequences of their work and extends the life and the effectiveness of their interventions.

PLANNED SHORT-TERM PSYCHOTHERAPY AND MANAGED CARE

The last several years have witnessed the beginnings of a profound change in the organization and financing of medical care in the United States. The traditional system of fee-for-service health care is being replaced by a variety of innovative organized health care systems. More than 100 million Americans are now covered by some form of organized health care (Hoyt, 1995), and the number is rapidly increasing. While the specific characteristics of the U.S. health care delivery system of the future are far from clear, there seems to be general agreement that fee-for-service health care is far too inefficient and expensive (Giles, 1993, Chapter 2).

The cost of health care is growing at a rate three or four times that of the general inflation rate, and its unrestricted continuing growth cannot be sustained.

In the last decade for which figures are available, expenditures for health care have more than doubled, reaching $884 billion in 1993. This amount represents 14 percent of the gross domestic product and an average of $3300 per person per year.

As the cost of health care increases, the cost of health insurance increases as well. As a consequence, access to health care is eroding. A growing number of Americans are not only unable to afford out-of-pocket medical expenses; they are also unable to afford to pay for health insurance. Ours is the most costly health care system in the world. Some 40 million people in the United States have no health insurance, and an additional million people a year lose the health insurance they have.

In addition, insufficient attention is paid to the supply, quality, and distribution of health care services, as well as to the fundamental beliefs governing contemporary health care policy. It is not at all clear, for example, that the huge increases in expenditures for health care of the past two decades have yielded a commensurate improvement in our health status. The decision to create more health care resources might not have been the best way to improve the general health of Americans.

These problems are as true for mental health services as they are for general health services (Christianson & Osher, 1994; Feldman & Fitzpatrick, 1992; Shaffer, Cutler, & Wellstone, 1994). The organization and financing of mental health care have to be reformed, or, to put this statement into more contemporary vocabulary, "managed." Planned short-term psychotherapy is playing a rapidly growing role in the thinking of health care policy analysts as they consider the implications of managed health care theory for the treatment of psychological disorders.

The major alternative to unrestricted fee-for-service mental health care is the health maintenance organization, of which there are two general types. In one, mental health-related services are provided as part of a comprehensive health maintenance organization (Altman & Goldstein, 1988; Bittker, 1992; Bloom, 1988; Feldman & Goldman, 1987; La Court, 1988; Siddall, Haffey, & Feinman, 1987). In the other, mental health-related services are provided through a separate mental health maintenance organization that may or may not be affiliated with a health maintenance organization. (Cummings, 1986; Cummings & Duhl, 1987; Feldman & Fitzpatrick, 1992).

These alternatives to fee-for-service medical care share a number of important fiscal similarities: (1) The cost of care is prepaid and entirely predictable to the patient, (2) the cost is essentially independent of the amount or nature of services that are provided, (3) the amount of income to the health care provider system is fixed and predictable, and (4) a variety of mechanisms are introduced in order to control expenditures. While the traditional fee-for-service health care delivery system profits whenever services are provided, health maintenance organizations profit from providing only those services that are judged to be necessary.

Comprehensive health maintenance organizations and specialized mental health maintenance organizations each have their potential advantages and disadvantages. With the evidence of the strong connection between mental and physical well-being (Bloom, 1988, 1990) and the evidence that brief psychotherapy can result in significant reductions in medical care utilization and expenditures (see Chapter 20), the idea of embedding mental health and substance abuse services in the same service delivery system that provides general health care has special appeal. Goldman (1988) has described this appeal eloquently:

> Comprehensive mental health and substance abuse services in a prepaid, managed health care system offers one of the few opportunities available today to serve most, if not all, members of a community. HMOs hold the potential for both excellence and comprehensiveness of services. For the vast majority of its members HMOs can reduce barriers to care for both physical and psychological needs. At their best and most innovative, these plans can provide rational, individual treatment plans that manifest commitment to professional ideals, to improved patient care and to cost consciousness. (p. 200)

The primary advantage of the mental health maintenance organization is that it is governed by mental health professionals who can potentially provide the best services possible, rather than by physicians who might ordinarily think of mental health services as a minor adjunct to general medical care.

At the moment the move toward managed mental health care is far from smooth. Many health maintenance and mental health maintenance organizations are underfunded, poorly conceptualized, and excessively concerned about profitability. There are concerns about the possible loss of the confidentiality of the relationship between health care provider and client. Managed care organizations appear and disappear. Their survival depends on the ongoing search for contracts with employer groups and on market forces that often result in unpredictable changes in ownership.

The competitive environment among organized mental health care delivery systems has resulted in considerable instability, so that the possibility of multiple brief episodes of psychotherapy within an ongoing therapeutic relationship (suggested earlier in this chapter) is not always present. An ongoing therapeutic relationship is not possible when, for example, employers negotiate periodically with competing health care service delivery systems and move their employees wholesale from one set of health care providers to another. Under these circumstances, therapeutic relationships are inevitably severed.

There are many components to managing the financing and organization of health care. No responsible health care practitioner objects to the ongoing efforts to eliminate fraudulent billing. Few health care practitioners object to efforts to eliminate unnecessary duplication of services or even to eliminate reimbursement for services that are clearly ineffective. Accomplishing these objectives will save billions of dollars each year.

But the most common and most serious objection that has been raised by mental health professionals to managed care is the possibility that patients will be undertreated, that is, that there will be too much attention to managed cost and too little attention to managed care (Hoyt, 1995). Managed mental health organizations are at financial risk. If the costs that are incurred in delivering mental health services exceed the income that is derived from fixed prepaid fees, the managed mental health organization cannot survive. Under these circumstances there may be considerable pressure to reduce mental health treatment across the board or to disallow more costly interventions—a practice antithetical to responsible planned short-term psychotherapy, which avoids overtreatment in order to conserve resources so that undertreatment can also be avoided. To put it differently, while a fee-for-service medical care system can run the risk of overtreating patients, there is a fear that a managed care system can run the risk of undertreating patients. A well-functioning health care delivery system should minimize both risks.

Reducing these risks depends precisely on a greater understanding of the concept of sufficiency discussed earlier in this chapter, that is, how to know when enough treatment has been delivered. It is the rare professional training program that provides even token attention to this issue. Many, perhaps a majority of, mental health professionals continue to believe, in spite of all the evidence to the contrary, that longer treatment episodes inevitably result in significantly greater clinical improvement.

Until such time as our training programs produce mental health professionals who appreciate what they can accomplish in brief periods of time, who routinely assess therapeutic progress and outcome (e.g., Savitz, 1992), and who develop a stronger knowledge

base for identifying those clients who require longer episodes of care, success in making effective use of short-term psychotherapy will depend on wise staff recruitment and ongoing supervision and continuing education, on thoughtful program planning and implementation, and on a reward system that is tied to evidence of increasing clinical skill.

Recruitment and Continuing Education

A new generation of therapists is on the horizon—clinicians who are well trained in brief psychotherapy techniques and who have confidence in the effectiveness of these techniques and in their own clinical competencies. If a therapist does not believe that time-limited psychotherapy can be effective and functions as if saying, in one way or another, "We only have six interviews available to us, so I do not think we can accomplish very much," then you have a prescription for failure. Put therapists who believe that they can be helpful to clients in a brief period of time together with patients who believe that they can and will be helped, and you have the perfect package for a good therapeutic outcome. The difference between failure and success in brief psychotherapy may well be the difference between "We only have an hour" and "We have a whole hour."

Recent surveys indicate that a significant portion of psychotherapists who now do planned short-term psychotherapy have had little or no training in brief therapy (Levenson, Speed, & Budman, 1995) and that being an experienced, traditionally trained psychotherapist does not guarantee equal effectiveness as a psychotherapist specializing in planned short-term psychotherapy (Budman & Armstrong, 1992; Strupp, 1980b, 1980c, 1993). Studies designed to evaluate the role of therapist training in determining therapy outcome (Pekarik, 1994; Stein & Lambert, 1995), however, suggest that outcome tends to be positively influenced by the level of training and expertise of therapists.

Accordingly, supervision and continuing education need to be thoughtfully provided by experienced staff members (or, less preferably, outside consultants) who are well trained in and committed to short-term psychotherapy strategies and techniques. Training and supervision can be offered in a variety of modalities—preemployment training programs, ongoing short-term therapy that is observed by trainees, regularly scheduled case consultation and case conferences, live observation and supervision of trainees engaged in time-limited psychotherapy, journal clubs, and more formal seminars and workshops (Haley, 1987, pp. 194 ff.; Walen, DiGiuseppe, & Dryden, 1992, pp. 323 ff.).

Budman and Armstrong (1992) have suggested that such training programs need to keep principles of adult education in mind, need to emphasize a flexible and pragmatic approach to short-term psychotherapy, and need to allocate sufficient resources to the task to ensure that training will have a long-term positive effect on therapy outcome.

Program Planning and Implementation

Agencies should move away as quickly as possible from a policy that sets an upper limit on the length or number of treatment episodes (Cummings, 1988). Preoccupation with time limits should be replaced with concern for how much treatment is necessary, paralleling what is done in the case of primary medical care. When there is a specified upper limit on the number of psychotherapy sessions to which a patient is entitled, patients will often feel cheated if they do not get their full entitlement. It would be far better to have no explicit limit, simply offering patients all the psychotherapy they need.

With this latter policy, clinicians can be allowed maximum flexibility in planning their own therapy schedules. Each clinician can be expected to meet an annual average number of sessions per therapeutic episode. The figure can be based on each clinician's years of experience and training, both prior to and after joining the staff, and on a measure of prior performance, with less experienced therapists being permitted a greater number of sessions per patient. Because it is an average number of sessions that constitutes the contracted standard, each therapist can then be allowed to deviate from that average depending on the nature of each patient's individual problem. Thus, some patients can be discharged after having fewer sessions than the anticipated average, while others may require more sessions than that expected average.

Flexibility should be encouraged not only in duration of therapy but also in the frequency of therapy

sessions; duration of sessions; plans for follow-up interviews (Malan, 1980a) or return visits; and in the use of alternatives to face-to-face interviews, such as contact by telephone or by letter. Initial interviews can be set up for 90 minutes or two hours, for example, and later interviews, if needed, can be shortened or lengthened and scheduled more or less frequently, depending on the nature of the presenting problem.

Patients should be encouraged to keep in touch with the agency, and therapists should be encouraged to check in with former patients from time to time. It should be clear to patients that they can return for additional therapeutic interviews whenever time they feel the need.

In addition to providing help to the patient, the therapist should be alert for opportunities to provide consultation regarding salient family-related or work-related issues. If the agency is part of a larger health maintenance organization or is embedded within a public general hospital, staff should be on the alert for other services that can be provided for the patient on the same occasion as the visit for mental health services. In the case of public general hospitals, for example, the prevalence of one-time visits is often so high that staff members might profitably assume that they will have but a single opportunity to be of help to the patient and they should "work the waiting room," trying to identify whatever other clinical, medical, or educational services are needed and making those services available on the spot.

Adjustable Reward Structure

Increasing clinical experience should bring with it increasing efficiency and effectiveness. This expectation provides the rationale for a reward structure for mental health personnel that can be tied to an appropriately calculated expected work product. Annual salary increments and job performance ratings could be related to work productivity during the previous year, for example, and that productivity can be calculated on the basis of whatever variables are crucial to an agency's mandate.

Thus, in some cases, salary increments can be tied to absolute average number of sessions per discharge. In other cases, increments can be tied to improvement compared to the previous year, or to total number of patients seen, or to recidivism rate, or to some combination of these or other variables. But clinical directors should be able to negotiate an annual plan for each clinician that sets agreed-upon standards for performance during the coming year and establishes salary increment levels that are associated with those standards.

The Near Future of Managed Care

The probable characteristics of managed care in the coming years can be extrapolated by examining recent trends in health care delivery. While such predictions must be presented with a good deal of caution, three major trends seem relatively clear. First, managed care is here to stay; in the future there are likely to be fewer but larger managed care companies.This development will allow for far greater stability of mental health care in the future. One consequence of this growing stability will be the increasing opportunity for both clients and staff to envision brief therapeutic episodes within an ongoing therapeutic relationship. Another consequence will be that managed care organizations will be able to devote more resources to those activities that have important but slow-to-appear consequences for improved physical and mental health. Now, with so much movement of clients in and out of health maintenance organizations, there is little incentive for the active development of, for example, stress management or social support enhancement programs. Such preventively oriented programs will more than likely benefit a different health maintenance organization than the one in which the programs were developed.

Second, medical care, particularly mental health care, will continue to become increasingly empirically based—treatment plans will be developed as a function of an increased knowledge base. There will probably be a continued decrease in inpatient treatment. Greater attention will be paid to the cost of mental health personnel, with a better match between level of skill and training of mental health personnel on the one hand and treatment outcome on the other. Mental health care should therefore become far more efficient and effective, while at the same time less costly. These developments should reduce the risk of undertreatment even more than might otherwise be the case.

Third, as mental health professionals become better trained in planned short-term psychotherapy and more secure about their abilities to be helpful to clients in brief periods of time, the need for external utilization review will diminish. As a consequence, mental health professionals will be able to resume their primary responsibility for evaluating patient care and for making decisions about the resources that will be needed to complete a therapeutic episode successfully, without as great a need for the onerous record-keeping that is now usually required.

What is less easy to predict is the future relationship between mental health and physical health care. The difficulty in being sanguine about such a prediction can be seen in the current state of affairs. While the research literature makes a persuasive case that mental and physical health are remarkably interdependent, most managed mental health care seems to be developing on its own, with little integration with physical health care.

These predictions are admittedly quite optimistic and suggest that managed care will become and then remain the primary mode for providing both physical and mental health services in the future. As time goes on, to continue this generally optimistic view, the risks of undertreatment and overtreatment should diminish, and mental health professionals should become increasingly comfortable about making the most efficient use of their time.

CONCLUDING COMMENTS

This final chapter has provided an overall assessment of the growing field of planned short-term psychotherapy and has considered a number of general issues that apply to the entire field. With remarkably few exceptions, short-term outpatient or inpatient psychotherapy appears to be equal in effectiveness to time-unlimited outpatient or inpatient care, and outpatient care appears to be equal in effectiveness to inpatient care. The implication of these conclusions for public policy is abundantly clear. In legal language, it is the policy of the *least restrictive alternative,* that is, the principle that psychotherapy should take place in the setting and the way that create the fewest personal restrictions on clients. Those restrictions are minimized by keeping the duration of treatment as short as possible.

We have seen that the field of planned short-term psychotherapy has become an important specialty area and that its clinical and research findings are having an increasing impact on the entire field of psychotherapy. Establishing standards by which clinicians can know when they have provided enough psychotherapy has been identified as one of the important empirical issues facing the field at this time. Avoiding overtreatment is the most compelling strategy for ensuring that additional treatment will be available when it is needed. Making sure that brief episodes of care are seen within the context of an ongoing therapeutic relationship can help ensure that additional treatment will be requested when needed.

We have also seen that the various approaches to planned short-term psychotherapy described in this volume have certain generally shared attributes. Careful consideration of these shared attributes may help define this complex field and chart its requirements for ongoing training and supervision.

The twin observations that planned short-term psychotherapy is indistinguishable from time-unlimited psychotherapy in its effects and that clients are generally quite satisfied with brief episodes of treatment are not only the most consistent findings in the psychotherapy literature; they are also the most affirmative. The repeatedly observed ability of mental health professionals to be helpful to their patients in remarkably short periods of time should bring an enormous sense of satisfaction to psychotherapists whose years of training have been designed to enhance their abilities to understand and be of help to troubled people. This book has been prepared in the hopes of making it easier for mental health professionals to find new and congenial ways of enhancing that effectiveness.

REFERENCES

Ahlers, C. (1992). Solution-oriented therapy for professionals working with physically impaired clients. *Journal of Strategic and Systemic Therapies, 11*, 53–68.

Aldrich, C. K. (1968). Brief psychotherapy: A reappraisal of some theoretical assumptions. *American Journal of Psychiatry, 125*, 585–592.

Alexander, F., & French, T. M. (1946). *Psychoanalytic therapy*. New York: Ronald.

Alford, B. A. (1993). Brief cognitive psychotherapy of panic disorder. In R. A. Wells & V. J. Giannetti (Eds.), *Casebook of the brief psychotherapies* (pp. 65–75). New York: Plenum Press.

Alpert, M. C. (1992). Accelerated empathic therapy: A new short-term dynamic psychotherapy. *International Journal of Short-Term Psychotherapy, 7*, 133–156.

Altman, L., & Goldstein, J. M. (1988). Impact of HMO model type on mental health service delivery: Variation in treatment and approaches. *Administration in Mental Health, 15*, 246–261.

American Psychiatric Association (1993). Practice guideline for major depressive disorder in adults. *American Journal of Psychiatry, 150(4) (Supp)*, 1–26.

American Psychiatric Association (1994). *Diagnostic and statistical manual of mental disorders: DSM-IV* (4th ed.). Washington, DC: American Psychiatric Association.

Applebaum, S. A. (1975). Parkinson's law in psychotherapy. *International Journal of Psychoanalytic Psychotherapy, 4*, 426–436.

Arkowitz, H., & Hannah, M. T. (1989). Cognitive, behavioral, and psychodynamic therapies: Converging or diverging pathways to change? In A. Freeman, K. M. Simon, L. E. Beutler, & H. Arkowitz (Eds.), *Comprehensive handbook of cognitive therapy* (pp. 143-167). New York: Plenum Press.

Atlas, J. A. (1994). Crisis and acute brief therapy with adolescents. *Psychiatric Quarterly, 65*, 79–87.

Auerbach, S. M., & Kilmann, P. R. (1977). Crisis intervention: A review of outcome research. *Psychological Bulletin, 84*, 1189–1217.

Avnet, H. H. (1965). How effective is short-term therapy? In L. R. Wolberg (Ed.), *Short-term psychotherapy* (pp. 7–22). New York: Grune & Stratton.

Baldwin, B. A. (1979). Crisis intervention: An overview of theory and practice. *Counseling Psychologist, 8*, 43–52.

Balint, E., & Norell, J. S. (Eds.) (1973). *Six minutes for the patient: Interactions in general practice consultation*. London: Tavistock Publications.

Balint, M. (1957). *The doctor, his patient and the illness*. New York: International Universities Press.

Balint, M., Ornstein, P. H., & Balint, E. (1972). *Focal psychotherapy: An example of applied psychoanalysis*. London: Lippincott.

Barber, J. P., & Crits-Christoph, P. (1991). Comparison of the brief dynamic therapies. In P. Crits-Christoph & J. P. Barber (Eds.), *Handbook of short-term dynamic psychotherapy* (pp. 323–352). New York: Basic Books.

Barkham, M. (1989a). Brief prescriptive therapy in two-plus-one sessions: Initial cases from the clinic. *Behavioural Psychotherapy, 17*, 161–175.

Barkham, M. (1989b). Exploratory therapy in two-plus-one sessions: I—Rationale for a brief psychotherapy model. *British Journal of Psychotherapy, 6(1)*, 81–88.

Barkham, M., & Shapiro, D. A. (1990). Brief psychotherapeutic interventions for job-related distress: A pilot study of prescriptive and exploratory therapy. *Counseling Psychology Quarterly, 3*, 133–147.

Barth, K., Nielsen, G., Havik, O. E., Haver, B., Mølstad, E., Rogge, H., Skåtun, M., Heiberg, A. N., & Ursin, H. (1988). Assessment for three different forms of short-term dynamic psychotherapy: Findings from the Bergen Project. *Psychotherapy and Psychosomatics, 49*, 153–159.

Bateson, G. (1972). *Steps to an ecology of mind*. New York: Ballantine.

Bateson, G. (1979). *Mind and nature: A necessary unity*. New York: Dutton.

Bauer, G. P., & Kobos, J. C. (1984). Short-term psychodynamic psychotherapy: Reflections on the past and current practice. *Psychotherapy, 21*, 153–170.

Bauer, G. P., & Kobos, J. C. (1987). *Brief therapy: Short-term psychodynamic intervention*. Northvale, NJ: Aronson.

Beck, A. T. (1967). *Depression: Clinical, experimental, and theoretical aspects*. New York: Hoeber.

Beck, A. T. (1976). *Cognitive therapy and the emotional disorders*. New York: International Universities Press.

Beck, A. T. (1991). Cognitive therapy: A 30-year retrospective. *American Psychologist, 46*, 368–375.

Beck, A. T., & Freeman, A. (Eds.) (1990). *Cognitive therapy of personality disorders*. New York: Guilford Press.

Beck, A. T., Rush, A. J., Shaw, B. F., & Emery, G. (1979). *Cognitive therapy of depression*. New York: Guilford Press.

Beck, A. T., Sokol, L., Clark, D. A., Berchick, R., & Wright, F. (1992). A crossover study of focused cognitive therapy for panic disorder. *American Journal of Psychiatry, 149,* 778–783.

Beck, A. T., Wright, F. D., Newman, C. F., & Liese, B. S. (1993). *Cognitive therapy of substance abuse.* New York: Guilford Press.

Bedrosian, R. C., & Bozicas, G. D. (1994). *Treating family of origin problems: A cognitive approach.* New York: Guilford Press.

Beeber, A. R. (1988). A systems model of short-term open-ended group therapy. *Hospital and Community Psychiatry, 39,* 537–542.

Bellak, L. (1984). Intensive brief and emergency psychotherapy. In L. Grinspoon (Ed.), *Psychiatry update: The American Psychiatric Association annual review (vol. 3)* (pp. 11–24). Washington, DC: American Psychiatric Press.

Bellak, L., & Siegel, H. (1983). *Handbook of intensive brief and emergency psychotherapy* (B.E.P.). Larchmont, NY: C.P.S. Inc.

Bellak, L., & Small, L. (1965). *Emergency psychotherapy and brief psychotherapy.* New York: Grune & Stratton.

Bellak, L., & Small, L. (1978). *Emergency psychotherapy and brief psychotherapy (2d ed.).* New York: Grune & Stratton.

Berg, I. K., & Miller, S. D. (1992). *Working with the problem drinker: A solution-focused approach.* New York: Norton.

Bergin, A. E., & Garfield, S. L. (1986). Introduction and historical review. In S. L. Garfield & A. E. Bergin (Eds.), *Handbook of psychotherapy and behavior change: An empirical analysis (3d ed.)* (pp. 3–22). New York: Wiley.

Bergler, E. (1949). *The basic neurosis, oral regression and psychic masochism.* New York: Grune & Stratton.

Bergman, J. S. (1985). *Fishing for barracuda: Pragmatics of brief systemic therapy.* New York: Norton.

Bergman, J. S. (1990). Clinical road maps for prescribing rituals. In J. K. Zeig & S. G. Gilligan (Eds.), *Brief therapy: Myths, methods, and metaphors* (pp. 124–134). New York: Brunner/Mazel.

Berman, J. S., & Norton, N. C. (1985). *Does professional training make a therapist more effective?* Psychological Bulletin, 98, 401–407.

Bierenbaum, H., Nichols, M. P., & Schwartz, A. J. (1976). Effects of varying session length and frequency in brief emotive psychotherapy. *Journal of Consulting and Clinical Psychology, 44,* 790–798.

Binder, J. L., Henry, W. P., & Strupp, H. H. (1987). An appraisal of selection criteria for dynamic psychotherapies and implications for setting time limits. *Psychiatry, 50,* 154–166.

Binder, J. L., Strupp, H. H., & Henry, W. P. (1995). Psychodynamic therapies in practice: Time-limited dynamic psychotherapy. In B. Bongar & L. F. Beutler (Eds.), *Comprehensive textbook of psychotherapy: Theory and practice* (pp. 48–63). New York: Oxford University Press.

Bittker, T. E. (1992). The emergence of prepaid psychiatry. In J. L. Feldman & R. J. Fitzpatrick (Eds.), *Managed mental health care: Administrative and clinical issues* (pp. 3–10). Washington, DC: American Psychiatric Press.

Blanck, G., & Blanck, R. (1988). The contribution of ego psychology to understanding the process of termination in psychoanalysis and psychotherapy. *Journal of the American Psychoanalytic Association, 36,* 961–984.

Bloch, S., Bond, G., Qualls, B., Yalom, I., & Zimmerman, E. (1977). Outcome in psychotherapy evaluated by independent judges. *British Journal of Psychiatry, 131,* 410–414.

Block, L. R. (1985). On the potentiality and limits of time: The single-session group and the cancer patient. *Social Work with Groups, 8,* 81–99.

Bloom, B. L. (1975). *Changing patterns of psychiatric care.* New York: Human Sciences Press.

Bloom, B. L. (1981). Focused single-session therapy: Initial development and evaluation. In S. Budman (Ed.), *Forms of brief therapy* (pp. 167–216). New York: Guilford Press.

Bloom, B. L. (1984). *Community mental health: A general introduction* (2nd ed.). Monterey, CA: Brooks/Cole.

Bloom, B. L. (1988). *Health psychology: A psychosocial perspective.* Englewood Cliffs, NJ: Prentice-Hall.

Bloom, B. L. (1990). Managing mental health services: Some comments for the overdue debate in psychology. *Community Mental Health Journal, 26,* 107–124.

Bloom, B. L. (1992a). *Planned short-term psychotherapy: A clinical handbook* (1st ed.). Boston: Allyn and Bacon.

Bloom, B. L. (1992b). Planned short-term psychotherapy: Current status and future challenges. *Applied & Preventive Psychology, 1,* 157–164.

Blowers, C., Cobb, J., & Mathews, A. (1987). Generalized anxiety: A controlled treatment study. *Behavior Research and Therapy, 25,* 493–502.

Bochner, R., Carruthers, G., Kampmann, J., Steiner, J., & Azarnoff, D. L. (1978). *Handbook of clinical pharmacology.* Boston: Little, Brown.

Boettcher, L. L., & Dowd, E. T. (1988). Comparison of rationales in symptom prescription. *Journal of Cognitive Psychotherapy, 2,* 179–195.

Booth, P. J. (1988). Strategic therapy revisited. In J. K. Zeig & S. R. Lankton (Eds.), *Developing Ericksonian therapy: State of the art* (pp. 39–58). New York: Brunner/Mazel.

Bornstein, M. T., Bornstein, P. H., & Walters, H. A. (1984). Children of divorce: A group treatment manual for research and application. *Journal of Child and Adolescent Psychotherapy, 2,* 267–273.

Boscolo, L., & Bertrando, P. (1993). *The times of time: A new perspective in systemic therapy and consultation.* New York: Norton.

Bouchard, M-A., Lecomte, C., Carbonneau, H., & Lalonde, F. (1987). Inferential communications of expert psycho-analytically oriented, gestalt and behaviour therapists. *Canadian Journal of Behavioral Science, 19,* 275–286.

Bowers, T. G., & Clum, G. A. (1988). Relative contribution of specific and nonspecific treatment effects: Meta-analysis of placebo-controlled behavior therapy research. *Psychological Bulletin, 103,* 315–323.

Brabender, V. M. (1985). Time-limited inpatient group therapy: A developmental model. *International Journal of Group Psychotherapy, 35,* 373–390.

Brabender, V. (1988). A closed model of short-term inpatient group psychotherapy. *Hospital and Community Psychiatry, 39,* 542–545.

Brabender, V., & Fallon, A. (1993). *Models of inpatient group psychotherapy.* Washington, DC: American Psychological Association.

Breuer, J., & Freud, S. (1895/1957). *Studies on hysteria.* New York: Basic Books.

Brockman, B., Poynton, A., Ryle, A., & Watson, J. P. (1987). Effectiveness of time-limited therapy carried out by trainees: Comparison of two methods. *British Journal of Psychiatry, 151,* 602–610.

Brodaty, H., & Andrews, G. (1983). Brief psychotherapy in family practice: A controlled prospective intervention trial. *British Journal of Psychiatry, 143,* 11–19.

Brown, D. Y. (1994). Private psychiatric hospital profile in 1990. In R. W. Manderscheid & M. A. Sonnenschein (Eds.), *Mental health, United States,* 1994 (pp. 135–147). Washington, DC: U. S. Government Printing Office.

Brown, J. S., & Kosterlitz, N. (1964). Selection and treatment of psychiatric outpatients. *Archives of General Psychiatry, 11,* 425–438.

Brown, L. M. (1984). A single consultation assessment clinic. *British Journal of Psychiatry, 145,* 558.

Budman, S. H. (1981). Looking toward the future. In S. H. Budman (Ed.), *Forms of brief therapy* (pp. 461–467). New York: Guilford Press.

Budman, S. (1990). The myth of termination in brief therapy: Or, it ain't over till it's over. In J. K. Zeig & S. G. Gilligan (Eds.), *Brief therapy: Myths, methods, and metaphors* (pp. 206–218). New York: Brunner/Mazel.

Budman, S. H., & Armstrong, E. (1992). Training for managed care settings: How to make it happen. *Psychotherapy, 29,* 416–421.

Budman, S. H., Bennett, M. J., & Wisneski, M. J. (1980). Short-term group psychotherapy: An adult developmental model. *International Journal of Group Psychotherapy, 30,* 63–76.

Budman, S. H., Bennett, M. J., & Wisneski, M. J. (1981). An adult developmental model of short-term group psychotherapy. In S. H. Budman (Ed.), *Forms of brief therapy* (pp. 305–342). New York: Guilford Press.

Budman, S. H., & Clifford, M. (1979). Short-term group therapy for couples in a health maintenance organization. *Professional Psychology: Research and Practice, 10,* 419–429.

Budman, S., Demby, A., & Feldstein, M. L. (1984). Insight into reduced use of medical services after psychotherapy. *Professional Psychology: Research and Practice, 15,* 353–361.

Budman, S., Demby, A., & Randall, M. (1980). Short-term group psychotherapy: Who succeeds, who fails? *Group, 4,* 3–16.

Budman, S. H., & Gurman, A. (1983). The practice of brief therapy. *Professional Psychology: Research and Practice, 14,* 277–292.

Budman, S. H., & Gurman, A. S. (1988). *Theory and practice of brief therapy.* New York: Guilford Press.

Budman, S. H., & Springer, T. (1987). Treatment delay, outcome, and satisfaction in time-limited group and individual psychotherapy. *Professional Psychology: Research and Practice, 18,* 647–649.

Budman, S. H., & Stone, J. (1983). Advances in brief psychotherapy: A review of recent literature. *Hospital and Community Psychiatry, 34,* 939–946.

Budson, R. D. (1994). Community residential and partial hospital care: Low-cost alternative systems in the spectrum of care. *Psychiatric Quarterly, 65,* 209–220.

Burke, J. D., White, H. S., & Havens, L. L. (1979). Which short-term therapy? *Archives of General Psychiatry, 36,* 177–186.

Burlingame, G. M., & Behrman, J. A. (1987). Clinician attitudes toward time-limited and time-unlimited therapy. *Professional Psychology: Research and Practice, 18,* 61–65.

Burlingame, G. M., & Fuhriman, A. (1987). Conceptualizing short-term treatment: A comparative review. *The Counseling Psychologist, 15,* 557–595.

Burns, D. D., & Nolen-Hoeksema, S. (1992). Therapeutic empathy and recovery from depression in cognitive-behavioral therapy: A structural equation model. *Journal of Consulting and Clinical Psychology, 60,* 441–449.

Butcher, J. N., & Koss, M. P. (1978). Research on brief and crisis-oriented therapies. In S. L. Garfield & A. E. Bergin (Eds.), *Handbook of psychotherapy and behav-*

ior change: An empirical analysis (2d ed.) (pp. 725–767). New York: Wiley.

Butcher, J. N., Stelmachers, Z. T., & Maudal, G. R. (1983). Crisis intervention and emergency psychotherapy. In I. Wiener (Ed.), Clinical methods in psychology (2nd ed.) (pp. 572–633). New York: Wiley.

Butler, G., Fennell, M., Robson, P., & Gelder, M. (1991). A comparison of behavior therapy and cognitive theory in the treatment of generalized anxiety disorder. Journal of Consulting and Clinical Psychology, 59, 167–175.

Cade, B., & O'Hanlon, W. H. (1993). A brief guide to brief therapy. New York: Norton.

Caffey, E. M., Galbrecht, C. R., & Klett, C. J. (1971). Brief hospitalization and aftercare in the treatment of schizophrenia. Archives of General Psychiatry, 24, 81–86.

Campbell, L. A., Kirkpatrick. S. E., Berry, C. C., Penn, N. E., Waldman, J. D., & Mathewson, J. W. (1992). Psychological preparation of mothers of preschool children undergoing cardiac catheterization. Psychology and Health, 7, 175–185.

Caplan, G. (1961). An approach to community mental health. New York: Grune & Stratton.

Cappon, D. (1964). Results of psychotherapy. British Journal of Psychiatry, 110, 35–45.

Carmona, P. E. (1988). Changing traditions in psychotherapy: A study of therapists' attitudes. Clinical Nurse Specialist, 2, 185–190.

Casanueva, E., Legarreta, D., Diaz-Barriga, M., Soberanis, Y., Cardenas, T., Iturriaga, A., Lartigue, T., & Vives, J. (1994). Weight gain during pregnancy in adolescents: Evaluation of a non-nutritional intervention. La Revista de Investigación Clínica, 46, 157–161.

Casey, R. J., & Berman, J. S. (1985). The outcome of psychotherapy with children. Psychological Bulletin, 98, 388–400.

Castelnuovo-Tedesco, P. (1965). The twenty-minute hour: A guide to brief psychotherapy for the physician. Boston: Little, Brown.

Castelnuovo-Tedesco, P. (1967). The twenty-minute hour: An approach to the postgraduate teaching of psychiatry. American Journal of Psychiatry, 123, 786–791

Castelnuovo-Tedesco, P. (1970). The "20-minute hour" revisited: A follow-up. Comprehensive Psychiatry, 11, 108–122.

Castelnuovo-Tedesco, P. (1971). Decreasing the length of psychotherapy: Theoretical and practical aspects of the problem. In S. Arieti (Ed.), The world biennial of psychiatry and psychotherapy (vol. 1) (pp. 55–71). New York: Basic Books.

Chapman, P. L. H., & Huygens, I. (1988). An evaluation of three treatment programmes for alcoholism: An exper-

imental study with 6- and 18-month follow-ups. British Journal of Addiction, 83, 67–81.

Chick, J., Ritson, B., Connaughton, J., Stewart, A., & Chick, J. (1988). Advice versus extended treatment for alcoholism: A controlled study. British Journal of Addiction, 83, 159–170.

Christianson, J. B. & Osher, F. C. (1994). Health maintenance organizations, health care reform, and persons with serious mental illness. Hospital and Community Psychiatry, 45, 898–905.

Ciarlo, J. A., Brown, T. R., Edwards, D. W., Kiresuk, T. J., & Newman, F. L. (1986). Assessing mental health treatment outcome measurement techniques. DHHS Pub. No. (ADM) 86–1301. Washington, DC: U.S. Government Printing Office.

Clarkin, J. F., & Frances, A. (1982). Selection criteria for the brief psychotherapies. American Journal of Psychotherapy, 36, 166–180.

Cochrane, A. L. (1972). Effectiveness and efficiency: Random reflections on health services. London: Nuffield Provincial Hospitals Trust.

Cole, N. J., Branch, C. H. H., & Allison, R. B. (1962). Some relationships between social class and the practice of dynamic psychotherapy. American Journal of Psychiatry, 118, 1004–1012.

Compton, A. B., & Purviance, M. (1992). Emotional distress in chronic medical illness: Treatment with time-limited group psychotherapy. Military Medicine, 157, 533–535.

Cook, N. R., & Ware, J. H. (1983). Design and analysis methods for longitudinal research. Annual Review of Public Health, 4, 1–23.

Cornes, C. (1990). Interpersonal psychotherapy of depression (IPT). In R. A. Wells & V. J. Giannetti (Eds.), Handbook of the brief psychotherapies (pp. 261–276). New York: Plenum Press.

Cornes, C. (1993). Interpersonal psychotherapy of depression: A case study. In R. A. Wells & V. J. Giannetti (Eds), Casebook of the brief psychotherapies (pp. 53–64). New York: Plenum.

Courtenay, M. (1968). Sexual discord in marriage: A field for brief psychotherapy. Philadelphia: Lippincott.

Cox, A., Rutter, M., & Holbrook, D. (1988). Psychiatric interviewing techniques: A second experimental study: Eliciting feelings. British Journal of Psychiatry, 152, 64–72.

Crits-Christoph, P. (1992). The efficacy of brief dynamic psychotherapy: A meta-analysis. American Journal of Psychiatry, 149, 151–158.

Crits-Christoph, P., & Connolly, M. B. (1993). Patient pretreatment predictors of outcome. In N. E. Miller, L. Luborsky, J. P. Barber, & J. P. Docherty (Eds.), Psychodynamic treatment research: A hand-

book for clinical practice (pp. 177–188). New York: Basic Books.

Croake, J. W., & Myers, K. M. (1989). Brief family therapy with childhood medical problems. *Individual Psychology, 45,* 159–177.

Cross, D. G., Sheehan, P. W., & Khan, J. A. (1982). Short- and long-term follow-up of clients receiving insight-oriented therapy and behavior therapy. *Journal of Consulting and Clinical Psychology, 50,* 103–112.

Cummings, N. A. (1977a). The anatomy of psychotherapy under national health insurance. *American Psychologist, 32,* 711–718.

Cummings, N. A. (1977b). Prolonged (ideal) versus short-term (realistic) psychotherapy. *Professional Psychology, 8,* 491–501.

Cummings, N. A. (1986). The dismantling of our health system: Strategies for the survival of psychological practice. *American Psychologist, 41,* 426–431.

Cummings, N. A. (1988). Emergence of the mental health complex: Adaptive and maladaptive responses. *Professional Psychology: Research and Practice, 19,* 308–315.

Cummings, N. A., & Duhl, L. J. (1987). The new delivery system. In L. J. Duhl & N. A. Cummings (Eds.), *The future of mental health services: Coping with crisis* (pp. 85–98). New York: Springer.

Cummings, N. A., & Follette, W. T. (1968). Psychiatric services and medical utilization in a prepaid health plan setting: Part II. *Medical Care, 6,* 31–41.

Cummings, N. A., & Follette, W. T. (1976). Brief psychotherapy and medical utilization. In H. Dorken & Associates (Eds.), *The professional psychologist today: New developments in law, health insurance and health practice* (pp. 165–174). San Francisco: Jossey-Bass.

Cummings, N., & Sayama, M. (1995). *Focused psychotherapy: A casebook of brief, intermittent psychotherapy throughout the life cycle.* New York: Brunner/Mazel.

Cummings, N. A., & VandenBos, G. R. (1979). The general practice of psychology. *Professional Psychology: Research and Practice, 10,* 430–440.

Curtis, J. T., & Silberschatz, G. (1986). Clinical implications of research on brief dynamic psychotherapy: I. Formulating the patient's problems and goals. *Psychoanalytic Psychology, 3,* 13–25.

Dacey, C. M. (1989). Inpatient group psychotherapy: Cohesion facilitates separation. *Group, 13,* 23–30.

Damon, L., Todd, J., & MacFarlane, K. (1987). Treatment issues with sexually abused young children. *Child Welfare, 66,* 125–137.

Davanloo, H. (Ed.). (1978a). *Basic principles and techniques in short-term dynamic psychotherapy.* New York: Spectrum.

Davanloo, H. (1978b). Evaluation, criteria for selection of patients for short-term dynamic psychotherapy: A metapsychological approach. In H. Davanloo (Ed.), *Basic principles and techniques in short-term dynamic psychotherapy* (pp. 9–34). New York: Spectrum.

Davanloo, H. (1978c). Short-term dynamic psychotherapy of one to two sessions' duration. In H. Davanloo (Ed.), *Basic principles and techniques in short-term dynamic psychotherapy* (pp. 307–326). New York: Spectrum.

Davanloo, H. (1979). Techniques of short-term dynamic psychotherapy. *Psychiatric Clinics of North America, 2,* 11–22.

Davanloo, H. (1980a). A method of short-term dynamic psychotherapy. In H. Davanloo (Ed.), *Short-term dynamic psychotherapy* (pp. 43–71). Northvale, NJ: Aronson.

Davanloo, H. (1980b). Response to interpretation. In H. Davanloo (Ed.), *Short-term dynamic psychotherapy* (pp. 75–91). Northvale, NJ: Aronson.

Davanloo, H. (Ed.) (1980c). *Short-term dynamic psychotherapy.* Northvale, NJ: Aronson.

Davanloo, H. (1980d). The technique of crisis evaluation and intervention. In H. Davanloo (Ed.), *Short-term dynamic psychotherapy* (pp. 245–281). Northvale, NJ: Aronson.

Davanloo, H. (1980e). Trial therapy. In H. Davanloo (Ed.), *Short-term dynamic psychotherapy* (pp. 99–128). Northvale, NJ: Aronson.

Day, A. (1993). Brief prescriptive psychotherapy for depression with an incarcerated young offender: An application of Barkham's 2 + 1 model. *Journal of Offender Rehabilitation, 19(1/2),* 75–87.

Day, A., Maddicks, R, & McMahon, D. (1993). Brief psychotherapy in two-plus-one sessions with a young offender population. *Behavioural and Cognitive Psychotherapy, 21,* 357–369.

de Bosset, F., & Styrsky, E. (1986). Termination in individual psychotherapy: A survey of residents' experience. *Canadian Journal of Psychiatry, 31,* 636–642.

Della Selva, P. C. (1992). Achieving character change in IS-TDP: How the experience of affect leads to the consolidation of the self. *International Journal of Short-Term Psychotherapy, 7,* 73–87.

Demos, V. C., & Prout, M. F. (1993). A comparison of seven approaches to brief psychotherapy. *International Journal of Short-Term Psychotherapy, 8,* 3–22.

de Shazer, S. (1979). On transforming symptoms: An approach to an Erickson procedure. *American Journal of Clinical Hypnosis, 22,* 17–28.

de Shazer, S. (1982). *Patterns of brief family therapy: An ecosystemic approach.* New York: Guilford Press.

de Shazer, S. (1985). *Keys to solution in brief therapy.* New York: Norton.

de Shazer, S. (1988). *Clues: Investigating solutions in brief therapy.* New York: Norton.

de Shazer, S. (1990). What is it about brief therapy that works? In J. K. Zeig & S. G. Gilligan (Eds.), *Brief therapy: Myths, methods, and metaphors* (pp. 90–99). New York: Brunner/Mazel.

de Shazer, S. (1991). *Putting difference to work.* New York: Norton.

de Shazer, S. (1994). *Words were originally magic.* New York: Norton.

de Shazer, S., Berg, I. K., Lipchik, E., Nunnally, E., Gingerich, W., & Weiner-Davis, M. (1986). Brief therapy: Focused solution development. *Family Process, 25,* 207–222.

de Shazer, S., & Molnar, A. (1984). Four useful interventions in brief family therapy. *Journal of Marital and Family Therapy, 10,* 297–304.

Dobson, K. S. (Ed.) (1988). *Handbook of cognitive-behavioral therapies.* New York: Guilford Press.

Dobson, K. (1989). A meta analysis of the efficacy of cognitive therapy for depression. *Journal of Consulting and Clinical Psychology, 57,* 414–419.

Dobson, K. S., & Block, L. (1988). Historical and philosophical bases of the cognitive-behavioral therapies. In K. S. Dobson (Ed.), *Handbook of cognitive-behavioral therapies* (pp. 3–38). New York: Guilford Press.

Donovan, J. M. (1987). Brief dynamic psychotherapy: Toward a more comprehensive model. *Psychiatry, 50,* 167–183.

Donovan, J. M., Bennett, M. J., & McElroy, C. M. (1981). The crisis group: Its rationale, format, and outcome. In S. Budman (Ed.), *Forms of brief therapy* (pp. 283–303). New York: Guilford Press.

Dorosin, D., Gibbs, J., & Kaplan, L. (1976). Very brief interventions: A pilot evaluation. *Journal of the American College Health Association, 24,* 191–194.

Dorwart, R. A., Schlesinger, M., Davidson, H., Epstein, S., & Hoover, C. (1991). A national study of psychiatric hospital care. *American Journal of Psychiatry, 148,* 204–210.

Dreiblatt, I. S., & Weatherley, D. (1965). An evaluation of the efficacy of brief-contact therapy with hospitalized psychiatric patients. *Journal of Consulting and Clinical Psychology, 29,* 513–519.

Dryden, W., & DiGiuseppe, R. (1990). *A primer on rational-emotive therapy.* Champaign, IL: Research Press.

Dryden, W., & Hill, L. K. (Eds.) (1993). *Innovations in rational-emotive therapy.* Thousand Oaks, CA: Sage.

Dubovsky, S. L. (1981). *Psychotherapeutics in primary care.* New York: Grune & Stratton.

Duckert, F. G., Amundsen, A., & Johnsen, J. (1992). What happens to drinking after therapeutic intervention? *British Journal of Addiction, 87,* 1457–1467.

Duncan, B. L., & Solovey, A. D. (1989). Strategic-brief therapy: An insight-oriented approach? *Journal of Marital and Family Therapy, 15,* 1–9.

Duncan, B. L., Solovey, A. D., & Rusk, G. S. (1992). *Changing the rules: A client-directed approach to therapy.* New York: Guilford Press.

Durham, R. C., Murphy, T., Allan, T., Richard, K., Treliving, L. R., & Fenton, G. W. (1994). Cognitive therapy, analytic psychotherapy and anxiety management training for generalised anxiety disorder. *British Journal of Psychiatry, 165,* 315–323.

Durlak, J. A. (1979). Comparative effectiveness of paraprofessional and professional helpers. *Psychological Bulletin, 86,* 80–92.

Eckert, P. A. (1993). Acceleration of change: Catalysts in brief therapy. *Clinical Psychology Review, 13,* 241–253.

Edbril, S. D. (1994). Gender bias in short-term therapy: Toward a new model for working with women patients in managed care settings. *Psychotherapy, 31,* 601–609.

Edwards, G., Orford, J., Egert, S., Guthrie, S., Hawker, A., Hensman, C., Mitcheson, M., Oppenheimer, E., & Taylor, C. (1977). Alcoholism: A controlled trial of "treatment" and "advice." *Journal of Studies on Alcohol, 38,* 1004–1031.

Eglau, U. (1992). Brief therapy for sexual dysfunction. *International Forum for Logotherapy, 15,* 108–110.

Eisenberg, J., & Wahrman, O. (1994). Brief strategic therapy in a child community clinic: A follow-up report. *Israeli Journal of Psychiatry and Related Sciences, 31,* 37–40.

Eisendrath, S. J. (1993). Brief psychotherapy in medical practice: Keys to success. *Western Journal of Medicine, 158,* 376–378.

Elkin, I. E., Parloff, M. B., Hadley, S. W., & Autry, A. H. (1985). NIMH treatment of depression collaborative research program: Background and research plan. *Archives of General Psychiatry, 42,* 305–316.

Elkin, I., Shea, M. T., Watkins, J. T., et al. (1989). National Institute of Mental Health treatment of depression collaborative research program: General effectiveness of treatment. *Archives of General Psychiatry, 46,* 971–983.

Ellis, A. (1962). *Reason and emotion in psychotherapy.* New York: Stuart.

Ellis, A. (1989). Using rational-emotive therapy (RET) as crisis intervention: A single session with a suicidal client. *Individual Psychology, 45,* 75–81.

Ellis, A. (1990). How can psychological treatment aim to be briefer and better? The rational-emotive approach to brief therapy. In J. K. Zeig & S. G. Gilligan (Eds.), *Brief therapy: Myths, methods, and metaphors* (pp. 291–302). New York: Brunner/Mazel.

Ellis, A. (1992). Brief therapy: The rational-emotive method. In S. H. Budman, M. F. Hoyt, & S. Friedman (Eds.), *The first session in brief therapy* (pp. 36–58). New York: Guilford Press.

Ellis, A. (1993). Fundamentals of rational-emotive therapy for the 1990s. In W. Dryden & L. K. Hill (Eds.), *Innovations in rational-emotive therapy* (pp. 1–32). Thousand Oaks, CA: Sage.

Ellis, A., & Abrahms, E. (1978). *Brief psychotherapy in medical and health practice.* New York: Springer.

Ellis, A., & Bernard, M. E. (Eds.) (1983). *Rational-emotive approaches to the problems of childhood.* New York: Plenum.

Ellis, A., & Grieger, R. (Eds.) (1977). *Handbook of rational-emotive therapy.* New York: Springer.

Ellis, A., & Harper, R. A. (1961). *A guide to rational living.* Englewood Cliffs, NJ: Prentice-Hall.

Endicott, J., Herz, M. I., & Gibbon, M. (1978). Brief versus standard hospitalization: The differential costs. *American Journal of Psychiatry, 135,* 707–712.

Epstein, N. B., Bishop, D. S., Keitner, G. I., & Miller, I. W. (1990). A systems therapy: Problem-centered systems therapy of the family. In R. A. Wells & V. J. Giannetti (Eds.), *Handbook of the brief psychotherapies,* (pp. 405–436). New York: Plenum.

Erickson, M. H. (1954). Special techniques of brief hypnotherapy. *Journal of Clinical and Experimental Hypnosis, 2,* 109–129.

Erickson, M. H. (1964). The confusion technique in hypnosis. *American Journal of Clinical Hypnosis, 6,* 183–207.

Erickson, M. H. (1977). Hypnotic approaches to therapy. American Journal of Clinical Hypnosis, 20, 20–35.

Erstling, S. S., & Devlin, J. (1989). The single-session family interview. *Journal of Family Practice, 28,* 556–560.

Eshet, I., Margalit, A., & Almagor, G. (1993). SFAT-AM: Short family therapy in ambulatory medicine. Treatment approach in 10–15 minute encounters. *Family Practice, 10,* 178–187.

Eshet, I., Margalit, A., Shalom, J., & Almagor, G. (1993). The use of short family therapy in ambulatory medicine (SFAT-AM) in Israel during the Gulf War. *Family Systems Medicine, 11,* 163–171.

Evans, T. D. (1989). Brief therapy: The tradition of individual psychology compared to MRI. *Individual Psychology, 45,* 48–56.

Ewing, C. P. (1978). *Crisis intervention as psychotherapy.* New York: Oxford University Press.

Ewing, C. P. (1990). Crisis intervention as brief psychotherapy. In R. A. Wells & V. J. Giannetti (Eds.), *Handbook of the brief psychotherapies* (pp. 277–294). New York: Plenum.

Faden, V. B., & Taube, C. A. (1977). *Length of stay of discharges from non-federal general hospital psychiatric inpatient units, United States, 1975* (Statistical Note No. 133. National Institute of Mental Health). Washington, D.C.: U.S. Government Printing Office.

Fago, D. P. (1980). Time-unlimited brief and longer-term psychotherapy with rural clients. *Journal of Rural Community Psychology, 1,* 16–23.

Fairburn, C. G. (1993). Interpersonal psychotherapy for bulimia nervosa. In G. L. Klerman & M. M. Weissman (Eds.), *New applications of interpersonal psychotherapy* (pp. 353–378). Washington, DC: American Psychiatric Press.

Farrelly, F., & Brandsma, J. (1974). *Provocative therapy.* Cupertino, CA: Meta Publications.

Feldman, J. B. (1994). A multischema model for combining Ericksonian and cognitive therapy. In S. R. Lankton & K. K. Erickson (Eds.), *The essence of a single-session success* (pp. 54–74). New York: Brunner/Mazel.

Feldman, J. L., & Fitzpatrick, R. J. (Eds.) (1992). *Managed mental health care: Administrative and clinical issues.* Washington, DC: American Psychiatric Press.

Feldman, S., & Goldman, B. (1987). Mental health care in HMOs: Practice and potential. In L. J. Duhl & N. A. Cummings (Eds.), *The future of mental health services: Coping with crisis* (pp. 71–84). New York: Springer.

Fiester, A. R., & Rudestam, K. E. (1975). A multivariate analysis of the early drop-out process. *Journal of Consulting and Clinical Psychology, 43,* 528–535.

Fine, S., & Gilbert, M. (1993). Short-term group therapy with depressed adolescents. In R. A. Wells & V. J. Giannetti (Eds.), *Casebook of the brief psychotherapies* (pp. 375–387). New York: Plenum.

Fine, S., Gilbert, M., Schmidt, L., Haley, G., Maxwell, A., & Forth, A. (1989). Short-term group therapy with depressed adolescent outpatients. *Canadian Journal of Psychiatry, 34,* 97–102.

Fisch, R. (1982). Erickson's impact on brief psychotherapy. In J. K. Zeig (Ed.), *Ericksonian approaches to hypnosis and psychotherapy* (pp. 155–162). New York: Brunner/Mazel.

Fisch, R. (1990). "To thine own self be true…": Ethical issues in strategic therapy. In J. K. Zeig & S. G. Gilligan (Eds.), *Brief therapy: Myths, methods, and metaphors* (pp. 429–436). New York: Brunner/Mazel.

Fisch, R. (1994). Basic elements in the brief therapies. In M. F. Hoyt (Ed.), *Constructive therapies* (pp. 126–139). New York: Guilford Press.

Fisch, R., Weakland, J. H., & Segal, L. (1982). *The tactics of change.* San Francisco: Jossey-Bass.

Fisher, S. G. (1980). The use of time limits in brief psychotherapy: A comparison of six-session, twelve-session, and unlimited treatment with families. *Family Process, 19,* 377–392.

Flegenheimer, W. V. (1982). *Techniques of brief psychotherapy.* Northvale, NJ: Aronson.

Flegenheimer, W. (1985). History of brief psychotherapy. In A. J. Horner (Ed.), *Treating the Oedipal patient in brief psychotherapy* (pp. 7–24). Northvale, NJ: Aronson.

Foa, E. B., Rothbaum, B. O., Riggs, D. S., & Murdock, T. B. (1991). Treatment of posttraumatic stress disorder in rape victims: A comparison between cognitive-behavioral procedures and counseling. *Journal of Consulting and Clinical Psychology, 59,* 715–723.

Fogelman, E. (1992). Intergenerational group therapy: Child survivors of the holocaust and offspring of survivors. *Psychiatria Hungarica, 7,* 255–269.

Foley, S. H., O'Malley, S., Rounsaville, B. J., Prusoff, B. A., & Weissman, M. M. (1987). The relationship of patient difficulty to therapist performance in interpersonal psychotherapy of depression. *Journal of Affective Disorders, 12,* 207–217.

Follette, W., & Cummings, N. A. (1967). Psychiatric services and medical utilization in a prepaid health plan setting. *Medical Care, 5,* 25–35.

Foote, B. (1992). Accelerated empathic therapy: The first self-psychological brief therapy? *International Journal of Short-Term Psychotherapy, 7,* 177–191.

Foote, J. (1992). Explicit empathy and the stance of therapeutic neutrality. *International Journal of Short-Term Psychotherapy, 7,* 193–198.

Fosha, D. (1992). The interrelatedness of theory, technique and therapeutic stance: A comparative look at intensive short-term dynamic psychotherapy and accelerated empathic therapy. *International Journal of Short-Term Psychotherapy, 7,* 157–176.

Frank, J. D. (1968). Methods of assessing the results of psychotherapy. In R. Porter (Ed.), *The role of learning in psychotherapy* (pp 38–60). Boston: Little, Brown.

Frank, J. D. (1984). The psychotherapy of anxiety. In L. Grinspoon (Ed.), *Psychiatry update: The American Psychiatric Association annual review* (vol. 3) (pp. 418–426). Washington, DC: American Psychiatric Press.

Fraser, J. S. (1986). Integrating system-based therapies: Similarities, differences, and some critical questions. In D. E. Efron (Ed.), *Journeys: Expansion of the strategic-systemic therapies* (pp. 125–149). New York: Brunner/Mazel.

Free, N. K., Green, B. L., Grace, M. C., Chernus, L. A., & Whitman, R. M. (1985). Empathy and outcome in brief focal dynamic therapy. *American Journal of Psychiatry, 142,* 917–921.

Freeman, M. A., & Trabin, T. (1994). *Managed behavioral healthcare: History, models, key issues, and future course.* Prepared for the U.S. Center for Mental Health Services, Substance Abuse and Mental Health Services Administration. Rockville, MD.

Freud, S. (1909/1953). Notes upon a case of obsessional neurosis. In A. Strachey & J. Strachey (Eds.), *Sigmund Freud, M.D., LL.D. Collected papers* (vol. 3) (pp. 293–383). London: Hogarth Press.

Freud, S. (1917/1953). Mourning and melancholia. In E. Jones (Ed.), *Sigmund Freud, M.D., LL.D. Collected papers* (vol. 4) (pp. 152–170). London: Hogarth Press.

Friedman, S., Budman, S. H., & Hoyt, M. F. (1992). Introduction to couple and family brief therapy approaches. In S. H. Budman, M. F. Hoyt, & S. Friedman (Eds.), *The first session in brief therapy* (pp. 183–185). New York: Guilford Press.

Friedrich, W. N., Berliner, L., Urquiza, A. J., & Beilke, R. L. (1988). Brief diagnostic group treatment of sexually abused boys. *Journal of Interpersonal Violence, 3,* 331–343.

Frings, J. (1951). What about brief services?—A report of a study of short-term cases. *Social Casework, 32,* 236–241.

Fuhriman, A., Paul, S. C., & Burlingame, G. M. (1986). Eclectic time-limited therapy. In J. C. Norcross (Ed.), *Handbook of eclectic psychotherapy* (pp. 226–259). New York: Brunner/Mazel.

Furman, B., & Ahola, T. (1988). The use of humour in brief therapy. *Journal of Strategic and Systemic Therapies, 7(2),* 3–20.

Furman, B., & Ahola, T. (1992). *Solution talk: Hosting therapeutic conversations.* New York: Norton

Gallagher, D. E., & Thompson, L. W. (1983). Effectiveness of psychotherapy for both endogenous and nonendogenous depression in older adult outpatients. *Journal of Gerontology, 38,* 707–712.

Gallagher, T. J. (1987). Accountability and implications for supervision and future training. In L. J. Duhl & N. A. Cummings (Eds.), *The future of mental health services: Coping with crisis* (pp. 117–131). New York: Springer.

Garfield, S. L. (1989). *The practice of brief psychotherapy.* New York: Pergamon Press.

Garfield, S. L., & Affleck, D. C. (1959). An appraisal of duration of stay in outpatient psychotherapy. *Journal of Nervous and Mental Disease, 129,* 492–498.

Garner, D. M., & Bemis, K. M. (1982). A cognitive-behavioral approach to anorexia nervosa. *Cognitive Therapy and Research, 6,* 123–150.

Garvin, C. D. (1990). Short-term group therapy. In R. A. Wells & V. J. Giannetti (Eds.), *Handbook of the brief psychotherapies* (pp. 513–536). New York: Plenum.

Gask, L. (1986). What happens when psychiatric outpatients are seen once only? *British Journal of Psychiatry, 148,* 663–666.

Gelso, C. J. (1992). Realities and emerging myths about brief therapy. *Counseling Psychologist, 20,* 464–471.

Gelso, C. J., & Johnson, D. H. (1983). *Explorations in time-limited counseling and psychotherapy.* New York: Teachers College Press.

Gerald, M. C. (1981). *Pharmacology: An introduction to drugs* (2d ed.). Englewood Cliffs, NJ: Prentice-Hall.

Getz, W. L., Fujita, B. N., & Allen, D. (1975). The use of paraprofessionals in crisis intervention: Evaluation of an innovative program. *American Journal of Community Psychology, 3,* 135–144.

Giles, T. R. (1993). *Managed mental health care: A guide for practitioners, employers, and hospital administrators.* Boston: Allyn and Bacon.

Gilliland, B. E., & James, R. K. (1993). *Crisis intervention strategies.* Pacific Grove, CA: Brooks/Cole.

Gillman, R. D. (1965). Brief psychotherapy: A psychoanalytic view. *American Journal of Psychiatry, 122,* 601–611.

Gilman, A. G., Goodman, L. S., Gilman, A., Mayer, S. E., & Melmon, K. L. (Eds.). (1980). *Goodman and Gilman's the pharmacological basis of therapeutics* (6th ed.). New York: Macmillan.

Glasscote, R., & Fishman, M. E. (1973). *Mental health on the campus: A field study.* Washington, DC: American Psychiatric Association.

Glick, I. D. (1994). Unbundling the function of an inpatient unit. *New Directions for Mental Health Services, 63,* 35–43.

Glick, I. D., Hargreaves, W. A., & Goldfield, M. D. (1974). Short vs. long hospitalization: A prospective controlled study: The preliminary results of a one-year follow-up of schizophrenics. *Archives of General Psychiatry, 30,* 363–369.

Glick, I. D., Hargreaves, W. A., Raskin, M., & Kutner, S. J. (1975). Short vs. long hospitalization: A prospective controlled study: II. Results for schizophrenic inpatients. *American Journal of Psychiatry, 132,* 385–390.

Glover, R., & Petrila, J. (1994). Can state mental health agencies survive health care reform? *Hospital and Community Psychiatry, 45,* 911–913.

Gluth, D. R., & Kiselica, M. S. (1994). Coming out quickly: A brief counseling approach to dealing with gay and lesbian adjustment issues. *Journal of Mental Health Counseling, 16,* 163–173.

Goldberg, D. A., Schuyler, W. R., Bransfield, D., & Savino, P. (1983). Focal group psychotherapy: A dynamic approach. *International Journal of Group Psychotherapy, 33,* 413–431.

Goldberg, I. D., Krantz, G., & Locke, B. Z. (1970). Effect of a short-term outpatient psychiatric therapy benefit on the utilization of medical services in a prepaid group practice medical program. *Medical Care, 8,* 419–428.

Goldberg, R. L., & Green, S. A. (1986). A learning-theory perspective of brief psychodynamic psychotherapy. *American Journal of Psychotherapy, 40,* 70–82.

Goldin, V., & Winston, A. (1985). The impact of short-term dynamic psychotherapy on psychoanalytic psychotherapy. In A. Winston (Ed.), *Clinical and research issues in short-term dynamic psychotherapy* (pp. 62–79). Washington, DC: American Psychiatric Press.

Goldman, W. (1988). Mental health and substance abuse services in HMOs. *Administration in Mental Health, 15,* 189–200.

Goldsmith, S. (1986). *Psychotherapy of people with physical symptoms: Brief strategic approaches.* Lanham, MD: University Press of America.

Gonzales, J. J., Magruder, K. M., & Keith, S. J. (1994). Mental disorders in primary care: An update. *Public Health Reports, 109,* 251–258,

Gottschalk, L. A., Mayerson, P., & Gottlieb, A. A. (1967). Prediction and evaluation of outcome in an emergency brief psychotherapy clinic. *Journal of Nervous and Mental Disease, 144,* 77–96.

Grand, S., Rechetnick, J., Podrug, D., & Schwager, E. (1985). *Transference in brief psychotherapy: An approach to the study of psychoanalytic process.* Hillsdale, NJ: Analytic Press.

Graves, E., & Lovato, C. (1981). Utilization of short-stay hospitals in the treatment of mental disorders: 1974-1978. *Vital and Health Statistics of the National Center for Health Statistics.* No. 70. May 22. Washington DC: U.S. Government Printing Office.

Greenstone, J. L., & Leviton, S. C. (1993). *Elements of crisis intervention: Crises and how to respond to them.* Pacific Grove, CA: Brooks/Cole.

Groddeck, G. (1951). *The unknown self.* New York: Funk & Wagnalls.

Gross, M. L. (1978). *The psychological society.* New York: Random House.

Grove, D. R., & Haley, J. (1993). *Conversations on therapy: Popular problems and uncommon solutions.* New York: Norton.

Gruenberg, E. M. (1974). Benefits of short-term hospitalization. In R. Cancro, N. Fox, & L. E. Shapiro (Eds.), *Strategic intervention in schizophrenia: Current developments in treatment* (pp. 251–259). New York: Behavioral Publications.

Guerney, B. (1990). Creating therapeutic and growth-inducing family systems: Personal moorings, landmarks, and guiding stars. In F. Kaslow (Ed.) *Voices in family psychology* (pp. 114-138). Thousand Oaks, CA: Sage.

Guerney, L. F., & Guerney, B. G. (1985). The relationship enhancement family of family therapies. In L. L'Abate & M. Milan (Eds.), *Handbook of social skills training and research.* (pp. 506–524). New York: Wiley.

Gurman, A. S. (1981). Integrative marital therapy: Toward the development of an interpersonal approach. In S. Budman (Ed.), *Forms of brief therapy* (pp. 415–457). New York: Guilford Press.

Gustafson, J. P. (1981). The complex secret of brief psychotherapy in the works of Malan and Balint. In S. Budman (Ed.), *Forms of brief therapy* (pp. 83–128). New York: Guilford Press.

Gustafson, J. P. (1986). *The complex secret of brief psychotherapy.* New York: Norton.

Gustafson, J. P. (1990). The great simplifying conventions of brief individual psychotherapy. In J. K. Zeig & S. G. Gilligan (Eds.), *Brief therapy: Myths, methods, and metaphors* (pp. 407–425). New York: Brunner/Mazel.

Gustafson, J. P. (1992). *Self-delight in a harsh world: The main stories of individual, marital, and family psychotherapy.* New York: Norton.

Gustafson, J. P. (1995). *The dilemmas of brief psychotherapy.* New York: Plenum.

Gustafson, J. P., & Cooper, L. W. (1990). *The modern contest: A systemic guide to the pattern that connects—individual psychotherapy, family therapy, group work, teaching, organizational life and large-scale social problems.* New York: Norton.

Hadley, S. W., & Strupp, H. H. (1976). Contemporary views on negative effects: An integrated account. *Archives of General Psychiatry, 33,* 1291–1302.

Haley, J. (1963). *Strategies of psychotherapy.* New York: Grune & Stratton.

Haley, J. (1967). *Advanced techniques of hypnosis and therapy: Selected papers of Milton H. Erickson.* New York: Grune & Stratton.

Haley, J. (1973). *Uncommon therapy: The psychiatric techniques of Milton H. Erickson, M. D.* New York: Norton.

Haley, J. (1984). *Ordeal therapy.* San Francisco: Jossey-Bass.

Haley, J. (1987). *Problem-solving therapy* (2d ed.). San Francisco: Jossey-Bass.

Haley, J. (1990). Why not long-term therapy? In J. K. Zeig & S. G. Gilligan (Eds.), *Brief therapy: Myths, methods, and metaphors* (pp. 3–17). New York: Brunner/Mazel.

Halligan, F. R. (1995). The challenge: Short-term dynamic psychotherapy for college counseling centers. *Psychotherapy, 32,* 113–121.

Hargreaves, W. A., Glick, I. D., Drues, J., Shaustack, J. A., & Feigenbaum, E. (1977). Short vs. long hospitalization: A prospective controlled study: VI: Two-year follow-up results for schizophrenics. *Archives of General Psychiatry, 34,* 305–311.

Hattie, J. A., Sharpley, C. F., & Rogers, H. J. (1984). Comparative effectiveness of professional and paraprofessional helpers. *Psychological Bulletin, 95,* 534–541.

Havens, L. (1986). *Making contact: Uses of language in psychotherapy.* Cambridge, MA: Harvard University Press.

Hawton, K., McKeown, S., Day, A., Martin, P., O'Connor, M., & Yule, J. (1987). Evaluation of outpatient counselling compared with general practitioner care following overdoses. *Psychological Medicine, 17,* 751–761.

Hazelrigg, M. D., Cooper, H. M., & Borduin, C. M. (1987). Evaluating the effectiveness of family therapies: An integrative review and analysis. *Psychological Bulletin, 101,* 428–442.

Held, B. S. (1986). The relationship between individual psychologies and strategic/systemic therapies reconsidered. In D. E. Efron (Ed.), *Journeys: Expansion of the strategic-systemic therapies* (pp. 222–260). New York: Brunner/Mazel.

Herz, M. I., Endicott, J., & Spitzer, R. L. (1975). Brief hospitalization of patients with families: Initial results. *American Journal of Psychiatry, 132,* 413–418.

Herz, M. I., Endicott, J., & Spitzer, R. L. (1976). Brief versus standard hospitalization: The families. *American Journal of Psychiatry, 133,* 795–801.

Hildebrand, H. P. (1986). Brief psychotherapy. *Psychoanalytic Psychology, 3,* 1–12.

Hill, C. E. (1992). Research on therapist techniques in brief individual therapy: Implications for practitioners. *Counseling Psychologist, 20,* 689–711.

Hill, C. E., Helms, J. E., Tichenor, V., Spiegel, S. B., O'Grady, K. E., & Perry, E. S. (1988). Effects of therapist response modes in brief psychotherapy. *Journal of Counseling Psychology, 35,* 222–233.

Hoch, P. H. (1965). Short-term versus long-term therapy. In L. W. Wolberg (Ed.), *Short-term psychotherapy* (pp. 51–66). New York: Grune & Stratton.

Hoffman, D. L., & Remmel, M. L. (1975). Uncovering the precipitant in crisis intervention. *Social Casework, 56,* 259–267.

Høglend, P. (1993). Suitability for brief dynamic psychotherapy: Psychodynamic variables as predictors of outcome. *Acta Psychiatrica Scandinavica, 88,* 104–110.

Høglend, P., Heyerdahl, O., Amlo, S., Engelstad, V., Fossum, A., Sørbye, Ø., & Sørlie, T. (1993). Interpretations of the patient-therapist relationship in brief dynamic psychotherapy. *Journal of Psychotherapy Practice and Research, 2,* 296–306.

Høglend, P., Sørbye, Ø., Sørlie, T., Fossum, A., & Engelstad, V. (1992). Selection criteria for brief dynamic psychotherapy: Reliability, factor structure and long-term predictive validity. *Psychotherapy and Psychosomatics, 57,* 67–74.

Hollon, S. D., & Najavits, L. (1988). Review of empirical studies of cognitive therapy. In A. J. Francis & R. E. Hales (Eds.), *American Psychiatric Press review of psychiatry* (vol. 7) (pp. 643–666). Washington, DC: American Psychiatric Press.

Hoppe, E. W. (1977). Treatment dropouts in hindsight: A follow-up study. *Community Mental Health Journal, 13,* 307–313.

Horner, A. J. (1985). The Oedipus complex. In A. J. Horner (Ed.), *Treating the Oedipal patient in brief psychotherapy* (pp. 25–54). Northvale, NJ: Aronson.

Horowitz, L. M., Rosenberg, S. E., & Bartholomew, K. (1993). Interpersonal problems, attachment styles, and outcome in brief dynamic psychotherapy. *Journal of Consulting and Clinical Psychology, 61,* 549–560.

Horowitz, L. M., Rosenberg, S. E., & Kalehzan, B. M. (1992). The capacity to describe other people clearly: A predictor of interpersonal problems in brief dynamic psychotherapy. *Psychotherapy Research, 2,* 37–51.

Horowitz, L. M., & Vitkus, J. (1986). The interpersonal basis of psychiatric symptoms. *Clinical Psychology Review, 6,* 443–469.

Horowitz, M. (1976). *Stress response syndromes.* Northvale, NJ: Aronson.

Horowitz, M. J. (1987). *States of mind: Configurational analysis of individual psychology* (2d ed.). New York: Plenum.

Horowitz, M. J. (1991). Short-term dynamic therapy of stress response syndromes. In P. Crits-Christoph & J. P. Barber (Eds.), *Handbook of short-term dynamic psychotherapy* (pp. 166–198). New York: Basic Books.

Horowitz, M., & Kaltreider, N. (1978). Brief therapy of the stress response syndrome. *Psychiatric Clinics of North America, 2,* 365–378.

Horowitz, M. J., Marmar, C., Krupnick, J., Wilner, N., Kaltreider, N., & Wallerstein, R. (1984). *Personality styles and brief psychotherapy.* New York: Basic Books.

Horowitz, M. J., Marmar, C., Weiss, D. S., DeWitt, K., & Rosenbaum, R. (1984). Brief psychotherapy of bereavement reactions: The relationship of process to outcome. *Archives of General Psychiatry, 41,* 438–448.

Horowitz, M., Marmar, C. R., Weiss, D. S., Kaltreider, N. B., & Wilner, N. R. (1986). Comprehensive analysis of change after brief dynamic psychotherapy. *American Journal of Psychiatry, 143,* 582–589.

Horowitz, M. J., Stinson, C., Curtis, D., Ewert, M., Redington, D., Singer, J., Bucci, W., Mergenthaler, E., Milbrath, C., & Hartley, D. (1993). Topics and signs: Defensive control of emotional expression. *Journal of Consulting and Clinical Psychology, 61,* 421–430.

Horowitz, M., Wilner, N., & Alvarez, W. (1979). Impact of event scale: A measure of subjective stress. *Psychosomatic Medicine, 41,* 209–218.

Howard, K. I., Kopta, S. M., Krause, M. S., & Orlinsky, D. E. (1986). The dose–effect relationship in psychotherapy. *American Psychologist, 41,* 159–164

Hoyt, M. F. (1979). Aspects of termination in a time-limited brief psychotherapy. *Psychiatry, 42,* 208–219.

Hoyt, M. F. (1985). Therapist resistances to short-term dynamic psychotherapy. *Journal of the American Academy of Psychoanalysis, 13,* 93–112.

Hoyt, M. F. (1987). Resistance to brief therapy. *American Psychologist, 42,* 408–409.

Hoyt, M. F. (1990). On time in brief therapy. In R. A. Wells & V. J. Giannetti (Eds.), *Handbook of the brief psychotherapies* (pp. 115–143). New York: Plenum.

Hoyt, M. F. (1994a). Characteristics of psychotherapy under managed healthcare. *Behavioral Healthcare Tomorrow, 3,* 59–62.

Hoyt, M. F. (1994b). Introduction: Competency-based future-oriented therapy. In M. F. Hoyt (Ed.), *Constructive therapies* (pp. 1–10). New York: Guilford Press

Hoyt, M. F. (1994c). Single-session solutions. In M. F. Hoyt (Ed.), *Constructive therapies* (pp. 140–159). New York: Guilford Press.

Hoyt, M. F. (1995). Brief therapy and managed care: Readings for contemporary practice. San Francisco: Jossey-Bass.

Hoyt, M. F., & Austad, C. S. (1992). Psychotherapy in a staff model health maintenance organization: Providing and assuring quality care in the future. *Psychotherapy, 29,* 119–129.

Hoyt, M. F., Rosenbaum, R., & Talmon, M. (1992). Planned single-session psychotherapy. In S. H. Budman, M. F. Hoyt, & S. Friedman (Eds.), *The first session in brief therapy* (pp. 59–86). New York: Guilford Press.

Hudson, P. O., & O'Hanlon, W. H. (1991). *Rewriting love stories: Brief marital therapy.* New York: Norton.

Hurley, D. J., & Fisher, S. G. (1993). A brief family therapy model for child guidance clinics. In R. A. Wells & V. J. Giannetti (Eds.), *Casebook of the brief psychotherapies* (pp. 259–270). New York: Plenum.

Husby, R. (1985). Short-term dynamic psychotherapy: IV. Comparison of recorded changes in 33 neurotic patients 2 and 5 years after end of treatment. Psychotherapy and Psychosomatics, 43, 23–27.

Husby, R., Dahl, A. A., Dahl, C-I., Heiberg, A. N., Olafsen, O. M., & Weisæth, L. (1985). Short-term dynamic psychotherapy: II. Prognostic value of characteristics of patients studied by a 2-year follow-up of 39 neurotic patients. *Psychotherapy and Psychosomatics, 43,* 8–16.

Imber, S. D., & Evanczuk, K. J. (1990). Brief crisis therapy groups. In R. A. Wells & V. J. Giannetti (Eds.), *Handbook of the brief psychotherapies* (pp. 565–582). New York: Plenum.

Isely, P. J. (1992). A time-limited group therapy model for men sexually abused as children. *Group, 16,* 233–246.

Jacobson, N. S., & Margolin, G. (1979). *Marital therapy: Strategies based on social learning and behavior exchange principles.* New York: Brunner/Mazel.

Jameson, J., Shuman, L. J., & Young, W. W. (1978). The effects of outpatient psychiatric utilization on the costs of providing third-party coverage. *Medical Care, 16,* 383–399.

Janosik, E. H. (1994). *Crisis counseling: A contemporary approach* (2d ed.). Boston: Jones and Bartlett.

Johnson, D. H., & Gelso, C. J. (1980). The effectiveness of time limits in counseling and psychotherapy: A critical review. *Counseling Psychologist, 9,* 70–83.

Jones, E. (1955). *The life and work of Sigmund Freud.* New York: Basic Books.

Jones, E. E., (1980). Multidimensional change in psychotherapy. *Journal of Clinical Psychology, 36,* 544–547.

Jones, E. E., Cumming, J. D., & Horowitz, M. J. (1988). Another look at the nonspecific hypothesis of therapeutic effectiveness. *Journal of Consulting and Clinical Psychology, 56,* 48–55.

Jones, E. E., & Pulos, S. M. (1993). Comparing the process in psychodynamic and cognitive-behavioral therapies. *Journal of Consulting and Clinical Psychology, 61,* 306–316.

Jones, K. R., & Vischi, T. R. (1979). Impact of alcohol, drug abuse and mental health treatment on medical care utilization: A review of the research literature. *Medical Care, 17 (Supp.),* 1–82.

Jones, R., Peveler, R. C., Hope, R. A., & Fairburn, C. G. (1993). Changes during treatment for bulimia nervosa: A comparison of three psychological treatments. *Behavior Research and Therapy, 31,* 479–485.

Joyce, A. S., & Piper, W. E. (1993). The immediate impact of transference interpretation in short-term individual psychotherapy. *American Journal of Psychotherapy, 47,* 508–526.

Kaffman, M. (1963). Short term family therapy. *Family Process, 2,* 216–234.

Kalpin, A. (1993). The use of time in intensive short-term dynamic psychotherapy. *International Journal of Short-Term Psychotherapy, 8,* 75–91.

Kanas, N. (1990). Short-term therapy groups for schizophrenics. In R. A. Wells & V. J. Giannetti (Eds.), *Handbook of the brief psychotherapies* (pp. 551–564). New York: Plenum.

Kane, J. M. (1991). Risk–benefit ratios in psychiatric treatment. In S. M. Mirin, J. T. Gossett, & M. C. Grob (Eds.), *Psychiatric treatment: Advances in outcome research* (pp. 15–20). Washington, DC: American Psychiatric Press.

Karasu, T. B. (1987). The psychotherapy of the future. *Psychosomatics, 28,* 380–381, 384.

Keilson, M. V., Dworkin, F. H., & Gelso, C. J. (1979). The effectiveness of time-limited psychotherapy in a university counseling center. *Journal of Clinical Psychology, 35,* 631–636.

Keller, A. (1984). Planned brief psychotherapy in clinical practice. *British Journal of Medical Psychology, 57,* 347–361.

Kemp, B. J., Corgiat, M., & Gill, C. (1991/1992). Effects of brief cognitive-behavioral group psychotherapy on older persons with and without disabling illness. *Behavior, Health, and Aging, 2,* 21–28.

Kendall, P. C., Vitousek, K. B., & Kane, M. (1991). Thought and action in psychotherapy: Cognitive-behavioral approaches. In M. Hersen, A. E. Kazdin, & A. S. Bellack (Eds.), *The clinical psychology handbook* (2d ed.) (pp. 596–626). New York: Pergamon Press.

Kiesler, C. A. (1982). Mental hospitals and alternative care: Noninstitutionalization as potential public policy for mental patients. *American Psychologist, 37,* 1051–1057.

King, M., Broster, G., Lloyd, M., & Horder, J. (1994). Controlled trials in the evaluation of counselling in general practice. *British Journal of General Practice, 44,* 229–232.

Kirkby, R. J., & Smyrnios, K. X. (1992). The psychological health of children, cost-effectiveness, and brief therapy. *Australian Psychologist, 27,* 78–82.

Kirshner, L. A. (1988). A model of time-limited treatment for the older patient. *Journal of Geriatric Psychiatry, 21,* 155–168.

Klar, H., & Coleman, W. L. (1995). Brief solution-focused strategies for behavioral pediatrics. *Pediatric Clinics of North America, 42,* 131–141.

Kleber, R. J., & Brom, D. (1987). Psychotherapy and pathological grief controlled outcome study. *Israeli Journal of Psychiatry and Related Sciences, 24,* 99–109.

Klerman, G. L. (1983). The efficacy of psychotherapy as the basis for public policy. *American Psychologist, 38,* 929–934.

Klerman, G. L., Budman, S., Berwick, D., Weissman, M. M., Damico-White, J., Demby, A., & Feldstein, M. (1987). Efficacy of a brief psychosocial intervention for symptoms of stress and distress among patients in primary care. *Medical Care, 25,* 1078–1088.

Klerman, G. L., & Weissman, M. M. (1982). Interpersonal psychotherapy theory and research. In A. J. Rush (Ed.),

Short-term psychotherapies for depression (pp. 88–106). New York: Guilford Press.

Klerman, G. L., & Weissman, M. M. (Eds.) (1993). *New applications of interpersonal psychotherapy.* Washington, DC: American Psychiatric Press.

Klerman, G. L., Weissman, M. M., Rounsaville, B. J., & Chevron, E. S. (1984a). Interpersonal psychotherapy for depression. In L. Grinspoon (Ed.), *Psychiatry update: The American Psychiatric Association annual review* (vol. 3) (pp. 56–67). Washington, DC: American Psychiatric Press.

Klerman, G. L., Weissman, M. M., Rounsaville, B. J., & Chevron, E. S. (1984b). *Interpersonal psychotherapy of depression.* New York: Basic Books.

Kline, M. V. (1992). *Short-term dynamic hypnotherapy and hypnoanalysis: Clinical research and treatment strategies.* Springfield, IL: Thomas.

Knight, B. G. (1992). *Older adults in psychotherapy: Case histories.* Thousand Oaks, CA: Sage.

Koegler, R. R. (1966). Brief-contact therapy and drugs in outpatient treatment. In G. J. Wayne & R. R. Koegler (Eds.), *Emergency psychiatry and brief therapy* (pp. 139–154). Boston: Little, Brown.

Kogan, L. S. (1957a). The short-term case in a family agency Part I: The study plan. *Social Casework, 38,* 231–238.

Kogan, L. S. (1957b). The short-term case in a family agency Part II: Results of study. *Social Casework, 38,* 296–302.

Kogan, L. S. (1957c). The short-term case in a family agency Part III: Further results and conclusion. Social Casework, 38, 366–374.

Koss, M. P., & Butcher, J. N. (1986). Research on brief psychotherapy. In A. E. Bergin & S. L. Garfield (Eds.), *Handbook of psychotherapy and behavior change: An empirical analysis* (3d ed.) (pp. 627–670). New York: Wiley.

Koss, M. P., Butcher, J. N., & Strupp, H. H. (1986). Brief psychotherapy methods in clinical research. *Journal of Consulting and Clinical Psychology, 54,* 60–67.

Koss, M. P., & Shiang, J. (1994). Research on brief psychotherapy. In A. E. Bergin & S. L. Garfield (Eds.), *Handbook of psychotherapy and behavior change* (pp. 664–700). New York: Wiley.

Kovacs, A. L. (1982). Survival in the 1980s: On the theory and practice of brief psychotherapy. *Psychotherapy: Theory, Research and Practice, 19,* 142–159.

Kral, R. (1992). Solution-focused brief therapy: Applications in the schools. In M. J. Fine & C. Carlson (Eds.), *The handbook of family-school intervention: A systems perspective* (pp. 330–346). Boston: Allyn and Bacon.

Kreilkamp, T. (1989). *Time-limited, intermittent therapy with children and families.* New York: Brunner/Mazel.

Krupnick, J. L., Elkin, I., Collings, J., Simmens, S.,

Sotsky, S. M., Pilkonis, P. A. & Watkins, J. T. (1994). Therapeutic alliance and clinical outcome in the NIMH treatment of depression collaborative research program: Preliminary findings. *Psychotherapy, 31,* 28–35.

Krupnick, J. L., & Horowitz, M. J. (1985). Brief psychotherapy with vulnerable patients: An outcome assessment. *Psychiatry, 48,* 223–233.

Kupers, T. A. (1988). *Ending therapy: The meaning of termination.* New York: New York University Press.

La Court, M. (1988). The HMO crisis: Danger/opportunity. *Family Systems Medicine, 6,* 80–93.

LaCrosse, M. B. (1994). Understanding change: Five-year follow-up of brief hypnotic treatment of chronic bruxism. *American Journal of Clinical Hypnosis, 36,* 276–281.

Laikin, M., Winston, A., & McCullough, L. (1991). Intensive short-term dynamic psychotherapy. In P. Crits-Christoph & J. P. Barber (Eds.), *Handbook of short-term dynamic psychotherapy* (pp. 80–109). New York: Basic Books.

Lambert, M. J. (1979). Characteristics of patients and their relationship to outcome in brief psychotherapy. *Psychiatric Clinics of North America, 2,* 111–123.

Lambert, M. J. (1989). The individual therapist's contribution to psychotherapy process and outcome. *Clinical Psychology Review, 9,* 469–485.

Lambert, M. J., Shapiro, D. A., & Bergin, A. E. (1986). The effectiveness of psychotherapy. In S. L. Garfield & A. E. Bergin (Eds.), *Handbook of psychotherapy and behavior change* (3d ed.) (pp. 157–211). New York: Wiley.

Land, J. M. (1993). Calumny and misrepresentation of intensive short-term dynamic psychotherapy: A critique of two articles. *International Journal of Short-Term Psychotherapy, 8,* 43–53.

Lankton, S. R. (1994). Introduction to the case: A woman with chronic anxiety and panic attacks. In S. R. Lankton & K. K. Erickson (Eds.), *The essence of a single-session success* (pp. 81–107). New York: Brunner/Mazel.

Lankton, S. R., & Erickson, K. K. (Eds.) (1994). *The essence of a single-session success.* New York: Brunner/Mazel.

Lavoritano, J. E., & Segal, P. B. (1992). Evaluating the efficacy of short-term counseling on adolescents in a school setting. *Adolescence, 27,* 535–543.

Lazare, A., Cohen, F., Jacobson, A. M., Williams, M. W., Mignone, R. J., & Zisook, S. (1972). The walk-in patient as a "customer": A key dimension in evaluation and treatment. *American Journal of Orthopsychiatry, 42,* 872–883.

Lazarus, L. W. (1988). Self psychology—its application to brief psychotherapy with the elderly. *Journal of Geriatric Psychiatry, 21,* 109–125.

Lefkovitz, P. M. (1988). The short-term program. *New Directions in Mental Health Services. No. 38,* 31–49.

Leibenluft, E., & Goldberg, R. L. (1987). Guidelines for short-term inpatient psychotherapy. *Hospital and Community Psychiatry, 38,* 38–43.

Leibenluft, E., Tasman, A., & Green, S. A. (1993). *Less time to do more: Psychotherapy on the short-term inpatient unit.* Washington, DC: American Psychiatric Press.

Lerner, A., Sigal, M., Bacalu, A., & Gelkopf, M. (1992). Short term versus long term psychotherapy in opioid dependence: A pilot study. *Israeli Journal of Psychiatry and Related Sciences, 29,* 114–119.

Lettieri-Marks, D. (1987). Research in short-term inpatient group psychotherapy: A critical review. *Archives of Psychiatric Nursing, 1,* 407–421.

Levenson, H., & Butler, S. F. (1994). Brief dynamic individual psychotherapy. In R. E. Hales, S. C. Yudofsky, & J. A. Talbott (Eds.), *The American Psychiatric Press textbook of psychiatry.* (2d ed.) (pp. 1009–1033). Washington, DC: American Psychiatric Press.

Levenson, H., Speed, J., & Budman, S. H. (1995). Therapist's experience, training, and skill in brief therapy: A bicoastal survey. *American Journal of Psychotherapy, 49,* 95–117.

Lewin, K. K. (1970). *Brief encounters: Brief psychotherapy.* St. Louis, MO: Green.

Lewinsohn, P. M., Sullivan, J. M., & Grosscup, S. J. (1982). Behavioral therapy: Clinical applications. In A. J. Rush (Ed.), *Short-term psychotherapies for depression* (pp. 50–87). New York: Guilford Press.

Liberzon, I., Goldman, R. S., & Hendrickson, W. J. (1992). Very brief psychotherapy in the psychiatric consultation setting. *International Journal of Psychiatry in Medicine, 22,* 65–75.

Lieberman, M. A., & Yalom, I. (1992). Brief group psychotherapy for the spousally bereaved: A controlled study. *International Journal of Group Psychotherapy, 42,* 117–132.

Lieberman, P. B., McPhetres, E. B., Elliott, B., Egerter, E., & Wiitala, S. (1993). Dimensions and predictors of change during brief psychiatric hospitalization. *General Hospital Psychiatry, 15,* 316–324.

Liese, B. S. (1995). Integrating crisis intervention, cognitive therapy, and triage. In A. R. Roberts (Ed.), *Crisis intervention and time-limited cognitive treatment* (pp. 28–53). Thousand Oaks, CA: Sage.

Lindemann, E. (1944). Symptomatology and management of acute grief. *American Journal of Psychiatry, 101,* 141–148.

Littlepage, G. E., Kosloski, K. D., Schnelle, J. F., McNees, M. P., & Gendrich, J. C. (1976). The problems of early outpatient terminations from community mental health centers: A problem for whom? *Journal of Community Psychology, 4,* 164–167.

Littrell, J. M., Malia, J. A., & Vanderwood, M. (1995). Single-session brief counseling in a high school. *Journal of Counseling and Development, 73,* 451–458.

Loar, L. (1994). Child sexual abuse: Several brief interventions with young perpetrators. *Child Abuse and Neglect, 18,* 977–986.

Lohnes, K. L., & Kalter, N. (1994). Preventive intervention groups for parentally bereaved children. *American Journal of Orthopsychiatry, 64,* 594–603.

Lorr, M., McNair, D. M., Michaux, W. W., & Raskin, A. (1962). Frequency of treatment and change in psychotherapy. *Journal of Abnormal and Social Psychology, 64,* 281–292.

Luborsky, L., Crits-Christoph, P., Mintz, J., & Auerbach, A. (1988). *Who will benefit from psychotherapy?: Predicting therapeutic outcomes.* New York: Basic Books.

Luborsky, L., Docherty, J. P., Miller, N. E., & Barber, J. P. (1993). What's here and what's ahead in dynamic therapy research and practice? In N. E. Miller, L. Luborsky, J. P. Barber, & J. P. Docherty (Eds.), *Psychodynamic treatment research: A handbook for clinical practice* (pp. 536–553). New York: Basic Books.

Lutz, S. (1991). Troubled times for psych hospitals. *Modern Health Care. December 16, 1991,* 26–27, 30, 32–33.

MacKenzie, K. R. (1988). Recent developments in brief psychotherapy. *Hospital and Community Psychiatry, 39,* 742–752.

MacMahon, B., & Pugh, T. F. (1970). *Epidemiology: Principles and methods.* Boston: Little, Brown.

Madanes, C. (1984). *Behind the one-way mirror: Advances in the practice of strategic therapy.* San Francisco, CA: Jossey-Bass.

Madanes, C. (1990). Strategies and metaphors of brief therapy. In J. K. Zeig & S. G. Gilligan (Eds.), *Brief therapy: Myths, methods, and metaphors* (pp. 18–35). New York: Brunner/Mazel.

Magnavita, J. J. (1993a). The evolution of short-term dynamic psychotherapy: Treatment of the future? *Professional Psychology: Research and Practice, 24,* 360–365.

Magnavita, J. J. (1993b). The treatment of passive-aggressive personality disorder: A review of current approaches. Part I. *International Journal of Short-Term Psychotherapy, 8,* 29–41.

Magnavita, J. J. (1993c). The treatment of passive-aggressive personality disorder: Intensive short-term dynamic psychotherapy. Part II: Trial therapy. *International Journal of Short-Term Psychotherapy, 8,* 93–106.

Mahrer, A. R. & Roberge, M. (1993). Single-session experiential therapy with any person whatsoever. In R. A.

Wells & V. J. Giannetti (Eds.), *Casebook of the brief psychotherapies* (pp. 179–196). New York: Plenum.

Malan, D. H. (1963). *A study of brief psychotherapy,* London: Tavistock.

Malan, D. H. (1976). *The frontier of brief psychotherapy: An example of the convergence of research and clinical practice.* New York: Plenum.

Malan, D. H. (1978a). Evaluation, criteria for selection of patients. In H. Davanloo (Ed.), *Basic principles and techniques in short-term dynamic psychotherapy* (pp. 85–97). New York: Spectrum.

Malan, D. H. (1978b). Principles of technique in short-term dynamic psychotherapy. In H. Davanloo (Ed.), *Basic principles and techniques in short-term dynamic psychotherapy* (pp. 332–342). New York: Spectrum.

Malan, D. H. (1979). *Individual psychotherapy and the science of psychodynamics.* London: Butterworth.

Malan, D. H. (1980a). Basic principles and technique of the follow-up interview. In H. Davanloo (Ed.), *Short-term dynamic psychotherapy* (pp. 349–377). Northvale, NJ: Aronson.

Malan, D. H. (1980b). The most important development in psychotherapy since the discovery of the unconscious. In H. Davanloo (Ed.), *Short-term dynamic psychotherapy* (pp. 13–23). Northvale, NJ: Aronson.

Malan, D. H. (1980c). The nature of science and the validity of psychotherapy. In H. Davanloo (Ed.), *Short-term dynamic psychotherapy* (pp. 319–347). Northvale, NJ: Aronson.

Malan, D. H., Heath, E. S., Bacal, H. A., & Balfour, F. H. G. (1975). Psychodynamic changes in untreated neurotic patients. II. Apparently genuine improvements. *Archives of General Psychiatry, 32,* 110–126.

Malan, D., & Osimo, F. (1992). *Psychodynamics, training, and outcome in brief psychotherapy.* Oxford: Butterworth-Heinemann.

Malan, D. H., Rayner, E. H., Bacal, H. A., Heath, E. S., & Balfour, F. H. G. (1968). Psychodynamic assessment of the outcome of psychotherapy. In R. Porter (Ed.), *The role of learning in psychotherapy* (pp. 61–67). Boston: Little, Brown.

Malcolm, J. (1987). J'appelle un chat un chat. *The New Yorker, April 20, 1987.* 84–92, 95–102.

Mallinckrodt, B. (1993). Session impact, working alliance, and treatment outcome in brief counseling. *Journal of Counseling Psychology, 40,* 25–32.

Manaster, G. J. (1989). Clinical issues in brief psychotherapy: A summary and conclusion. *Individual Psychology, 45,* 243–247.

Manderscheid, R. W., & Sonnenschein, M. A. (Eds.) (1990). *Mental health, United States, 1990.* DHHS Pub. No. (ADM) 90–1708. Washington, DC: U.S. Government Printing Office.

Mann, J. (1973). *Time-limited psychotherapy.* Cambridge, MA: Harvard University Press.

Mann, J. (1981). The core of time-limited psychotherapy: Time and the central issue. In S. Budman (Ed.), *Forms of brief therapy* (pp. 25–43). New York: Guilford Press.

Mann, J. (1984). Time limited psychotherapy. In L. Grinspoon (Ed.), *Psychiatry update: The American Psychiatric Association annual review* (vol. 3) (pp. 35–44). Washington, DC: American Psychiatric Press.

Mann, J. (1991). Time limited psychotherapy. In P. Crits-Christoph & J. P. Barber (Eds.), *Handbook of short-term dynamic psychotherapy* (pp. 17–44). New York: Basic Books.

Mann, J., & Goldman, R. (1982). *A casebook in time-limited psychotherapy.* New York: McGraw-Hill.

Margo, K. L., & Margo, G. M. (1994). The problem of somatization in family practice. *American Family Physician, 49,* 1873–1879.

Marks, I. (1986). Behavioural psychotherapy in general psychiatry: Helping patients to help themselves. *British Journal of Psychiatry, 150,* 593–597.

Marmar, C. R., Horowitz, M. J., Weiss, D. S., Wilner, N. R., & Kaltreider, N. B. (1988). A controlled trial of brief psychotherapy and mutual-help group treatment of conjugal bereavement. *American Journal of Psychiatry, 145,* 203–209.

Marmar, C. R., Weiss, D. S., & Gaston, L. (1989). Toward the validation of the California Therapeutic Alliance Rating System. *Psychological Assessment: A Journal of Consulting and Clinical Psychology, 1,* 46–52.

Marmor, J. (1968). New directions in psychoanalytic theory and therapy. In J. Marmor (Ed.), *Modern psychoanalysis: New directions and perspectives* (pp. 3–15). New York: Basic Books.

Marmor, J. (1979). Short-term dynamic psychotherapy. *American Journal of Psychiatry, 136,* 149–155.

Marmor, J. (1980). Crisis intervention and short-term dynamic psychotherapy. In H. Davanloo (Ed.), *Short-term dynamic psychotherapy* (pp. 237–243). Northvale, NJ: Aronson.

Marziali, E. A. (1987). People in your life: Development of a social support measure for predicting psychotherapy outcome. *Journal of Nervous and Mental Disease, 175,* 327–338.

Marziali, E., Marmar, C., & Krupnick, J. (1981). Therapeutic alliance scales: Development and relationship to psychotherapy outcome. *American Journal of Psychiatry, 138,* 361–364.

Mathews, B. (1988). Planned short-term therapy utilizing the techniques of Jay Haley and Milton Erickson: A guide for the practitioner. *Psychotherapy in Private Practice, 6,* 103–118.

Mattes, J. A., Rosen, B., & Klein, D. F. (1977). Comparison of the clinical effectiveness of "short" versus "long" stay psychiatric hospitalization. II. Results of a 3-year posthospital follow-up. *Journal of Nervous and Mental Disease, 165,* 387–394.

Mattes, J. A., Rosen, B., Klein, D. F., & Millan, D. (1977). Comparison of the clinical effectiveness of "short" versus "long" stay psychiatric hospitalization. III. Further results of a 3-year posthospital follow-up. *Journal of Nervous and Mental Disease, 165,* 395–402.

Maturana, H. R., & Varela, F. J. (1980). *Autopoiesis and cognition: The realization of the living.* Boston: Reidel.

McConkey, N. (1992). Working with adults to overcome the effects of sexual abuse: Integrating solution-focused therapy, systems thinking and gender issues. *Journal of Strategic and Systemic Therapies, 11 (3),* 4–19.

McDuff, D. R., & Solounias, B. L. (1992). The use of brief psychotherapy with substance abusers in early recovery. *Journal of Psychotherapy Practice and Research, 1,* 163–170.

McFarland, B. (1995). *Brief therapy and eating disorders.* San Francisco: Jossey-Bass.

McGuire, T. G., & Frisman, L. K. (1983). Reimbursement policy and cost-effective mental health care. *American Psychologist, 38,* 935–940.

McGuire, T. J. (1988). A time-limited dynamic approach to adolescent inpatient group psychotherapy. *Adolescence, 23 (90),* 373–382.

McKay, J. R., Murphy, R. T., & Longabaugh, R. (1991). The effectiveness of alcoholism treatment: Evidence from outcome studies. In S. M. Mirin, J. T. Gossett, & M. C. Grob (Eds.), *Psychiatric treatment: Advances in outcome research* (pp. 143–158). Washington, DC: American Psychiatric Press.

McLean, P. (1982). Behavior therapy: Theory and research. In A. J. Rush (Ed.), *Short-term psychotherapies for depression* (pp. 19–49). New York: Guilford Press.

Mc Mullin, R. E. (1986). *Handbook of cognitive therapy techniques.* New York: Norton.

Meltzoff, J., & Kornreich, M. (1970). *Research in psychotherapy.* New York: Atherton.

Mendel, W. M. (1967). Brief hospitalization techniques. In J. Masserman (Ed.), *Current psychiatric therapies: 1966* (vol. 6) (pp. 310–316). New York: Grune & Stratton.

Menninger, K. (1963). *The vital balance.* New York: Viking Press.

Messer, S. B., Tishby, O., & Spillman, A. (1992). Taking context seriously in psychotherapy research: Relating therapist interventions to patient progress in brief psychodynamic therapy. *Journal of Consulting and Clinical Psychology, 60,* 678–688.

Meyer, A-E., Bolz, W., Stuhr, U., & Burzig, G. (1981). VI. Outcome results by clinical evaluation based on the blind group ratings. *Psychotherapy and Psychosomatics, 35,* 199–207.

Meyer, N. G., & Taube, C. A. (1973). *Length of stay of admissions to state and county mental hospitals, United States, 1971* (Statistical Note 74, National Institute of Mental Health). Washington, D.C.: U.S. Government Printing Office.

Migone, P. (1985). Short-term dynamic psychotherapy from a psychoanalytic viewpoint. *Psychoanalytic Review, 72,* 615–634.

Mikkelsen, E. J., Bereika, G. M., & McKenzie, J. C. (1993). Short-term family-based residential treatment: An alternative to psychiatric hospitalization for children. *American Journal of Orthopsychiatry, 63,* 28–33.

Miller, W. R., & Hester, R. K. (1986). Inpatient alcoholism treatment: Who benefits? *American Psychologist, 41,* 794–805.

Mohl, P. C. (1988). Brief supportive psychotherapy by the primary care physician. Texas Medicine, 84, 28–32.

Mumford, E., & Schlesinger, H. J. (1987). Assessing consumer benefit: Cost offset as an incidental effect of psychotherapy. *General Hospital Psychiatry, 9,* 360–363.

Mumford, E., Schlesinger, H. J., & Glass, G. V. (1982). The effects of psychological intervention on recovery from surgery and heart attacks: An analysis of the literature. *American Journal of Public Health, 72,* 141–151.

Mumford, E., Schlesinger, H. J., Glass, G. V., Patrick, C., & Cuerdon, T. (1984). A new look at evidence about reduced cost of medical utilization following mental health treatment. *American Journal of Psychiatry, 141,* 1145–1158.

Nahmias, J. (1991). Selection criteria in short-term dynamic psychotherapy: Part II. Trial therapy. *International Journal of Short-Term Psychotherapy, 6,* 259–275.

National Center for Health Statistics (1989). *Health, United States, 1988.* DHHS Pub. No. (PHS) 89–1232. Washington, DC: U.S. Government Printing Office.

Nehls, N. (1994). Brief hospital treatment plans: Innovations in practice and research. *Issues in Mental Health Nursing, 15,* 1–11.

Neu, C., Prusoff, B. A., & Klerman, G. L. (1978). Measuring the interventions used in the short-term interpersonal psychotherapy of depression. *American Journal of Orthopsychiatry, 48,* 629–636.

Neumann, M., & Hudson, P. O. (1994). Solution-oriented therapy techniques for women's health nurses. *Journal of Obstetric, Gynocologic, and Neonatal Nursing, 23,* 16–20.

Nielsen, G., & Barth, K. (1991). Short-term anxiety-provoking psychotherapy. In P. Crits-Christoph & J. P.

Barber (Eds.), *Handbook of short-term dynamic psychotherapy* (pp. 45–79). New York: Basic Books.

Nielsen, G., Barth, K., Haver, B., Havik, O. E., Mølstad, E., Rogge, H., & Skåtun, M. (1988). Brief dynamic psychotherapy for patients presenting physical symptoms. *Psychotherapy and Psychosomatics, 50,* 35–41.

Norcross, J. C. (1986). Eclectic psychotherapy: An introduction and overview. In J. C. Norcross (Ed.), *Handbook of eclectic psychotherapy* (pp. 3–24). New York: Brunner/Mazel.

Norcross, J. C., & Freedheim, D. K. (1992). Into the future: Retrospect and prospect in psychotherapy. In D. K. Freedheim (Ed.), *History of psychotherapy: A century of change* (pp. 881–900). Washington, DC: American Psychological Association.

Nunnally, E. (1993). Solution focused therapy. In R. A. Wells & V. J. Giannetti (Eds.), *Casebook of the brief psychotherapies* (pp. 271–286). New York: Plenum.

Nunnally, E., de Shazer, S., Lipchik, E., & Berg, I. (1986). A study of change: Therapeutic theory in process. In D. E. Efron (Ed.), *Journeys: Expansion of the strategic-systemic therapies* (pp. 77–96). New York: Brunner/Mazel.

O'Hanlon, W. (1985). A study guide of frameworks of Milton Erickson's hypnosis and therapy. In J. K. Zeig (Ed.), *Ericksonian psychotherapy: Vol. I: Structures* (pp. 33–51). New York: Brunner/Mazel.

O'Hanlon, W. H. (1990). A grand unified theory for brief therapy: Putting problems in context. In J. K. Zeig & S. G. Gilligan (Eds.), *Brief therapy: Myths, methods, and metaphors* (pp. 78–89). New York: Brunner/Mazel.

O'Hanlon, W. H., & Hexum, A. L. (1990). *An uncommon casebook: The complete clinical work of Milton H. Erickson.* New York: Norton.

O'Hanlon, W. H., & Hudson, P. O. (1994). Coauthoring a love story: Solution-oriented marital therapy. In M. F. Hoyt (Ed.), *Constructive therapies* (pp. 160–188). New York: Guilford Press.

O'Hanlon, W. H., & Weiner-Davis, M. (1989). *In search of solutions; A new direction in psychotherapy.* New York: Norton.

Oldham, J. M., & Russakoff, L. M. (1987). *Dynamic therapy in brief hospitalization.* Northvale, NJ: Aronson.

O'Leary, M. G. (1995). Therapists' estimation of client satisfaction with services: Implications in an era of managed care. *Crisis Intervention and Time-Limited Treatment, 2,* 13–22.

Olfson, M., & Pincus, H. A. (1994). Outpatient psychotherapy in the United States: II. Patterns of utilization. *American Journal of Psychiatry, 151,* 1289–1294.

Oppenheimer, B. T. (1984). Short-term small group intervention for college freshmen. *Journal of Counseling Psychology, 31,* 45–53.

Oremland, J. D. (1976). A curious resolution of a hysterical symptom. *International Review of Psycho-Analysis, 3,* 473–477.

O'Shea, M. D., Bicknell, L., & Wheatley, D. (1991). Brief multifamily psychoeducation programs for schizophrenia: Strategies for implementation and management. *American Journal of Family Therapy, 19,* 33–44.

Öst, L-G. (1989). One-session treatment for specific phobias. *Behavior Research and Therapy, 7,* 1–7.

Parad, H. J., & Parad, L. G. (1968). A study of crisis-oriented planned short-term treatment: Part I. *Social Casework, 49,* 346–355.

Parad, H. J. & Parad, L. G. (1990). Crisis intervention: An introductory overview. In H. J. Parad & L. G. Parad (Eds.), *Crisis intervention Book 2: The practitioner's sourcebook for brief therapy* (pp. 3–66). Milwaukee, WI: Family Service America.

Parad, L. G. (1971). Short-term treatment: An overview of historical trends, issues, and potentials. *Smith College Studies in Social Work, 41,* 119–146.

Parad, L. G., & Parad, H. J. (1968). A study of crisis-oriented planned short-term treatment: Part II. *Social Casework, 49,* 418–426.

Parloff, M. B. (1982). Psychotherapy research evidence and reimbursement decisions: Bambi meets Godzilla. *American Journal of Psychiatry, 139,* 718–727.

Pavan, L., & Mangini, E. (1992). Brief psychotherapy focused on separation. *International Journal of Short-Term Psychotherapy, 7,* 231–242.

Peake, T. H., Borduin, C. M., & Archer, R. P. (1988). *Brief psychotherapies: Changing frames of mind.* Thousand Oaks, CA: Sage.

Pekarik, G. (1983). Follow-up adjustment of outpatient dropouts. *American Journal of Orthopsychiatry, 53,* 501–511.

Pekarik, G. (1994). Effects of brief therapy training on practicing psychotherapists and their clients. *Community Mental Health Journal, 30,* 135–144.

Pekarik, G., & Wierzbicki, M. (1986). The relationship between clients' expected and actual treatment duration. *Psychotherapy, 23,* 532–534.

Perris, C. (1988). *Cognitive therapy with schizophrenics.* New York: Guilford Press.

Persons, J. B. (1989). *Cognitive therapy in practice: A case formulation approach.* New York: Norton.

Phillips, E. L. (1985a). *A guide for therapists and patients to short-term psychotherapy.* Springfield, IL: Thomas.

Phillips, E. L. (1985b). *Psychotherapy revised: New frontiers in research and practice.* Hillsdale, NJ: Erlbaum.

Phillips, E. L., Gershenson, J., & Lyons, G. (1977). On time-limited writing therapy. *Psychological Reports, 41,* 707–712.

Phillips, E. L., & Wiener, D. N. (1966). *Short-term psychotherapy and structured behavior change.* New York: McGraw-Hill.

Pinkerton, R. S., & Rockwell, W. J. K. (1994). Very brief psychological interventions with university students. *Journal of American College Health, 42,* 156–162.

Piper, W. E., Azim, H. F. A., McCallum, M., & Joyce, A. S. (1990). Patient suitability and outcome in short-term individual psychotherapy. *Journal of Consulting and Clinical Psychology, 58,* 475–481.

Piper, W. E., Debbane, E. G., Bienvenu, J. P., & Garant, J. (1984). A comparative study of four forms of psychotherapy. *Journal of Consulting and Clinical Psychology, 52,* 268–279.

Piper, W. E., Joyce, A. S., McCallum, M., & Azim, H. F. A. (1993). Concentration and correspondence of transference interpretations in short-term psychotherapy. *Journal of Consulting and Clinical Psychology, 61,* 586–595.

Piper, W. E., McCallum, M., & Azim, H. F. A. (1992). *Adaptation to loss through short-term group psychotherapy.* New York: Guilford Press.

Popchak, G. K., & Wells, R. A. (1993). Brief family therapy with a low-socioeconomic family. In R. A. Wells & V. J. Giannetti (Eds.), *Casebook of the brief psychotherapies* (pp. 303–314). New York: Plenum.

Powers, R. L., & Griffith, J. (1989). Single-session psychotherapy involving two therapists. *Individual Psychology, 45,* 99–125.

Prazoff, M., Joyce, A. S., & Azim, H. F. A. (1986). Brief crisis group psychotherapy: One therapist's model. *Group, 10,* 34–40.

Propst, A., Paris, J., & Rosberger, Z. (1994). Do therapist experience, diagnosis and functional level predict outcome in short term psychotherapy? *Canadian Journal of Psychiatry, 39,* 168–176.

Puryear, D. A. (1979). *Helping people in crisis.* San Francisco, CA: Jossey-Bass.

Quintana, S. M. (1993). Toward an expanded and updated conceptualization of termination: Implications for short-term, individual psychotherapy. *Professional Psychology: Research and Practice, 24,* 426–432.

Rabkin, R. (1977). *Strategic psychotherapy: Brief and symptomatic treatment.* New York: Basic Books.

Rasmussen, A., & Messer, S. B. (1986). A comparison and critique of Mann's time-limited psychotherapy and Davanloo's short-term dynamic psychotherapy. *Bulletin of the Menninger Clinic, 50,* 163–184.

Rauch, S. P., Brack, C. J., & Orr, D. P. (1987). School-based, short-term group treatment for behaviorally disturbed young adolescent males: A pilot intervention. *Journal of School Health, 57,* 19–22.

Regier, D. A., Goldberg, I. D., & Taube, C. A. (1978). The de facto U.S. mental health services system. *Archives of General Psychiatry, 35,* 685–693.

Reich, J., & Neenan, P. (1986). Principles common to different short-term psychotherapies. *American Journal of Psychotherapy, 40,* 62–69.

Reider, N. (1955). A type of psychotherapy based on psychoanalytic principles. *Bulletin of the Menninger Clinic, 19,* 111–128.

Reitav, J. (1991). The treatment of character pathology with Davanloo's intensive short-term dynamic psychotherapy: Part I: Management of resistance. *International Journal of Short-Term Psychotherapy, 6,* 3–25.

Rempel, K., Hazelwood, E., & McElheran, N. (1993). Brief therapy group for mothers of troubled children. *Journal of Systemic Therapies, 12,* 32–48.

Rhodes, J. (1993). The use of solution-focused brief therapy in schools. *Educational Psychology in Practice, 9,* 27–34.

Richmond, R., Heather, N., Wodak, A., Kehoe, L., & Webster, I. (1995). Controlled evaluation of a general practice-based brief intervention for excessive drinking. *Addiction, 90,* 119–132.

Riessman, C. K., Rabkin, J. G., & Struening, E. L. (1977). Brief versus standard psychiatric hospitalization: A critical review of the literature. *Community Mental Health Review, 2(2),* 1, 3–10.

Robbins, S. B., & Zinni, V. R. (1988). Implementing a time-limited treatment model: Issues and solutions. *Professional Psychology: Research and Practice, 19,* 53–57.

Roberts, A. R. (1990). *Crisis intervention handbook: Assessment, treatment, and research.* Belmont, CA: Wadsworth.

Roberts, A. R. (Ed.) (1991). *Contemporary perspectives on crisis intervention and prevention.* Englewood Cliffs, NJ: Prentice Hall.

Roberts, A. R. (Ed.) (1995a). *Crisis intervention and time-limited cognitive treatment.* Thousand Oaks, CA: Sage.

Roberts, A. R. (1995b). Crisis intervention units and centers in the United States: A national survey. In A. R. Roberts (Ed.), *Crisis intervention and time-limited cognitive treatment* (pp. 54–70). Thousand Oaks, CA: Sage.

Roberts, A. R., & Dziegielewski, S. F. (1995). Foundation skills and applications of crisis intervention and cognitive therapy. In A. R. Roberts (Ed.), *Crisis intervention and time-limited cognitive treatment.* (pp. 3–27). Thousand Oaks, CA: Sage.

Roberts, J. (1986). An evolving model: Links between the Milan approach and strategic models of family therapy. In D. E. Efron (Ed.), *Journeys: Expansion of the strategic-systemic therapies* (pp. 150–173). New York: Brunner/Mazel.

Robinson, H. A., Redlich, F. C., & Myers, J. K. (1954). Social structure and psychiatric treatment. *American Journal of Orthopsychiatry, 24,* 307–316.

Rockwell, W. J. K., & Pinkerton, R. S. (1982). Single-session psychotherapy. *American Journal of Psychotherapy, 36,* 32–40.

Rogawski, A. S. (1982). Current status of brief psychotherapy. *Bulletin of the Menninger Clinic, 46,* 331–351.

Rosegrant, J. (1988). A dynamic/expressive approach to brief inpatient group psychotherapy. *Group, 12,* 103–112.

Rosen, B., Katzoff, A., Carrillo, C., & Klein, D. F. (1976). Clinical effectiveness of "short" vs "long" psychiatric hospitalization. I. Inpatient results. *Archives of General Psychiatry, 33,* 1316–1322.

Rosen, J. C., & Wiens, A. N. (1979). Changes in medical problems and use of medical services following psychological intervention. *American Psychologist, 34,* 420–431.

Rosenbaum, C. P. (1964). Events of early therapy and brief therapy. *Archives of General Psychiatry, 10,* 506–512.

Rosenbaum, C. P., & Beebe, J. E. (1975). *Psychiatric treatment: Crisis/clinic/consultation.* New York: McGraw-Hill.

Rosenbaum, R. (1990). Strategic psychotherapy. In R. A. Wells & V. J. Giannetti (Eds.), *Handbook of the brief psychotherapies* (pp. 351–403). New York: Plenum.

Rosenbaum, R. (1993). Heavy ideals: Strategic single-session hypnotherapy. In R. A. Wells & V. J. Giannetti (Eds.), *Casebook of the brief psychotherapies* (pp. 109–128). New York: Plenum.

Rosenbaum, R. (1994). Single-session therapies: Intrinsic integration? *Journal of Psychotherapy Integration, 4,* 229–252.

Rosenbaum, R., Hoyt, M. F., & Talmon, M. (1990). The challenge of single-session therapies: Creating pivotal moments. In R. A. Wells & V. J. Giannetti (Eds.), Handbook of the brief psychotherapies (pp. 165–189). New York: Plenum.

Rosenthal, A. J., & Levine, S. V. (1970). Brief psychotherapy with children: A preliminary report. *American Journal of Psychiatry, 127,* 646–651.

Rosenthal, A. J., & Levine, S. V. (1971). Brief psychotherapy with children: Process of therapy. *American Journal of Psychiatry, 128,* 141–146.

Rosenthal, D., & Frank, J. D. (1958). The fate of psychiatric clinic outpatients assigned to psychotherapy. *Journal of Nervous and Mental Disease, 127,* 330–343.

Rothschild, B. H. (1993). RET and chronic pain. In W. Dryden & L. K. Hill (Eds.), *Innovations in rational-emotive therapy* (pp. 91–115). Thousand Oaks, CA: Sage.

Rounsaville, B. J., & Carroll, K. (1993). Interpersonal psychotherapy for patients who abuse drugs. In G. L. Klerman & M. M. Weissman (Eds.), *New applications of interpersonal psychotherapy* (pp. 319–352). Washington, DC: American Psychiatric Press.

Rounsaville, B. J., & Chevron, E. S. (1982). Interpersonal psychotherapy: Clinical applications. In A. J. Rush (Ed.), *Short-term psychotherapies for depression* (pp. 107–142). New York: Guilford Press.

Rounsaville, B. J., Chevron, E. S., Prusoff, B. A., Elkin, I., Imber, S., Sotsky, S., & Watkins, J. (1987). The relation between specific and general dimensions of the psychotherapy process in interpersonal psychotherapy of depression. *Journal of Consulting and Clinical Psychology, 55,* 379–384.

Rounsaville, B. J., Gawin, F., & Kleber, H. (1985). Interpersonal psychotherapy adapted for ambulatory cocaine abusers. *American Journal of Drug and Alcohol Abuse, 11,* 171–191.

Rounsaville, B. J., O'Malley, S., Foley, S., & Weissman, M. M. (1988). Role of manual-guided training in the conduct and efficacy of interpersonal psychotherapy for depression. *Journal of Consulting and Clinical Psychology, 56,* 681–688.

Rubin, Z., & Mitchell, C. (1976). Couples research as couples counseling. *American Psychologist, 36,* 17–25.

Rudolph, B., Datz-Weems, H., Marrie, S., Cusack, A., Beerup, C., & Kiel, S. (1993). Assessment interview processes: A successful and a failed brief therapy. *Psychotherapy in Private Practice, 12(2),* 17–35.

Rush, A. J. (Ed.). (1982). *Short-term psychotherapies for depression.* New York: Guilford Press.

Rush, A. J. (1984). Cognitive therapy. In L. Grinspoon (Ed.), Psychiatry update: *The American Psychiatric Association annual review* (vol. 3) (pp. 44–56). Washington, DC: American Psychiatric Press.

Rush, A. J., & Giles, D. E. (1982). Cognitive therapy: Theory and research. In A. J. Giles (Ed.), *Short-term psychotherapies for depression* (pp. 143–181). New York: Guilford Press.

Ryder, D. (1988). Minimal intervention: A little quality for a lot of quantity? *Behaviour Change, 5,* 100–107.

Ryle, A., Poynton, A. M., & Brockman, B. J. (1990). *Cognitive-analytic therapy: Active participation in change.* New York: Wiley.

Sabin, J. E. (1981). Short-term group psychotherapy: Historical antecedents. In S. H. Budman (Ed.), *Forms of brief therapy* (pp. 271–282). New York: Guilford Press.

Sachs, J. S. (1983). Negative factors in brief psychotherapy: An empirical assessment. *Journal of Consulting and Clinical Psychology, 51,* 557–564.

Saunders, B., Wilkinson, C., & Phillips, M. (1995). The impact of brief motivational intervention with opiate users attending a methadone programme. *Addiction, 90,* 415–424.

Savitz, S. A. (1992). Measuring quality of care and quality maintenance. In J. L. Feldman & R. J. Fitzpatrick

(Eds.), *Managed mental health care: Administrative and clinical issues* (pp. 143–158) Washington, DC: American Psychiatric Press.

Scheidlinger, S. (1984). Short-term group psychotherapy for children: An overview. *International Journal of Group Psychotherapy, 34,* 573–585.

Schlesinger, H. J. (1984). Research in dynamic psychotherapy. *Psychoanalytic Psychology, 1,* 83–84.

Schlesinger, H. J. (1994). Keeping psychotherapy efficient: How much is enough? Unpublished manuscript.

Schlesinger, H. J., Mumford, E., Glass, G. V., Patrick, C., & Sharfstein, S. (1983). Mental health treatment and medical care utilization in a fee-for-service system: Outpatient mental health treatment following the onset of a chronic disease. *American Journal of Public Health, 73,* 422–429.

Schuyler, D. (1991). *A practical guide to cognitive therapy.* New York: Norton.

Scrignar, C. B. (1979). One-session cure of a case of speech anxiety with a 10 year follow-up. *Journal of Nervous and Mental Disease, 167,* 315–316.

Seagull, A. A. (1966). Must the deeply disturbed have long-term treatment? *Psychotherapy: Theory, research, and practice, 3,* 36–42.

Selekman, M. D. (1993). *Pathways to change: Brief therapy solutions with difficult adolescents.* New York: Guilford Press.

Seligman, M. E. P. (1995). The effectiveness of psychotherapy: The Consumer Reports study. *American Psychologist, 50,* 965–974.

Selvini Palazzoli, M., Boscolo, L., Cecchin, G. F., & Prata, G. (1978). *Paradox and counterparadox.* Northvale, NJ: Aronson.

Selvini Palazzoli, M., Cirillo, S., Selvini, M., & Sorrentino, A. M. (1989). *Family games: General models of psychotic processes in the family.* New York: Norton.

Shadish, W. R., Montgomery, L. M., Wilson, P., Wilson, M. R., Bright, I., & Okwumabua, T. (1993). Effects of family and marital psychotherapies: A meta-analysis. *Journal of Consulting and Clinical Psychology, 61,* 992–1002.

Shaffer, E. R., Cutler, A. J., & Wellstone, P. D. (1994). Coverage of mental health and substance abuse services under a single-payer health care system. *Hospital and Community Psychiatry, 45,* 916–919.

Shapiro, D. A., Barkham, M., Hardy, G. E., & Morrison, L. A. (1990). The second Sheffield psychotherapy project: Rationale, design and preliminary outcome data. *British Journal of Medical Psychology, 63,* 97–108.

Shapiro, D. A., & Shapiro, D. (1983). Comparative therapy outcome research: Methodological implications of meta-analysis. *Journal of Consulting and Clinical Psychology, 51,* 42–53.

Shapiro, L. E. (1984). *The new short-term therapies for children: A guide for the helping professions and parents.* Englewood Cliffs, NJ: Prentice-Hall.

Shapiro, L. E., & Henderson, J. G. (1992). Brief therapy for encopresis: A case study. *Journal of Family Psychotherapy, 3(3),* 1–12.

Sharfstein, S. S. (1991). Assessing the outcome of managed costs: An exploratory approach. In S. M. Mirin, J. T. Gossett, & M. C. Grob (Eds.), *Psychiatric treatment: Advances in outcome research* (pp. 311–320). Washington, DC: American Psychiatric Press.

Shectman, F. (1986). Time and the practice of psychotherapy. *Psychotherapy, 23,* 521–525.

Shepherd, M., Lader, M., & Rodnight, R. (1968). *Clinical psychopharmacology.* Philadelphia: Lea & Febiger.

Shiang, J., & Bongar, B. (1995). Brief and crisis psychotherapy in theory and practice. In B. Bongar & L. E. Beutler (Eds.), *Comprehensive textbook of psychotherapy: Theory and practice* (pp. 380–401). New York: Oxford University Press.

Shiffman, S. (1987). Clinical psychology training and psychotherapy interview performance. *Psychotherapy, 24,* 71–84.

Shulman, B. H. (1989). Single-session psychotherapy: A didactic demonstration. *Individual Psychology, 45,* 82–98.

Shyne, A. W. (1957). What research tells us about short-term cases in family agencies. *Social Casework, 38,* 223–231.

Siddall, L. B., Haffey, N. A., & Feinman, J. A. (1988). Intermittent brief psychotherapy in an HMO setting. *American Journal of Psychotherapy, 42,* 96–106.

Sifneos, P. E. (1967). Two different kinds of psychotherapy of short duration. *American Journal of Psychiatry, 123,* 1069–1074.

Sifneos, P. E. (1968). Learning to solve emotional problems: A controlled study of short-term anxiety-provoking psychotherapy. In R. Porter (Ed.), *The role of learning in psychotherapy* (pp. 87–99). Boston: Little, Brown.

Sifneos, P. E. (1972). *Short-term psychotherapy and emotional crisis.* Cambridge, MA: Harvard University Press.

Sifneos, P. E. (1978). Evaluation, criteria for selection of patients. In H. Davanloo (Ed.), *Basic principles and techniques in short-term dynamic psychotherapy* (pp. 81–85). New York: Spectrum.

Sifneos, P. E. (1979). *Short-term dynamic psychotherapy: Evaluation and technique.* New York: Plenum.

Sifneos, P. E. (1980). Motivation for change. In H. Davanloo (Ed.), *Short-term dynamic psychotherapy* (pp. 93–98). Northvale, NJ: Aronson.

Sifneos, P. E. (1981a). Short-term anxiety-provoking psychotherapy: Its history, technique, outcome, and instruction. In S. Budman (Ed.), *Forms of brief therapy* (pp. 45–81). New York: Guilford Press.

Sifneos, P. E. (1981b). Short-term dynamic psychotherapy: Its history, its impact and its future. *Psychotherapy and Psychosomatics, 35,* 224–229.

Sifneos, P. E. (1984). Short-term anxiety-provoking psychotherapy. In L. Grinspoon (Ed.), *Psychiatry update: The American Psychiatric Association annual review* (vol. 3) (pp. 24–35). Washington, DC: American Psychiatric Press.

Sifneos, P. E. (1985). Short-term dynamic psychotherapy of phobic and mildly obsessive-compulsive patients. *American Journal of Psychotherapy, 39,* 314–322.

Sifneos, P. E. (1987). *Short-term dynamic psychotherapy: Evaluation and technique* (2d ed.). New York: Plenum.

Sifneos, P. (1990). Short-term anxiety-provoking psychotherapy (STAPP) termination-outcome and videotaping. In J. K. Zeig & S. G. Gilligan (Eds.), *Brief therapy: Myths, methods, and metaphors* (pp. 318–326). New York: Brunner/Mazel.

Sifneos, P. E. (1991). Short-term dynamic psychotherapy. In J. F. Masterson, M. Tolpin, & P. E. Sifneos (Eds.), *Comparing psychoanalytic psychotherapies* (pp. 77–95, 185–222). New York: Brunner/Mazel.

Sifneos, P. E. (1992). *Short-term anxiety-provoking psychotherapy: A treatment manual.* New York: Basic Books.

Silberschatz, G., & Curtis, J. T. (1991). Time-limited psychodynamic therapy with older adults. In W. A. Myers (Ed.), *New techniques in the psychotherapy of older patients* (pp. 95–108). Washington, DC: American Psychiatric Press.

Silberschatz, G., & Curtis, J. T. (1993). Measuring the therapist's impact on the patient's therapeutic progress. *Journal of Consulting and Clinical Psychology, 61,* 403–411.

Silberschatz, G., Fretter, P. B., & Curtis, J. T. (1986). How do interpretations influence the process of psychotherapy? *Journal of Consulting and Clinical Psychology, 54,* 646–652.

Silverman, W. H., & Beech, R. P. (1979). Are dropouts, dropouts? *Journal of Community Psychology, 7,* 236–242.

Simon, F. B., Stierlin, H., & Wynne, L. C. (1985). *The language of family therapy: A systemic vocabulary and sourcebook.* New York: Family Process Press.

Sledge, W. H., Moras, K., Hartley, D., & Levine, M. (1990). Effect of time-limited psychotherapy on patient dropout rates. *American Journal of Psychiatry, 147,* 1341–1347.

Sloves, R., & Peterlin, K. B. (1986). The process of time-limited psychotherapy with latency-aged children.

Journal of the American Academy of Child Psychiatry, 25, 847–851.

Small, L. (1979). *The briefer psychotherapies* (rev. ed). New York: Brunner/Mazel.

Smith, M. L., Glass, G. V., & Miller, T. I. (1980). *The benefits of psychotherapy.* Baltimore, MD: Johns Hopkins University Press.

Smyrnios, K. X., & Kirkby, R. J. (1993). Long-term comparison of brief versus unlimited psychodynamic treatments with children and their parents. *Journal of Consulting and Clinical Psychology, 61,* 1020–1027.

Snyder, M., & Guerney, B. G. (1993). Brief couple/family therapy: The relationship enhancement approach. In R. A. Wells & V. J. Giannetti (Eds.), *Casebook of the brief psychotherapies* (pp. 221–234). New York: Plenum.

Snyker, E. C. (1992). Treatment of exhibitionism in intensive short-term dynamic psychotherapy. *International Journal of Short-Term Psychotherapy, 7,* 13–30.

Sperry, L. (1987). ERIC: A cognitive map for guiding brief therapy and health care counseling. *Individual Psychology, 43,* 237–241.

Sprang, G. (1992). Utilizing a brief EAP-based intervention as an agent for change in the treatment of depression. *Employee Assistance Quarterly, 8(2),* 57–65.

Springmann, R. R. (1982). Some remarks on psychotherapy by a single interpretation. *Journal of Psychiatric Treatment and Evaluation, 4,* 327–332.

Starr, A., & Weisz, H. S. (1989). Psychodramatic techniques in the brief treatment of inpatient groups. *Individual Psychology, 45,* 143–147.

Steenbarger, B. N. (1992a). A multicontextual model of counseling: Bridging brevity and diversity. *Journal of Counseling and Development, 72,* 8–15.

Steenbarger, B. N. (1992b). Toward science–practice integration in brief counseling and therapy. *Counseling Psychologist, 20,* 403–450.

Steenbarger, B. N. (1993). Intentionalizing brief college student psychotherapy. *Journal of College Student Psychotherapy, 7(2),* 47–61.

Stein, D. M., & Lambert, M. J. (1995). Graduate training in psychotherapy: Are therapy outcomes enhanced? *Journal of Consulting and Clinical Psychology, 63,* 182–196.

Sterba, R. (1951). A case of brief psychotherapy by Sigmund Freud. *Psychoanalytic Review, 38,* 75–80.

Stern, T. A. (1987). Psychiatric management of acute myocardial infarction in the coronary care unit. *American Journal of Cardiology, 60,* 59J–67J.

Stiles, W. B., & Shapiro, D. A. (1989). Abuse of the drug metaphor in psychotherapy process-outcome research. *Clinical Psychology Review, 9,* 521–543.

Straker, G. (1986). Brief-term psychodynamic psychotherapy: A contradiction in terms? *South African Journal of Psychology, 16,* 57–61.

Straker, M. (1980). An overview. In H. Davanloo (Ed.), *Short-term dynamic psychotherapy* (pp. 221–236). Northvale, NJ: Aronson.

Strassberg, D. S., Anchor, K. N., Cunningham, J., & Elkins, D. (1977). Successful outcome and number of sessions: When do counselors think enough is enough? *Journal of Counseling Psychology, 24,* 477–480.

Strupp, H. H. (1980a). Problems of research. In H. Davanloo (Ed.), *Short-term dynamic psychotherapy* (pp. 379–392). Northvale, NJ: Aronson.

Strupp, H. H. (1980b). Success and failure in time-limited psychotherapy. *Archives of General Psychiatry, 37,* 595–603.

Strupp, H. H. (1980c). Success and failure in time-limited psychotherapy: A systematic comparison of two cases, Comparison 2. *Archives of General Psychiatry, 37,* 708–716.

Strupp, H. H. (1980d). Success and failure in time-limited psychotherapy: Further evidence (Comparison 4). *Archives of General Psychiatry, 37,* 947–954.

Strupp, H. H. (1980e). Success and failure in time-limited psychotherapy with special reference to the performance of a lay counselor. *Archives of General Psychiatry, 37,* 831–841.

Strupp, H. H. (1989). Psychotherapy: Can the practitioner learn from the researcher? *American Psychologist, 44,* 717–724.

Strupp, H. H. (1993). The Vanderbilt psychotherapy studies: Synopsis. *Journal of Consulting and Clinical Psychology, 61,* 431–433.

Strupp, H. H., & Binder, J. L. (1984). *Psychotherapy in a new key: A guide to time-limited dynamic psychotherapy.* New York: Basic Books.

Stuart, M. R., & Lieberman, J. A. (1986). The *fifteen minute hour: Applied psychotherapy for the primary care physician.* New York: Praeger.

Stuart, M. R., & Mackey, K. J. (1977). Defining the differences between crisis intervention and short-term therapy. *Hospital & Community Psychiatry, 28,* 527–529.

Stuhr, U., Meyer, A-E., & Bolz, W. (1981). V. Outcome results in psychological tests. *Psychotherapy and Psychosomatics, 35,* 138–198.

Sue, S., Allen, D. B., & Conaway, L. (1978). The responsiveness and equality of mental health care to Chicanos and Native Americans. *American Journal of Community Psychology, 6,* 137–146.

Svartberg, M. (1993). Characteristics, outcome, and process of short-term psychodynamic psychotherapy: An updated overview. *Nordic Journal of Psychiatry, 47,* 161–167.

Svartberg, M., Seltzer, M. H., Stiles, T. C., & Khoo, S. T. (1995). Symptom improvement and its temporal course in short-term dynamic psychotherapy: A growth curve analysis. *Journal of Nervous and Mental Disorders, 183,* 242–248.

Svartberg, M., & Stiles, T. C. (1991). Comparative effects of short-term psychodynamic psychotherapy: A meta-analysis. *Journal of Consulting and Clinical Psychology, 59.* 704–714.

Svartberg, M., & Stiles, T. C. (1992). Predicting patient change from therapist competence and patient-therapist complementarity in short-term anxiety-provoking psychotherapy: A pilot study. *Journal of Consulting and Clinical Psychology, 60,* 304–307.

Swartzburg, M., & Schwartz, A. (1976). A five-year study of brief hospitalization. *American Journal of Psychiatry, 133,* 922–924.

Talley, J. E. (1992). *The predictors of successful very brief psychotherapy: A study of differences by gender, age, and treatment variables.* Springfield, IL: Thomas.

Talley, J. E., Butcher, T., & Moorman, J. C. (1992). Client satisfaction with very brief psychotherapy. In J. E. Talley (Ed.), *The predictors of successful very brief psychotherapy: A study of differences by gender, age, and treatment variables* (pp. 46–84). Springfield, IL: Thomas.

Talmon, M. (1990). *Single-session therapy: Maximizing the effect of the first (and often only) therapeutic encounter.* San Francisco: Jossey-Bass.

Tannenbaum, S. A. (1919). Three brief psychoanalyses. *American Journal of Urology and Sexology, 15,* 145–151.

Task Force on Promotion and Dissemination of Psychological Procedures (1995). Training in and dissemination of empirically-validated psychological treatments: Report and recommendations. *Clinical Psychologist, 48,* 3–23.

Tasman, A. (1993). Application of therapeutic community principles in short-stay units. In E. Leibenluft, A. Tasman, & S. A. Green (Eds.), *Less time to do more: Psychotherapy on the short-term inpatient unit* (pp. 3–24). Washington, DC: American Psychiatric Press.

Taube, C. A., & Barrett, S. A. (1985). *Mental health, United States, 1985.* DHHS Pub. No. (ADM) 85–1378. Washington, DC: U.S. Government Printing Office.

Tedeschi, D. H., & Tedeschi, R. E. (Eds.) (1968). *Importance of fundamental principles in drug evaluation.* New York: Raven.

Teitelbaum, M. L., & Kettl, P. (1988). Brief psychotherapy with a patient suffering from Guillain-Barr syndrome. *Psychosomatics, 29,* 231–233.

Tennov, D. (1975). *Psychotherapy: The hazardous cure.* New York: Abelard-Schuman.

Thompson, L. W., Gallagher, D., & Breckenridge, J. S. (1987). Comparative effectiveness of psychotherapies for depressed elders. *Journal of Consulting and Clinical Psychology, 55,* 385–390.

Thorpe, S. A. (1987). An approach to treatment planning. *Psychotherapy, 24,* 729–735.

Tidwell, R. (1992). Crisis counseling: A right and a necessity for members of the underclass. *Counseling Psychology Quarterly, 5,* 245–249.

Tomm, K. (1984a). One perspective on the Milan systemic approach: Part I. Overview of development, theory and practice. *Journal of Marital and Family Therapy, 10,* 113–125.

Tomm, K. (1984b). One perspective on the Milan systemic approach: Part II. Description of session format, interviewing style and interventions. *Journal of Marital and Family Therapy, 10,* 253–271.

Trad, P. V. (1991). The application of developmental strategies to short-term psychotherapy. *International Journal of Short-Term Psychotherapy, 6,* 219–235.

Trad, P. V. (1993). *Short-term parent-infant psychotherapy.* New York: Basic Books.

True, P. K., & Benway, M. W. (1992). Treatment of stress reaction prior to combat using the "BICEPS" model. *Military Medicine, 157,* 380–381.

Tuyn, L. K. (1992). Solution-oriented therapy and Rogerian nursing science: An integrated approach. *Archives of Psychiatric Nursing, 6(2),* 83–89.

Ursano, R. J., & Dressler, D. M. (1977). Brief versus long-term psychotherapy: Clinician attitudes and organizational design. *Comprehensive Psychiatry, 18,* 55–60.

Ursano, R. J., & Hales, R. E. (1986). A review of brief individual psychotherapies. *American Journal of Psychiatry, 143,* 1507–1517.

Vardi, D. J., & Buchholz, E. S. (1994). Group psychotherapy with inner-city grandmothers raising their grandchildren. *International Journal of Group Psychotherapy, 44,* 101–122.

Walen, S. R., DiGiuseppe, R., & Dryden, W. (1992). *A practitioner's guide to rational-emotive therapy* (2d ed.). New York: Oxford University Press.

Walter, J. L., & Peller, J. E. (1992). *Becoming solution-focused in brief therapy.* New York: Brunner/Mazel.

Waring, E. M., Chamberlaine, C. H., McCrank, E. W., Stalker, C. A., Carver, C., Fry, R., & Barnes, S. (1988). Dysthymia: A randomized study of cognitive marital therapy and antidepressants. *Canadian Journal of Psychiatry, 33,* 96–99.

Washburn, P. (1994). Advantages of a brief solution oriented focus in home based family preservation services. *Journal of Systemic Therapies, 13(2),* 47–58.

Watzlawick, P. (1978). *The language of change: Elements of therapeutic communication.* New York: Basic Books.

Watzlawick, P. (1983). *The situation is hopeless but not serious: The pursuit of unhappiness.* New York: Norton.

Watzlawick, P. (Ed.) (1984). *The invented reality: How do we know what we believe we know?* New York: Norton.

Watzlawick, P. (1990). *Munchhausen's pigtail: Psychotherapy and "reality."* New York: Norton.

Watzlawick, P., Beavin, J., & Jackson, D. (1967). *Pragmatics of human communication: A study of interactional patterns, pathologies, and paradoxes.* New York: Norton.

Watzlawick, P., Weakland, J., & Fisch, R. (1974). *Change: Principles of problem formation and problem resolution.* New York: Norton.

Wayne, G. J. (1966). How long?—an approach to reducing the duration of inpatient treatment. In G. J. Wayne & R. R. Koegler (Eds.), *Emergency psychiatry and brief therapy.* (pp. 107–117). Boston: Little, Brown.

Weakland, J. (1990). Myths about brief therapy; myths of brief therapy. In J. K. Zeig & S. G. Gilligan (Eds.), *Brief therapy: Myths, methods, and metaphors* (pp. 100–107). New York: Brunner/Mazel.

Weakland, J. H., & Fisch, R. (1992). Brief therapy—MRI style. In S. H. Budman, M. F. Hoyt, & S. Friedman (Eds.), *The first session in brief therapy* (pp. 306–323). New York: Guilford Press.

Weakland, J., Fisch, R., Watzlawick, P., & Bodin, A. M. (1974). Brief therapy: Focused problem resolution. *Family Process, 13,* 141–168.

Weakland, J. H., & Jordan, L. (1992). Working briefly with reluctant clients: Child protective services as an example. *Journal of Family Therapy, 14,* 231–254.

Weishaar, M. E. (1993). *Aaron T. Beck.* Thousand Oaks, CA: Sage.

Weiss, R. L., & Jacobson, N. S. (1981). Behavioral marital therapy as brief therapy. In S. Budman (Ed.), *Forms of brief therapy* (pp. 387–414). New York: Guilford Press.

Weissman, M. M. (1979). The psychological treatment of depression: Evidence for the efficacy of psychotherapy alone, in comparison with and in combination with pharmacotherapy. *Archives of General Psychiatry, 36,* 1261–1269.

Weissman, M. M., & Klerman, G. L. (1993). Interpersonal counseling for stress and distress in primary care settings. In G. L. Klerman & M. M. Weissman (Eds.), *New applications of interpersonal psychotherapy* (pp. 295–318). Washington, DC: American Psychiatric Press.

Wells, R. A. (1993). Clinical strategies in brief psychotherapy. In R. A. Wells & V. J. Giannetti (Eds.), *Casebook of the brief psychotherapies* (pp. 3–17). New York: Plenum.

Wells, R. A. (1994). *Planned short-term treatment.* (2d ed) New York: Free Press.

Wells, R. A., & Phelps, P. A. (1990). The brief psychotherapies: A selective overview. In R. A. Wells & V. J. Giannetti (Eds.), *Handbook of the brief psychotherapies* (pp. 3–26). New York: Plenum.

Werner, M. J. (1995). Principles of brief intervention for adolescent alcohol, tobacco, and other drug use. *Pediatric Clinics of North America, 42,* 335–349.

Whale, J. (1992). The use of brief focal psychotherapy in the treatment of chronic pain. *Psychoanalytic Psychotherapy, 6,* 61–72.

White, H. S., Burke, J. D., & Havens, L. L. (1981). Choosing a method of short-term therapy: A developmental approach. In S. Budman (Ed.), *Forms of brief therapy* (pp. 243–267). New York: Guilford Press.

White, M., & Epston, D. (1990). *Narrative means to therapeutic ends.* New York: Norton.

Wiener, D. N. (1988). *Albert Ellis: Passionate skeptic.* New York: Praeger.

Wierzbicki, M., & Pekarik, G. (1993). A meta-analysis of psychotherapy dropout. *Professional Psychology: Research and Practice, 24,* 190–195.

Williamson, P. S. (1987). Psychotherapy by family physicians. *Primary Care, 14,* 803–816.

Wilson, G. T. (1978). On the much discussed nature of the term "behavior therapy." *Behavior Therapy, 9,* 89–98.

Wilson, G. T. (1981). Behavior therapy as a short-term therapeutic approach. In S. H. Budman (Ed.), Forms of brief therapy (pp. 131–166). New York: Guilford Press.

Winer-Elkin, J. I., Weissberg, R. P., & Cowen, E. L. (1988). Evaluation of a planned short-term intervention for schoolchildren with focal adjustment problems. *Journal of Clinical Child Psychology, 17,* 106–115.

Winston, A., Laikin, M., Pollack, J., Samstag, L. W., McCullough, L., & Muran, J. C. (1994). Short-term psychotherapy of personality disorders. *American Journal of Psychiatry, 151,* 190–194.

Winston, A., Pollack, J., McCullough, L. Flegenheimer, W., Kestenbaum, R., & Trujillo, M. (1991). Brief psychotherapy of personality disorders. *Journal of Nervous and Mental Disease, 179,* 188–193.

Wolberg, L. (1965a). Methodology in short-term therapy. *American Journal of Psychiatry, 122,* 135–140.

Wolberg, L. R. (1965b). *Short-term psychotherapy,* New York: Grune & Stratton.

Wolberg, L. R. (1965c). The technic of short-term therapy. In L. R. Wolberg (Ed.), *Short-term psychotherapy* (pp. 127–200). New York: Grune & Stratton.

Wolberg, L. R. (1968). Short-term psychotherapy. In J. Marmor (Ed.), *Modern psychoanalysis* (pp. 343–354). New York: Basic Books.

Wolberg, L. R. (1980). *Handbook of short-term psychotherapy.* New York: Thieme-Stratton.

Woody, G. E., McLellan, A. T., Luborsky, L., & O'Brien, C. P. (1987). Twelve-month follow-up of psychotherapy for opiate dependence. *American Journal of Psychiatry, 144,* 590–596.

Worchel, J. (1993). Pathological mourning in short-term dynamic psychotherapy. In R. A. Wells & V. J. Giannetti (Eds.), *Casebook of the brief psychotherapies* (pp. 197–218). New York: Plenum.

Wortman, P. M. (1983). Evaluation research: A methodological perspective. *Annual Review of Psychology, 34,* 223–260.

Wynne, L. C., McDaniel, S. H., & Weber, T. T. (1987). Professional politics and the concepts of family therapy, family consultation, and systems consultation. *Family Process, 26,* 153–166.

Yapko, M. D. (1988). *When living hurts: Directives for treating depression.* New York: Brunner/Mazel.

Young, J. E., & Beck, A. T. (1982). Cognitive therapy: Clinical applications. In A. J. Giles (Ed.), *Short-term psychotherapies for depression* (pp. 182–214). New York: Guilford Press.

Zabarenko, R. N., Merenstein, J., & Zabarenko, L. (1971). Teaching psychological medicine in the family practice office. *Journal of the American Medical Association, 218,* 392–396.

Zeig, J. K. (Ed.) (1982). *Ericksonian approaches to hypnosis and psychotherapy.* New York: Brunner/Mazel.

Zeig, J. K. (1985). Ethical issues in hypnosis: Informed consent and training standards. In J. K. Zeig (Ed.), *Ericksonian psychotherapy: Volume I: Structures* (pp. 459–473). New York: Brunner/Mazel.

Zilbergeld, B. (1983). *The shrinking of America: Myths of psychological change.* Boston: Little, Brown.

Zirkle, G. A. (1961). Five-minute psychotherapy. *American Journal of Psychiatry, 118,* 544–546.

Zweben, A., Pearlman, S., & Li, S. (1988). A comparison of brief advice and conjoint therapy in the treatment of alcohol abuse: The results of the marital systems study. *British Journal of Addiction, 83,* 899–916.

AUTHOR INDEX

SUBJECT INDEX

Note: PSTP = Planned short-term psychotherapy